FACT ORIENTED MO

WITH

FCO-IM

Capturing Business Semantics in Data Models with Fully Communication Oriented Information Modeling

first edition

Jan Pieter Zwart

Marco Engelbart

Stijn Hoppenbrouwers

Published by:

2 Lindsley Road
Basking Ridge, NJ 07920 USA
https://www.TechnicsPub.com

Cover design by Mark Brye

ISBN, print ed. 9781634620864

ISBN, Kindle ed. 9781634620871

ISBN, ePub ed. 9781634620888

ISBN, PDF ed. 9781634620895

First Printing 2015

Library of Congress Control Number: 2015945578

Table of Contents

Foreword
By Guido Bakema

I am sure that this book on Fact Oriented Modeling (FOM), and especially on the latest and most powerful FOM dialect called Fully Communication Oriented Information Modeling (FCO-IM), will find its way into university and college level education about information modeling and relational database design. The authors are convinced that this new book on FCO-IM will suit self-study more than the preceding course book (see Appendix B1, [1]), not only by leaving out some of the more sophisticated (but, for operational practice, less important issues), but even more by adding chapters on basic skills, like verbalizing elementary facts, and applying their long university teaching experience with respect to information modeling and database design. In my opinion they really succeeded to deliver the self-study book they had in mind, and I proudly recommend it.

After my friend Harm van der Lek and I had already applied and taught FOM successfully in practice (in the Dutch system house BSO) and in higher education (at the HAN University of Applied Sciences in the Netherlands), we concluded in 1991 that the then just-published FOM-method NIAM/ORM (see Appendix B2 [10], [11]), though powerful as such, had to be criticized to some extent from the point of view of elegance (not based on a minimum number of basic concepts) and internal consistency (violating the principle of single point of definition). We came up with suggestions how FOM could be improved with respect to these flaws, and we founded a group of which two of the authors became members as well. This group evolved into the university research group that I had the privilege to lead until my retirement as professor of applied sciences in 2011. Apart from being members of the development group, without any doubt both authors are also the most experienced university lecturers on FCO-IM.

FCO-IM found its way into operational practice because it was supported from the start by powerful modeling tools that were developed by several small Dutch software companies including Ascaris Software, Mattic Software and BCP Software. The state-of-the-art FCO-IM modeling and database generation tool CaseTalk Developer (see Appendix B1 [2]) not only matches one-to-one with the approach to FCO-IM as treated in this book, but BCP Software also offers a fully functional free educational version for non-commercial higher educational institutes as well. This FCO-IM modeling tool, in some cases together with an FCO-IM Bridge toolset for model transformations (developed by my research group in HAN University of Applied Sciences), was successfully used in a number of large projects for developing big transactional and/or business intelligence systems at the Dutch Railway Company, Royal Dutch Airlines, Erasmus Medical Centre, etc.

This book discusses the basics of the FCO-IM modeling process and illustrates the transformation of such information models to other techniques: not only to relational models, but also to Entity-Relationship diagrams, UML Class diagrams, Dimensional models, Data Vaults, etc. Full details of these transformations go beyond the scope of this book, which mainly intends to be an introductory book to advocate the advantages of FOM modeling techniques and for learning the FCO-IM modeling procedure. I hope the authors will find time to write a second book in which these transformation algorithms will be explained further. Moreover, I hope that BCP Software will be able to develop FCO-IM based bridge tools for the transformation of CaseTalk FCO-IM models towards all before mentioned models in supporting state-of-the art tools. I hope this even more because I am convinced that at the moment FCO-IM is the highest level conceptual modeling method available, and as a consequence all other desired information/data models should be derived from conceptual FCO-IM models.

Guido Bakema

Professor of Data Architectures and Metadata Management

HAN University of Applied Sciences

Wijchen, The Netherlands, June 2015

Chapter 1
Information Modeling in Context

This chapter explains what information modeling is. It shows how information modeling relates to businesses, business processes, business communication and business language on the one hand and the functionality an information system should offer on the other. It briefly ponders on what information is, how it can be handled, and what is required if computational machinery is to be used to help us capture, convey, store and process it. This chapter also explains the role of models of various flavors and how they relate to one specific sort of design document: the information model. It concludes by discussing the importance of always keeping close to the actual communication that takes place on the work floor to avoid 'getting lost in concept space'.

Wherever possible in this introductory chapter, examples will be given related to the case study used throughout this book about the reservation and booking system of Serviceton Music Theater, which is presented in Chapter 2.

1.1 Business Information and Communication Systems

Organizations (or businesses or enterprises) are all around us, and communication is one of the key things that make them work. Some people even go so far as to see communication as the *essential* ingredient that *defines* an organization: when two people agree—typically in a conversation—that one of them will do something for the other (usually getting something in return), an organization is born (see Appendix B, [22]). Scaling this up, we get complex combinations of people, hierarchies, networks, departments, locations, policies, business strategies, enterprise architectures and so on and so forth, but the basics are still people cooperating, establishing and realizing their cooperation through, at least for a large part, communication.

For thousands of years, boosted by the emergence of writing, communication has been explicitly, and sometimes rigidly, harnessed to help organizations along. Implicitly or explicitly, people have created and used conventions for their organization, including agreements on 'who does what for whom, when and how', but also 'who talks to whom, when, and how'. At the core of these conventions are *languages*: not just national languages like Finnish or Chinese, but also endlessly nuanced, detailed variations in language between companies, departments, professional groups and so on. Specific situations require specific concepts (words, phrases) to fit the thinking and communication required (see Appendix B, [23]). While it is clear that organizational communication is not the main purpose of a business, it is an indispensable element like the warp in the art of weaving (the warp consists of the longitudinal, neutral strings). Furthermore, writing (contrary to oral language use) adds something to the communication: it makes it last better than if people just try to remember what was said. Writing creates *texts*. In this sense, clay tablets used for administration in ancient Egypt are on a par with modern spreadsheets and databases. So organizations rely on and are shaped by *structured communication*, and language is part of this structure.

This also holds for the expected or even mandatory order in which pieces of information are exchanged as they support some activity that is taking place. For centuries, business communication has been organized increasingly tightly using things like ledgers, messaging and reporting conventions and so on. Mechanical machines (from the late 19th century on) and digital devices (from the mid-20th century on) have played a huge part in enabling an increasingly advanced and intensive organizing of communication. This development has led to our current dependence on and indulgence in computer-based information systems. And yet, the bottom line is still 'who talks to whom, when and how'.

Below, six distinct but related views or perspectives on business communication are presented. These views are used by information system analysts and developers in the process of designing information systems as supporters and enablers of structured business communication. In the world of IT, these views are often related to *models* or *design artifacts* of a particular type. One of these six views is central in this book, which is why it will be discussed first: information models.

1.2 Views on Business Communication

1.2.1 Information Model

In the second half of the 20th century, the understanding emerged that it is pretty important to know the structure of the language people use to communicate about some specific area of business; for example, claim processing in an insurance company, stock keeping in a store or reserving a seat in a theater. This is particularly so if an effective information system is to be created that fits well in its context of use. This context of use always concerns some sort of communication in support of some specific business goal. In plain English: information modeling is making a model (i.e. a nicely structured and useful description; a *chart*, if you like) of the language used to communicate about some specific domain of business in a more or less fixed way. This involves not only the words used (like 'client', 'order' or, in our theater example, 'show' or 'performer'), but also the typical phrases and patterns that combine these words into meaningful standard statements about the domain (for example, "Client K. Johanson orders the article called power wrench." or, in the theater domain, "There is a show *Tiger Feet, The Musical* performed by Jungle Town."). The information system, or the database, is a pre-structured machine dedicated to holding, managing and sharing a special and rather dynamic sort of text. It is designed following a kind of specialized *grammar* of the language used in this one special communication domain (for example, the Serviceton Music Theater and its booking and reservation operations). Indeed, information models are sometimes technically called 'information grammars'.

1.2.2 BUSINESS VOCABULARY

Information models do not capture all aspects of language; they provide terms (like 'show') and phrase structures (like "There is a show ... performed by ... ."), but they do not explain the meanings of the individual terms as such. However, this is needed, too, if it is important that no misunderstandings arise as to what a term or phrase means in the domain concerned. This may not seem all that urgent in the case of a ticket reservation system (though you might be surprised how easily things can go wrong), but if your domain is strewn with jargon and includes phrases like "Fluctures epibrate Hypermodals." (a fictional example), a dictionary of some sort is indispensable. After all, it is still communication conventions that are being dealt with here, so knowing what terms mean is rather important to everyone involved. Such dictionaries were called 'data dictionaries' in the early days of information systems. Nowadays their use has broadened, so people prefer to talk about 'business vocabularies', 'business dictionaries' or 'business ontologies'.

1.2.3 GRAPHICAL USER INTERFACE (GUI)

Information systems typically have a database at their core. Since the 1990s, users usually access this database through a *graphical user interface (GUI)*: a screen containing a number of well laid-out phrases and terms matching the information model (in the form of fields in which they can be read or entered) as well as gizmos like pop-ups, menus, buttons and so on, which are also partly based on the information grammar. For example, menu choices are often based on options that are represented in the database.

1.2.4 BUSINESS PROCESS MODEL

However, most contemporary information systems are more than just databases accessed through an interface; they may be part of a workflow supporting setup (the 'who does what and communicates with whom, when' part) or of a case management setup (for example, medical treatment). To use the jargon term for this, they are part of a *business process*, and the information system specifically supports the tasks and activities that constitute the execution of this business process.

Business processes (typically the sequences or 'flows' of activities in a business) can also be captured nicely and usefully in diagrams. Such diagrams are called 'business process models'. Process modeling techniques widely used are, for example, BPMN (see Appendix B, [18]) and UML Activity Diagrams (see Appendix B, [13]). Commonly, such models include the messages or documents (sometimes called 'business objects') sent between activities in the process via 'information flows' or 'data flows'. Zooming in on the details of these flows, they can be described by their information structure: the language items they consist of (their information grammar).

1.2.5 BUSINESS RULES

Processes, however, do not always nicely fit standardized flows. For example, what if we know which activities may—or even have to—take place, but we cannot predict the order in which they will take place? Medical treatment is a case in point: what to do at some particular moment depends on how the patient is doing and how she has responded to previous steps. As an alternative to data flows, such activities can be organized by means of *rules.* In fact, rules can be used to capture, guide or even automate many sorts of decisions to be taken when running a business.

Organizational rules (in particular the ones that guide the activities on a pretty detailed, operational level) are called *business rules*. Every organization works by them, but often implicitly so. When made explicit, business rules can be effectively used to organize and manage many different things: not just when to do what ("Ticket reservations for a performance must be made at least two hours before the beginning of that performance."), but also how to carry out calculations (e.g., discounts, pricing), make classifications (what is meant by a 'weekday'?) and provide support for all sorts of other decisions to be taken while running a business, whether automated or not.

Although business rules are usually given in terms of vague verbal descriptions (if any) rather than as precise formal diagrams, they should be considered as just another type of model. To put business rules together effectively, in particular when they are to be supported by an information system, clear building blocks are needed: neatly defined terms and phrases, preferably linked unambiguously to a database. So this turns out to be yet another link with information modeling; the terms and phrases in business rules are precisely those found in an information model. For example, consider the following business rule (see also Appendix A3.1):

BR 08: Customers who order tickets for *at least six* performances *before the start of the theater season get* season tickets.

This rule means: if you buy tickets for six or more performances, you are entitled to a price reduction for all of these tickets in the form of cheaper season tickets. The underlined parts in this business rule are also part of the underlying information model; they can be checked in a database (if there is one) to see if the rule holds in a specific case. The italics parts are logical elements that glue the phrases together into a rule. Please note that as it is stated now, the rule is far too vague to be implemented straightaway. For instance, what happens if a customer has bought tickets for five performances last month and buys some more for a sixth performance today? This rule will have to be made precise before the procedures to calculate prices can be designed as part of the functionality the database should provide (i.e. the information processing routines to be implemented in the database). Designing the detailed database procedures is, however, outside the scope of this book (see also the remark in Appendix A3.1 for BR 08).

1.2.6 USE CASES

There is one last view on business communication in relation to information systems worth mentioning. So far, activities and their order in time (business processes, business rules) have been discussed. They describe how the business works. However, more closely tied to the information system to be designed, *the way we say things to this system* and *what this system may say back* need to be considered. This is sometimes called 'interaction flow' and is quite different from the 'activity flow' in process models. An interaction flow is the essential part of what a user-computer interface does, step by step. It describes the dynamics of the interactions with the information system that a user can perform through the GUI. An interaction flow is often specified by a *use case,* i.e. a description of the actions involved when a user performs a small task *using* the information system. Use cases are yet another type of model. A single use case is a sensibly grouped set of interactions that is needed to complete some activity (for example: 'Enter reservation request'). Indeed, often an activity in a business process can be matched 1:1 to a use case. In a use case diagram (as is shown in Figure 2.7) the various Serviceton use cases are shown together with the actors that may execute them when using the system. For example, use case 'Enter reservation request' can be executed by either a customer (for example, online) or by a clerk (for example, during a telephone conversation with a customer). Each individual use case is described in detail according to a template. The core description is the interaction flow (also known as the 'Basic Course of Events'). Here's an example assuming everything runs smoothly and a single request is entered on the website:

1. User selects a performance to attend including all details required.
2. System confirms the possibility to enter a request for this performance.
3. System asks how many tickets are to be reserved for this performance.
4. User states the number of tickets requested.
5. System confirms the reservation.

So the interaction flow in a use case is a detailed description of how the information system is part of the communication structure that supports and shapes the business. You could replace 'system' with 'box office employee' in the use case example above and the communication taking place during an 'Enter reservation request' activity in a 19th century, computer-free ticket booth would not be all that different. So what is the link between use cases and information models? Suppose that customer Mary Higgins wants three tickets for the show Tiger Feet, The Musical performed by Jungle Town on March 8, 2015, at 3:00 PM. In this example the information items exchanged (facts to be retrieved from or added to the database) would be:

- "Reservation request 7801 was made by customer 512."
- "The surname of customer 512 is: Higgins."
- "The first name of customer 512 is: Mary."
- "Part 1 of reservation request 7801 concerns performance 108."
- "Performance 108 features Tiger Feet, The Musical performed by Jungle Town."
- "Performance 108 is planned on March 8, 2015."
- "Performance 108 starts at 3:00 PM."
- "Part 1 of reservation request 7801 claims 3 seats."

Let's assume that Mary Higgins is already registered as a customer (if not, further facts containing her address are needed as well). The information model provides a more detailed information structure than the compound lump sentence given first, namely in the form of smaller, *elementary* chunks (individual facts), and so complements the use case 'Enter reservation request'.

1.2.7 SUMMARY OF VIEWS

In a nutshell, we have now talked you through the basic kinds of descriptions commonly used in functional information system design. Since this is a book about information modeling, the information model is the central point of focus here (see Figure 1.1). Please note that it is quite possible to take other descriptions as a starting point for information system analysis and design; in particular, business process models are a good candidate for this. Indeed, making a rough process model before any information modeling is done is almost indispensable (see Section 3.2). The art lies in when to elaborate which view, and how much.

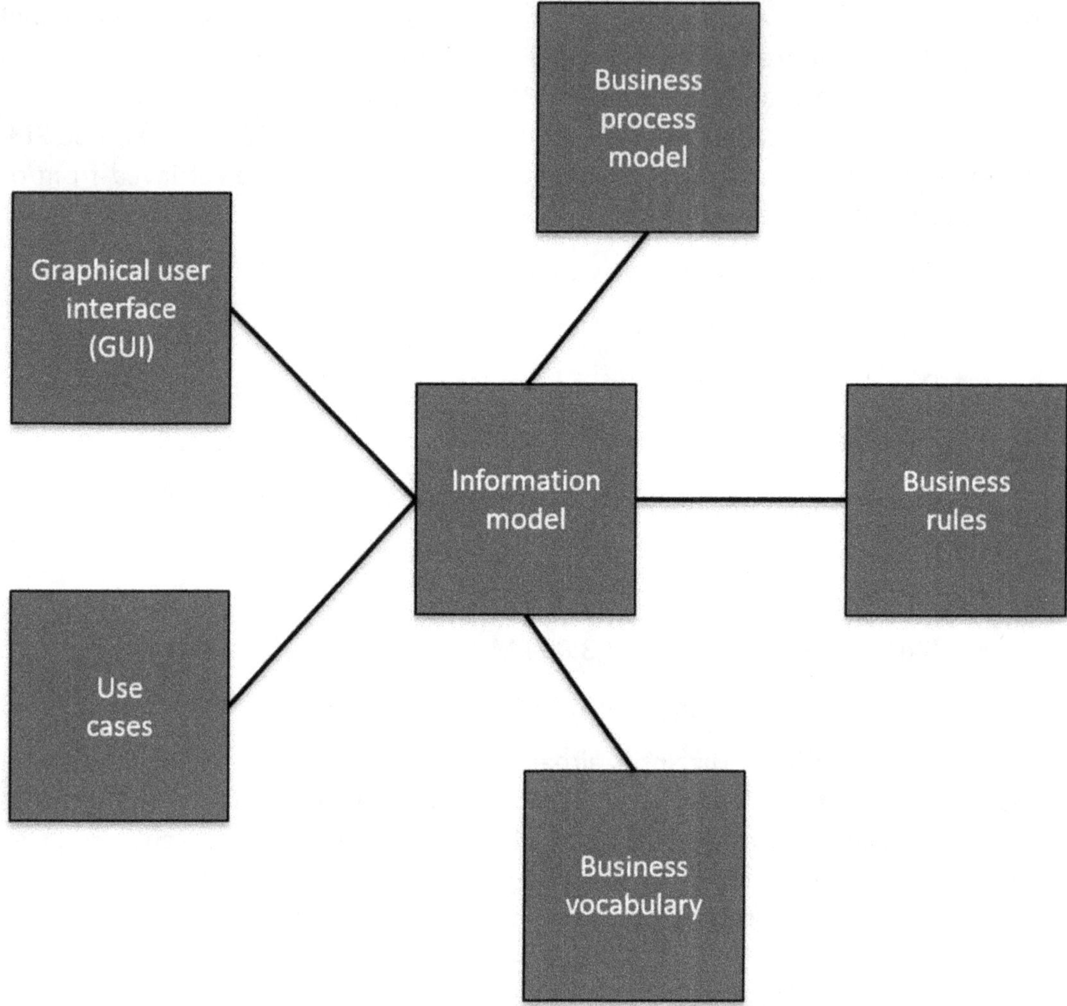

Figure 1.1 The several views on business communication in relation to the information model

So far, it was shown how various kinds of business models fit together in information system analysis and design. Below, once more the main links between these models are spelled out, now focusing on the relationships between each of these deliverables with the information model.

- **Information Model and Business Process Model**. If an activity requires or produces a document, message or piece of information, this is indicated in a business process model as a 'data object' or 'message' (for details, take a look at any business process modeling book). Putting such a document or message or piece of information under an information modeling magnifying glass would show the words and phrases (information grammar with individual fact types) conventionally used.

- **Information Model and Business Rules**. A business rule that applies to a domain is usually stated informally before an information model is made up (in what will be called 'Domain Style'; see Section 4.1.1). The information model, however, will be more strictly structured (in 'Model Style'; see Section 4.1.1 and further sections) and, in addition to the terms and phrases, include model-specific constraints. Such constraints are the logical expressions that give a rule its limiting (indeed, constraining) meaning. For example, 'at least six' is not just a phrase, it is a calculable restrictive condition; it describes exactly what needs to be the case for the rule to come into effect. In the end, the Statements expressed in Domain Style and Model Style may look a bit different, but their meaning should match completely. So to ensure a good correspondence with the information model, each business rule should eventually be stated in terms of building blocks that match the information model (see Appendix A3, in which this is done for the complete information model for Serviceton Music Theater).
- **Information Model and Use Cases**. In the interaction flow of a use case, the dialogue between the user and the system is described. This description involves words and phrases (individual facts) contained in the information model (see the examples given in Section 1.2.6).
- **Information Model and Graphical User Interface (GUI)**. The GUI includes a number of fields that correspond directly to items (individual facts) in the information model.
- **Information Model and Business Vocabulary**. Every word in the information model should in principle be defined in the business vocabulary or business dictionary. This holds in particular for the nouns (like 'show' and 'performer'). Defining verbs and other relational items (like 'performed by') is a bit harder and is often seen as less urgent.

1.3 Fact Oriented Modeling (FOM)

To conclude this introductory chapter, an explanation is given of what distinguishes Fact Oriented information Modeling (FOM) from other main types of information modeling or data modeling. In some cases, the term 'Fact Based Modeling' is used instead of 'Fact Oriented Modeling'; the terms are as good as synonymous. The 'Fact Orientation' feature lends its name not only to the technique further explained in this book (FCO-IM: Fully Communication Oriented Information Modeling, see Appendix B, [1] through [9]), but also to its parent technique NIAM (Natural language Information Analysis Method, see Appendix B, [11] and [1, appendix B therein]) and its sibling techniques, ORM (Object Role Modeling, see Appendix B, [10]) and CogNIAM (Cognition enhanced NIAM, see Appendix B, [11]). These are all Fact Oriented Modeling approaches. Finally, the unique characteristics of FCO-IM are briefly discussed.

1.3.1 HALLMARKS OF FOM TECHNIQUES

The most important hallmarks of Fact Oriented Modeling (abbreviated as FOM from here on) are:

- Use of *verbalizations of concrete examples of facts* as a basis for modeling instead of a general description (the latter is always vague and incomplete).
- A good *procedure* (cookbook) telling you *how* to model instead of just *what* to model.
- Focus on *elementary facts* instead of attributes (half facts) or entities (clusters of facts).

Each point is explained further below.

1.3.1.1 Verbalizations of Concrete Examples of Facts

So what is meant by 'verbalizations of concrete examples of facts'? They are sentences in natural language used by people who are exchanging information about their work (they're called 'domain experts'), as in a telephone conversation. For example, "The price of a single ticket for performance 108 is $27.50." is such a verbalization. Such sentences that express one actual fact are used by domain experts many times daily and mean much more to them and to information modelers than abstract generalizations like 'performance tickets have prices'. They are a *big* help in making domain experts (pros in their own field, but usually unfamiliar with information modeling) and information modelers (pros in information modeling, but usually unfamiliar with the domain) understand each other. This point is elaborated further below because the fact orientation aspect is so crucial to this book.

Technically, 'performance 108' (one specific thing) is called an *instance*, whereas 'performance' (without a number) is a kind of thing, or a *type*. Similarly, 'Jungle Town' is an instance of the type 'performer', just as 'Fido' can be an instance of the type 'dog'. Practically speaking, type level descriptions like 'performance tickets have prices' ideally give you what you need to create *empty* tables in a database. That is fine in itself (the type level is crucial in FOM as well), but it leaves out the explicit link with the instance level communicational payload. By including instances in the modeling and providing concrete means to analyze instance level items (examples of real fact communication), it is assured that there is a full, well described match between instance level and type level.

So what makes FOM approaches Fact Oriented is that they take the instance level very seriously and incorporate it into their modeling. Other techniques of information modeling (for example ERM, see appendix B, [12], or UML Class Diagrams, see Appendix B, [13]) do not do this. This has implications for the logical technicalities underlying FOM, but it also, and perhaps primarily, reflects a *way of looking at information structures*. Using concrete and realistic examples is stressed because it is considered indispensable for analyzing domain communication and designing information systems in order to support business communication.

Briefly consider what we mean by 'model' in the context of information system analysis and design. The six core types of model (or design artifacts) discussed in Section 1.2 (information models, business rules, use cases, etc.) each represent a particular lens through which one can view a business domain or its supporting information system. Many more such lenses (modeling techniques) exist and are used in many different branches of analysis, design and engineering. Applying each lens requires and enforces a *conceptual filter* on the way we look at the domain; it helps us, but also requires us to leave things out of our view and focus instead on a particular aspect (information grammar, business decisions and so on).

When communicating with business stakeholders (i.e. the people in the business who may not know much about designing information systems but surely know a lot about their business!), we cannot simply assume they can easily and readily cope with the various concepts involved in using the various lenses. This depends on the talents, education and experience of each business stakeholder. But even when working with business stakeholders who are quite good at abstract thinking, it is highly recommendable to keep a solid footing in the concrete world of the communication that really takes place in the domain at all times in everyday work and interactions. In other words, always complement your abstractions with plenty of *real or realistic examples.*

In the FOM approach explained in this book, the use of concrete examples is implemented in such a way that it cannot be left out. The abstractions are always explicitly rooted in clear examples of business communication. This not only helps a great deal in clarifying and describing information grammars while co-designing these with domain experts, but it also prevents the dreaming up of terms and phrases that do not match the domain language actually used in the business. In other words, using real examples greatly helps in assuring a good fit of the central information model to business operations.

In short, using concrete examples has the following advantages (see also Section 3.3.1):

- They make the *meaning* of the data much clearer than general descriptions.
- They are the common ground between domain experts and information modelers.
- They serve as the firm basis (instance level) on which all modeling decisions (type level) are based.
- They automatically bring out many modeling details (how a performer is identified, etc.).
- They make validation of the model easy (see Section 5.1).

This is the core idea behind Fact Oriented Modeling, but it is not the whole story. Without going into as much detail, here are some other features typical to FOM.

1.3.1.2 A Good Procedure for How to Model

Less typically in FOM, but still a strong characteristic of all FOM approaches, is that an extensive *process of modeling* is included in them. Many forms of modeling heavily emphasize the modeling language as such: its concepts (entities, relationships, classes, attributes, tables, keys, etc.), its syntax and semantics, its notation. While the FOM approaches are, without exception, fully worked out in this respect (including underlying math), they also provide an extensive, stepwise description of *how* to perform an analysis and create an information model (the modeling process or procedure). Of course, all information modeling techniques are clear in *what* a model should contain, but students and other interested parties are rather left in the cold if they aren't shown *how* this can be achieved. This FOM book also follows this FOM tradition: Chapters 3-6 are devoted to the modeling procedure. In the case of FCO-IM and the main tool that goes with it (CaseTalk, see Appendix B, [2]), the process of conceptualizing is explicitly built in and supported.

1.3.1.3 Focus on Elementary Facts

Fact Oriented Modeling techniques consider *one complete fact at a time*. This contrasts sharply with other modeling techniques like ERM (see Appendix B, [12]), UML class diagrams (see Appendix B, [13]) or Relational tables (see Appendix B, [14]). These techniques use concepts like *attribute* (at best, half a fact) and *entity, class* or *table* (clusters of several facts). Historically, these concepts may have been quite useful from a software engineering perspective, but for considering information structures, they are rather arbitrary and do not match how language and logic are actually structured. By enforcing the attribute-entity distinction, a software engineering view (lens) is imposed on information structures. The scientists behind the creation of the FOM family of information modeling techniques did not approve of this (see Section 1.3.2.1) as it needlessly fouls up the essence of what information modeling stands for: entities overshoot the mark and attributes fall short. The essential building blocks for information structures are solitary whole facts. One single complete fact is called an *elementary fact*: it is the smallest unit of information that can be meaningfully exchanged.

Using elementary facts has the following benefits (see also Section 3.3.3.2):

- They are the simplest to model; if clusters are modeled in one go, the risk of errors is much greater. If incomplete facts are modeled, information loss might occur (see Section 3.3.3.2, especially Textbox 3.11 and Figure 3.12).
- They don't need extra concepts, like NULL values in tables, which you do need if you want to model clusters. So FOM techniques are simpler and leaner than other techniques, yet have the same modeling power.
- They can be easily combined in desired clusters later, whether on a computer interface screen (an elementary fact is either completely on it or not at all) or in entities, classes or table structures without making mistakes (even automatically, see Chapter 7).
- They prevent modelers and others from continually considering just fact *parts* (attributes). Seeing *pairs of columns* or attributes (or larger groups,

depending on the number of components in the elementary facts) as indivisible units of information is far more fruitful (see Section 7.1.1).

1.3.2 WHAT MAKES FCO-IM SPECIAL?

As mentioned previously, FCO-IM stands firmly in the tradition of Fact Oriented Modeling that was established by NIAM, the 'Natural language Information Analysis Method' as conceived by Sjir Nijssen and cohorts as early as the late 1960s. However, there are some specific features of FCO-IM that distinguish it from its kin (most notably, CogNIAM (see Appendix B, [11]) and ORM (see Appendix B, [10]).

An extensive history of developments in NIAM and FCO-IM can be found in Appendix B [1, appendix B therein]. A few highlights are mentioned here. NIAM, the root of the tree of FOM, originated from a project on information modeling in 1967 by Control Data Nederland under the supervision of G.M. Nijssen. It is named Natural language Information Analysis Method to stress that its basic principle is the verbalization of information in natural language. Nijssen was appointed at the University of Queensland, Australia, in 1982, where he and Terry Halpin developed NIAM further, resulting in their book *Conceptual Schema and Relational Database Design* (see Appendix B, [11]). In 1989, Nijssen returned to the Netherlands and continued to develop NIAM into its present form, CogNIAM (see Appendix B, [11]). In Australia, and later at Neumont University, USA, and INTI University, Malaysia, Halpin also continued the development of FOM under the name of Object Role Modeling (ORM) and supported it with several CASE tools, of which Norma is the present powerful incarnation.

1.3.2.1 Crucial Distinction between FCO-IM and Other FOM Techniques

The first book on FCO-IM (see Appendix B, [1]) was co-authored by Harm van der Lek, who used NIAM in 1989 in a large project for the Dutch Railways. He was building a software tool to store NIAM models in, because "The then available NIAM-tools were not capable of precisely regenerating the verbalizations that the domain experts had given of their facts, which strongly hampered the validation of NIAM information grammars by the domain experts." (see Appendix B, [1, Appendix B therein: "FCO-IM and NIAM"]), and to transform a NIAM model to a Relational schema. He found that this transformation could be simplified considerably by viewing information grammars and relational schemas as different manifestations of a single information model that is generic for both FCO-IM and the Relational Model. Building this tool, he encountered some difficulties. For example, NIAM uses two different sorts of object types (as does ORM). He found he could solve this by abolishing the distinction between fact types and object types, seeing object types as fact types as well. This is the crucial distinction between FCO-IM and the other FOM techniques. Whereas ORM models both objects in the real world *and* the facts about them, FCO-IM does not model real-world objects, but *only* facts about them. In spite of its name, an FCO-IM 'object type' is actually only a collection of sentences *about* objects (like "There is a show Tiger Feet, The Musical performed by Jungle Town.") but *not those objects themselves* (the actual show you can watch is not modeled).

As a result of unifying object types and fact types, the formalization of FCO-IM needs fewer fundamental concepts than NIAM or ORM do (see Appendix B, [1, appendix B therein]) and allows advanced modeling concepts (like subtyping and generalization) to be added in the same way as ordinary object types and fact types. This simple metamodel is even capable of modeling genuinely recursive identification structures (see Appendix B, [1, Section 6.2.5] and [9]).

In a nutshell, the distinction between FCO-IM and other FOM techniques is given in the Key Point below.

Key Point

- **FCO-IM does not model things in the real world, but only *the facts people communicate* about things in the real world.**

1.4 Why This Book?

This book is essentially an update of a book that was published in 1996: *Volledig Communicatiegeoriënteerde Informatiemodellering* (authors were Guido Bakema, Jan Pieter Zwart and Harm van der Lek), written in Dutch and translated into English in 2002 (see Appendix B, [1]). Guido Bakema was teaching NIAM in 1986 at what is now HAN University of Applied Sciences, Arnhem, Netherlands. He incorporated Harm van der Lek's innovation into the curriculum and developed FCO-IM further; in particular he added the fact expression types to the models, enabling the automatic regeneration of the original verbalizations. These developments resulted in a Master of Science training program centered on FOM with FCO-IM. Guido was the driving force behind the development of the book and of CASE tools implementing FCO-IM, of which CaseTalk (see Appendix B, [2]) is the present version. As Professor of Data Architectures and Metadata Management at HAN University, Guido has led research and development in many areas based on the FCO-IM metamodel and automatic transformations to other metamodels (see Chapter 7).

Since then, FCO-IM has been taught and used for almost twenty years. It was felt by some prominent figures in the data modeling community (both in the United States and in Europe) that an updated textbook was due, taking into account new insights gained in use, teaching and research. Jan Pieter Zwart, third author of the FCO-IM book in Appendix B, [1] and main author of this book, and Marco Engelbart, co-author of this book, divide their time between teaching and further development of FCO-IM in the Model-Based Information Systems research group at HAN University of Applied Sciences, led by Professor Stijn Hoppenbrouwers, the third co-author of this book. The research group is part of the HAN Faculty of Engineering and closely related to ICA, its Academy of Communication and Information Technology.

Some aspects concerning FCO-IM as such were improved and simplified in this book (for example, terminology). The way of introducing and explaining FCO-IM to readers and students has evolved over time, and this is also reflected in the book, in particular in sections about collecting concrete examples of facts (see Section 3.2) and how to verbalize these examples (see Section 3.3). Finally, explicit relations with other main methods and techniques used in information system analysis and design are now included (in this chapter), as is a broader, contemporary perspective on information modeling in view of developments in society and ICT (Information and Communication Technology) (in the final chapter). We believe that though FCO-IM itself has not changed much in twenty years, the outlook presented in this book places it even more firmly in the current context of information, communication, organization and the development of digital systems that support them in this day and age.

Chapter 2
Serviceton Music Theater

The case study that will be used throughout the book is presented here. It concerns the reservation and booking system of Serviceton Music Theater. This chapter contains concrete examples of all the relevant information to be modeled, and a few typical specimens from other perspectives as well (process model, business rules, use cases and mockup for a GUI).

2.1 Description of the Domain

Serviceton Music Theater is a 1500-seat theater located in a medium-sized city in the United States. The theater hosts more than 200 live performances a year, from pop and rock legends to classical music and from musicals to comedians.

The theater season runs from September to July. In May, four months before the start of the next theater season, the program is published in a brochure and on the theater's website. A part of the performance schedule for March 2015 is shown in Figure 2.1 as an example.

March 2015						
Day	**Time**	**Performance**	**Show**	**Genre**	**Price**	
					Single ticket	**Season ticket**
Sun 1	7:30PM	104	Big Train – Movin' and Groovin'	Oldies	$29.00	$26.00
Mon 2						
Tue 3	7:30PM	105	Kelly Turner – Cats and Dogs	Comedy	$35.00	$31.50
Wed 4						
Thu 5	8:00PM	106	Fireball – Fools Parade	Pop/Rock	$55.00	$50.00
Fri 6	8:00PM	107	Fireball – Fools Parade	Pop/Rock	$60.00	$55.00
Sat 7						
Sun 8	3:00PM	108	Jungle Town – Tiger Feet, The Musical	Musical, Family	$27.50	$24.00
	8:00PM	109	Jungle Town – Tiger Feet, The Musical	Musical, Family	$27.50	$24.00
Mon 9						
Tue 10	7:30PM	110	James Rutherford – Lucky Number	Comedy	$32.00	$29.00
Wed 11						
Thu 12	7:00PM	111	The East Side Gang – Mystery	Musical	$35.00	$30.00

			Hotel			
Fri 13	7:00PM	112	The East Side Gang – Mystery Hotel	Musical	$39.00	$35.00
Sat 14	7:00PM	113	The East Side Gang – Mystery Hotel	Musical	$39.00	$35.00
Sun 15	7:30PM	114	The Serviceton Symphony Orchestra – Magic Spell	Classical	$69.00	$64.00
Mon 16						
Tue 17						
Wed 18	7:30PM	115	Kathleen Menotti – Girl Next Door	Comedy	$29.00	$26.00
Thu 19						
Fri 20	8:00PM	116	The Tim Spencer Tribute Band – I Feel Good	Pop/Rock	$32.00	$29.00
Sat 21	7:30PM	117	The Cadillacs – Hot Rods	Oldies	$29.00	$26.00
Sun 22	7:30PM	118	The Serviceton Symphony Orchestra – Magic Spell	Classical	$69.00	$64.00
Mon 23						
Tue 24						
Wed 25	7:30PM	119	Russell Bloom – Tic Tac Toe	Comedy	$32.00	$29.00
Thu 26						
Fri 27	8:00PM	120	Blue Mask – The Nuggets Tour	Pop/Rock, Oldies	$55.00	$50.00
Sat 28	8:00PM	121	Blue Mask – The Nuggets Tour	Pop/Rock, Oldies	$55.00	$50.00
Sun 29	7:30PM	122	The Serviceton Symphony Orchestra – Magic Spell	Classical	$69.00	$64.00
Mon 30						
Tue 31	7:30PM	123	Daniel Bauer – Thunderbolt	Comedy	$29.00	$26.00

Figure 2.1 Example of the performance schedule

Each show has a title and a performer. For example, the show Fools Parade is performed by the rock band Fireball. A show belongs to one or more genres, like Pop/Rock, Oldies, Classical, Musical, Family and Comedy. A show can have multiple performances, which are identified by a unique performance number. For example, performances 106 and 107 both feature the show Fools Parade by Fireball. The first two columns of the schedule above contain the date and time of the performances.

Serviceton Music Theater sells two kinds of ticket: a single ticket (normal price) and a season ticket (reduced price). Each performance has a single ticket price and a season ticket price, as seen in the performance schedule in Figure 2.1. The same show can have different performance prices (e.g., a lower price on slow days). Customers who order tickets for at least six performances before the start of the theater season get season tickets. In all other cases they have to pay the single ticket price. On the website of Serviceton Music Theater, the details of a show are presented like in the example in Figure 2.2.

Fools Parade	**Genre**	Pop/Rock
	Performance date and time	**Ticket price (single / season)**
Fireball	Thursday March 5, 2015 8:00 PM	$55.00 / $50.00
	Friday March 6, 2015 8:00 PM	$60.00 / $55.00

Fireball is an American rock band formed in Los Angeles, in 1978. Their latest album, *Fools Parade*, was released in 2014. During the Fools Parade tour, the band will play songs from the new album and their greatest hits like 'Burn and Shine', 'Highway' and 'Judy'.

Figure 2.2 Example of a show

Customers can send in a request for tickets for several performances by either using the paper reservation form in the brochure or the digital form on the theater's website. It is also possible to buy tickets at the Serviceton Music Theater Box Office. Figure 2.3 shows a filled out (paper) reservation form. The reservation number and customer number are added by a member of the administrative staff of the theater.

Serviceton Music Theater Reservation Form
Season 2014/2015

Customer name: Leonard Reed
Address: 1255 Blue Mansions
Lake Area
Town: Pine Mound, Texas
ZIP code: TX 75105
Country: USA

Email address:: LeonardReed@ip4me.com
Phone number(s): +1-6-5432-6789

To be filled in by Serviceton:
Reservation number: 7795
Customer number: 436

	Performance	Show	Date and time	Nr of tickets
1	41	Ronald Young and the Shakers – Golden Years Of Rock 'n Roll	October 24, 2014 8:00 PM	4

2	75	The Maryland Orchestra – Russian Masterpieces	December 20, 2014 3:00 PM	2
3	104	Big Train - Movin' and Groovin'	March 1, 2015 7:30 PM	4
4	115	Kathleen Menotti – Girl Next Door	March 18, 2015 7:30 PM	2
5	122	The Serviceton Symphony Orchestra - Magic Spell	March 29, 2015 7:30 PM	2
6	138	Jonathan Tickner – Straight Up North	April 26, 2015 8:00 PM	2
7				
8				
9				
10				

Figure 2.3 Example of a reservation form

Reservation requests are processed every week and approved if possible. A reservation request part might, for instance, concern a performance that is already fully booked, in which case it would not be approved. For each approved request part, seats are assigned to customers and tickets for these seats are printed and sent to the customer's home address. Figure 2.4 shows an example of a ticket.

Figure 2.4 Example of a ticket

Each ticket has a unique ticket number (in the example, 7749026) and is for one specific seat (in the example in Figure 2.4, seat 25 in row 13). The rows of seats in Serviceton Music Theater are numbered from 1 to 30 from the stage side up. The seats are numbered from left to right. In every row, seat 1 is located on the left hand side (when you face the stage).

Figure 2.5 shows an example of an invoice sent to a customer. The customer pays the invoice, and payments are handled by the cashier.

S♫T Serviceton Music Theater

Date: July 25, 2015 **Reservation number:** 7795

Bill to **Customer:** Jeff Reed **Customer number:** 436
Address: 1255 Blue Mansions
Lake Area
Town Pine Mound, Texas
ZIP code: TX 75105
Country USA

	Perfor-mance	**Show**	**Date Time**	**Nr of tickets**	**Price**	**Subtotal**
1	41	Ronald Young and the Shakers Golden Years Of Rock 'n Roll	Oct 24, 2014 8:00 PM	4	$32.00	$128.00
2	75	The Maryland Orchestra Russian Masterpieces	Dec 20, 2014 3:00 PM	0	*not available*	*not available*
3	104	Big Train Movin' and Groovin'	Mar 1, 2015 7:30 PM	4	$26.00	$104.00
4	115	Kathleen Menotti Girl Next Door	Mar 18, 2015 7:30 PM	2	$26.00	$104.00
5	122	The Serviceton Symphony Orchestra Magic Spell	Mar 29, 2015 7:30 PM	2	$64.00	$128.00
6	138	Jonathan Tickner Straight Up North	Apr 26, 2015 8:00 PM	2	$32.50	$65.00
Total due						**$529.00**

Total payment due in 30 days. Please include the reservation number on your check

Figure 2.5 Example of an invoice

2.2 The Information System Development Perspective

To support the business processes of the theater, a new information system will be developed. This section gives an impression of several artifacts describing functional properties of the information system that is to be delivered during the analysis phase of the system development lifecycle (see also Section 1.2): business process model in Figure 2.6, use case diagram in Figure 2.7, with a mockup for it in Figure 2.8, and concludes with remarks about the information model and list of business rules.

2.2.1 Serviceton Music Theater Business Process Model

The requirements engineer involved in the development of this new information system started by making an overview of the main business processes in a Business Process Model and Notation (BPMN) schema (see Appendix B, [18]), presented in Figure 2.6. It shows the *tasks* Serviceton Music Theater carries out as rounded rectangles.

In the swim lane marked 'Planner', which contains all the tasks the planner does, you can see that the task 'Register shows and set up performance schedule' starts four months before the beginning of the season. It produces data that are stored in the data store 'Schedule'. Next, the task 'Display schedule' is carried out, which reads the data from data store 'Schedule', and displays it (in the brochure or on the website) so the customer (top swim lane) can read the schedule via data flow 'Schedule'. After this task has completed the chain of tasks for the planner ends, indicated by the symbol with a big dot in a circle.

The swim lane 'Clerk' shows that the task 'Receive reservation request' starts when a message from the customer arrives via data flow 'Reservation request' (this can be on paper or via the website, not shown in Figure 2.6). The requests are stored in data store 'Reservation requests and assigned seats'. Next, starting once a week, the task 'Process reservation requests' is done. Although there are several subtasks in this task, like approving a reservation request part and assigning seats, these are not shown on this top level process model. It is easy to expand the task (zoom in) later and reveal those subtasks on a lower level. Next, the task 'Create invoice and tickets' is carried out, and the chain of tasks ends by sending the customer a message with the tickets and an invoice via the data flow 'Tickets and invoice'. Data stores 'Reservation requests and assigned seats' and 'Financial data' are used by the clerk's tasks.

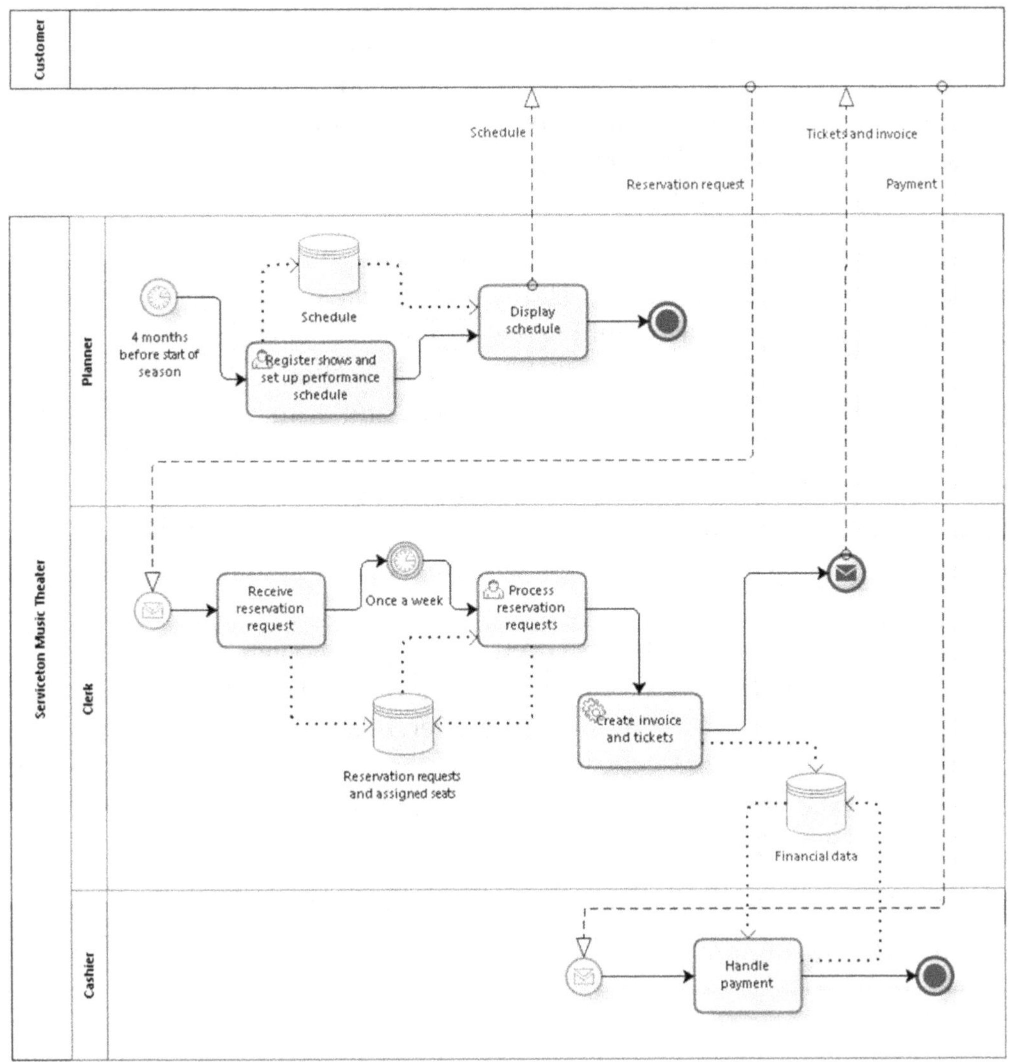

Figure 2.6 Business process model

Finally, in the swim lane 'Cashier', the task 'Handle payment' starts when a message from the customer arrives (via data flow 'Payment'). The cashier performs this task using data store 'Financial data'. Several subtasks are involved in this task, which can be zoomed in on later.

Such a top-level BPMN schema as shown in Figure 2.6 can also be useful in determining the *scope* of the future information system. In this case, the requirements engineer and the client (Serviceton Music Theater) decided to leave out the financial part for the time being (everything in the 'Cashier' swim lane, in data flow 'Payment' and in data store 'Financial data'). The reason is that the management wants to change from sending tickets and invoices first and receiving payments later to a form in which the customer pays first and gets the tickets afterwards. Many details of this change are not clear yet (Credit card? PayPal?), so it was decided to focus on the rest first.

A BPMN schema as in Figure 2.6 is also very useful for the information modeling to be done. *All* data flows and data stores in the schema within the determined scope (see the previous paragraph) serve as sources of concrete examples of the information to be modeled, as will be seen in Section 3.2 (here, data flows 'Schedule', 'Reservation request' and 'Tickets and invoice', and data stores 'Schedule' and 'Reservation requests and assigned seats'). Indeed, all the example documents from the domain description in Section 2.1 (the performance schedule in Figure 2.1, the show in Figure 2.2, the reservation form in Figure 2.3, the ticket in Figure 2.4 and the invoice in Figure 2.5) were taken from these flows and stores.

2.2.2 SERVICETON MUSIC THEATER USE CASE DIAGRAM AND BRIEF DESCRIPTION

With the scope determined (which tasks in the BPMN schema should be supported by the new information system: everything except 'Handle payment'), the requirements engineer translated these tasks into separate functions the information system should perform. She displayed these in the use case diagram (see Appendix B, [19]) given in Figure 2.7.

For each use case, a brief description was drawn up. For example:

Use case: Register Show
Brief description The planner creates a show or edits an already existing show. The planner enters the show name, the name of the performer, a show description and at least one genre. After confirmation by the planner, the system stores the show. Optionally, the planner can remove an existing show.

Servicetom Music Theater
Booking System
Register Show
Set up performance schedule
Enter reservation request
<<include>>
Register customer
Process reservation request
Generate invoice and tickets
Planner
Customer
Clerk

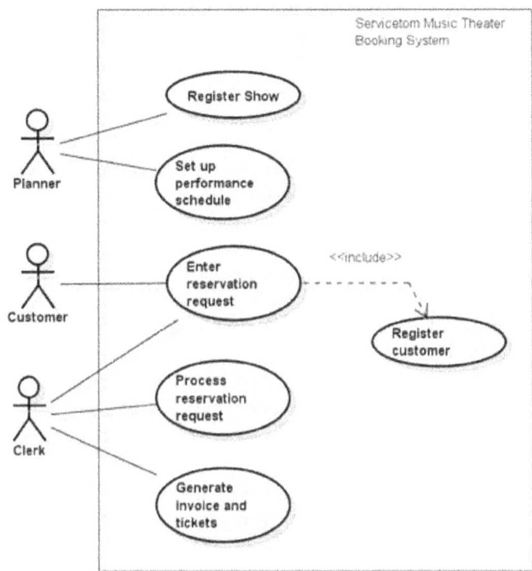

Figure 2.7 Serviceton Music Theater use case diagram

2.2.3 SERVICETON MUSIC THEATER GRAPHICAL USER INTERFACE

The requirements engineer also produced fully dressed (see Appendix B, [19]) descriptions for some of the use cases (not shown here). She also created a quick mockup (screen design) of the use case 'Register Show' (see Figure 2.8) to make it more tangible for the management of the theater.

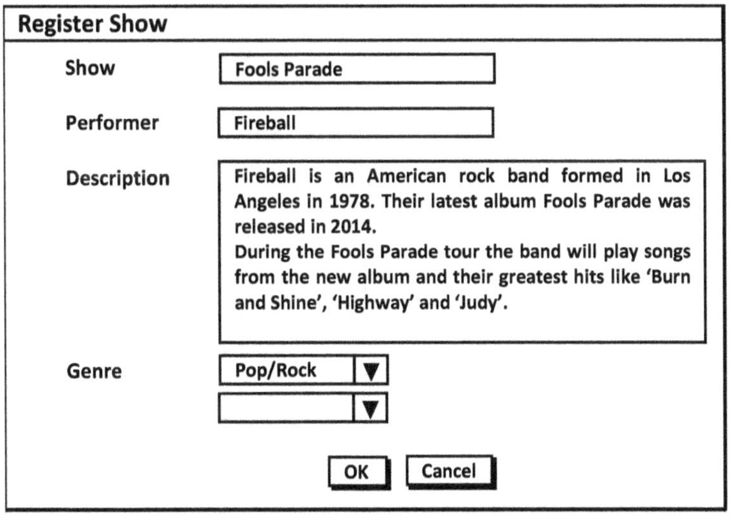

Register Show
Show
Fools Parade
Performer
Fireball
Description
Fireball is an American rock band formed in Los Angeles in 1978. Their latest album Fools Parade was released in 2014.
During the Fools Parade tour the band will play songs from the new album and their greatest hits like 'Burn and Shine', 'Highway' and 'Judy'.
Genre
Pop/Rock
OK
Cancel

Figure 2.8 Mockup for use case 'Register Show'

2.2.4 SERVICETON MUSIC THEATER INFORMATION MODEL

One of the main tasks of the analysis phase is setting up a conceptual information model. The development team decided to use FCO-IM. The complete information model for the theater is presented in Appendix A. Chapters 3 through 6 describe in detail how to create such an information model.

2.2.5 SERVICETON MUSIC THEATER BUSINESS RULES

A list of business rules was made as well. A few examples of business rules are as follows (see Appendix A3 for the complete set of rules):

BR 04 A show can have multiple performances.

BR 07 Each performance has a single ticket price and a season ticket price.

BR 08 Customers who order tickets for at least six performances before the start of the theater season get season tickets prices.

BR 24 To be able to contact a customer, an email address and/or a phone number must be known for each customer.

Chapter 3
How to Model the Facts

Key Points

- **The key to the abstract model is the concrete Fact.**
- **FCO-IM has a good procedure to draw up a conceptual information model.**
- **Concrete examples of Facts are Collected, Verbalized, Sorted and Analyzed.**

Terms with a specific meaning in FCO-IM like 'Fact', 'Object Type' or 'Analyzing' will from here on be capitalized to distinguish them from their run-of-the-mill homonyms. One of the most valuable and rewarding tricks of the trade of information modeling is to always use *concrete examples of Facts*. Never be satisfied with a general description, an abstract account or a blank form. Always ask for concrete specimens of the information that is described, reported about or supposed to be filled in. If a domain expert says "Customers can send in reservation requests.", then do not rest before you have several concrete examples like the one shown in Figure 2.3 with actual data filled in by a customer.

The power of such examples to make things clear can hardly be overstated. They help to avoid misunderstandings (two people can talk about an abstract concept without realizing that they actually have different meanings in mind), prevent accidental or intentional vagueness (an abstract description is almost always quite incomplete) and force both domain expert and modeler to always get down to brass tacks. Therefore, using concrete examples is a hallmark of all Fact Oriented Modeling techniques, not only FCO-IM. Indeed, concrete examples can and should be used in all other information modeling techniques as well (they often are, but unfortunately not always).

In FCO-IM, the abstract level of the information model is built up exclusively from the concrete level of the concrete examples of Facts. Not a single modeling decision is made without being firmly rooted in concrete Facts. In addition to the benefits stated above, this has the following advantages as well: the modeler can only build the information model together with the domain expert (no ivory tower work) and the domain expert is not bothered with technical information modeling jargon or arcane diagrams. Everything is done using concrete examples of Facts, which both modeler and domain expert understand.

Section 3.1 briefly summarizes the FCO-IM procedure, which is then elaborated extensively in the rest of the book. How to draw up the basic information structure is covered in the rest of Chapter 3: Collecting concrete examples of Facts (Section 3.2), Verbalizing these examples (Section 3.3) and Sorting these Verbalizations (Section 3.4). Next, the basic concepts of FCO-IM are discussed by showing how the original Verbalizations can be read back from an FCO-IM diagram (Section 3.5). This is a didactical approach that we have found fruitful in our classes. Then the modeling process is resumed by Analyzing the Verbalizations (Section 3.6). A few common pitfalls (Section 3.7) and typical cases (Section 3.8) conclude this chapter. Further steps in the FCO-IM procedure are discussed in later chapters.

3.1 The FCO-IM Information Modeling Procedure

Textbox 3.1 lists the steps in the FCO-IM procedure to draw up a conceptual information model. They should be carried out in this order even if they are discussed in a slightly different order in this book for didactical reasons.

---

1 **Collecting** (see Section 3.2).
Collect or draw up concrete examples of the data to be modeled.

2 **Verbalizing** (see Section 3.3).
Verbalize the examples in clear and correct sentences that express one complete Fact each.

3 **Sorting** (see Section 3.4).
Sort the verbalizations into Fact Types and give each Fact Type a meaningful name.

4 **Analyzing** (see Section 3.6).
Analyze the Fact Types to determine the Object Types and Label Types that occur in them.

5 **Determining Uniqueness Constraints** (see Section 4.2).
For each Fact Type, systematically find all the Uniqueness Constraints that apply to it.

6 **Checking** (see Chapter 5, especially Sections 5.3 and 5.4).
Use the Uniqueness Constraints to correct the information model, if necessary.

7 **Determining Totality Constraints** (see Section 4.3).
For each Object Type, semi-systematically find all Totality Constraints that apply to it.

8 **Subtyping** (see Section 6.2).
For each Object Type, find all (if any) subtypes of it.

9 **Determining Other Constraints** (see Section 4.5).
Incorporate all Business Rules that have not been modeled yet.

Textbox 3.1 Steps in the FCO-IM procedure to draw up a conceptual information model

3.2 Collecting: Finding or Drawing up Examples of Facts

When you start to make an information model, it is often very helpful to make a rough (i.e. without too many details) process model first like the Business Process Model for Serviceton Music Theater shown in Figure 2.6. Such a model serves to capture the important data flows as well, and can therefore be used as a starting point to Collect concrete examples of the relevant information to be modeled. For every data flow or data store in the process model, samples of the actual data in the flow or store should be Collected. This also helps to ensure that the information model will contain all the relevant data. In this way, the example of the performance schedule in Figure 2.1 was taken from the data store 'Schedule' in Figure 2.6, the example reservation form in Figure 2.3 from the data flow 'Reservation request' in Figure 2.6 and so on.

If other data sources turn up, during interviews or otherwise, samples should be Collected immediately from these as well. It is usually easy to find concrete examples like this. However, sometimes the organization doesn't yet have concrete examples because the data concerned is to be used in the future and is not available yet. In such a case, the modeler and domain expert should make up realistic artificial concrete examples, as in the dialogue shown in Textbox 3.2. This dialogue is used here only to illustrate making up examples of data, it was not used for the actual information model for Serviceton Music Theater.

Domain expert:	In the future, we'd like to offer discounts for different types of customers in the form of a percentage of the total cost for reservations, independent from the usual arrangement for season ticket prices.
Analyst:	Can you give me an example of such a discount?
Domain expert:	Well, something like VIP customers get a 10% reduction.
Analyst:	OK, then you'd have to know which customers are VIPs as well, I suppose.
Domain expert:	Yes, of course.
Analyst:	(Quickly scribbling two tables on a piece of paper) Like this?

Customer type	reduction (%)
Ordinary	0
Frequent	5
VIP	10

Customer	is of type
111	VIP
112	Ordinary
113	Ordinary

Domain expert:	Exactly! Good idea to use 'Ordinary', too; then we're sure we didn't forget to specify a type for a customer. Let's make that the default type.
Analyst:	That's why I always like to make examples; they often help to make things a lot more clear.

Textbox 3.2 Drawing up concrete examples of Facts that are new

3.3 VERBALIZING: PUTTING THE CONCRETE EXAMPLES INTO WORDS

Step 2 in the FCO-IM procedure to draw up a conceptual information model (see Section 3.1) is *Verbalizing*: putting the Collected concrete examples of the data to be modeled into words so that a set of correct sentences is obtained in which each sentence expresses exactly one complete Fact. Such sentences that express exactly one complete Fact are called Fact Expressions in FCO-IM.

3.3.1 WHY VERBALIZE?

Key Points

- **Verbalizing concrete examples prevents vagueness and misunderstandings.**
- **A good Verbalization makes the *meaning* of the Facts clear.**
- **Verbalizing clarifies how persons, things or concepts are *identified*.**

One of the main problems with data models is that they are very hard to *validate*: How can domain experts verify that an information model is correct and give their approval? They usually cannot read such arcane models, and while the information modelers may be experts in data structures, they are usually not familiar with the data itself. If this problem is not dealt with, an information model can have serious flaws and nobody will notice until the implementation fails to work.

One reason is that information models contain a lot of *metadata* (i.e. statements *about* the data to be modeled; see also Section 4.4.1), in terms of Object Types, Fact Types, cardinalities and other such abstract data structure concepts, but they usually do not show the 'ordinary' data itself. This leaves the door wide open to vagueness (the abstract concepts seem quite plausible) and misunderstandings (people can interpret the abstract concepts differently and so talk at cross-purposes without realizing it).

Using Verbalizations of concrete examples of the data to be modeled helps to avoid such problems in two important ways:

- The first way is that good Verbalizations make the *meaning* of the data clear. Data examples are often in abbreviated form (diagrams, tables, etc.) in which much of their meaning is tacitly understood by the domain experts, but unknown to the information modeler. This 'hidden' semantics is brought out by Verbalizing them. Because Verbalizations are expressions of Facts in natural language, they put both domain expert and modeler on common ground.
- The second way is that these Verbalizations are the foundation on which the abstract information model will be built. All abstract data structures are gradually added to this concrete layer in a constant dialogue between

the information modeler and the domain expert (Sections 3.4 and 3.6 describe how this is done).

Another benefit from using such Verbalizations is that several crucial information modeling issues are automatically and inextricably dealt with as well. For instance, how are all the persons/things/concepts that the Facts refer to *identified*? Verbalizing a concrete Fact forces you to use the actual numbers, names, codes, etc. that unambiguously make clear which individual things, persons or concepts the Fact is about. Identification is one of the most important aspects of information models, and is so taken along automatically in a natural way.

Because the Verbalizations are incorporated lock, stock and barrel into the information model, the connection between the concrete ordinary data of the domain expert and the abstract metadata of the information modeler is always clear. This makes validation a lot easier and greatly reduces the risk of vagueness and misunderstandings.

3.3.2 GOOD VERBALIZATIONS FOR SERVICETON

A part of the performance schedule of Serviceton Music Theater (see Chapter 2) is repeated in Figure 3.3. Good Verbalizations for two shows (highlighted in Figure 3.3) are given in Table 3.4.

March 2015						
Day	**Time**	**Performance**	**Show**	**Genre**	**Price**	
					Single ticket	**Season ticket**
Sun 1	7:30PM	104	Big Train – Movin' and Groovin'	Oldies	$29.00	$26.00
Mon 2						
Tue 3	7:30PM	105	Kelly Turner – Cats and Dogs	Comedy	$35.00	$31.50
...	...	...	....	...	...	...
Sun 8	3:00PM	108	Jungle Town – Tiger Feet, The Musical	Musical, Family	$27.50	$24.00
	8:00PM	109	Jungle Town – Tiger Feet, The Musical	Musical, Family	$27.50	$24.00
Mon 9						
Tue 10	7:30PM	110	James Rutherford – Lucky Number	Comedy	$32.00	$29.00
...	...	...	...	...	...	...

Figure 3.3 Part of the performance schedule

"There is a show Cats and Dogs performed by Kelly Turner."	"There is a show Tiger Feet, The Musical performed by Jungle Town."
"The show Cats and Dogs by Kelly Turner is briefly described as: Stand-up comedy."	"The show Tiger Feet, The Musical by Jungle Town is briefly described as: A sparkling show for the whole

	family."
"The show Cats and Dogs by Kelly Turner is in the genre Comedy."	"The show Tiger Feet, The Musical by Jungle Town is in the genre Musical." "The show Tiger Feet, The Musical by Jungle Town is in the genre Family."
"Performance 105 features Cats and Dogs by Kelly Turner."	"Performance 108 features Tiger Feet, The Musical by Jungle Town."
"Performance 105 is planned on March 3, 2015."	"Performance 108 is planned on March 8, 2015."
"March 3, 2015 is a Tuesday."	"March 8, 2015 is a Sunday."
"Performance 105 starts at 7:30 PM."	"Performance 108 starts at 3:00 PM."
"The price of a single ticket for performance 105 is $35.00."	"The price of a single ticket for performance 108 is $27.50."
"The price of a season ticket for performance 105 is $31.50."	"The price of a season ticket for performance 108 is $24.00."

Table 3.4 Verbalizations of the highlighted parts in Figure 3.3

3.3.3 GUIDELINES FOR VERBALIZING

Key Points

- **A good Verbalization is a grammatically correct complete sentence that**
  - **expresses a concrete Fact that can be highlighted in the concrete examples,**
  - **expresses exactly one Fact (no clusters of Facts, no half Facts),**
  - **does not refer to other sentences and**
  - **expresses the meaning of this Fact as clearly as possible.**

This section presents guidelines for Verbalizing and gives examples of good and bad Verbalizations.

All Verbalizations must always be stated in complete sentences with correct spelling and grammar. This basic requirement is assumed to be fulfilled throughout this book. Such sentences, which express exactly one Fact, are called Fact Expressions from now on. Such Fact Expressions are always written as quoted sentences: they start with a double quote mark (to signify the start of the quotation), and end with a period (to signify the end of the sentence) followed by another double quote mark (to signify the end of the quotation).

Figure 3.5 shows a few examples of the body weight data of members of the SlimSlim Fitness and Weight Reducing Club. These examples will be used to illustrate the guidelines for Verbalizing.

SlimSlim body weight data:

Member:	M47 John
Date	**Weight (lb)**
May 4, 2015	198.4
May 5, 2015	197.9
May 8, 2015	198.3
May 9, 2015	197.9

Member:	M58 Lisa
Date	**Weight (lb)**
April 29, 2015	201.3
May 5, 2015	198.3
May 10, 2015	196.6

Figure 3.5 Examples of body weight data

3.3.3.1 Express Concrete Facts That Can Be Highlighted

Express only what you see *directly* in the concrete examples. You should be able to highlight every component in the Fact Expressions in the concrete examples with a marker.

Good Verbalizations	Why good?
`"The first name of member M47 is John."`	Both concrete components 'M47' and 'John' are listed directly in the examples in Figure 3.5.

"Member M58 weighed 198.3 lb on May 5, 2015."	All concrete components 'M58', '193.3 lb' and 'May 5, 2015' can be highlighted in the examples in Figure 3.5.

Table 3.6 Good Verbalizations

Bad Verbalizations	**Why bad?**
"Weights are to be recorded for members."	This Fact Expression expresses a generality, not a concrete Fact. It is *metadata*: an expression *about* the data, not an expression *of* the data in Figure 3.5.
"3 measurements have been recorded for M58."	The '3' can't be highlighted directly in the examples in Figure 3.5. This is a conclusion drawn from looking at the basic Facts and counting them. A very large number of other conclusions can be drawn from them as well (like "Lisa lost 1.7 pounds in 5 days."), and it would be absurd to state them all. That's what we have query languages for: to derive all sorts of interesting things from the basic Facts. In information modeling we only model the indispensable basic Facts.

Table 3.7 Bad Verbalizations

3.3.3.2 Express Exactly One Fact: No Clusters of Facts, No Incomplete Facts

The goal of modeling *elementary* Facts is to have Facts that each express exactly one concrete Fact. The reasons are:

- **Elementary Facts are the simplest to model**. Modeling the smallest units of information one at a time prevents biting off more than you can chew. If you try to model clusters of Facts in one go, the risk of making mistakes is much bigger. Moreover, you would need to use extra, more complicated concepts. For example, in FCO-IM only one concept is needed (namely Fact Type), whereas Entity-Relationship Modeling (ERM, see Appendix B, [12]) needs *three* concepts (entity type, attribute, relationship type) to model the same information.

- **Elementary Facts can be easily combined into desired clusters later.** It is easy to group elementary Facts into a table or on a user interface screen. When these 'Lego' building blocks are all available, any desired compound structure can be built with them. Clustering elementary Facts prematurely reduces flexibility in making clusters and introduces extra concepts (like NULL values) that are not needed at the conceptual level of modeling; NULL values can arise only when elementary Fact Types are combined. In an elementary Fact Type, all components are always present (or the Fact simply doesn't exist at all), so no NULL values are needed.
- **Considering incomplete Facts (partial Facts, half Facts) leads to information loss.** See the examples in Table 3.9 below.
- **A table column (attribute) is almost always an incomplete Fact and not enough to use as an independent unit.** Using elementary Facts prevents modelers from considering just Fact *parts*. An attribute is only half a Fact Type at best, so it cannot be used as a separate building block. Seeing *pairs of columns* (or sets of three or more, depending on the number of components in an elementary Fact Type) as indivisible units of information is far more fruitful.

Good Verbalizations	Why good?
"The first name of member M47 is John."	A complete elementary Fact with two concrete components 'M47' and 'John'.
"Member M58 weighed 198.3 lb on May 5, 2015."	A complete elementary Fact with three concrete components 'M58', '198.3 lb' and 'May 5, 2015'.

Table 3.8 Good elementary Verbalizations

Bad Verbalizations	Why bad?
"The first names of members M47 and M58 are	This expression combines two separate Facts. It should be split into two separate Fact Expressions,

John and Lisa."	each stating only one single Fact: "The first name of member M47 is John." "The first name of member M58 is Lisa." In addition, in the compound sentence it isn't entirely clear which member has which first name. Adding 'respectively' would solve that but not the bigger problem of expressing two Facts in one go.
S1: "Member M58 was weighed on May 5, 2015." S2: "Member M58 was weighed on May 10, 2015." S3: "Member M58 weighed 196.6 lb." S4: "Member M58 weighed 198.3 lb."	Fact Expressions S1 and S2 seem OK, but if you look at S3 and S4, you can't tell *when* Lisa weighed 196.6 lb. Does Fact Expression S3 go together with S1 or S2, neither or both? S4 has the same problem. It is necessary to have the member, the weight and the date in one Fact Expression, otherwise the connection is lost and only partial Facts remain. S14: "Member M58 weighed 198.3 lb on May 5, 2015." S23: "Member M58 weighed 196.6 lb on May 10, 2015." In Fact Expressions S14 and S23, the correct members, weights and dates are combined, so no information is lost. S14 and S23 can replace S1, S2, S3 and S4. It is also possible to keep S1, S2, S14 and S23, even though S1 and S2 give no extra information when S14 and S23 are there as well, but S3 and S4 surely are incomplete. Reasons to keep S1 and S2 will be discussed later (see Section 4.4).

Table 3.9 Bad Verbalizations, compound or incomplete

How can you tell whether a Fact is elementary? Here's a test:

Test for elementaryness

Suppose you have a Verbalization in the form of a sentence.
Count the number of components in this sentence (e.g. it is four).

IF	you can split this sentence into two other complete sentences that *both* have fewer components (e.g. you can split it into two sentences, each having three components)
THEN	the sentence is not elementary. Split it into these smaller sentences and run the test again.
ELSE	the sentence is indeed elementary, and it is a genuine Fact Expression.

Textbox 3.10 Test for elementariness

Table 3.9 above shows an example of applying this test. Suppose you have only S14, and you wonder whether it is elementary. S14 has three components (member, weight, date):

`S14: "Member M58 weighed 198.3 lb on May 5, 2015."`

You can split it into S1 and S4, which *both* have fewer components (namely two).

`S1: "Member M58 was weighed on May 5, 2015."`

`S4: "Member M58 weighed 198.3 lb."`

But then you have an incomplete Fact: S4. This is even clearer if you consider S14 and S23, split them into S1, S2, S3, and S4, and find you no longer can tell when Lisa weighed what.

Alternatively, you can split S14 into S1 and S4, but repair S4 by adding the date to it and so get:

`S1: "Member M58 was weighed on May 5, 2015."`

`S5: "On May 10, 2015, member M58 weighed 198.3 lb."`

But S5 is just the same as S14, only with a different order of the three components. So this is not a split after which *both* new sentences have fewer than three components, and S1 and S5 together fail the test condition.

All other possibilities of splitting sentence S14 into two sentences with less than three components also yield incomplete Facts, so it is an elementary Fact Expression after all.

How can you tell whether a sentence that expresses a Fact is incomplete? Here's a test:

Test for completeness

Suppose you have Verbalized all the Facts from a concrete example.
Try to reconstruct the example *from these Verbalizations alone*.

IF you can reconstruct the example

THEN these Verbalizations do not express any incomplete Facts, and therefore, if they are not compound (see the test for elementariness in Textbox 3.10), they are genuine Fact Expressions.

ELSE the Verbalizations are incomplete, and you have to Verbalize the underlying Facts with more components.

Textbox 3.11 Test for completeness

As an example of applying this test, suppose you have Verbalized the right half of Figure 3.5, and you wonder whether these Verbalizations express complete Facts or not. All Verbalizations (sentences) are given in Figure 3.12 for completeness, though only S1, S2, S3 and S4 would be enough to carry out the test. Now make an empty example that looks like the ones in Figure 3.5. There is no problem in reconstructing the part of the figure that corresponds to sentences S6, S0, S1 and S2 (see Figure 3.12).

```
S0: Member M58 was weighed on
     April 29, 2015."
S1: "Member M58 was weighed on May
     5, 2015."
S2: "Member M58 was weighed on May
     10, 2015."
S3: "Member M58 weighed 196.6 lb."
S4: "Member M58 weighed 198.3 lb."
S5: "Member M58 weighed 201.3 lb."
S6: "The first name of member M58
    is Lisa."
```

Member:	**M58 Lisa**
Date	**Weight (lb)**
April 29, 2015 May 5, 2015 May 10, 2015	

Figure 3.12 Applying the test for completeness

But when you try to add S3, S4 and S5, the problem becomes clear: You can't tell where the weights have to go. So the test shows that these last three sentences express incomplete Facts. Table 3.9 discusses the same sentences S1, S2, S3 and S4 more abstractly but arrives at the same conclusion.

3.3.3.3 Use Sentences That Do Not Depend on Other Sentences

Every Verbalized Fact must be a stand-alone sentence, which needs no other sentences to be understood.

Good Verbalizations	**Why good?**
S1: "The first name of member M47 is John." S2: "Member M47 weighed 198.3 lb on May 8, 2015."	Two complete stand-alone Verbalizations of elementary Facts.

Table 3.13 Good Verbalizations

Bad Verbalizations	**Why bad?**
S1: "The first name of member M47 is John." S3: "This member weighed 198.3 lb on May 8, 2015."	Sentence S3 does not state explicitly which member it refers to. S3 needs S1 (as immediate predecessor) to know which member is meant, so it depends on S1. It should be corrected by explicitly identifying which member is meant (see S2 in Table 3.13).

Table 3.14 Bad Verbalizations, referring to other sentences

3.3.3.4 Use Sentences That Make the Meaning of the Facts as Clear as Possible

The clearer a Fact is expressed, the better. It is well worth the time and effort to search for phrases that make the *meaning* of the expressed Facts as clear as possible. Here are a few general guidelines, which should be used judiciously as rules of thumb, not as strict laws, each followed by some examples of poor and better ways of Verbalizing.

G1: Where possible and convenient, use the name of the *kind of person/thing/concept* together with the concrete identifier.

This provides context and so leads to a much better understanding. Units of physical quantities such as length (inches, feet, miles, etc.), weight (pounds, kilograms, metric tons, etc.) and time duration (seconds, minutes, years, etc.) must of course always be given.

Poor Verbalizations	Better Verbalizations
"M47 weighed 198.3 on May 8, 2015." "926R785 is held by Zwrtj."	"Member M47 weighed 198.3 lb on May 8, 2015." "Staff card 926R785 is held by employee Zwrtj."

Table 3.15 Poor and better Verbalizations

G2 Use verbs that are as specific as possible.

A common lazy way of Verbalizing is to use 'has' in almost every expression. This only satisfies the requirement for grammatically correct sentences, but doesn't make the meaning any clearer and makes the expressions indistinguishable on the metalevel (i.e. several Fact Expressions Types (see Section 3.5) contain the same predicate: "...has..."). Choose 'has' only if you really can't think of anything else.

Poor Verbalizations	Better Verbalizations
"Member M47 has first name John."	"The first name of member M47 is John."
"Member M47 has city Miami, Florida, USA."	"Member M47 presently lives in the city of Miami, Florida, USA."
"Employee E1257 has room A3.12."	"Employee E1257 uses room A3.12 for experiments."
"The car with license plate Colorado 521 ACJ has service date 3 March 2014."	"The car with license plate Colorado 521 ACJ was last serviced on 3 March 2014."

Table 3.16 Poor and better Verbalizations

3.4 Sorting

Step 3 in the FCO-IM procedure to draw up a conceptual information model (see Section 3.1) is *Sorting*: putting Fact Expressions that express similar Facts into the same Fact Type and giving each Fact Type a meaningful name.

Key Points

- **Sorting consists of two steps: Typing and Naming.**
- **In the Typing step, Facts of the same type are placed together in Fact Types.**
- **In the Naming step, each Fact Type is given a meaningful name.**

3.4.1 VERBALIZATIONS FOR SERVICETON

A part of the performance schedule of Serviceton Music Theater (see Figure 2.1) is repeated in Figure 3.17. Good Verbalizations are given in Table 3.18 for two shows (highlighted) in the form of Fact Expressions. They are the same as were presented in Section 3.3 above.

March 2015						
Day	Time	Performance	Show	Genre	Price	
					Single ticket	Season ticket
Sun 1	7:30PM	104	Big Train – Movin' and Groovin'	Oldies	$29.00	$26.00
Mon 2						
Tue 3	7:30PM	105	Kelly Turner – Cats and Dogs	Comedy	$35.00	$31.50
...	...	...	....	...	...	...
Sun 8	3:00PM	108	Jungle Town – Tiger Feet, The Musical	Musical, Family	$27.50	$24.00
	8:00PM	109	Jungle Town – Tiger Feet, The Musical	Musical, Family	$27.50	$24.00
Mon 9						
Tue 10	7:30PM	110	James Rutherford – Lucky Number	Comedy	$32.00	$29.00
...	...	...	...	...	...	...

Figure 3.17 Part of the performance schedule

"There is a show Cats and Dogs performed by Kelly Turner."	"There is a show Tiger Feet, The Musical performed by Jungle Town."
"The show Cats and Dogs by Kelly Turner is briefly described as: Stand-up comedy."	"The show Tiger Feet, The Musical by Jungle Town is briefly described as: A sparkling show for the whole family."
"The show Cats and Dogs by Kelly Turner is in the genre Comedy."	"The show Tiger Feet, The Musical by Jungle Town is in the genre Musical."

	"The show Tiger Feet, The Musical by Jungle Town is in the genre Family."
"Performance 105 features Cats and Dogs by Kelly Turner."	"Performance 108 features Tiger Feet, The Musical by Jungle Town."
"Performance 105 is planned on March 3, 2015."	"Performance 108 is planned on March 8, 2015."
"March 3, 2015 is a Tuesday."	"March 8, 2015 is a Sunday."
"Performance 105 starts at 7:30 PM."	"Performance 108 starts at 3:00 PM."
"The price of a single ticket for performance 105 is $35.00."	"The price of a single ticket for performance 108 is $27.50."
"The price of a season ticket for performance 105 is $31.50."	"The price of a season ticket for performance 108 is $24.00."

Table 3.18 Verbalizations of highlighted parts in Figure 3.17

For each row in the performance schedule in Figure 3.17, nine or ten Facts were Verbalized. These Verbalizations are shown side by side in Table 3.18. Similar Verbalizations can be made for all other rows in the performance schedule, which would yield a new set of nine or ten Fact Expressions for each row. Although each of these Fact Expressions would express a new, different Fact, obviously all of these Facts would be of the same *kinds* as those already shown in Table 3.18.

Fact Oriented Modeling techniques use Verbalizations of concrete Facts as the solid foundation on which to build the abstract conceptual information model. Because a conceptual information model is concerned with the *kinds of Facts (Fact Types)* rather than the "plain" concrete Facts, Verbalizing more rows would not help any further. The Verbalizations given in Figure 3.18 of the two rows in Figure 3.17 will suffice for the first step to build the conceptual level from the concrete level.

3.4.2 SORTING: TYPING AND NAMING

There are two easy substeps in Sorting: Typing and Naming. In Typing, Fact Expressions that seem to express Facts of the same type of Fact are put together in groups called Fact Types. In Naming, each Fact Type is given a clear and meaningful name. The result of Typing and Naming for the Fact Expressions in Table 3.18 is shown in Textbox 3.19.

```
Show:
   "There is a show Cats and Dogs performed by Kelly Turner."
   "There is a show Tiger Feet, The Musical performed by Jungle
    Town."

Brief Description of Show:
   "The show Cats and Dogs by Kelly Turner is briefly described as:
    Stand-up comedy."
   "The show Tiger Feet, The Musical by Jungle Town is briefly
    described as: A sparkling show for the whole family."

Show in Genre:
   "The show Cats and Dogs by Kelly Turner is in the genre Comedy."
   "The show Tiger Feet, The Musical by Jungle Town is in the genre
    Musical."
   "The show Tiger Feet, The Musical by Jungle Town is in the genre
    Family."

Performance Features Show:
   "Performance 105 features Cats and Dogs by Kelly Turner."
   "Performance 108 features Tiger Feet, The Musical by Jungle
    Town."

Performance Planned Date:
   "Performance 105 is planned on March 3, 2015."
   "Performance 108 is planned on March 8, 2015."

Calendar Day Is Weekday:
   "March 3, 2015 is a Tuesday."
   "March 8, 2015 is a Sunday."

Performance Starting Time:
   "Performance 105 starts at 7:30 PM."
   "Performance 108 starts at 3:00 PM."

Performance Price:
   "The price of a single ticket for performance 105 is $35.00."
   "The price of a season ticket for performance 105 is $31.50."
   "The price of a single ticket for performance 108 is $27.50."
   "The price of a season ticket for performance 108 is $24.00."
```

Textbox 3.19 Result of Typing and Naming Fact Expressions from Table 3.18

In Typing, there can be some freedom of choice in certain cases. For example, in Textbox 3.19, all four Fact Expressions that refer to a price of a ticket have been assigned to one Fact Type named 'Performance Price'. But it is also possible to assign these Fact Expressions to two different Fact Types, one for single tickets and one for season tickets, as is shown in Textbox 3.20.

```
Performance Price of Single Ticket:
   "The price of a single ticket for performance 105 is $35.00."
   "The price of a single ticket for performance 108 is $27.50."

Performance Price of Season Ticket:
   "The price of a season ticket for performance 105 is $31.50."
   "The price of a season ticket for performance 108 is $24.00."
```

Textbox 3.20 Alternative way of Typing the last four Fact Expressions from Textbox 3.19

Choices such as this will result in different information models (one Fact Type named 'Performance Price' versus two Fact Types named 'Performance Price of Single Ticket' and 'Performance Price of Season Ticket') although both models will contain exactly the same Facts. At this point, no preference for either way of Typing is given, and both ways can be considered as equally valid. However, such choices do have consequences for the flexibility of the information model and for the structure of the Relational Schema that can be derived (see Chapter 7). Pros and cons for making one choice or the other will be given later (see Section 6.1.1).

The name for a Fact Type should be chosen as specifically and meaningfully as possible, so it is clear from its name alone what kind of Facts it contains.

3.5 Reading Back Fact Expressions From an FCO-IM Diagram

Key Points

- **An FCO-IM information model contains as Population the concrete Fact Expressions from which it was built.**
- **These Fact Expressions can be read back from an FCO-IM diagram with a simple rule:**
  1. **Choose a Fact Type with a Fact Expression Type and one of its Tuples.**
  2. **Fill in the blanks:**

     IF a blank refers to a Role played by an Object Type

     THEN enter the indicated Object Expression Type
and fill in its blanks in the same way

     ELSE fill in the appropriate Label from the chosen Tuple.

In Section 3.4 (Sorting), Facts Expressions, which live on the concrete level of the data, were sorted into Fact Types, which live on the abstract level of the information model (the metadata level). This section introduces other main FCO-IM concepts by showing how the Fact Expressions from Section 3.4 can be read back from an FCO-IM diagram. These concepts are:

- Fact, Fact Type, Role
- Fact Expression, Fact Expression Type
- Tuple, Population
- Object, Object Type
- Object Expression, Object Expression Type
- Label, Label Type

These FCO-IM concepts belong to two different levels, namely the *concrete level* of the Facts themselves and the *abstract level* of the information model. In Table 3.21, there's an overview of which concept belongs to which level:

Concrete level of Fact Expressions	**Abstract level of information model**
Fact	Fact Type
[no counterpart]	Role
Fact Expression	Fact Expression Type
Tuple	*[no counterpart]*
Population	*[no counterpart]*
Object	Object Type
Object Expression	Object Expression Type
Label	Label Type

Table 3.21 FCO-IM concepts and levels

The diagram in Figure 3.22 shows an intermediate stage of the complete FCO-IM information model for Serviceton Music Theater. It contains the structure of the performance schedule part of the information model and all the Fact Expressions from Section 3.4 without any Constraints (Business Rules) added yet.

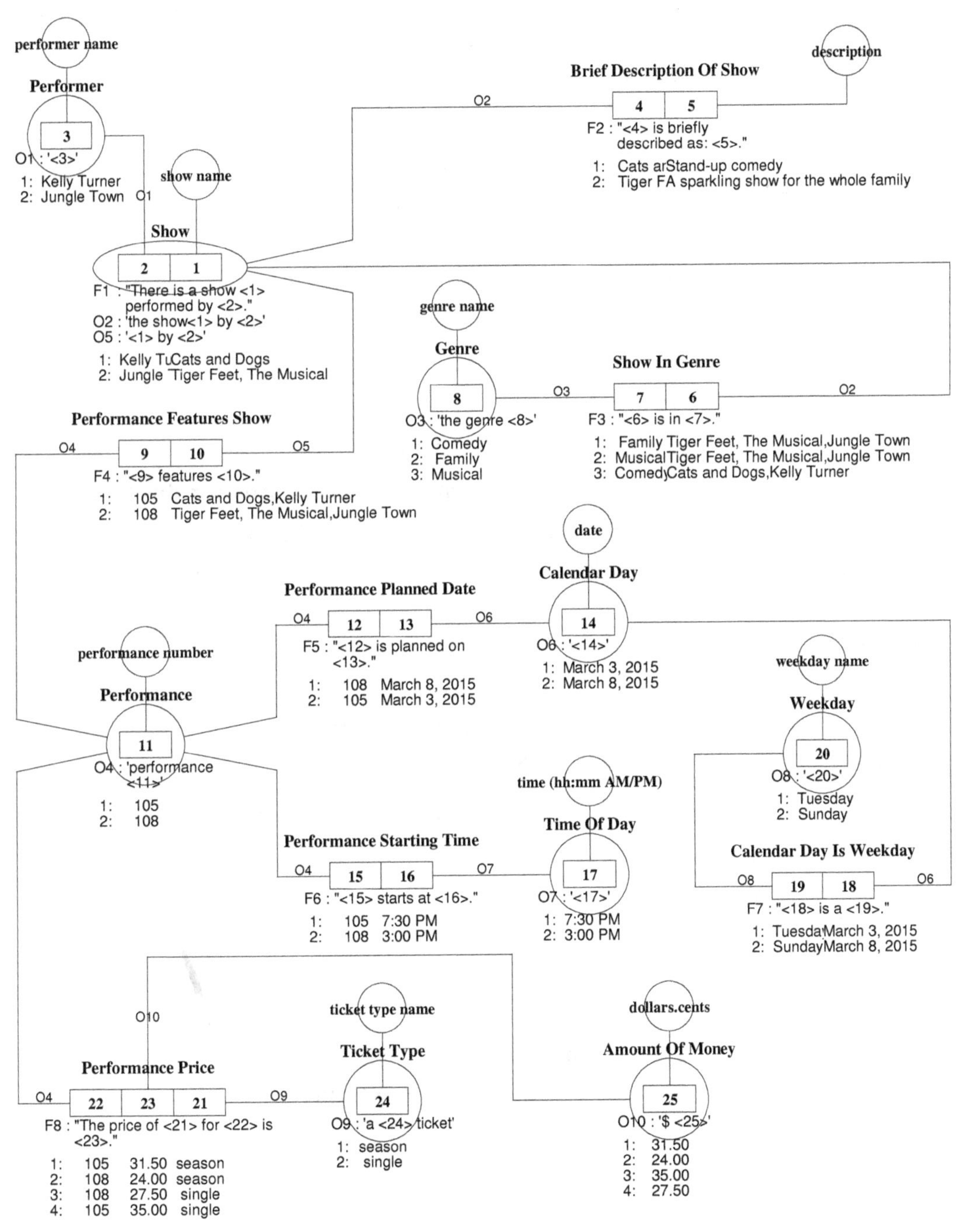
performer name
Performer
3
O1 : '<3>'
1: Kelly Turner
2: Jungle Town
O1
show name
Show
2 1
F1 : "There is a show <1> performed by <2>."
O2 : 'the show<1> by <2>'
O5 : '<1> by <2>'
1: Kelly TuCats and Dogs
2: Jungle Tiger Feet, The Musical
description
Brief Description Of Show
O2
4 5
F2 : "<4> is briefly described as: <5>."
1: Cats arStand-up comedy
2: Tiger FA sparkling show for the whole family
genre name
Genre
8
O3 : 'the genre <8>'
1: Comedy
2: Family
3: Musical
Show In Genre
O3
7 6
O2
F3 : "<6> is in <7>."
1: Family Tiger Feet, The Musical,Jungle Town
2: MusicalTiger Feet, The Musical,Jungle Town
3: ComedyCats and Dogs,Kelly Turner
Performance Features Show
O4
9 10
O5
F4 : "<9> features <10>."
1: 105 Cats and Dogs,Kelly Turner
2: 108 Tiger Feet, The Musical,Jungle Town
date
Calendar Day
14
O6 : '<14>'
1: March 3, 2015
2: March 8, 2015
Performance Planned Date
O4
12 13
O6
F5 : "<12> is planned on <13>."
1: 108 March 8, 2015
2: 105 March 3, 2015
performance number
Performance
11
O4 : 'performance <11>'
1: 105
2: 108
weekday name
Weekday
20
O8 : '<20>'
1: Tuesday
2: Sunday
time (hh:mm AM/PM)
Time Of Day
17
O7 : '<17>'
1: 7:30 PM
2: 3:00 PM
Performance Starting Time
O4
15 16
O7
F6 : "<15> starts at <16>."
1: 105 7:30 PM
2: 108 3:00 PM
Calendar Day Is Weekday
O8
19 18
O6
F7 : "<18> is a <19>."
1: TuesdaMarch 3, 2015
2: SundayMarch 8, 2015
O10
ticket type name
Ticket Type
24
O9 : 'a <24> ticket'
1: season
2: single
dollars.cents
Amount Of Money
25
O10 : '$ <25>'
1: 31.50
2: 24.00
3: 35.00
4: 27.50
Performance Price
O4
22 23 21
O9
F8 : "The price of <21> for <22> is <23>."
1: 105 31.50 season
2: 108 24.00 season
3: 108 27.50 single
4: 105 35.00 single

Figure 3.22 FCO-IM diagram for the performance schedule; no constraints added yet

From this diagram, the original Fact Expressions can be read back using the following procedure. All steps are illustrated below, and the new FCO-IM terms are explained as they are encountered.

Procedure to read Fact Expressions from a diagram

1	Choose a Fact Type that has a Fact Expression Type.	
2	Choose one of the Tuples in the Population of the Fact Type.	
3	Write the Fact Expression Type down including the double quote marks.	
4	Choose a blank in the Expression Type.	
5	Find the Role the blank refers to.	
6	IF	this Role is played by an Object Type
7	THEN	Find the Object Expression Type that is indicated for this Role.
8		Write the Object Expression Type into the blank, deleting the old single quote marks, the chevrons (angle brackets) and the role number.
9	ELSE	Find the Label Type that plays this Role.
10		Write the appropriate Label from the chosen Tuple into the blank, deleting the chevrons and the role number.
11	ENDIF	
12	IF	there is still at least one blank in the developing Fact Expression
13	THEN	go to line 4.
14	ELSE	We're done!
15	ENDIF	

Textbox 3.23 Procedure to read Fact Expressions back from an FCO-IM diagram

In Figure 3.24, Fact Type 'Performance Planned Date' is copied. It will be used to illustrate the procedure in Textbox 3.23 as a first example.

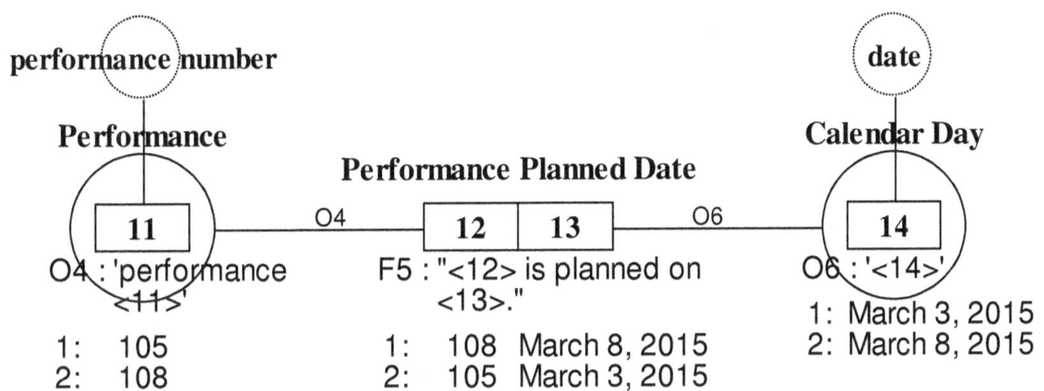

Figure 3.24 Fact Type 'Performance Planned Date'

3.5.1 FACT, FACT TYPE, ROLE, FACT EXPRESSION, FACT EXPRESSION TYPE

Line 1 from the procedure in Textbox 3.23:

1 Choose a Fact Type that has a Fact Expression Type.

Fact Types are familiar from Section 3.4. In an FCO-IM diagram, a Fact Type is depicted as a number of small rectangles in a row (1, 2, 3 or more), with its name written above the rectangles. These rectangles are called *Roles*. Each Role has a unique *role number* to distinguish it from other Roles in the same information model. In Figure 3.24, there are three Fact Types: 'Performance', which consists of one Role with number 11; 'Performance Planned Date', which consists of two Roles with numbers 12 and 13; and 'Calendar Day', which has one Role with number 14.

Fact Expressions are familiar from Section 3.3. They are sentences that state exactly one elementary Fact. Fact Expressions that belong to the same Fact Type are all very much alike:

```
"Performance 105 is planned on March 3, 2015."
"Performance 108 is planned on March 8, 2015."
```

The common part of Fact Expressions of the same Fact Type is a sort of skeleton for every sentence of this type. This skeleton can be written down explicitly if the varying parts are removed and replaced by blanks that can be filled in differently for each concrete Fact Expression. These blanks are indicated by chevrons (angle brackets: '<' and '>'). What remains is a *Fact Expression Type*:

"<...> is planned on <...>."

In an FCO-IM diagram, every Fact Expression Type is given a unique number that starts with 'F'. To show what is to be entered into the blanks, a *role number* is written in each blank.

F5: "<12> is planned on <13>."

From the diagram, it is then clear what should be entered in each blank: a performance (number) in <12>, because Role 12 is connected to 'Performance', and a calendar day (date) in <13>.

In Figure 3.24, only Fact Type 'Performance Planned Date' has a Fact Expression Type.

Result of line 1:

We choose Fact Type 'Performance Planned Date' with Fact Expression Type 'F5'.

3.5.2 TUPLE, POPULATION

Lines 2-5 from the procedure in Textbox 3.23:

2 Choose one of the Tuples in the Population of the Fact Type.
3 Write the Fact Expression Type down including the double quote marks.
4 Choose a blank in the Expression Type.
5 Find the Role the blank refers to.

There are two lines with performance numbers and dates written under Roles 12 and 13 of Fact Type 'Performance Planned Date' in Figure 3.24. The values in each line belong together, and such a line is called a *Tuple*. Each Tuple represents one concrete Fact. All the Tuples combined are called the *Population of the Fact Type*. The values under one Role are called the *Population of the Role*.

Result of lines 2-5:

We arbitrarily choose Tuple number 1 with the values '108' and 'March 8, 2015'.

We copy the Fact Expression Type: "<12> is planned on <13>."

Let's choose blank <12>. We find Role 12 in Figure 3.24.

3.5.3 OBJECT, OBJECT TYPE, OBJECT EXPRESSION, OBJECT EXPRESSION TYPE

In FCO-IM, every Role of a Fact Type is connected to something. Role 12, which we have just found (see the **Result of lines 2-5** above, and Figure 3.24), is connected to a solid circle named 'Performance'. The FCO-IM-way of stating this connection is: Role 12 is *played by* 'Performance', a metaphor that comes from the stage world. For a further explanation of this metaphor, see **Don't 2** in Section 3.6.6.2.

Lines 6-8 from the procedure in Textbox 3.23:

```
6  IF    this Role is played by an Object Type
7  THEN  Find the Object Expression Type that is indicated for this Role.
8        Write the Object Expression Type into the blank, deleting the
         old single quote marks, the chevrons and the role number.
```

An *Object* is a concrete person/thing/concept that can be uniquely identified. Examples are one individual customer, one specific seat somewhere in Serviceton Music Theater and one particular show. The part of a Fact Expression that uniquely identifies an Object is called an *Object Expression*. Examples are 'customer 436', 'seat 14 in row 3' and 'the show Cats and Dogs by Kelly Turner'. Note that whereas complete Fact Expressions are written between double quotes (see Section 3.5.1), Object Expressions are written between single quote marks, to make clear they are just *parts* of a Fact Expression. Each Object Expression refers to exactly one Object (so it *identifies* the Object).

Just like Facts can be sorted into Fact Types, Objects can be sorted into Object Types.

- 'customer 436', 'customer 437', and 'customer 123' are three different persons that can all be sorted into one Object Type 'Customer'.
- 'seat 3 in row 4', 'seat 14 in row 3', and 'seat 8 in row 12' are three different seats that can all be sorted into one Object Type 'Seat'.
- 'the show Cats and Dogs by Kelly Turner', 'the show Tiger Feet, The Musical by Jungle Town' and 'the show Lucky Number by James Rutherford' are three different shows that can all be sorted into one Object Type 'Show'.

In FCO-IM, almost every Object Type is shown as a Fact Type enclosed in a solid circle (or ellipse). See Object Types 'Performance' and 'Calendar Day' in Figure 3.24. See also Section 1.3.2.1 for some further remarks on why this is so in FCO-IM.

Just like the common part (skeleton) of Fact Expressions of the same Fact Type can be given in the form of a Fact Expression Type with a unique number that starts with 'F' and blanks that refer to Roles, so also can Object Expressions of the same

Object Type be given in the form of an Object Expression Type with a unique number that starts with 'O' and blanks that refer to Roles. Examples are `O15`: '`customer <34>`' (see the diagram in Figure A1.2), `O26`: '`seat <74> in <75>`' (see the diagram in Figure A1.4) and `O2`: '`the show <1> by <2>`' (see Figures 3.22 and A1.1).

Object Expression Types are written below every Object Type (= enclosed Fact Type) in FCO-IM diagrams. See `O4`: '`performance <11>`' and `O6`: '`<14>`' in Figure 3.24, for instance. If a Role is played by an Object Type, then the number of the Object Expression Type that applies to this Role is written next to the line that connects the Role to the Object Type. This is because an Object Type can have more than one Object Expression Type, so we need to know which one applies here. See Object Type 'Show' in Figure 3.22, which has two Object Expression Types O2 and O5, of which O2 applies to Roles 4 and 6, whereas O5 applies to Role 10.

Result of lines 6-8 for Role 12:

Role 12 is played by an Object Type (namely 'Performance'), and the Object Expression Type number O4 is written next to the connecting line between Role 12 and 'Performance'. So we find O4:

'`performance <11>`'.

We replace blank <12> with O4:

"`<12> is planned on <13>.`" becomes

"`Performance <11> is planned on <13>.`"

We have now completed lines 6-8 for Role 12 and skip to line 12 in the procedure in Textbox 3.23.

Lines 12-13 from the procedure in Textbox 3.23:

12 IF there is still at least one blank in the developing Fact Expression

13 THEN go to line 4.

Result of lines 12-13:

There are still blanks in the developing Fact Expression (namely <11> and <13>), so we go to line 4, and this time we choose blank <11>.

3.5.4 LABEL, LABEL TYPE

Lines 4-10 from the procedure in Textbox 3.23:

4 Choose a blank in the Expression Type.
5 Find the Role the blank refers to.
6 IF this Role is played by an Object Type
7 THEN ...
9 ELSE Find the Label Type that plays this Role.
10 Write the appropriate Label from the chosen Tuple into the blank, deleting the chevrons and the role number.

Blank <11> was chosen, which refers to Role 11. Role 11 is not played by an Object Type; it is played by 'performance number' (see Figure 3.24), which is not shown as an enclosed Fact Type. It is instead a *Label Type.* In FCO-IM, a *Label* is anything you can write down and which can be entered into an information system: It is a *name, number, code, text string,* or anything else that can be typed on a keyboard. Labels are used for several purposes; most importantly, they are used to *identify Objects with* in Fact Expressions (sentences) and/or information systems. Obviously, real people/things/concepts cannot be entered into a database, but the names/numbers/codes/etc. by which we identify them in speech or writing can! This distinction between the people/things/concepts and their names/numbers/codes is crucial in every information modeling technique including FCO-IM.

In FCO-IM, Labels like customer numbers '436', '437', '103' etc. can be sorted into a Label Type 'customer number', and seat numbers like '1', '14', '8' into a Label Type 'seat number' and performer names like 'Kelly Turner' and 'Jungle Town' into a Label Type 'performer name'. Label Types are shown as dotted circles in FCO-IM diagrams.

Result of lines 4-10 for Role 11:

Role 11 is played by Label Type 'performance number'. So we find the appropriate performance number in the Tuple '108 March 8, 2015' and replace the blank with it.

"Performance <11> is planned on <13>." becomes

"Performance 108 is planned on <13>."

3.5.5 READING BACK THE COMPLETE FACT EXPRESSIONS

Once more lines 12-13 make us go back to line 4, because there is still one blank to filled in (<13>).

Role 13 is played by an Object Type (namely 'Calendar Day'), and the Object Expression Type number O6 is written next to the connecting line between Role 13 and 'Calendar Day'. So we find O6:

'<14>'.

We replace blank <13> with O6:

"Performance 108 is planned on <13>." becomes

"Performance 108 is planned on <14>."

Again we go back to line 4 to fill in the blank <14>.

Role 14 is played by Label Type 'date', so we find the appropriate Label 'March 8, 2015' in the chosen Tuple, and replace the blank with this value:

"Performance 108 is planned on <14>." becomes

"Performance 108 is planned on March 8, 2015."

This is exactly the Fact Expression we started from in Section 3.4.

As a second example, please find below the results of several steps for reading back Tuple 2 from Fact Type 'Brief Description Of Show' (see Figure 3.22, at the top), without comment:

We choose 'Brief Description Of Show' with F2 and Tuple 2: '((Tiger Feet, The Musical), Jungle Town), A sparkling show for the whole family'.

"<4> is briefly described as: <5>"

"The show <1> by <2> is briefly described as: <5>."

"The show <1> by <3> is briefly described as: <5>."

"The show Tiger Feet, The Musical by Jungle Town is briefly described as: A sparkling show for the whole family."

You can verify that *all* the original Fact Expressions from Section 3.4 (down to the very last comma, quote mark, etc.) can be read back from the diagram in Figure 3.22 in the same way.

3.6 Analyzing

Step 4 in the FCO-IM procedure (see Section 3.1) to draw up a conceptual information model is *Analyzing*: finding out what *kind of people/things/concepts* (*Object Types*) play a Role in the Fact Types that were determined in step 3 (Sorting), by what *names/numbers/codes (Label Types)* these Object Types are *identified* and what other Label Types (if any) are used. Step 4 is the most important one in the FCO-IM procedure, so it will be discussed in detail with several examples.

Key Points

- **For each Fact Type:**
  - **Take its concrete Fact Expressions, and find the Object Expressions and/or Labels these contain.**
  - **Determine the corresponding Fact Expression Type, Object Types, Object Expression Types, and Label Types.**
  - **Add the Fact Type, Fact Expression Type, Object Types, Object Expression Types, Label Types and Population to the diagram.**
- **Rule of Thumb for Analyzing a Fact Expression:**

  IF an Expression part identifies an Object

  THEN mark it as an Object Expression

  ELSE mark it as a Label

  ENDIF

  For each Object Expression found, continue analyzing its parts according to this Rule of Thumb until only Labels are found.

Section 3.5 shows how concrete Fact Expressions can be read back from a given abstract FCO-IM information model. Here, the opposite direction is taken: how to build the abstract information model from these concrete Fact Expressions. The structure of the Fact Expressions will be analyzed in terms of which Object Expressions and/or Labels they contain.

The whole process of Analyzing is done by at least two persons in constant dialogue: the modeler and the domain expert. The modeler is an expert in information modeling, but usually unfamiliar with the domain (i.e. the organization for which the information system is being designed). In contrast, the domain expert knows everything about the domain, but is usually unfamiliar with information modeling. The modeler can only draw up a correct information model if he constantly consults the domain expert and verifies all information modeling decisions with him. To illustrate what questions the modeler can ask the domain expert without using technical lingo, several dialogues are given below as examples of such discussions.

Textbox 3.25 repeats the result of Sorting the Fact Expressions from Section 3.4.

```
Show:
   "There is a show Cats and Dogs performed by Kelly Turner."
   "There is a show Tiger Feet, The Musical performed by Jungle
    Town."

Brief Description of Show:
   "The show Cats and Dogs by Kelly Turner is briefly described as:
    Stand-up comedy."
   "The show Tiger Feet, The Musical by Jungle Town is briefly
    described as: A sparkling show for the whole family."

Show in Genre:
   "The show Cats and Dogs by Kelly Turner is in the genre Comedy."
   "The show Tiger Feet, The Musical by Jungle Town is in the genre
    Musical."
   "The show Tiger Feet, The Musical by Jungle Town is in the genre
    Family."

Performance Features Show:
   "Performance 105 features Cats and Dogs by Kelly Turner."
   "Performance 108 features Tiger Feet, The Musical by Jungle
    Town."

Performance Planned Date:
   "Performance 105 is planned on March 3, 2015."
   "Performance 108 is planned on March 8, 2015."

Calendar Day Is Weekday:
   "March 3, 2015 is a Tuesday."
   "March 8, 2015 is a Sunday."

Performance Starting Time:
```

```
  "Performance 105 starts at 7:30 PM."
  "Performance 108 starts at 3:00 PM."

Performance Price:
  "The price of a single ticket for performance 105 is $35.00."
  "The price of a season ticket for performance 105 is $31.50."
  "The price of a single ticket for performance 108 is $27.50."
  "The price of a season ticket for performance 108 is $24.00."
```

Textbox 3.25 Result of Typing and Naming Fact Expressions from Table 3.18

3.6.1 ANALYZING FACT TYPE 'SHOW'

Let's start with the first Fact Type: 'Show'. Its Fact Expressions have several words in common, and there are a few places where sentence parts can vary. To show what can vary and what the fixed parts are, the Fact Expressions have been copied below, with ditto marks highlighting the fixed parts.

```
Show:
  "There is a show Cats and Dogs
                             performed by Kelly Turner."
  "   "    " "   "  Tiger Feet, The Musical
                                   "      " Jungle Town."
```

The main concerns of the modeler at this point are what kinds of persons/things/concepts (Objects) are these sentences referring to and how are they identified? In these Fact Expressions, there are two places with varying contents: one after the word 'show' and the other after the word 'by'. The modeler has only two options for each of these places: either such a place contains an Object Expression or it contains a Label. The difference is an Object Expression *identifies an Object* and a Label does not.

There are two guidelines the modeler will satisfy while deciding on Object Expression versus Label:

G1 A Label always concerns only one varying part, but an Object Expression might concern more than one varying part (see several examples below).

G2 Any candidate Object Expression must concern *fewer* than the total number of varying parts in the Expressions that are being Analyzed.

Guideline G1 is always valid. Guideline G2 holds for all the Expressions discussed in this chapter. The only exception concerns *Subtypes*, which will be discussed separately in Section 6.2.

Some of the Objects (persons/things/concepts) the sentences in Textbox 3.25 refer to will be familiar even to a layman in the field of the domain. For example, in Fact Type 'Performance Planned Date', there are parts like '`March 3, 2015`' and '`January 23, 2016`'. Obviously, these are *dates*. As everybody knows, each date identifies a time period of 24 hours, and we are all familiar with diaries and calendars that have separate sections for such periods: they are called (calendar) *days*.

Other persons/things/concepts will be less familiar to a layman in the field of the domain, maybe even completely unknown. The modeler cannot be as sure about the sentence parts in Fact Type 'Show' that contain '`Cats and Dogs`' or '`Jungle Town`' as he would be about dates. He may have a strong intuition that these names identify a show and a performer, but he cannot be sure until he verifies this hunch with the domain expert. So the modeler and domain expert might have the dialogue in Textbox 3.26 to make this clear.

Analyst:	These names here, '`Cats and Dogs`' and '`Tiger Feet, The Musical`', do they identify a show? Are they unique, referring to just one show?
Domain expert:	Well, almost yes, but there are exceptions now and then.
Analyst:	Ah, could you give me an example of such an exception, please?
Domain expert:	We had the musical '`Cats`' a few years ago, but we also hosted a stand-up comedian, who had a show with the same name.
Analyst:	So how do you distinguish between those two shows? Do you use '`Cats, The Musical`' and '`Cats, The Stand-up Comedy`'?
Domain expert:	We could do that I suppose, because we do record the genre of every show, but now we use the name of the show together with the name of the performer. We think this appeals more to our customers, who are often fans of a performer. By the way, '`Tiger Feet, The Musical`' is actually the full show name, not a show name combined with a genre.
Analyst:	Could you give me two sentences like the ones here for those 'Cats'-shows?
Domain expert:	`"There is a show Cats performed by The Victoria Musical Company." "There is a show Cats performed by David Hardinger."`
Analyst:	Thanks. So a show is completely identified only by a

	combination of a show name and a performer name?
Domain expert:	Yes.
Analyst:	OK. About those performers: Kelly Turner and David Hardinger seem to be one person, but Jungle Town and The Victoria Musical Company seem to be a group of people. Does that difference matter?
Domain expert:	No, sometimes the performer is one person, sometimes a band, sometimes a group of actors or dancers or even an orchestra. We just use the name of the group or the solo performer.
Analyst:	Could you ever have two different performers with the same name?
Domain expert:	No, performers would get into big legal trouble if they used the same name.

Textbox 3.26 Dialogue about the identifications of 'Show' and 'Performer'

The modeler concludes that a *combination* of a show name and a performer identifies a show. However, he cannot mark this combination as an Object Expression:

```
Show (with Wrong Object Expression marked):
  "There is a show Cats and Dogs
                                  performed by Kelly Turner."
  "  "     " "   "  Tiger Feet, The Musical
                                       "       " Jungle Town."
```

This does not comply with guideline G2 above. The combination includes *all* varying parts instead of fewer than the total number of varying parts. So the modeler turns to the separate parts instead.

The modeler concludes that a name like 'Cats and Dogs' and 'Tiger Feet, The Musical' does not *by itself* identify a show. Therefore he will not mark this part as an Object Expression but as a Label. In contrast, a name like 'Kelly Turner' and 'Jungle Town' does indeed *by itself* identify a performer. So he will mark this last sentence part as an Object Expression.

In an FCO-IM diagram (see Section 3.5), Label Types are shown as *dotted circles (or ellipses)*. In contrast, Object Types are shown as Fact Types with a *solid circle (or ellipse)* around it. It would be nice if the Fact Expression parts could be marked in the same way, but unfortunately the distinction between dotted lines and solid lines is not clear if the sentence parts are too short. Therefore, the convention for underlining written text is that a *single underlining* corresponds to a Label and a *double underlining* corresponds to an Object Expression.

```
Show:
  "There is a show Cats and Dogs
                                   performed by Kelly Turner."
  "  "     "  "    "  Tiger Feet, The Musical
                                        "        " Jungle Town."
                            show name              Performer:O1

        F1: "There is a show <1> performed by <2>."
```

The name of the corresponding Label Type or Object Type is written directly below the underlining (here: 'show name' and 'Performer'). The Object Expressions above the double underlining all belong to one Object Expression Type, which has to be analyzed further (see below). But it is already given a unique code at this point (here: 'O1'). These codes start with 'O' followed by a unique number. In the software tool CaseTalk (see Appendix B, [2]), with which the diagrams in this book were made, these numbers start with '1' and are incremented automatically.

The last line in the Analysis above gives the Fact Expression Type. Fact Expression Types have a code that starts with 'F' followed by a unique number (here the code is 'F1' since this Fact Type is the first to be analyzed). The fixed text parts common to all the Fact Expressions (the parts that are not underlined) are written down, and each underlined part is represented as a numbered blank between chevrons (angle brackets). Each blank in the Fact Expression Type corresponds to a Role in the Fact Type (see Section 3.5). These Roles each get a unique number, and the corresponding Role number is written between the chevrons in the blank (here, <1> and <2>).

Here are the results of the Analysis of this Fact Type so far (halfway):

- There's a Fact Type called 'Show'.
- It has two Roles (two places have been underlined), with Role numbers 1 and 2.
- It has a Fact Expression Type F1.
- Role 1 is *played by* (a stage metaphor for 'is connected to', see also **Don't 2** in Section 3.6.6.2) a Label Type. This Label Type is called 'show name'.

- Role 2 is played by an Object Type. This Object Type is called 'Performer'. The corresponding Object Expression Type has the code 'O1'.

A diagram showing the results so far is given in Figure 3.27.

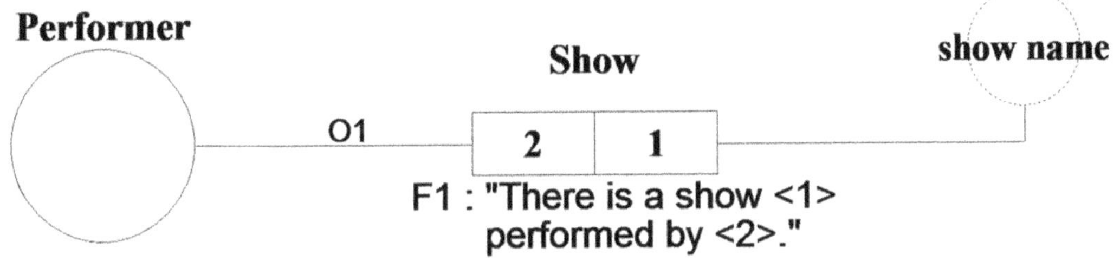

Figure 3.27 FCO-IM diagram with results of the Analysis of Fact Type 'Show' halfway

Now the structure of the Object Type 'Performer' with its Object Expression Type 'O1' still has to be determined. The modeler has to establish whether there are separate components in the Object Expressions used to identify a performer, and what kind of names/numbers/codes etc. (Labels) are used in these Object Expressions.

An Object Expression might consist of several separately varying compounds. For example, a hotel room could be identified by Object Expressions like '`room 27 on floor number 6`' or '`room 14 on floor number 3`', which contain a room number *and* a floor number. In such cases, it is necessary to look for *smaller* Object Expressions within the one being analyzed. In the hotel room example, '`floor number 6`' and '`floor number 3`' identify a floor in the hotel building, and so there is a new, smaller Object Expression that identifies a floor within each original one that identifies a room. In contrast, if there are no separate compounds, then no new Object Expressions can be found, and the modeler only has to determine the Label Type(s) used to identify the Object Type.

So the modeler copies all Object Expressions and analyzes these further with the domain expert. He includes one from the earlier dialogue (see Textbox 3.26). He encloses the Object Expressions in single quotes, because he is dealing with a sentence part instead of a complete sentence. There is no fixed text this time; otherwise, he would have used ditto marks again.

```
'Kelly Turner'
'Jungle Town'
'David Hardinger'
```

Modeler and analyst now have the dialogue shown in Textbox 3.28.

Analyst: These names that identify a performer, do they have any compounds like a first name and a surname or something like that?

Domain expert: Some performers have both, yes, but some have only a surname or a stage name, and there are groups and bands with completely different names like '`The Victoria Musical Company`', or '`Texornia`' or '`Swipe Swipe Swipe`', etc.

Analyst: So you don't separate these names into components?

Domain expert: No, we just write the full name down as it is.

Analyst: I guess you call them 'performer names'?

Domain expert: We usually just put 'Performer' in our ads and in our program, but yeah, those names are performer names.

Textbox 3.28 Dialogue about performer names

The modeler concludes that the performer names have no systematic underlying structure and thus belong to one Label Type 'performer name'. So he marks the Object Expressions accordingly.

```
'Kelly Turner'
'Jungle Town'
'David Hardinger'
 performer name

 O1: '<3>'
```

The last line above gives the Object Expression Type. Object Expression Types have a code that starts with 'O' followed by a unique number (here, 'O1'). The fixed text parts common to all the Object Expressions (the parts that are not underlined) are written down (O1 happens to have no fixed text), and each underlined part is represented as a numbered blank between chevrons (angle brackets). Each blank in the Object Expression Type corresponds to a Role in a Fact Type (see Section 3.5). This Fact Type is contained inside the solid circle that represents the Object Type. In FCO-IM, *all* Object Types contain a Fact Type. This Fact Type has as many Roles are there are underlined parts in the Object Expression (here, only one). Roles each get a unique number, and the corresponding role number is written between the chevrons in the blank (here, <3>).

The result so far is then (omitting the third Fact Expression with 'David Hardinger'):

```
Show:
  "There is a show Cats and Dogs
                              performed by Kelly Turner."
  "   "    " "   "  Tiger Feet, The Musical
                              "           " Jungle Town."
                     show name              Performer:O1

           F1: "There is a show <1> performed by <2>."

                                           'Kelly Turner'
                                           'Jungle Town'
                                           performer name

                                              O1: '<3>'
```

Here are the results of the Analysis of the Object Expression:

- Object Type 'Performer' contains a Fact Type with one Role (only one part is underlined in O1) with Role number 3.
- This Role 3 is played by a Label Type called 'performer name'.
- The structure of its Object Expression Type O1 is now clear (just a blank, no fixed text).

A diagram showing the results of the whole Analysis is given in Figure 3.29.

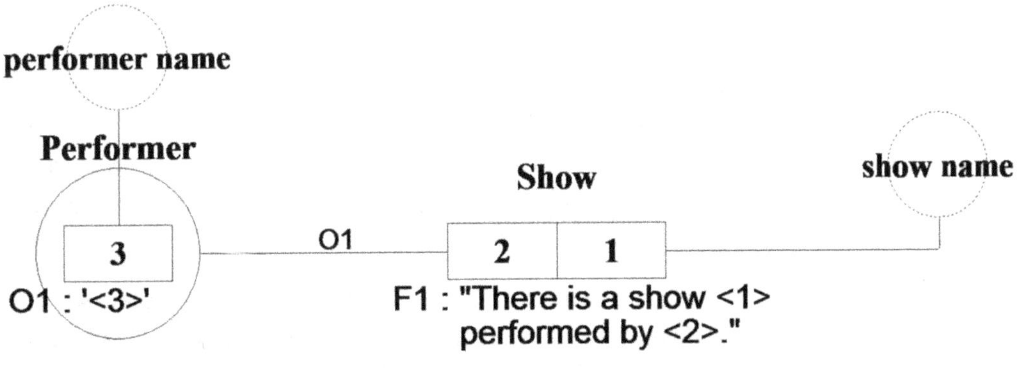

Figure 3.29 FCO-IM diagram showing the results of the Analysis, abstract level only

Everything you see in Figure 3.29 belongs to the abstract level of the information model. It was built entirely from the concrete Fact Expressions obtained in Section

3.3.2 and the dialogue between the modeler and the domain expert. Indeed these concrete Fact Expressions are the foundation of the entire information model, and they carry the *meaning* (semantics) of the modeled information. Therefore, no FCO-IM information model is complete without them. They can be added to the diagram in the form of a *population* of the Fact Types (see Section 3.5). This has been done in Figure 3.30. Please verify that the concrete Fact Expressions can be read back exactly (down to every comma, space character, etc.) from this figure using the procedure explained in Section 3.5. You can also compare it with the bigger diagram in Figure 3.22, where you will find exactly the same Fact Type, but with a few extra things that will be explained later.

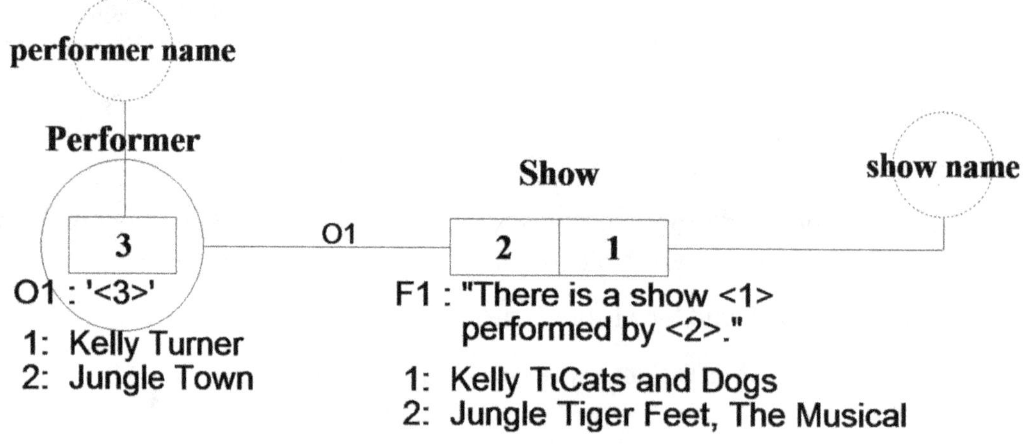

Figure 3.30 Complete FCO-IM diagram showing the result of the Analysis, with Population

3.6.2 RULE OF THUMB AND PROCEDURE FOR ANALYZING

Section 3.6.1 presented an example of performing the Analysis step of the FCO-IM procedure to draw up a conceptual information model (see Section 3.1). In this section, a Rule of Thumb for Analyzing is given as a practical guideline on how to perform this step. This rule works well in most cases. Another example of applying this rule is given in Section 3.6.3.

The following Textbox 3.31 contains a brief statement of this rule. A more elaborate procedure for carrying it out is given in Textbox 3.32 below. Examples of applying this procedure to Analyze Fact Types are given in Sections 3.6.3 – 3.6.5.

IF   an Expression part identifies an Object
THEN mark it as an Object Expression

ELSE mark it as a Label
ENDIF
For each Object Expression found,
continue analyzing its parts according to this Rule of Thumb
until only Labels are found.

Textbox 3.31 Rule of thumb for Analyzing

Textbox 3.32 below contains a detailed procedure for carrying out the Analysis step for a Fact Type.

Procedure for Analyzing

1 Choose one Fact Type and several (at least two) of its Fact Expressions.
2 Determine which parts of these Expressions vary.
3 If in doubt, find or make up extra Expressions to show which parts can and cannot vary.
4 Use ditto marks to highlight all the non-varying parts.

5 Suppose there are N varying parts in the Expression.
(N is often 2 or 3, but other numbers are possible too.)
6 Looking at all the varying parts, find (combinations of these) parts that identify an Object, but with *fewer* than the original N parts. Such (combinations of) parts are Object Expressions.
7 Look for the *largest* (combinations of) parts first.

8 FOR EACH Object Expression found in lines 5-7:
9 Find the *longest* part of the sentence that *only identifies an Object*. This may include some fixed text parts, like the name of the Object Type, or small words like 'the'.
10 Mark it with a double underlining.
11 Give the corresponding Object Type a meaningful name. If the Object Type is the same as one that was analyzed earlier, use the same name.
12 Add an Object Expression Type code ('O' followed by a unique number). If the Object Expression Type is exactly the same as one that was analyzed earlier, use the same code.

13 FOR EACH remaining varying part that does not belong to an Object Expression:

14 Mark *only the varying part* as a Label by giving it a single underlining.
15 Give the corresponding Label Type a meaningful name.

16 FOR EACH Object Type found in lines 5-12 above:
17 IF *exactly the same* Object Expression Type has already been analyzed earlier,
THEN write 'MATCH' below its code.
The Analysis is complete for this Object Type.
ELSE Repeat the procedure in lines 2-17 for its corresponding Object Expressions.

18 The procedure is finished when all found Object Types have been processed and no new Object Types have been found. You will finally find only Label Types or the word 'MATCH' at the lowest level.

Textbox 3.32 Detailed procedure for Analyzing

3.6.3 ANALYZING FACT TYPE 'PERFORMANCE FEATURES SHOW'

To illustrate the Procedure for Analyzing in Textbox 3.32, let's take the Analysis of Fact Type 'Performance Features Show'. The discussion of the Analyses of Fact Types 'Brief Description Of Show' and 'Show In Genre' (see Textbox 3.25 in Section 3.6.2) is skipped for now but will be summarized in Section 3.6.5.

Result of lines 1-4:

```
Performance Features Show:
  "Performance 105 features
                   Cats and Dogs             by Kelly Turner."
  "       "     108    "
                   Tiger Feet, The Musical   " Jungle Town."
```

There are three places where the text can vary: after the words 'Performance', 'features' and 'by'.

Result of lines 5-12 for the first varying place:

The modeler has a hunch that numbers like '105' and '108' identify a performance, but he cannot be sure until he checks this with the domain expert. They might have a dialogue about this like the one in Textbox 3.33.

Analyst:	These numbers here, '105' and '108', do they identify a performance?

Domain expert:	Yes, they do.
Analyst:	Is there really only one performance with number '105', or do you have several performances with this number, only in different years, or something like that?
Domain expert:	No, we have a unique number for each performance now. We did have a number per season some time ago, but this led to many misunderstandings ("You have sent me tickets for performance 12 in the spring season, but I meant performance 12 in the winter season."), and so we decided last year to give all performances their own unique number.

Textbox 3.33 Dialogue about the identification of 'Performance'

The modeler therefore decides to mark the first varying part as Object Expressions since there are no other varying parts that are needed to identify a performance. This one part also complies with the rule that an Object Expression must contain *fewer* than the total number of varying parts in the sentences. For the underlining, Line 9 in the procedure in Textbox 3.32 says:

> 9 Find the *longest* part of the sentence that *only identifies an Object*. This may include some fixed text parts, like the name of the Object Type, or small words like 'the'.

So the modeler includes the word 'Performance' in the underlining. Finally he adds the name of the Object Type: 'Performance', and a code for the Object Expression Type: '04'. (In the Analysis that led to the diagram in Figure 3.22, this was indeed the fourth Object Expression Type encountered).

```
Performance Features Show:
  "Performance 105 features
                 Cats and Dogs            by Kelly Turner."
  "       "      108      "
                 Tiger Feet, The Musical  " Jungle Town."
  Performance:04
```

Result of lines 5-12 for the second and third varying places:

From the dialogue in Textbox 3.26, the modeler already knows that 'Kelly Turner' is a performer name that identifies a performer and that 'Cats and Dogs' is a show name, which does not by itself identify a show, but together with a performer name does identify a show. Line 7 of the Procedure for Analyzing (see Textbox 3.32) says about varying parts that identify an Object:

7 Look for the *largest* (combination of) parts first.

So it would be wrong to underline the last two varying parts in the following way:

```
Performance Features Show
  (with wrong underlining of the last two parts):
  “Performance 105 features
                         Cats and Dogs            by Kelly Turner.”
  “       "       108        "
                         Tiger Feet, The Musical   " Jungle Town.”
   Performance:05              show name            Performer:01
```

The reason is that the combination of show name and performer identifies a show. Therefore this combination should be underlined first because the combination is larger than the two parts it consists of. In addition, the rule is satisfied that an Object Expression must contain *fewer* than the total number of parts in the Expression under consideration (see guideline G2 in Section 3.6.1, or line 6 in the Procedure for Analyzing in Textbox 3.32). Here, there are three varying parts. Only two identify a show, so these parts can be marked as one Object Expression. In contrast, when Fact Type ‘Show’ was Analyzed in Section 3.6.1, there were only two varying parts in the Expression. These two parts cannot be marked as an Object Expression in Fact Type ‘Show’, because these two parts do not concern fewer than the total number of varying parts in Fact type ‘Show’.

The modeler therefore underlines both varying places, adds the name of the Object Type (‘Show’) and an Object Expression code (‘05’):

```
Performance Features Show:
  “Performance 105 features
                         Cats and Dogs            by Kelly Turner.”
  “       "       108        "
                         Tiger Feet, The Musical   " Jungle Town.”
   Performance:04                           Show:05

               F4: “<9> features <10>.”
```

The last line above gives the Fact Expression Type. Here the code is ‘F4’ since this Fact Type was the fourth to be analyzed when the Analysis that lead to the diagram in Figure 3.22 was carried out. The Roles are numbered ‘9’ and ‘10’ for the same reason. The FCO-IM diagram with the results so far is shown in Figure 3.34.

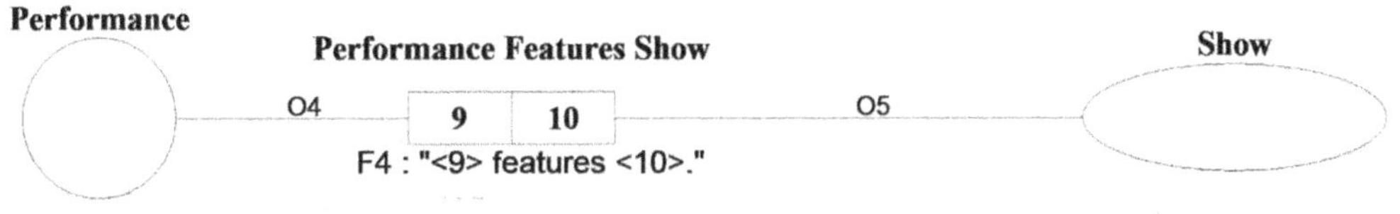

Figure 3.34 FCO-IM diagram of the Analysis of 'Performance Features Show' halfway

Result of lines 13-15:

These lines are not applicable here, since all varying parts were marked as Object Expressions, and so no Labels can be underlined yet.

Result of lines 16-17:

Since neither Object Expression Type O4 nor Object Expression Type O5 has been analyzed earlier, the procedure in lines 2-17 must now be repeated for the Object Expressions belonging to 'Performance' and for those belonging to 'Show'.

Result of lines 2-15 for the Object Expressions belonging to 'Performance':

The word '`performance`' is fixed text, and there seems to be only one varying place in these Object Expressions. Note the single quotes that enclose the Object Expressions:

```
'performance 105'
'     "      108'
```

Please ignore the use of capital letters to mark the beginning of a sentence when analyzing Object Expressions; an Object Expression might happen to be situated at the beginning of a sentence (as is the case here) or find itself located somewhere in the middle of a sentence. Therefore the convention used in this book is that we strip an Object Expression of its initial capital, but *only if this capital comes from the beginning of a sentence.* Names that require an initial capital retain it regardless of their location in a sentence. It is tacitly assumed that the initial capital is restored when a complete sentence is (re)generated from a diagram.

If there really is only one place where the text can vary, then the modeler can only mark it as Labels. This is the consequence of the condition in line 6 of the Procedure in Textbox 3.32 (and of guideline G2 in Section 3.5) because an Object Expression would then have to have fewer than one varying part, which is obviously impossible. But maybe there are really two separate places directly next to each other that can vary independently. Maybe the first digit '1' means something, and the other two digits '05'or '08' mean something else. So the modeler decides to check this with the domain expert; see the dialogue in Textbox 3.35.

Analyst:	These numbers that identify a performance, like '105' and '108', do they have any internal structure, like the first digit stands for a season and the others for a sequence number within that season or something like that?
Domain expert:	No, we've just started from 1 last year, and every new performance gets a new sequence number even if it concerns the same show. We're going to have a special promotion show when we reach number 1000.
Analyst:	OK. Do you call them 'performance numbers', 'performance codes' or something else?
Domain expert:	Performance numbers.

Textbox 3.35 Dialogue about the structure of performance numbers

Please note that in other cases, there could well be such a structure. For example, the rooms in a hotel might have unique room numbers, used in Object Expressions like 'room 215', 'room 708' or 'room 1208', in which the first digits identify the floor and the last two are a sequence number *on that floor*. In such a case, a correct Analysis of these Object Expressions would be that they contain *two* varying places. One place *by itself* identifies a floor and is therefore marked as Object Expressions (with 'Floor' as the Object Type), the other does not *by itself* identify anything (there are several rooms with a room number ending in '08') and so marked as Labels (with 'room seqno' as the Label Type).

```
  'room  215'
  '  "   708'
  '  "  1208'

Floor:O23  room seqno
```

Here, the modeler is satisfied that the performance numbers do not have such a structure, and therefore he marks them as Labels with corresponding Label Type 'performance number'.

```
Performance Features Show:
  "Performance 105 features
                   Cats and Dogs          by Kelly Turner."
  "       "    108     "
                   Tiger Feet, The Musical  "  Jungle Town."
   Performance:O4                        Show:O5

          F4: "<9> features <10>."

  'performance 105'
  '      "     108'
   performance number

  O4: 'performance <11>'
```

The structure of the Object Expression Type is clear as well now: the fixed text is 'performance', and the single Role gets number 11. Figure 3.36 shows the FCO-IM diagram with the results so far.

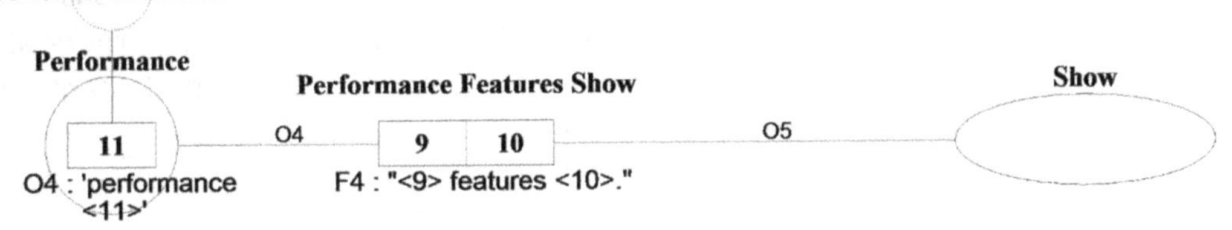

Figure 3.36 FCO-IM diagram of the Analysis of 'Performance Features Show' with 'Performance' filled in

Result of lines 2-17 for the Object Expressions belonging to 'Show':

For the further Analysis of 'Show', the modeler remembers the dialogue in Textbox 3.26, from which he knows that 'Tiger Feet, The Musical' is a show name, which is not always unique for a show, and 'Jungle Town' is a performer name that identifies a performer. So he can finish the analysis without unnecessarily consulting the domain expert further, as follows:

```
Performance Features Show:
  "Performance 105 features
                    Cats and Dogs            by Kelly Turner."
  "     "     108     "
                    Tiger Feet, The Musical   " Jungle Town."
   Performance:O4                          Show:O5

          F4: "<9> features <10>."

  'performance 105''Cats and Dogs           by Kelly Turner'
  '     "      108''Tiger Feet, The Musical  " Jungle Town'
   performance number      show name           Performer:O1
                                                  MATCH

  O4: 'performance <11>'             O5: '<1> by <2>'
```

The word 'MATCH' means that this Object Expression Type (O1) was already Analyzed earlier (see Section 3.6.1) and so does not need to be considered again. The modeler could not use 'MATCH' for the Analysis of Object Expression Type O5 because this is the first time O5 is encountered. Although the Analysis of O5 is very similar to the Analysis of Fact Expression Type F1, given in Section 3.6.1, there are differences too: F1 is a complete sentence, not a sentence part that identifies something, it contains different fixed words than O5 and it does not contain an Object Expression Type like O5.

The last part of the Analysis above can be added to the empty Object Type 'Show' in Figure 3.36.

- Object Type 'Show' contains a Fact Type with two Roles.
- One Role is played by a Label Type called 'show name'.
- The other Role is played by an Object Type called 'Performer'.

The above three points sound familiar; there already is a Fact Type called 'Show' with Roles that satisfy them all in Figure 3.30 with Role 1 playing 'show name' and Role 2 playing 'Performer'. So Object Type 'Show' contains Fact Type 'Show'! This feature, that every Object Type contains a Fact Type with the same name, is a unique property of FCO-IM as was elaborated on earlier (see Section 1.3.2.1). Such a Fact Type can be either a new one or an already existing one as this example illustrates. With the recognition that Object Type 'Show' contains Fact type 'Show', the structure of Object Expression Type O5 is clear too, and the result in diagram form is given in Figure 3.37.

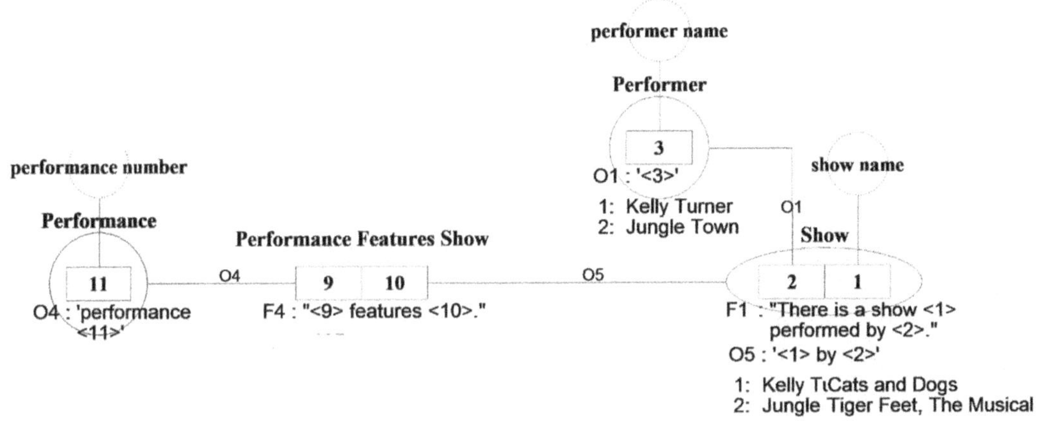

Figure 3.37 FCO-IM diagram of the Analysis of 'Performance Features Show' with 'Show' filled in

Result of lines 16-18 for the Object Expressions belonging to 'Performance' and 'Show':

No new Object Types were found, and the bottom level of the Analysis above has either Label Types ('performance number', and 'show name') or the word 'MATCH' (below Object Type 'Performer'). So finally, we can add the population to Fact Type 'Performance Features Show', to obtain the end result of the Analysis so far, shown in Figure 3.38. You can also compare it with the bigger diagram in Figure 3.22, where you will find exactly the same Fact Type but with a few extra things that will be explained later.

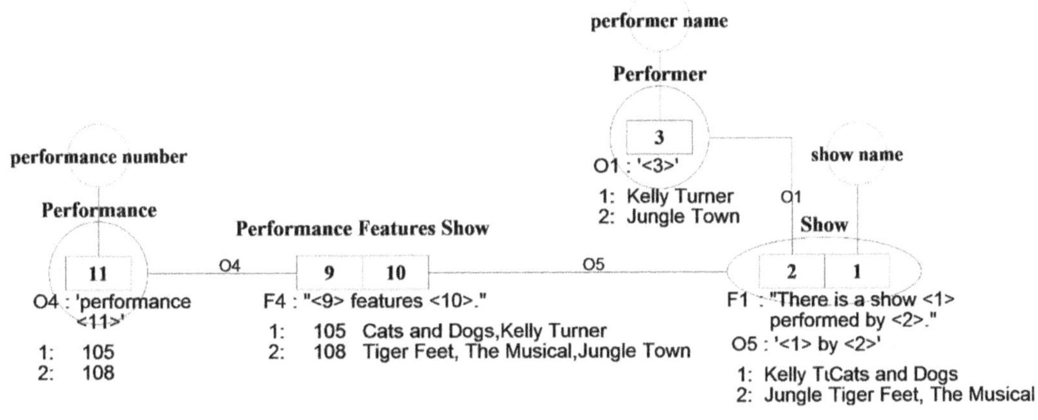

Figure 3.38 FCO-IM diagram of the complete Analysis of 'Performance Features Show'

Please note that 'Show' has both a Fact Expression Type `F1`, which is used for Verbalizations of Fact Type 'Show', and an Object Expression Type `O5`, which is used as part of the Verbalizations *of Fact Type 'Performance Features Show', with Fact Expression Type F4. Please* check that all the original Verbalizations of these two Fact Types can be regenerated from this diagram using the procedure described in Section 3.5.

3.6.4 ANALYZING FACT TYPE 'PERFORMANCE PRICE'

As another illustration of using the Procedure for Analyzing (see Textbox 3.32 in Section 3.6.2), let's take the Analysis of Fact Type 'Performance Price'. The discussion of the Analyses of Fact Types 'Performance Planned Date', 'Performance Starting Time' and 'Calendar Day Is Weekday' (see Textbox 3.25) is skipped for now, but it will be summarized in Section 3.6.5.

Result of lines 1-17, before Analyzing new Object Expression Types further:

```
Performance Price:
  "The price of a single ticket for performance 105 is $35.00."
  "  "    "    " " season    "    "       "       105  " "31.50."
  "  "    "    " " single    "    "       "       108  " "27.50."
  "  "    "    " " season    "    "       "       108  " "24.00."
```

There are three places with varying text. The modeler recognizes the Object Expressions that belong to Object Type 'Performance' ('`performance 105`' and '`performance 108`'), but perhaps these are a part of a larger Object Expression in these sentences. So he checks this with the domain expert, in a dialogue like the one in Textbox 3.39.

Analyst:	These sentences seem to say: "`The price of X is Y.`" with '`X`' being a combination of a ticket type and a performance. Does this combination, like '`a season ticket for performance 105`', mean something special here? Is there, for example, a clear difference between '`a season ticket for performance 105`', '`a season ticket for performance 106`' and '`a single ticket for performance 106`'?
Domain expert:	I'm not sure I understand your question completely. Of course performances 105 and 106 are two different performances, and a single ticket has a higher price than a season ticket, but other than that I don't know what you mean.
Analyst:	OK, and I get that you want to be able to price your tickets depending on both the performance and the ticket type. Are there properties specifically for '`a season ticket for`

	performance 105' that you need to record other than the price?
Domain expert:	No, I can't think of any.
Analyst:	OK, fine. Are 'season ticket' and 'single ticket' indeed ticket types, and do you have others?
Domain expert:	Yes they are, and we have a few others, like a 'complimentary ticket', or a 'special promotion ticket' and so on, but we usually don't advertise those.
Analyst:	A rather technical question (I need to know for the information model I'm drawing up): would 'ticket type name' be a good term for phrases like 'season ticket' and 'complementary ticket', or would you rather use another one?
Domain expert:	Sounds fine to me.

Textbox 3.39 Dialogue about Object Expressions in Fact Type 'Performance Price'

The modeler concludes from the dialogue in Textbox 3.39 that he does not need to create a separate Object Type for the combination of ticket type and performance (however, if this conclusion turned out to be wrong after all, see Sections 6.1.3 and 5.4 for how to fix that). The modeler decides not to check the other two possible combinations (ticket type + price, and performance + price). He knows from experience that a price (or any other amount of money) is almost never a part of a larger Object Expression. The reason is that a phrase like 'a season ticket of $35.00' does not identify a meaningful Object: it cannot refer to one individual ticket, because there will be several such tickets, and it is not perceived as a clearly different Object from 'a season ticket of $34.00'. The combination of performance and price is even more far-fetched ('performance 108 costing $35.00' or 'performance 108 costing $34.00' are hardly meaningful at all). The modeler might make a mistake by not checking these two possibilities, but he does want to bother the domain expert with seemingly pointless and tedious questions. It is part of the art of drawing up a good information model that a modeler can find the right balance between being too strict (needlessly verifying the obvious) and being too sloppy (missing important information structures). Fortunately there is a check in a later step in the FCO-IM procedure (see Section 3.1) to draw up a conceptual information model that will correct any mistake made here (see Section 5.4).

From the dialogue in Textbox 3.39, the modeler concludes that 'a single ticket' and 'a season ticket' are Object Expressions that identify an Object of an Object Type called ‘Ticket Type’. He already knows from the earlier Analysis that ‘performance 108’ and ‘performance 105’ identify Objects from Object Type ‘Performance’. He also knows from experience that ‘$35.00’, ‘$31.50’, ‘$27.50’ and ‘$24.00’ are Object Expressions because they identify an amount of money (you know exactly how much you have to pay when you read ‘$31.50’). So he underlines as follows:

```
Performance Price:
  “The price of a single ticket for performance 105 is $35.00.”
  “ "     "    " " season   "     "       "     105  " "31.50."
  “ "     "    " " single   "     "       "     108  " "27.50."
  “ "     "    " " season   "     "       "     108  " "24.00."
                 Ticket Type:09     Performance:04   Amount Of
                                        MATCH        Money:O10
          F8: “The price of <21> for <22> is <23>.”
```

The Object Type Expressions for ‘Ticket Type’ and ‘Amount Of Money’ are new and get codes ‘O9’ and ‘O10’, but the one for ‘Performance’ has been Analyzed before, so it gets its old code ‘O4’, and the word ‘MATCH’ is added to show that its Analysis has been completed earlier. The Fact Expression Type gets a new code ‘F8’ with Roles 21, 22 and 23 (see Section 3.6.5 for a summary of the Analysis of F5, F6 and F7). The corresponding FCO-IM diagram is given in Figure 3.40. Please note that Role 22 can be connected without further ado to the already existing Object Type ‘Performance’.

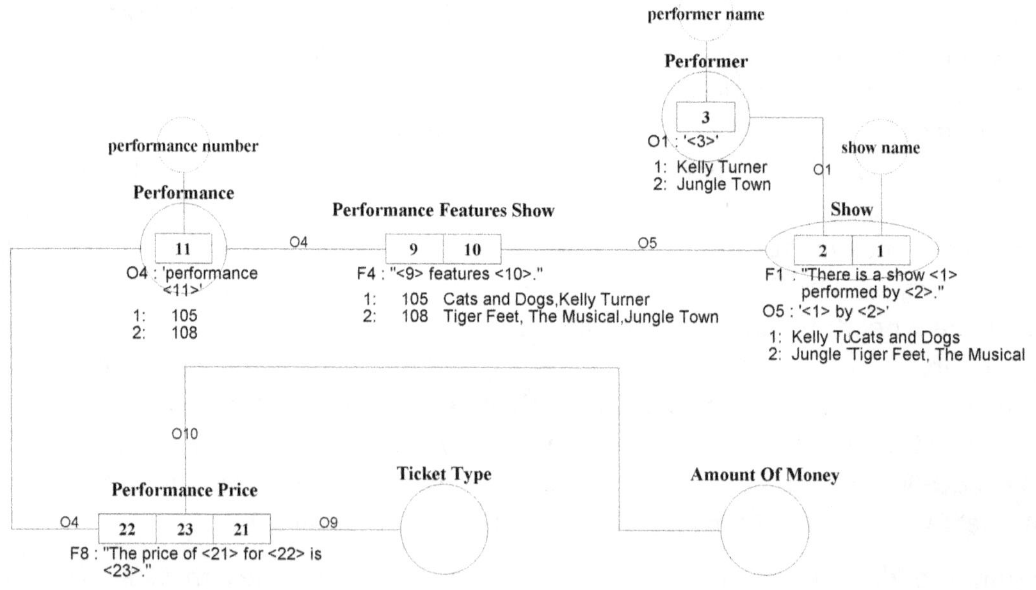

Figure 3.40 FCO-IM diagram of the Analysis of ‘Performance Price’ halfway

Result of lines 2-18, for the new Object Expression Types O9 and O10:

The modeler now looks at the new Object Expression Types O9 for 'Ticket Type' and O10 for 'Amount Of Money'. He knows from the dialogue in Textbox 3.39 that a ticket type is identified by a ticket type name, which obviously has no further internal structure; the names 'complementary', 'season', 'single', etc. are clear enough.

For the amounts of money, the modeler knows from experience that in '$31.50', the dollar sign is fixed text, after which the number of dollars and cents is given (dollars before the dot, and cents after it). He could see this as two different places where information varies—one for the dollars, and one for the cents—but decides to leave these two components unspecified for the time being. He can zoom in on these components later if necessary. There is a certain arbitrariness in the level of detail chosen for any information modeling. Many very common concepts, like dates or amounts of money, are best modeled using a single Label Type because most implementation platforms offer a good set of standard tools to manipulate dates and amounts of money. Domain-specific things however are best modeled in a greater level of detail because implementation platforms do not offer standard tools for those.

So the Analysis is completed as follows:

```
Performance Price:
  "The price of a single ticket for performance 105 is $35.00."
   "  "     "    " " season    "    "         "    105  "  "31.50."
   "  "     "    " " single    "    "         "    108  "  "27.50."
   "  "     "    " " season    "    "         "    108  "  "24.00."
                   Ticket Type:O9    Performance:O4    Amount Of
                                          MATCH        Money:O10
        F8: "The price of <21> for <22> is <23>."

               'a single ticket'                          '$35.00'
               '" season    "  '                          '"31.50'
               '" single    "  '                          '"27.50'
               '" season    "  '                          '"24.00'
             ticket type name                         dollars.cents

          O9: 'a <24> ticket'                         O10: '$<25>'
```

Figure 3.41 shows these results in diagram form with all the Facts added as Population as well. You can also compare it with the bigger diagram in Figure 3.22, where you will find exactly the same Fact Type, but with a few extra things that will be explained later.

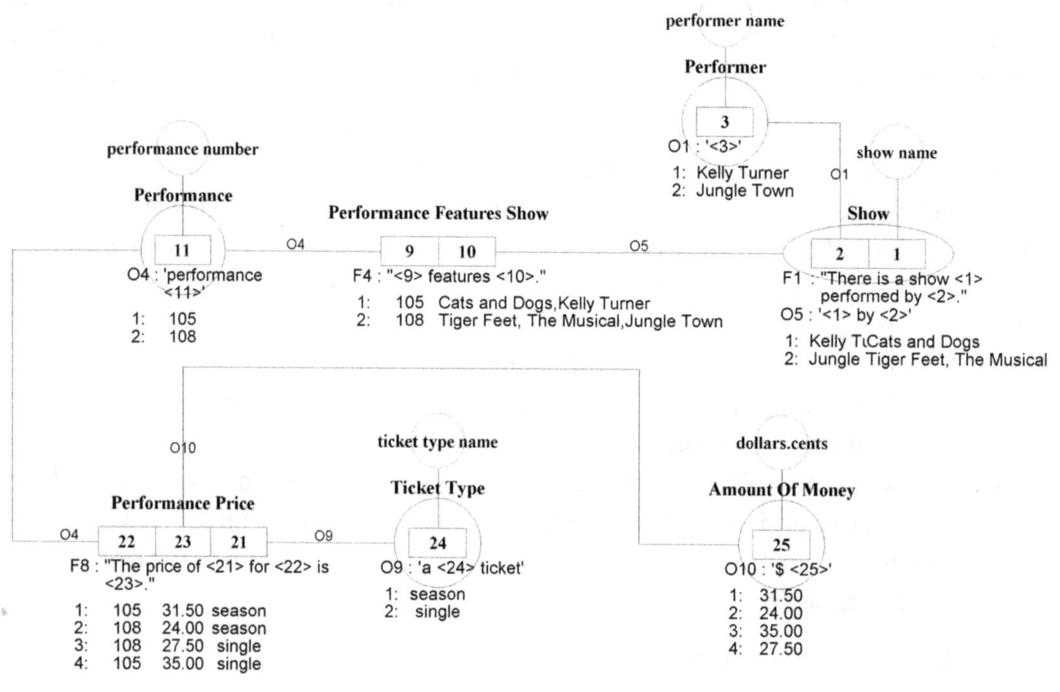

Figure 3.41 FCO-IM diagram of the complete Analysis of 'Performance Price'

3.6.5 SUMMARY OF ANALYZING THE OTHER PERFORMANCE SCHEDULE FACT TYPES

The results of Analyzing the Fact Types from Textbox 3.25 that have not been discussed yet in Sections 3.6.1 – 3.6.4 are given below with only a few comments.

Figure 3.42 repeats the diagram from Figure 3.22. You can verify that the result of the Analysis of the three Fact Types discussed so far, with Fact Expression Types F1, F4 and F8, is shown there. This section gives a brief summary of the Analysis of the other Fact Types from Textbox 3.25. The results of these Analyses, with Fact Expression Types F2, F3, F5, F6 and F7, can also be seen in the diagram in Figure 3.42.

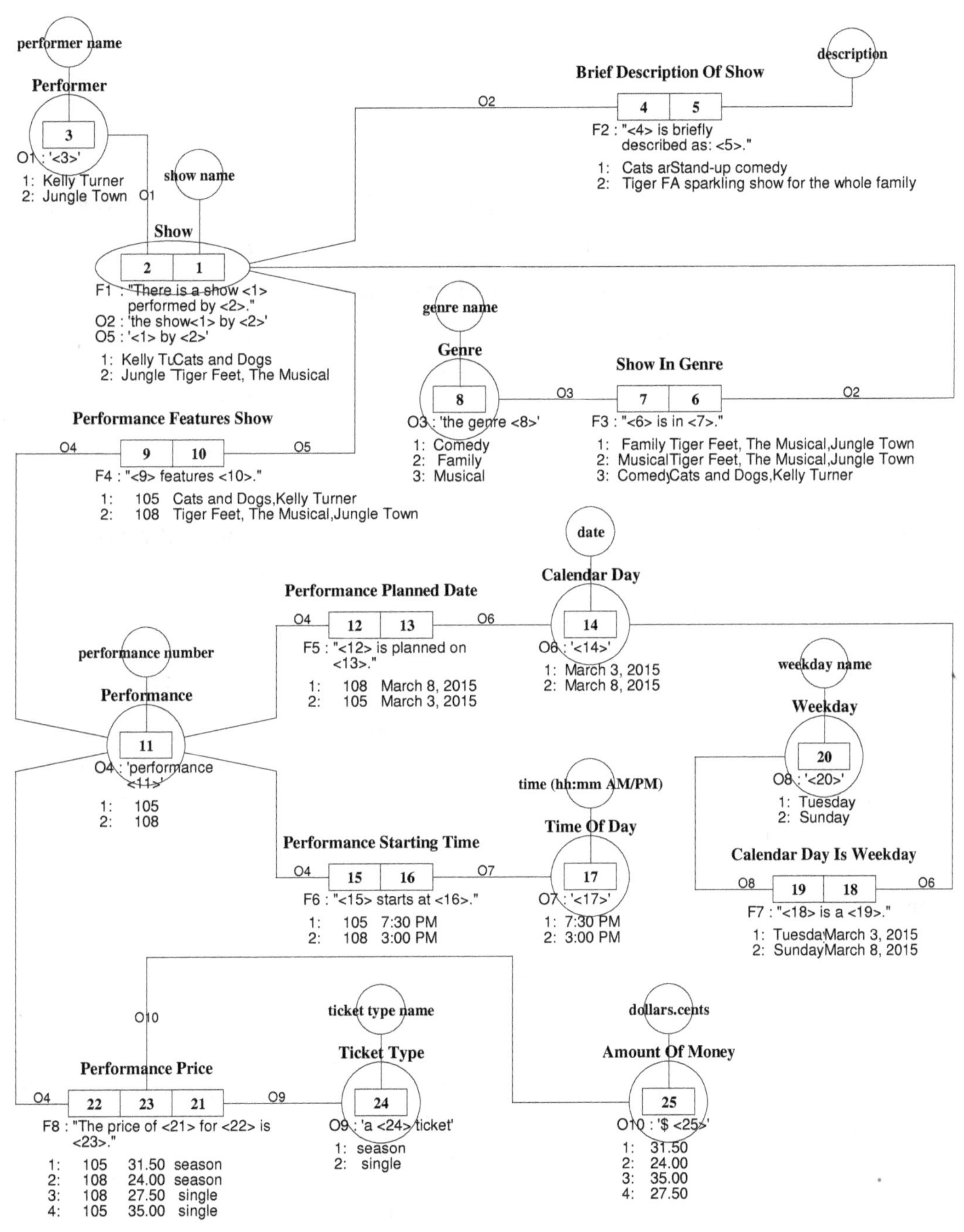

Figure 3.42 FCO-IM diagram for the performance schedule; no constraints added yet

Analysis of 'Brief Description Of Show' with F2.

```
Brief Description Of Show:

  "The show Cats and Dogs            by Kelly Turner is briefly
          described as: Stand-up comedy."
  " "      " Tiger Feet, The Musical   " Jungle Town    "     "
             "      " A sparkling show for the whole family."
                  Show:O2              description

              F2: "<1> is briefly described as: <2>."

  'the show Cats and Dogs            by Kelly Turner'
  ' "      " Tiger Feet, The Musical  " Jungle Town'
                  show name            Performer:O1
                                         MATCH

              O2: 'the show <1> by <2>
```

As discussed in Section 3.6.1, the combination of a show name and a performer identifies a show, and so phrases like 'the show Cats and Dogs by Kelly Turner' were recognized as Object Expressions. They contain only two of the three places with varying text and so comply with the condition in guideline G2 (see Section 3.6.1) and line 6 of the procedure for Analyzing (see Textbox 3.32).

Please note that Object Expression Type O2 is different from Object Expression Type O5, which was found in Section 3.6.3. It contains the two extra words 'the show'. In FCO-IM, an Object Type can have several Object Expression Types. This is often convenient and even necessary for more complex information structures like Generalization (see Appendix B, [1, Chapter 6]) and for transforming an FCO-IM information model into a model in another modeling technique like ERM, UML, Relational, Data Vault, etc. (see Chapter 7). This is the reason that Object Expression Type codes must be written next to the lines connecting Roles with Object types: You have to know which one to choose. Here, O2 is used for Fact Expressions from F2 and F3, and O5 for F4 (see Figure 3.42). In the Serviceton Theater model, having two Object Expression Types for 'Show' is not really necessary, but they serve as an example of the general case.

The last place with varying text was marked as a Label Type because the domain expert explained that a phrase like 'stand-up comedy' can be used for several different shows, and it does not identify a show category or something like that. Sometimes a show has a more specific description like 'a dazzling virtuoso on unusual musical instruments'.

Analysis of Fact Type 'Show In Genre' with F3.

```
Show In Genre:
  "The show Cats and Dogs            by Kelly Turner is in
                                               the genre Comedy."
  " "     "  Tiger Feet, The Musical  " Jungle Town    "  "
                                                "    "   Musical."
  " "     "  Tiger Feet, The Musical "  Jungle Town    "  "
                                                "    "   Family."
                    Show:O2                         Genre:O3
                     MATCH

              F3: "<6> is in <7>."

                                               'the genre Comedy'
                                               ' "     "   Musical'
                                               ' "     "   Family'
                                                        genre name

                                           O3: 'the genre <8>'
```

The previously Analyzed Object Expression Type O2 was recognized and marked with 'MATCH'. The domain expert confirmed that 'Comedy', 'Musical' etc. are names for specific genres, and that every show is tagged with one or more of these genres.

Analysis of Fact Type 'Performance Planned Date' with F5.

```
Performance Planned Date:
  "Performance 105 is planned on March 3, 2015."
  "       "    108  "     "     " March 8, 2015."
  "       "    457  "     "     " January 23, 2016."
   Performance:O4                Calendar Day:O6
        MATCH

          F5: "<12> is planned on <13>."

                                'March 3, 2015'
                                'March 8, 2015'
                                'January 23, 2016'
                                      date

                                O6: '<14>'
```

The previously Analyzed Object Expression Type O4 was recognized and marked with 'MATCH'.

The modeler knows from experience that 'March 3, 2015' etc. are dates that identify a calendar day. So he marked these as Object Expressions. The modeler also knows that each date has actually a further structure: it contains a month name, a day number and a year, but he decides to leave these three components unspecified for the time being. He can zoom in on these components later if necessary. As stated earlier in Section 3.6.4, where 'Amount Of Money' was Analyzed, there is a certain arbitrariness in the level of detail chosen for modeling. Many very common concepts like amounts of money, or dates, are best modeled with a single Label Type because standard implementation platforms offer a good set of tools to manipulate dates and amounts of money, whereas domain-specific things are best modeled in a greater level of detail because standard implementation platforms do not offer tools for those.

Analysis of Fact Type 'Performance Starting Time' with F6.

```
Performance Starting Time:
  "Performance 105 starts at 7:30 PM."
  "     "      108    "     " 3:00 PM."
   Performance:O4          Time Of Day:O7
        MATCH

          F6: "<15> starts at <16>."

                             '7:30 PM'
                             '3:00 PM'
                        time (hh:mm AM/PM)

                             O7: '<17>'
```

The previously Analyzed Object Expression Type O4 was recognized and marked with 'MATCH'. The modeler knows from experience that notations like '7:30 PM' are used to identify a time of day. So he marked these as Object Expressions. As with 'Amount of Money' and 'Calendar Day', the modeler also knows that each time of day has actually a further structure—it contains separate parts for the hours, the minutes and an AM/PM indicator—but he decides to leave these three components unspecified for the time being because standard implementation platforms also offer a good set of tools to manipulate times of day.

Analysis of Fact Type 'Calendar Day Is Weekday' with F7.

```
Calendar Day Is Weekday:
  "March 3, 2015 is a Tuesday."
  "March 8, 2015  " "  Sunday."
   Calendar Day:O6     Weekday:O8
        MATCH

          F7: "<18> is a <19>."

                         'Tuesday'
                         'Sunday'
                       weekday name

                        O8: '<20>'
```

The previously Analyzed Object Expression Type O6 was recognized and marked with 'MATCH'. The modeler knows from experience that 'Tuesday' etc. are names that identify one of the seven days of the week, with no further detailed structure. So he marked these as Object Expressions and gave the corresponding Object Type and Label Type clear and meaningful names.

This completes the Analysis of all the Fact Expressions in Textbox 3.25. The corresponding FCO-IM diagram, which also contains all the Verbalized Facts from Textbox 3.25 as its Population, is given in Figure 3.42. All details in this diagram should now be clear..

3.6.6 DOS AND DON'TS WHEN ANALYZING

Here are a few tips for doing the Analysis step in the FCO-IM procedure to draw up a conceptual information model (see Section 3.1). Positive suggestions are given first and negative ones later.

3.6.6.1 Dos When Analyzing

Do 1: How to model dates and amounts of money.

If a part of a Fact Expression concerns a date or an amount of money (it is hard to find an information model that doesn't contain at least one of them, and most contain both!), then model exactly one Object Type called 'Calendar Day', which will cater for *all the dates in the entire information model*, and exactly one Object Type 'Amount Of Money', which will cater for *all the sums of money in the entire information model*. See Figure 3.42, which contains both Object Types. See also the 'Don'ts when analyzing' below, where it is explained why you should never model *more than one* Object Type for either dates or amounts of money. Also, (almost) always model dates or sums of money as *single Object Types*, not combined with any other sentence parts into any compound Object Type.

Do 2: How to model quantities that have units.

If a part of a Fact Expression concerns a quantity that has a unit, always model it as an Object Type (without any other sentence part) with the unit as part of the Object Expression Type. Examples (see also the corresponding Figure 3.43) with the Label part underlined and the Object Expression Type part not underlined: '5.6 inches', '17.5 lb', '120 V', '8.4 gal'. Please note that quantities of different kinds should be modeled as separate Object Types; it would not be meaningful to put '5.6 inches' and '17.5 lb' into the same Object Type because you can't compare lengths with weights. There's no conversion possible between them. If you have a quantity that can be measured with different units, like length measured in inches or in centimeters, choose just one of these units and use that as the standard unit for the basic facts in the information system. If desired, it is easy to augment the system with a small conversion program that calculates the values in other units later (for example, using the conversion factor 1 inch = 2.54 cm).

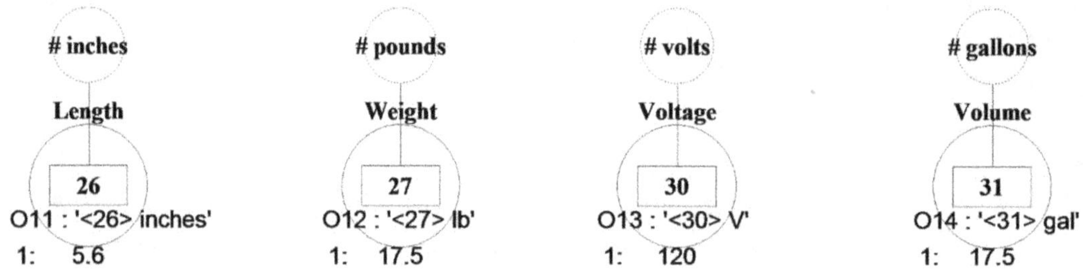

Figure 3.43 Object Types for quantities with units

Do 3: How to model quantities without units.

The quantity 'number' occurs in parts of Fact Expressions like '25 seats', '20 persons', '63 items', '3 USB slots', etc. It is used for things you can count and does not have a true unit like 'inches' or 'gallons'. The words 'seats', 'persons' 'items' and 'USB slots' tell us what is being counted. But contrary to inches and gallons, which cannot be compared in a meaningful way (is your car longer than its tank capacity?), you *can* compare the number of persons and seats in a meaningful way (is there a seat for everyone?). Since there is no fixed text (no unit), it is a matter of taste whether you model 'number' as an Object Type or as a Label Type. Do you and/or the domain expert perceive a certain number of things, like '5', as a meaningful Object that is identified by an integer? Most people will not think so; therefore, both ways are correct as shown in Figures 3.46 and 3.47. However, it is recommended to use an Object Type. That is more in style with how quantities that do have units are modeled (see **Do 2**) and avoids the Label Type with more than one connection, which is often an indication of bad modeling (see **Don't 1** and **Don't 2** below).

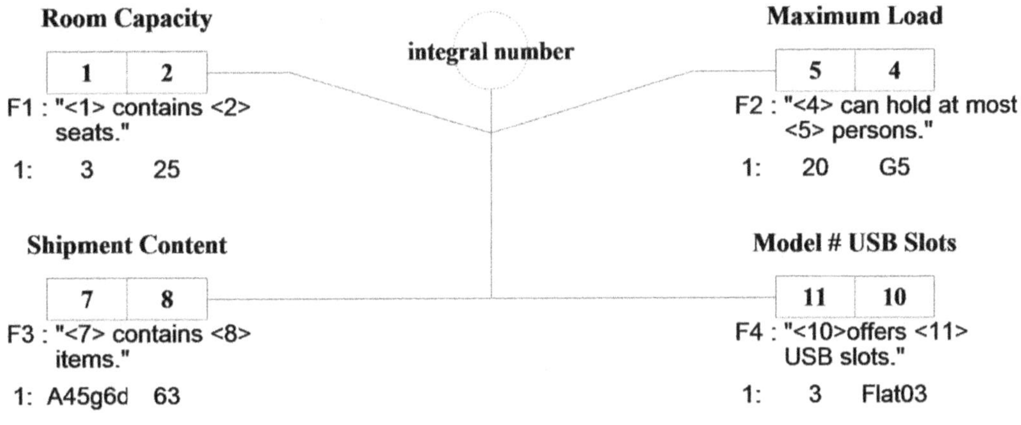

Figure 3.44 Correct but not preferred model: 'number' as Label Type

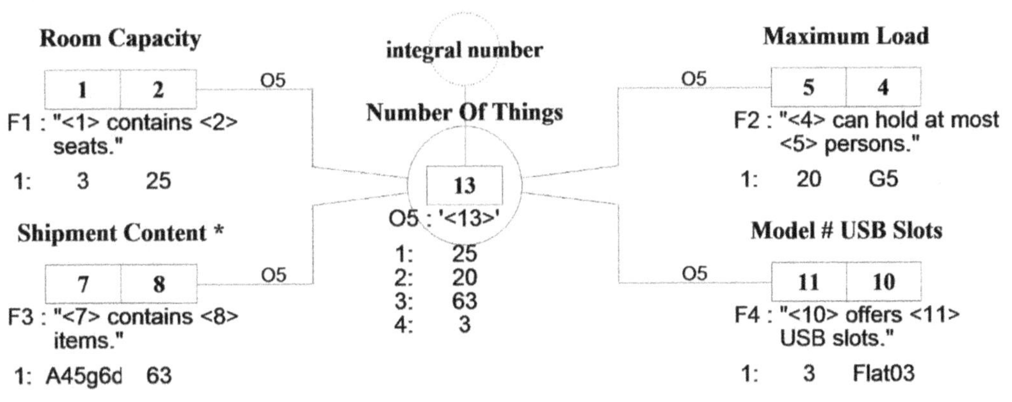

Figure 3.45 Correct and preferred model: 'number' as Object Type

Do 4: Prefer Object Type to Label Type.

When you are in doubt about whether you should model a sentence part as an Object Expression or as a Label, it is usually best to choose Object Expression. In a developing information model, it is easier to get rid of a superfluous Object Type than to insert a missing one. So: better one Object Type too many than one too few.

3.6.6.2 Don'ts When Analyzing

Don't 1: Don't use only a Label Type where an Object Type is needed.

Figure 3.46 shows several Fact Types to be recorded for patients. Please note: a patient is identified by his/her patient number, and all Fact Expressions about patients contain the fixed text 'patient'. Both observations should lead the modeler to recognize a phrase like 'patient 123' as an Object Expression. An identifier is always a good reason to model something as an Object Type; if people in the domain area have taken the trouble to introduce a unique name, number, code or other identifier for some 'things', then those 'things' are surely important Objects that should be modeled with an Object Type. Moreover, the common part in the Fact Expressions about 'things' in all of these sentences (namely '*patient* 123') should be modeled only once as part of an Object Expression as shown in Figure 3.47.

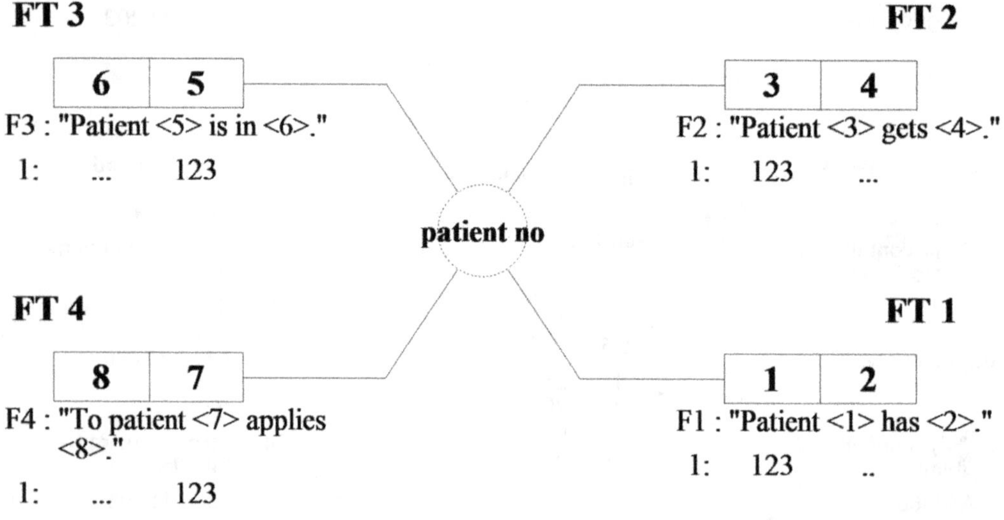

Figure 3.46 Wrong model: missing Object Type 'Patient'

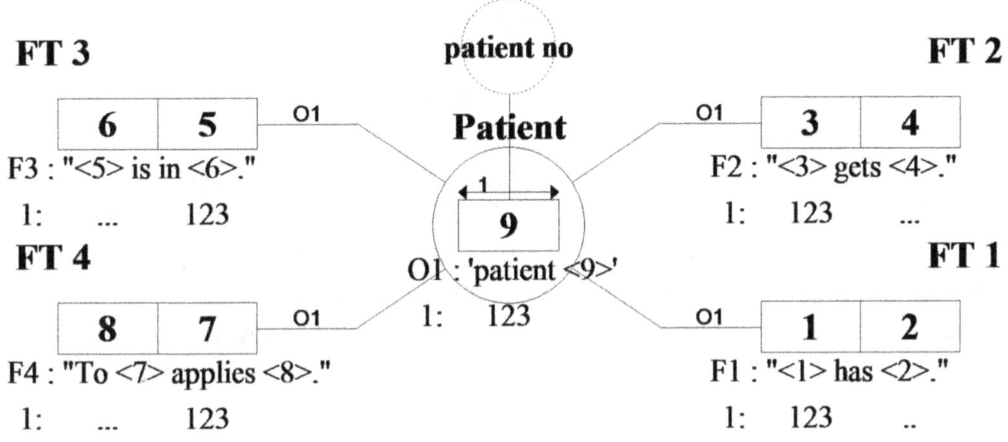

Figure 3.47 Correct model: with Object Type 'Patient'

Suppose it would be deemed to be socially undesirable to call someone with an illness or ailment a 'patient' any longer because this word would now be regarded as stigmatizing and derogatory. Instead, the term 'health client' would now be preferred. If we were to change the communication about such people in this way, then the model in Figure 3.46 would require an update in every single Fact Expression (only four are shown in the figure, but there could be many more in a realistic health care database), whereas the model in Figure 3.47 would require only one update in the Object Expression Type to achieve the same changes. This is the most important reason to use Object Types with Object Expression Types: to have just one place to store the standard way of speaking about these objects: *single point of definition*. A warning flag that you might have missed an Object Type is that your model contains a Label Type that connects to more than one Fact Type. Although a Label Type with several connections is not impossible in a valid information model, it should always trigger you to check for a possibly forgotten Object Type.

Don't 2: Don't use two Object Types for one Object.

Figure 3.48 shows an information model that contains facts about prices of articles. There are two Object Types, one for the cost prices and one for the selling prices. Please note that the *same* object can occur in the population of both these Object Types (in Figure 3.48, '`$10.00`') and that both Object Types are identified by the same Label Type 'dollars.cents'. In a good information model, however, any individual Object will occur by itself only in the population of just one Object Type though it can occur several times in the populations of Fact Types played by this Object Type. See, for example, ‘`article A2`’, which is used in the populations of both Fact Types ‘Article Cost Price’ and ‘Article Selling Price’ but occurs only once by itself in the population of Object Type ‘Article’. In other words, any individual Object can belong to only one Object Type (with the exception of Subtypes; see Section 6.2). Since ‘`$10.00`’ is exactly the same amount of money, regardless of whether it is a cost price or a selling price, the model in Figure 3.48 is wrong. Incidentally, that’s why those parts of Fact Types drawn as numbered small rectangles are called ‘Roles’: if a certain amount of money is present in the population of Role 2, then it *plays the role of* a cost price, and if this (same) amount of money is present in the population of Role 6, then it *plays the role of* a selling price.

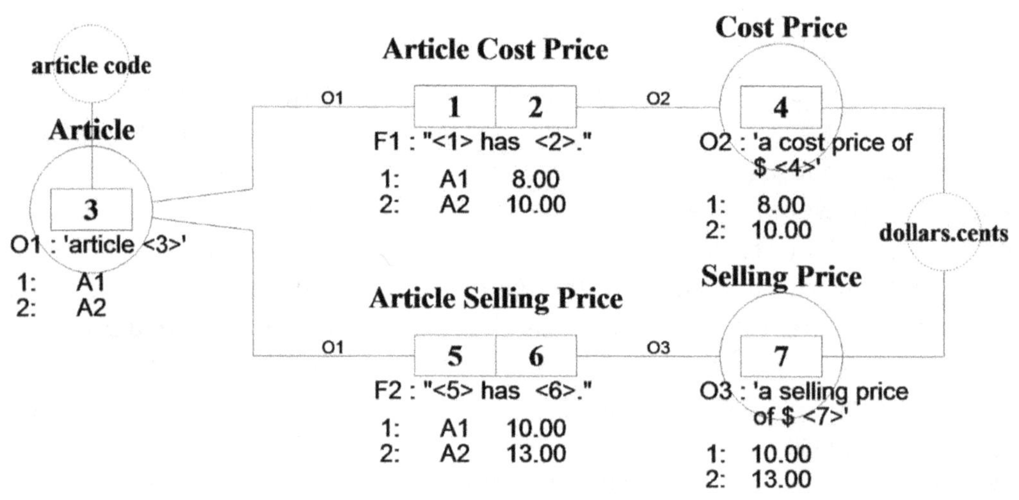

Figure 3.48 Wrong model: two Object Types for amounts of money

So it is better to model just one Object Type for *all* amounts of money as is shown in Figure 3.49. Please note that ‘`$10.00`’ by itself now belongs to just one Object Type though it is used in two Fact Types played by this Object Type. The Fact Expression Types and Object Expression Type have been adapted as well to model the exact same Fact Expressions.

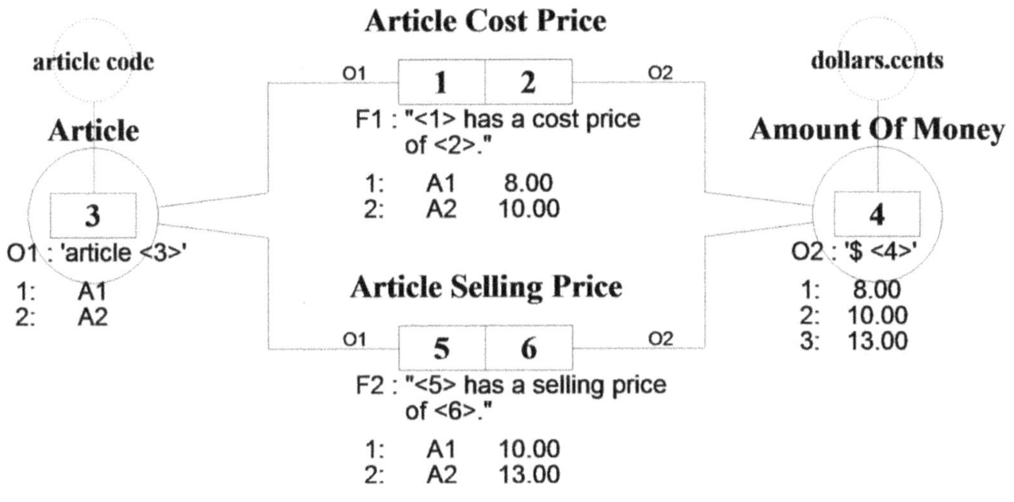

Figure 3.49 Correct model: only one Object Type for amounts of money

As in **Don't 1** above, the Label Type with more than one connection in Figure 3.48 can serve as a warning flag that something might be wrong. Indeed, one label Type that identifies more than one Object Type is a very strong indication that a modeling mistake has been made.

Don't 3: Don't make a new Fact Type for an Object Type when there already is one.

Suppose the model in Figure 3.50 has already been correctly made. The modeler proceeds to extend the model with Fact Expressions like "`The area of room 715 is 310 sq ft.`" that belong to Fact Type 'Room Area'. This Fact Expression contains an Object Expression, '`room 715`', that identifies a room and another varying part (for the area). So an Object Type 'Room' must be added (see the procedure for Analyzing in Section 3.1). This is done in a wrong way in Figure 3.51.

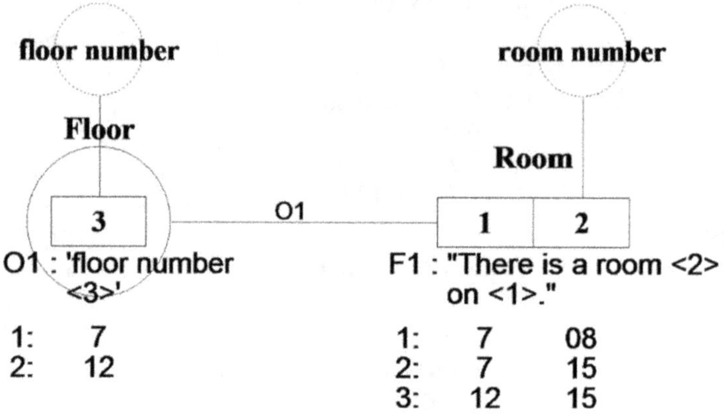

Figure 3.50 Room as fact Type

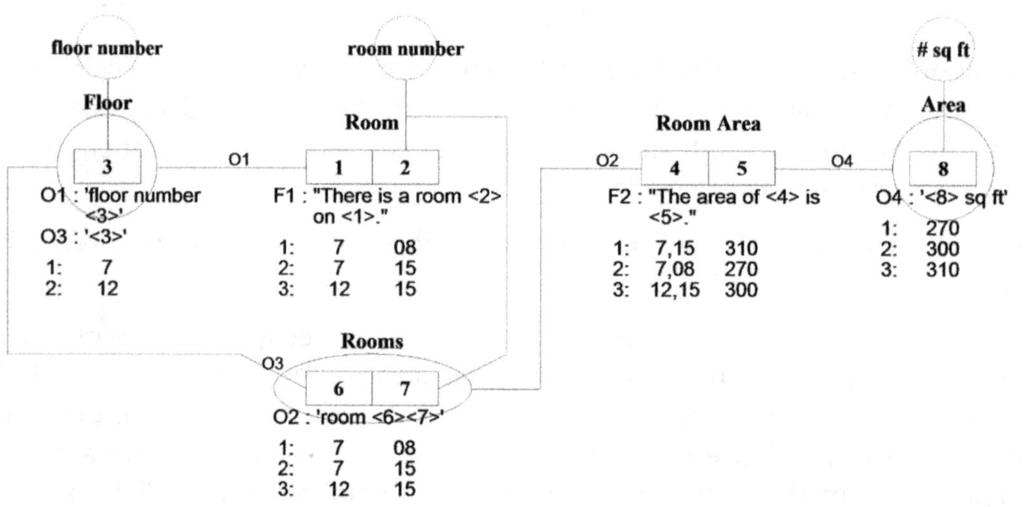

Figure 3.51 Wrong model: Room as Fact Type and Rooms as Object Type

In Figure 3.51, an Object Type 'Rooms' was added, containing a Fact Type with the same name although there already was a Fact Type 'Room' present in the model. The modeler couldn't use the same name 'Room' again (names of Fact Types and Label Types are unique in FCO-IM), so he used the plural 'Rooms' instead. This cheap trick alone should be a sure sign that something is going wrong, but there are other problems too.

Suppose a new Fact is to be added to Fact Type 'Room Area': "`The area of room 809 is 290 sq ft.`" Then '`room 809`' is added to the population of Role 4 and also automatically to Object Type 'Rooms' because Role 4 is played by this Object Type. But '`room 809`' is not yet present in the population of Fact Type 'Room'. This cannot be because if '`room 809`' has an area, then it must exist, and all existing rooms must be in the population of this Fact Type as its Fact Expression Type asserts. So a Fact must be added in a separate action there as well: "`There is a room 09 on floor number 8.`" Not only is this awkward, but it also shows that the Population of Object Type 'Room' contains *all* the rooms. The population of the other Object Type 'Rooms' adds nothing to the model; its Population is always at least a part of the Population of 'Room', and at best the two Populations are identical.

These problems arise from the modeler's failure to use the already present Fact Type 'Room' as the internal Fact Type of the new Object Type. Figure 3.52 shows the correct situation with Role 4 played by 'Room' instead of 'Rooms'. Now if the new fact "`The area of room 809 is 290 sq ft.`" is added, '`room 809`' is added to the population of Role 4 and also automatically to Object Type 'Room' because Role 4 is played by this Object Type. The fact "`There is a room 09 on floor number 8.`" is implicitly and automatically added as well.

Modelers should use an already existing Fact Type for a new Object Type whenever possible.

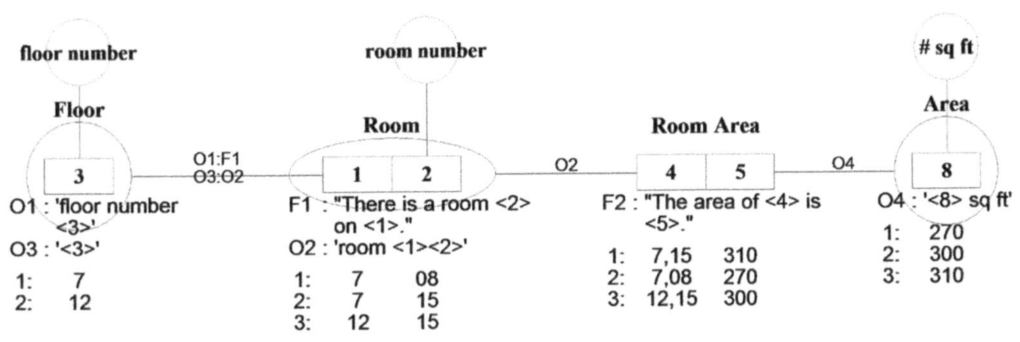

Figure 3.52 Correct model: Room as both Fact Type and Object Type

In several Fact Oriented Modeling techniques, a powerful feature is that some Object Types can be made by 'promoting' Fact Types in the way shown above. It is a unique property of FCO-IM that *all* Object Types are such promoted Fact Types. This makes FCO-IM both leaner (fewer concepts) and more powerful (able to model recursive structures, for instance; see the advanced FCO-IM book (Appendix B, [1])) than other FOM techniques.

3.6.7 AN OBJECT EXPRESSION MUST BE A CONNECTED SENTENCE PART

Finally, one requirement on Object Expressions and Object Expression Types should be highlighted. In the present version of FCO-IM, supported by the modeling tool CaseTalk (see Appendix B, [2]), an Object Expression must be a connected, unbroken part of a sentence. In natural language, however, it is quite possible to break an Object Expression up into several disconnected sentence parts. For example, the following two Fact Expressions verbalize the same Fact. In FE1a the Object Expression for an Object of Object Type 'Reservation Request Part' is a connected sentence part, but in the second expression FE1b, the Object Expression is broken up into two disconnected parts (double underlined parts):

```
FE1a: "Part 3 of reservation request 7795 claims 4 seats."
           Reservation Request Part: O22
FE1b: "Reservation request 7795 claims 4 seats for part 3."
```

If a verbalization like FE1b was made at first, then it should be rephrased as soon as it is recognized that the disconnected parts actually form one Object Expression.

In an improved and extended version of FCO-IM, this restriction has been removed so that even disconnected sentence parts can be marked as one Object Expression; see the research paper in Appendix B: [7] for further details.

Chapter 4
How to Keep the Facts Sound Using Constraints

One aspect of *data quality* (an important issue nowadays; see Appendix B, [21]) is to keep the Facts that are stored in a database sound. Data pollution (Facts that are wrong or missing) is a constant threat. Although it is impossible to guarantee that the Facts stored are 100% correct (e.g., someone deliberately enters an overoptimistic body weight figure), many measures can be taken to prevent data pollution.

Most of these measures follow from *Business Rules*: domain requirements that the Facts should satisfy at all times like "A show belongs to one or more genres." or "The sum of the average annual sales percentages must be 100%." Such Business Rules can be incorporated into the information model in the form of *Constraints*: model-specific requirements that the Facts in the model should satisfy at all times.

Chapter 3 shows how to follow steps 1-4 in the FCO-IM procedure to draw up a conceptual information model (see Section 3.1). Starting from verbalizations of concrete examples of Facts, a network of Fact Types and Object Types with their Expression Types and Population is built. That is the first half (and also the hard part) of the work to be done. In the remaining steps 5-9, several important types of Constraints on the Populations of the Fact Types and Object Types are added to the model.

In this chapter, the three most important kinds of Constraints are discussed in detail, and a procedure to determine them is given as well. Other kinds of Constraints are presented by showing a typical case, together with a Population that illustrates what the Constraint intends to prevent. Their correspondence with the domain Business Rules is made clear.

4.1 INTRODUCTION TO BUSINESS RULES AND CONSTRAINTS

Key Points

- **Business Rules are the laws by which an organization operates.**
- **Business Rules that concern Facts translate into Constraints in the information model.**
- **Business Rules can be Stated informally in Domain Style, and Constraints can be Stated informally in Model Style.**

All organizations use Business Rules, which define or constrain anything the business does, makes or uses ("We have a complete money-back guarantee.", "The annual performance report must be authorized by the chair of the board.", "A show belongs to one or more genres.", etc.). Business Rules can be about any aspect of an organization, but only those that concern the Facts used by an organization will be considered here.

Business Rules in the organization translate into Constraints in the information model. Please keep this distinction in mind: Business Rules live in the world of the organization, whereas Constraints live in the world of the information model. Therefore Business Rules are model-independent, whereas Constraints are model-specific; the same Business Rule could translate in an ERM (see Appendix B, [12]) model into quite different Constraints than in an FCO-IM model, for instance (see also Section 7.2). This translation is not a simple one-to-one affair either; one Business Rule can translate into several different Constraints and vice versa (see the example in Section 4.1.1. below).

There are always many restrictions on the whole set of allowed Facts in an information system. Here are a few examples from Serviceton Music Theater:

BR 1: "A performance concerns exactly one show."

This Business Rule constrains the allowed Facts in the two Fact Types 'Performance' and 'Performance Features Show' (see Figure 3.42 or 4.14). No performance is allowed to feature two or more shows, and every performance must feature a show. BR 1 corresponds in FCO-IM with two Constraints: Uniqueness Constraint 12 on Role 9 (see Section 4.2) and Totality Constraint 4 on Role 9 (see Section 4.3).

BR 2: "A show can have multiple performances."

This Business Rule corresponds in FCO-IM with the *absence* of a Uniqueness Constraint on Role 10 (see Section 4.2).

BR 3: "The gender is either male or female."

This Business Rule corresponds in FCO-IM with a Value Constraint on Label Type 'gender name' (see Section 4.4).

BR 4: "A customer can have an address line 2 only if there is an address line 1 as well."

This Business Rule corresponds in FCO-IM with a Subset Constraint from Role 45 to Role 43 (see Figure 4.39 in Section 4.5.2).

4.1.1 STATING BUSINESS RULES AND CONSTRAINTS

Business Rules can be Stated more or less formally. There are several special languages to express Business Rules formally, like Semantics of Business Vocabulary and Business Rules (SBVR, see Appendix B, [20]) or Second Order Predicate Logic (see any textbook on mathematical logic). However, those languages are beyond the scope of this book, which will use only informally Stated Business Rules.

Business Rules will be Stated in this book in English sentences in Domain Style. Such sentences can be understood by all domain experts, and they do not refer directly to anything in an information model. An example is:

BR 1: "A performance concerns exactly one show."

Constraints (which are information modeling technique specific) will be Stated in this book in English sentences in Model Style. Such sentences can be understood by all domain experts, while using verbs from Fact Expression Types and names of Object Types and Fact Types as much as possible. For example, BR 1 above translates into these two Constraints in FCO-IM (or ERM, see Appendix B, [12]):

C 1a: "A performance can feature at most one show."

C 1b: "A performance must feature at least one show."

C 1a corresponds with Uniqueness Constraint 12 on Role 9 (see Section 4.2 and Figure 4.14), and C 1b corresponds with Totality Constraint 4 on Role 9 (see Section 4.3 and Figure 4.32).

Please note the verb 'feature' in both C 1a and C 1b, from the Fact Expression Type that belongs to Fact Type 'Performance Features Show', whereas BR 1 used 'concerns', which is a verb not found in the verbalizations. The nouns 'performance' and 'show' are the names of the corresponding Object Types, used in C 1a, C 1b and BR 1 as well (but if BR 1 had used other nouns, C 1a and C 1b would still have used these).

How Business Rules translate into Constraints depends on the information modeling technique used; the same Business Rule can lead to completely different Constraints in FCO-IM than in for example ERM (see Appendix B, [12]); see also Section 7.2. Conversely, concepts from these modeling techniques (like Uniqueness Constraints in FCO-IM and cardinalities in ERM) can translate into zero, one or many Business Rules. In the following sections, it is indicated how the discussed types of Constraint correspond with Business Rules.

4.2 Uniqueness Constraints (UCs)

Key Points

- **A Uniqueness Constraint (UC) allows no duplicates under the Roles it is placed on.**
- **UCs are the most important type of constraint and should be determined carefully.**
- **There is a procedure that guarantees finding all UCs on a Fact Type with a minimum amount of work.**

Business Rules like "We will record only one email address (if any) for a customer." or "A reservation request part cannot concern more than one performance." occur very often. In FCO-IM, they translate into Uniqueness Constraints. (Other information modeling techniques have different concepts for the same thing. Relational databases (see Appendix B, [14]) use keys, ERM (see Appendix B, [12]) uses identifiers or cardinalities, etc.). The corresponding Statements in Model Style (see Section 4.1.1) are: “A customer can have at most one email address.” and “A reservation request part can concern at most one performance.”

Uniqueness Constraints (UCs for brevity; the term Uniqueness Constraint is abbreviated from here on as UC) are the most important type of Constraint in an FCO-IM information model. Therefore, when step 4 (Analyzing) in the procedure to draw up an information model (see Section 3.1) has been completed and all Fact Types and Object Types have been determined, the next step is to determine all UCs. UCs specify that *no duplicate values* are allowed under the Roles they are placed on. In other words, the values under a UC must be *unique*, hence the name.

In an FCO-IM diagram like the one in Figure 4.1, UCs are shown as double pointed arrows, each arrow above one or more Roles. A UC (arrow) above just one Role means *no duplicates allowed in the Population under me*, or in other words, *under me, every value must be unique*. A UC (arrow) above a combination of Roles means *no duplicates allowed in the Population under me*, or in other words, *under me every combination of values must be unique*.

Every Fact Type in FCO-IM has at least one UC, and at most as many as it has Roles. So the modeler needs to find out for each Fact Type which UCs it actually has. For this purpose an airtight procedure has been developed to systematically find all UCs on a Fact Type with a minimum of effort (see our research paper in Appendix B, [6]). For example, a Fact Type with three Roles will be tested for the three possibilities of a UC on a combination of two Roles. Each candidate UC can either be present or absent. The result of each test should be Stated in Model Style (see the examples in Sections 4.2.1–4.2.4 below), which allows the modeler to easily compare the presence or absence of a UC with Business Rules Stated in Domain Style (see Section 4.1.1) and also to compare them with Constraints in other modeling techniques like ERM (see Appendix B, [12]), if desired. However, in an FCO-IM diagram, only the actually existing UCs are entered as double pointed arrows above the Roles they concern.

In this book, an informal way of Stating the presence or absence of a UC in Model Style is used. Each such Statement concerns the presence or absence of exactly one candidate UC. So a Fact Type with N Roles always gets N Statements about the presence or absence of UCs on it. There is one exception: a Fact Type inside an Object Type can have only one UC on all its Roles (see Section 5.3.1), and for such Fact Types only one special Statement for the single UC on all the Roles is used even if this Fact type has more than one Role. See the examples in Section 4.2.4 below. Section 4.2.1 below illustrates what UCs are and how they are determined for Fact Types with two Roles. Section 4.2.2 gives the general procedure, which is illustrated in more complex cases in Section 4.2.3. Section 4.2.4 gives a summary of the UC-determination for the performance schedule part of the information model of Serviceton Music Theater.

4.2.1 ILLUSTRATIONS OF HOW UNIQUENESS CONSTRAINTS ARE DETERMINED

This section illustrates all possibilities for Uniqueness Constraints (UCs) on Fact Types with two roles (binary Fact Types). It also informally shows how the modeler and domain expert determine UCs in an interview session. This way of working is formalized in the next section, which gives a precise procedure to find all UCs within any one Fact Type. Figure 4.1 illustrates everything discussed in this section with examples from a different context than Serviceton Music Theater. It already shows all the UCs to be determined although the analyst of course starts with a model without any UC in it yet. All of these UCs will be explained in this section.

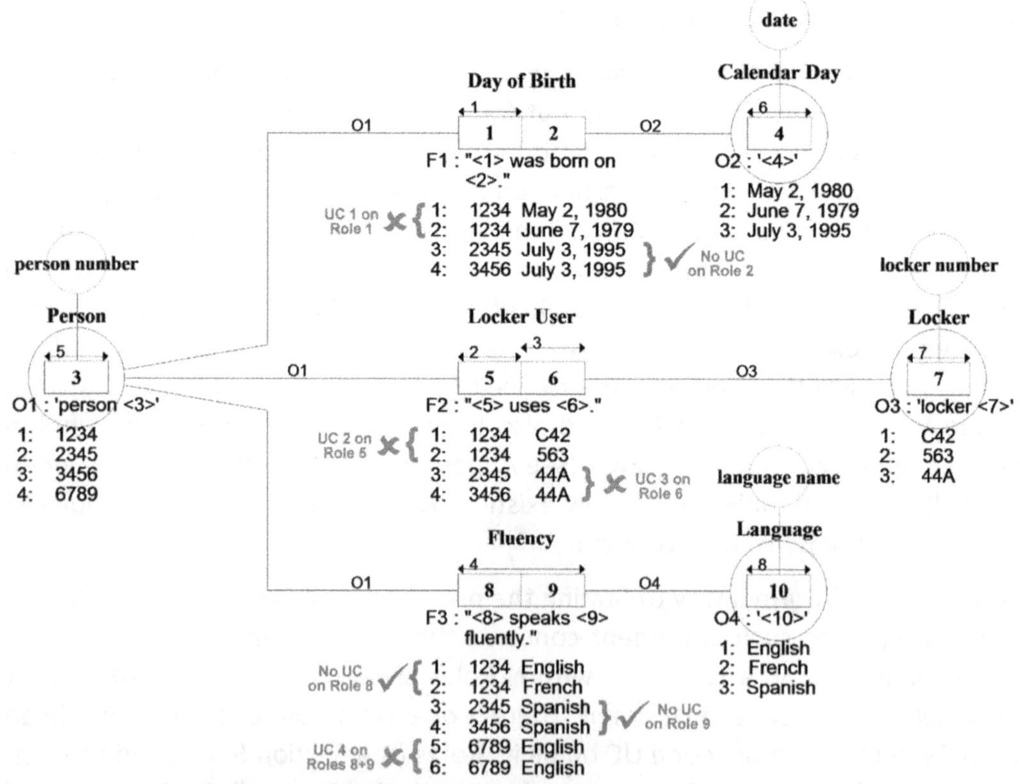

Figure 4.1 FCO-IM diagram illustrating UCs on Fact Types with 2 Roles, and how they are determined

UCs on Fact Type 'Day Of Birth'

Let's start with Fact Type 'Day of Birth'. Of course, everybody knows that each person can have only one day of birth and that several people can be born on the same calendar day. Still, for the sake of starting with an easy example, let's pretend the modeler and domain expert are only vaguely aware of this. The modeler wants to find all the UCs that apply to this Fact Type. To achieve this, he has the dialogue with the domain expert shown in Textbox 4.2. See Figure 4.1, Fact Type 'Day of Birth', for a summary of this dialogue in an FCO-IM diagram.

Modeler: Let's consider the days of birth to be recorded. Suppose I have the following two Facts (he draws the small table below and shows it to the domain expert): "Person 1234 was born on May 2, 1980." and "Person 1234 was born on June 7, 1979.".

Fact	Person	Day of Birth
1	1234	May 2, 1980
2	1234	June 7,1979

Could these two Facts both be present in your database at the same time?

Domain expert: No, the same person can't have two different birthdays. So either one or both of these is false.

Modeler: OK, and how about these next two Facts, 3 and 4? They are "Person 2345 was born on July 3, 1995." and "Person 3456 was born on July 3, 1995."

Fact	Person	Day of Birth
~~1~~	~~1234~~	~~May 2, 1980~~
~~2~~	~~1234~~	~~June 7,1979~~
3	2345	July 3, 1995
4	3456	July 3, 1995

Can they both be in your information system at the same time?

Domain expert: Yes, they could be. I hope so, actually; that's two pieces of cake then (laughs).

Textbox 4.2 Dialogue to determine the UCs for Fact Type 'Day of Birth'

From the dialogue in Textbox 4.2, the modeler concludes two things:

1 Any particular person can have only one day of birth. This can be Stated as a Constraint in Model Style (see Section 4.1.1) as: "A person can be born on at most one calendar day.". It is shown in the model in Figure 4.1 as UC 1 on Role 1 since the same person cannot occur in the Population of Role 1 more than once.

2 Any particular day can be the birthday of several persons. This can be Stated in Model Style (see Section 4.1.1) as: "A calendar day can be the birthday of several persons.". This is shown in the model in Figure 4.1 by the *absence* of a UC on Role 2 since the same calendar day can be in the Population of Role 2 several times.

Although in FCO-IM the absence of a UC is not seen as a Constraint (the Population of Role 2 is *not* constrained), this should still be Stated explicitly in Model Style as "A calendar day can be the birthday of several persons.". So, in an FCO-IM diagram, the absence of a UC is not marked explicitly (there is no graphical indication that says "A UC does not exist here."). But since in FCO-IM this does mean that we know for sure the UC isn't there, it still should be Stated explicitly in Model Style. This is a clear example of whether 'absence of evidence' is to be understood as 'evidence of absence' or not. In an FCO-IM diagram, the absence of a UC is indeed to be interpreted as evidence of its absence (see any reference to the Closed World Assumption for further background information). In contrast, other Fact Oriented Modeling techniques do require the modeler in similar cases to explicitly enter an appropriate symbol into the diagram (in ERM (see Appendix B, [12]), by entering a maximum cardinality of 'many', see also Section 7.2). This is another reason to formulate the absence of UCs explicitly in Model Style.

The modeler enters the UC on Role 1 as shown in Figure 4.1, which also shows the Facts used in Textbox 4.2 in the Population of Fact Type 'Day of Birth'.

UCs on Fact Type 'Locker Use'

Next, let's consider Fact Type 'Locker User'. Here, the modeler cannot be sure without consulting the domain expert whether a person can use just one or possibly several lockers. Conversely, he might suspect that a locker can be used by just one person, but again he cannot be sure without consulting the domain expert. The modeler wants to find all the UCs that apply to this Fact Type. To achieve this, he has the dialogue with the domain expert shown in Textbox 4.3. See Figure 4.1, Fact Type 'Locker User', for a summary of this dialogue in the FCO-IM diagram.

Modeler: Let's consider the use of lockers. Suppose I have the following two Facts (he draws the small table below and shows it to the domain expert): "Person 1234 uses locker C42." and "Person 1234 uses locker 563.".

Fact	Person	Locker
1	1234	C42
2	1234	563

Could these two Facts both be present in your database at the same time?

Domain expert: No, we don't have too many lockers, so locker use is limited to just one per employee.

Modeler: OK, then maybe people can share a locker? Could the following two Facts both be present in your database at the same time? They are "Person 2345 uses locker C42." and "Person 3456 uses locker C42.".

Fact	Person	Locker
~~1~~	~~1234~~	~~C42~~
~~2~~	~~1234~~	~~563~~
3	2345	C42
4	3456	C42

Domain expert: We're not that desperate for more lockers, so if you have one it's all yours.

Textbox 4.3 Dialogue to determine the UCs for Fact Type 'Locker User'

From the dialogue in Textbox 4.3, the modeler concludes two things:

1 Any particular person can have only one locker. This can be Stated as a Constraint in Model Style (see Section 4.1.1) as: "A person can use at most one locker.". It is shown in the model in Figure 4.1 as UC 2 on Role 5 since the same person cannot occur in the Population of Role 5 more than once.

2 Any particular locker can be used by only one person. This can be Stated as a Constraint in Model Style as: "A locker can be used by at most one person.". It is shown in the model in Figure 4.1 as UC 3 on Role 6 since the same locker cannot occur in the Population of Role 6 several times.

UCs on Fact Type 'Fluency'

Finally, let's consider Fact Type 'Fluency'. The modeler cannot be sure without consulting the domain expert whether it is the intention to record only one or several languages a person is fluent in. Conversely, he is pretty sure that one language can be fluently spoken by several people, but will formally check this nevertheless. The modeler wants to find all the UCs that apply to this Fact Type. To achieve this, he has the dialogue with the domain expert shown in Textbox 4.4. See Figure 4.1, Fact Type 'Fluency', for a summary of this dialogue in the FCO-IM diagram.

Modeler: Let's consider fluency in speaking languages. Suppose I have the following two Facts (he draws the small table below and shows it to the domain expert): "Person 1234 speaks English Fluently." and "Person 1234 speaks French fluently.".

Fact	Person	Language
1	1234	English
2	1234	French

Could these two Facts both be present in your database at the same time?

Domain expert: Yes, we want to record all the languages a person can speak fluently.

Modeler: OK, and of course these additional two facts, 3 and 4, can also both be present in your database at the same time? They are "Person 2345 speaks Spanish fluently." and "Person 3456 speaks Spanish fluently.".

Fact	Person	Language
1	1234	English
2	1234	French
3	2345	Spanish
4	3456	Spanish

Domain expert: Yes, of course.

Textbox 4.4 Dialogue to determine the UCs for Fact Type 'Fluency'

From the conversation in Textbox 4.4, the modeler concludes *three* things:

1 Any particular person can speak several languages fluently. This is shown in the model in Figure 4.1 by the *absence* of a small UC on Role 8 only (see point 3 below for the big UC on Roles 8+9), since the same person can be in the Population of Role 8 several times. Statement of this absence in Model Style (see also the second conclusion below Textbox 4.2): "A person can speak several languages fluently.". Other modeling techniques like ERM (see Appendix B, [12]) will require the explicit addition of a maximum cardinality of 'many', see also Section 7.2).

2 Any particular language can be spoken fluently by several persons. This is shown in the model in Figure 4.1 by the *absence* of a small UC on Role 9 only (see point 3 below for the big UC on Roles 8+9), since the same language can be in the Population of Role 9 several times. Statement of this absence in Model Style (see the second conclusion below Textbox 4.2): "A language can be spoken fluently by several people.". Other modeling techniques like ERM (see Appendix B, [12]) will require the explicit addition of a maximum cardinality of 'many', see also Section 7.2).

3 There is a UC on the *combination of Roles 8+9*. The reason is illustrated in Figure 4.1 by Tuples 5 and 6 of Fact Type Fluency. These are the same, so both Tuples represent the same Fact "Person 6789 speaks English fluently.". It would introduce *redundancy* (i.e. storing the same Fact more than once) into the information model if this would be possible. Although the controlled use of redundancy can be beneficial for performance reasons at the logical level of a Relational database schema (see Appendix B, [14]) or at the physical level of an implemented database, it should be strictly avoided at the conceptual level of the information model.

   Therefore UC 4 is placed on the combination of Roles 8+9, which means that the combination of values can occur only once in the Population, preventing the same Tuple from being entered more than once. The modeler doesn't bother the domain expert with Tuples 5 and 6. Rather, he enters UC 4 into the diagram after the conversation in Textbox 4.4. He has established there is no small UC on Role 8 alone and no small UC on Role 9 alone, so there must be a UC on the combination of Roles. This UC 4 doesn't really constrain the Population of the Fact Type apart from preventing the same Fact to be recorded more than once.

Figure 4.1 shows the three possibilities for UCs on a Fact Type with two Roles: one small UC, two small UCs or one big UC. The Population gives examples of Tuples that are allowed and not allowed under these UCs. The conversations in Textboxes 4.2, 4.3 and 4.4 illustrate how the modeler finds these UCs in dialogues with the domain expert. A detailed procedure to determine UCs for any Fact Type is given in the next section.

4.2.2 PROCEDURE TO FIND ALL UCS IN AN INFORMATION MODEL

UCs are the most important Constraints in FCO-IM; every Fact type has at least one Uniqueness Constraint (UC), and possibly more. A Fact Type with two Roles can have one or two UCs, a Fact Type with three Roles can have one, two or three UCs, and so on. UCs correspond to identifiers and cardinalities in ERM (see Appendix B, [12]) and to keys in the Relational model (see Appendix B, [14]), so it is crucial for the data modeler to find all the UCs in an information model.

Suppose there is a Fact Type with N Roles (N is often 1, 2 or 3, but other numbers are possible too). There is at least a UC on all its N roles to prevent redundancy (see the third conclusion the modeler draws from the dialogue in Textbox 4.4 in Section 4.2.1.). But maybe there is a UC on *fewer* than all its N Roles. If so, then such a smaller UC replaces the wider UC. This is because such a smaller UC is *more restrictive* than that wider UC (please try this out yourself by making valid Populations in a Fact Type with two Roles, first with a UC on both Roles, next with a UC on just one Role).

Therefore the strategy to find all the UCs on a Fact Type with N roles is:

1 Check all the possibilities for a UC on N-1 Roles.

2 If no UC on N-1 roles is found, then there must be one on all N Roles.

3 If any UCs on N-1 Roles are found, these UCs are entered instead of a UC on all Roles.

4 If necessary (see below for details), check for still smaller UCs on N-2 Roles or less.

This strategy is worked out in the detailed procedure in Textboxes 4.5 and 4.6 below. It guarantees that the modeler will find all the UCs within every Fact Type. For a further discussion of UCs, see our earlier book on FCO-IM (Appendix B, [1]), and our research paper on the procedure to find them all with the least amount of work (Appendix B, [6]).

The procedure given in Textbox 4.5 is divided into cases depending on the number of roles in the Fact Type, so for each Fact Type only one case needs to be worked out. Lines 2-4 deal with the trivial case of a Fact Type with one Role, lines 5-10 discuss Fact Types with two Roles and lines 11-34 Fact types with three Roles. Finally lines 35-36 refer for Fact Types with more than three Roles to the research paper (see Appendix B, [6]) with a complete but more abstract algorithm covering all cases.

Procedure to find all UCs on one Fact Type

1 For each Fact Type, only one case below applies depending on the number of its Roles.

2 Case 1: The Fact Type has only one Role.

3 Put a UC on this Role. (Obviously, there cannot be any UCs on less than one Role, and there should be one UC, so this is the only possibility. This could be done automatically.)

4 Done!

5 Case 2: The Fact Type has two Roles.

6 Test for the two possible UCs on just one Role (see Textbox 4.6 for details).

7 IF no UC on just one Role is found

8 THEN enter a single UC on the combination of both roles into the model.

9 ELSE enter the found UC(s) on just one Role into the model.

10 Done!

11 Case 3: The Fact Type has three Roles.

12 Test for all three possible UCs on combinations of two Roles (see Textbox 4.6 for details).

13 IF no UC on a combination of two Roles is found

14 THEN enter one UC on the combination of all three roles into the model.

15 Done!

16 ELSE IF only one UC on a combination of two roles is found

17 THEN enter this UC on the combination of two Roles into the model.

18 Done!

19 ELSE IF two UCs on combinations of two Roles are found

20 THEN test for a UC on the single Role that both UCs have in common

```
21            (Example: if the Fact Type has Roles 31, 32 and 33 and two UCs
              are found, namely on Roles 31+32 and on 32+33, then test for a
              UC on just Role 32)
22            IF     no UC on this one Role is found
23            THEN enter the two UCs on the two combinations of two Roles
                     into the model.
24                   Done!
25            ELSE   enter only this UC on just one Role into the model, and
26                   see Section 5.3.2 (N-1 Rule) for further steps to be taken.
27    ELSE IF three UCs on combinations of two Roles are found.
28    THEN    test for all three possibilities of a UC on just one Role
29            IF     no UC on just one Role is found
30            THEN enter the three UCs on the three combinations of two Roles
                     into the model
31            Done!
32            ELSE   enter all the found UCs on just one Role into the model, and
33            see Section 5.3.2 (N-1 Rule) for further steps to be taken.
34    Done!
35    Case 4: The Fact Type has four or more Roles.
36    This case is rare and is therefore not discussed in detail here. It is done in
      an analogous way to case 3 above. See the paper in Appendix B, [6] for a
      complete algorithm that covers all cases.
```

Textbox 4.5 Procedure to determine the UCs for one Fact Type.

For Fact Types with three Roles, if more than one UC on combinations of two Roles is found, further tests for UCs on just one Role must be done. The reason is that in such a case a still smaller UC might be present. There is just one test if two UCs on combinations of two Roles are found (lines 19-26) and three tests if three UCs on combinations of two Roles are found (lines 27-33). For a further explanation of why this must be done, see the paper in Appendix B, [7]. It has also been proven in this paper that this way of working requires the minimum number of tests.

In practice, we advise determining the UCs for Fact Types that have been Analyzed already as soon as possible. It is not necessary to wait for other Fact Types to be Verbalized or Analyzed; UCs can be determined for each Fact Type independently. In this way, the information model can grow incrementally. Of course, in the end the procedure in Textboxes 4.5 and 4.6 must have been applied to all the Fact Types in the model.

The procedure to test for one particular UC, given in Textbox 4.6, uses *pairs of concrete Facts* that are presented to the domain expert. Experience from practice has shown that this way of working is much better than asking the domain expert abstract questions like "Can the same performance have two different prices for a certain type of ticket?", which are highly likely to be misinterpreted. Moreover, in this way, with no extra effort, concrete examples of what is *not* allowed are built up. It is a good practice for every Constraint to have a concrete example of a *violation* of this Constraint. Such examples of violations of Constraints are a lot easier to understand and communicate than abstract formulations of Constraints (see Section 4.5 for several examples).

Procedure to test for one particular Uniqueness Constraint (UC)

1 The modeler uses the FCO-IM diagram as a reference but does not show it to the domain expert. To test whether a candidate UC on a certain Fact Type exists, the modeler draws up two concrete Facts in the Population of this Fact Type. These Facts should satisfy the following conditions (see the figure below with illustrations from Serviceton Music Theater, in which the Fact Expression Types have been expanded a bit for easy reading):

   a The values in the Population of the Role(s) below the UC should be identical.

   b The values in the Population of the other Role(s) should be different.

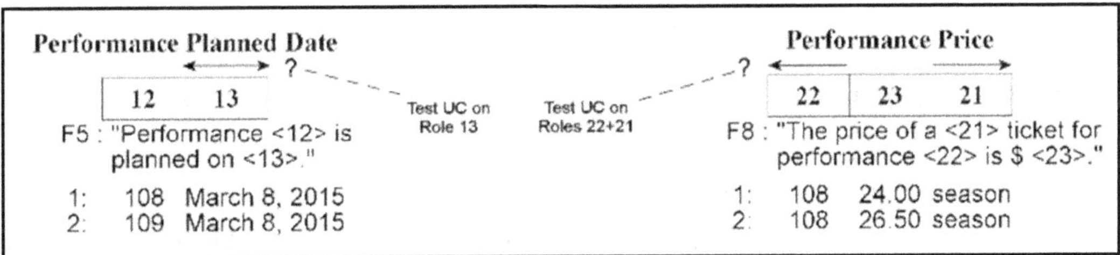

2 The modeler presents these concrete Facts to the domain expert in an easily readable form, for example in a table format as illustrated below (the order of the components of the facts about prices has been changed so the domain expert can read them more easily):

Fact	Perfor-mance	Date
1	108	March 8, 2015
2	109	March 8, 2015

Fact	Perfor-mance	Ticket Type	Price ($)
1	108	season	24.00
2	108	season	26.50

3 The modeler verbalizes both Facts, using the appropriate Fact Expression Type and all the relevant Object Expression Types from the model, so the verbalizations correspond exactly with the ones used to draw up the model. Here:

"Performance 108 is planned on March 8,2015."
"Performance 109 is planned on March 8,2015."
and
"The price for a season ticket for performance 108 is $24.00."
"The price for a season ticket for performance 108 is $26.50."

4 The modeler asks the domain expert whether these two Facts can exist in the Population of the information system *at the same time.*

5 IF the answer is YES,
THEN the duplicate values are allowed, and the UC DOES NOT EXIST.

6 IF the answer is NO,
THEN the duplicate values are NOT allowed, and the UC DOES EXIST.

Textbox 4.6 Procedure to test for one particular UC

4.2.3 PROCEDURE APPLIED TO FACT TYPES WITH THREE ROLES

The procedure in Section 4.2.2 is illustrated here in two examples of Fact Types with three Roles. See Section 4.2.1 for illustrations of its application to Fact Types with two roles.

4.2.3.1 First Example

Figure 4.7 shows a part of an information model for a conference. It concerns the schedule of the workshops in the conference. It is shown below how the modeler determines the UCs, which have been added to the figure already for easy reference, but of course the modeler starts without them.

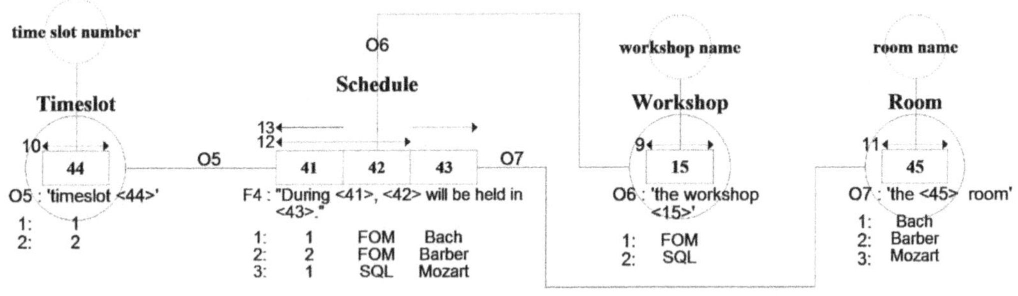

Figure 4.7 UCs on Fact Type 'Schedule'

UCs 10 on Role 44, 9 on Role 15 and 11 on Role 45 follow from lines 2-4 from the procedure in Textbox 4.5. Table 4.8 summarizes the procedure applied to Fact Type 'Schedule' and the dialogue between the modeler and the domain expert.

Fact Type 'Schedule': "During timeslot <41>, workshop <42> will be held in the <43> room.							
Test UC on:	**Fact**	**Time-slot**	**Work-shop**	**Room**	**Allowed?**	**Domain Expert Comment**	**Conclusion**
Roles 41+42	1: 2:	1 1	FOM FOM	Bach ***Pärt***	} ✗	Every workshop session in one room	UC 12 on Roles 41+42
Roles 41+43	3: 4:	1 1	FOM ***AI***	Bach Bach	} ✗	Workshops sessions cannot share a room	UC 13 on Roles 41+43
Roles 42+43	5: 6:	1 **2**	FOM FOM	Bach Bach	} ✓	The same workshop can be held twice	No UC on Roles 42+43
Role 41	7: 8:	1 1	FOM ***SQL***	Bach ***Mozart***	} ✓	No problem	No UC on Role 41 only
Because there is no UC on Role 41 only, UCs 12 and 13 are correct.							
Statements in Model Style: "A combination of a time slot and a workshop can be held in at most one room." "A combination of a time slot and a room can hold at most one workshop." "A combination of a workshop and a room can be held in several timeslots."							

Table 4.8 Summary of procedure applied to Fact Type 'Schedule'

Facts 1 – 6 illustrate line 12 of the procedure in Textbox 4.5: the three possible UCs on combinations of two Roles are tested. The modeler cannot be sure in advance about any of these UCs—for instance, whether one workshop session can be held in two rooms (using monitors) or not—so he must test this explicitly (Facts

1 and 2). The same holds for the other possible UCs on 2 Roles. The answers and comments from the domain expert lead to the conclusions shown.

Since two UCs were found using Facts 1 – 6, lines 19 – 21 in the procedure apply and a test for a UC on Role 41 (the Role that UCs 12 and 13 have in common) is needed. No UC is found, so lines 22-24 in the procedure apply and the conclusion is that UCs 12 and 13 are correct. The modeler enters them into the model and is done with the UC-determination for this Fact Type.

4.2.3.1 Second Example

As a second example, Figure 4.9 shows a part of an information model for a business. It concerns the office rooms where employees work. It is shown below how the modeler determines the UCs, which have been added to the figure already for easy reference, but of course the modeler starts without them.

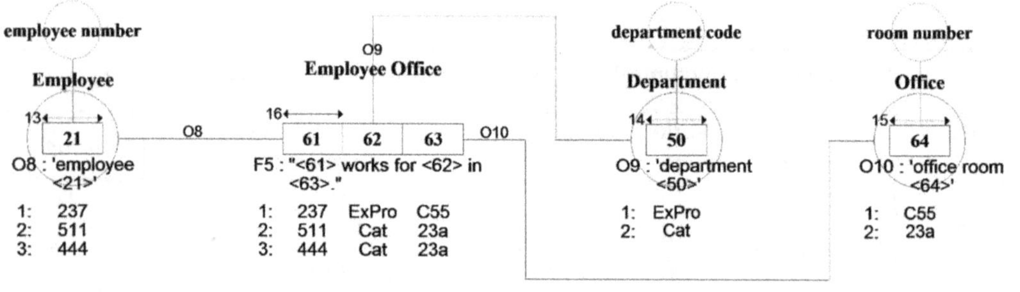

Figure 4.9 UCs on Fact Type 'Employee Office'

UCs 13 on Role 21, 14 on Role 50 and 15 on Role 64 follow from lines 2-4 from the procedure in Textbox 4.5. Table 4.10 summarizes the procedure applied to Fact Type 'Employee Office' and the dialogue between the modeler and the domain expert.

Fact Type Employee Office: "Employee <61> works for department <62> in office room <63>."							
Test UC on:	**Fact**	**Emp**	**Dept**	**Office**	**Allowed?**	**Domain Expert Comment**	**Conclusion**
Roles 61+62	1:	511	Cat	23a	} ✗	One office room is enough	UC 17 on Roles 61+62
	2:	511	Cat	***78***			
Roles 61+63	3:	237	ExPro	C55	} ✗	All employees work for 1 department	UC 18 on Roles 61+63
	4:	237	***Cat***	C55			
Roles 62+63	5:	511	Cat	23a	} ✓	Employees can share an office	No UC on Roles 62+63
	6:	***444***	Cat	23a			

<table>
<tr><td>Role 61</td><td>7: 237 ExPro C55
8: 237 <u>Cat</u> <u>78</u></td><td>} ✗</td><td>Each employee: 1 department, 1 office</td><td>UC 16 on Role 61 only</td></tr>
<tr><td colspan="5">Because there is a UC on Role 61 only, UCs 17 and 18 (not shown) are replaced by it.</td></tr>
<tr><td colspan="5">Statements in Model Style:
Postponed until the modeling error has been corrected (see Section 5.3.2).</td></tr>
</table>

Table 4.10 Summary of procedure applied to Fact Type 'Employee Office'

Facts 1 – 6 illustrate line 12 of the procedure in Textbox 4.5: the three possible UCs on combinations of two Roles are tested. The modeler cannot be sure in advance about any of these UCs—for instance, whether an employee can work for several departments or not—so he must test this explicitly (Facts 3 and 4). The same holds for the other possible UCs on 2 roles. The answers and comments from the domain expert lead to the conclusions shown.

Since two UCs were found using Facts 1 – 6, lines 19 – 21 in the procedure apply and a test for a UC on Role 61 (the Role that UCs 17 and 18, not shown in Figure 4.9, have in common) is needed. Indeed this UC is found, so lines 25-26 in the procedure apply and the conclusion is that UCs 17 and 18 must be replaced by UC 16. The modeler enters it into the model and is done with the UC-determination for this Fact Type.

However, see Section 5.3.2 because it is explained there that this UC-determination has revealed a modeling error that must be corrected. Sections 5.3 and 5.4 discuss three tests for possible modeling errors that should be performed as step 6 in the FCO-IM procedure to draw up a conceptual information model (see Section 3.1), after the UCs have been determined.

4.2.4 SUMMARY OF DETERMINING UCS FOR THE REMAINING FTS OF THE PERFORMANCE SCHEDULE

Figure 4.14 shows the performance schedule part of the information model for Serviceton Music Theater. It is the same as Figure 3.42, but with the UCs added. Below, the Statements in Model Style of all the UCs in Figure 4.14 are given, and for some Fact Types also a summary of the procedure to determine the UC(s). Of course, the procedure was actually carried out analogously for the other Fact Types too, but the summaries have been omitted here for brevity (see Appendix A2.1 for a complete account).

In practice, such a summary should be written down explicitly for every Fact Type with two or more Roles. Such a summary is an important part of the information model documentation because it gives a complete account of the presence or absence of every possible UC. Because the modeler follows the procedure in Textboxes 4.5 and 4.6 during the dialogues with domain experts, this documentation arises naturally and with no extra effort. So there is no excuse to fail to deliver a proper documentation for this step! This is how Appendix A2.1 was made.

All the UCs on Fact Types with one Role (UCs 1 through 8) follow from lines 2–4 in the procedure from Textbox 4.5. These are all Fact type inside an Object Type, and therefore the Statements in Model Style are phrased in a different way. However, the other way can be used here as well; then the first Statement below would be "A Performer can have at most one performer name.". See Fact Type 'Show' for an illustration of why this way of Stating is clearer. Statements in Model Style:

> "A performer is identified by a performer name."
>
> "A genre is identified by a genre name."
>
> "A performance is identified by a performance number."
>
> "A calendar day is identified by a date."
>
> "A time of day is identified by a time (hh:mm AM/PM)."
>
> "A weekday is identified by a weekday name."
>
> "A ticket type is identified by a ticket type name."
>
> "An amount of money is identified by a number of dollars.cents."

Below, several tables summarize the UC-determination for some Fact Types with more than one Role. A few extra explanatory remarks are given above the tables. The UCs on the other Fact Types in Figure 4.14 have been determined analogously (see Appendix A2.1).

UCs for Fact Type 'Show'

Fact Type 'Show' is inside an Object Type but must nevertheless be tested explicitly for UCs (see also Section 5.3.1). Also, because this Fact Type is inside an Object Type, there is only one Statement in Model Style: "A show is identified by the combination of a show name and a performer.". The meaning of this Statement is clear. It is equivalent to the awkward-sounding pair of Statements phrased in the other way, which do not easily convey the same meaning, as "A performer can perform shows with several show names." and "A show name can belong to shows performed by several performers.".

Fact Type 'Show': "There is a show <1> performed by <2>."						
Test UC on:	**Fact**	**Show name**	**Performer**	**Allowed?**	**Domain Expert Comment**	**Conclusion**
Role 1	1: 2:	Cats and Dogs Cats and Dogs	Kelly Turner ***Animals!***	} ✓	We had 2 shows with the same name once	No UC on Role 1 only
Role 2	3: 4:	Cats and Dogs ***Home Again***	Kelly Turner Kelly Turner	} ✓	Proud to host the same artist again	No UC on Role 2 only
Because there is no UC on just one Role, UC 9 on the combination of Roles 1+2 is added.						
Statements in Model Style: "A show is identified by the combination of a show name and a performer." The above Statement is equivalent to the pair of Statements (not recommended): "A performer can perform shows with several show names." "A show name can belong to shows performed by several performers."						

Table 4.11 Summary of procedure applied to Fact Type 'Show'

UCs for Fact Type 'Brief Description Of Show'

Please note that the Population of Role 4 contains a combination of values: a show is identified by a combination of a show name and a performer.

Fact Type 'Brief Description Of Show': "The show <4> is briefly described as: <5>."						
Test UC on:	**Fact**	**Show**	**Description**	**Allowed?**	**Domain Expert Comment**	**Conclusion**
Role 4	1: 2:	Cats..., Kelly... Cats..., Kelly...	Stand-up... ***Drama***	} ✗	Only one description for each show	UC 10 on Role 4
Role 5	3: 4:	Cats..., Kelly... ***Ouch!, Ron...***	Stand-up... Stand-up...	} ✓	We have many stand-up comedy shows	No UC on Role 5
Only UC 10 on Role 4.						
Statements in Model Style: "A show can be briefly described by at most one description." "A description can briefly describe several shows."						

Table 4.12 Summary of procedure applied to Fact Type 'Brief Description Of Show'

UCs for Fact Type 'Show In Genre'

Please note that the Population of Role 6 contains a combination of values: a show is identified by a combination of a show name and a performer.

Fact Type 'Show In Genre': "The show <6> is in the genre <7>."						
Test UC on:	**Fact**	**Show**	**Genre**	**Allowed?**	**Domain Expert Comment**	**Conclusion**
Role 6	1: 2:	Cats..., Kelly... Cats..., Kelly...	Musical ***Family***	} ✓	A show can be in several genres	No UC on Role 6 only
Role 7	3: 4:	Cats..., Kelly... ***Tiger..., Jungle...***	Musical Musical	} ✓	Many shows can be in the same genre	No UC on Role 7 only
Because there is no UC on just one Role, UC 11 on the combination of Roles 6+7 is added.						
Statements in Model Style: "A show can be in several genres." "A genre can contain several shows."						

Table 4.13 Summary of procedure applied to Fact Type 'Show'

UCs for Fact Type 'Performance Features Show'

In Model Style: "A performance can feature at most one show."
"A show can be featured in several performances."

UCs for Fact Type 'Performance Planned Date'

In Model Style: "A performance can be planned on at most one calendar day."
"A calendar day can be the planned day of several performances."

UCs for Fact Type 'Performance Starting Time'

In Model Style: "A performance can start on at most one time of day."
"A time of day can be the starting time of several performances."

UCs for Fact Type 'Calendar Day Is Weekday'

In Model Style: "A calendar day can be at most one weekday."
"A weekday can be the weekday of several calendar days."

UCs for Fact Type 'Performance Price'

The order of the components in the Fact Type has been changed for easy reading. For Facts 5 and 6, the domain expert says she wants to have complete freedom for ticket type prices; for promotion reasons or special occasions a special ticket type like ‘promotion ticket’ might be made available with a price that is the same as or even lower than a season ticket price.

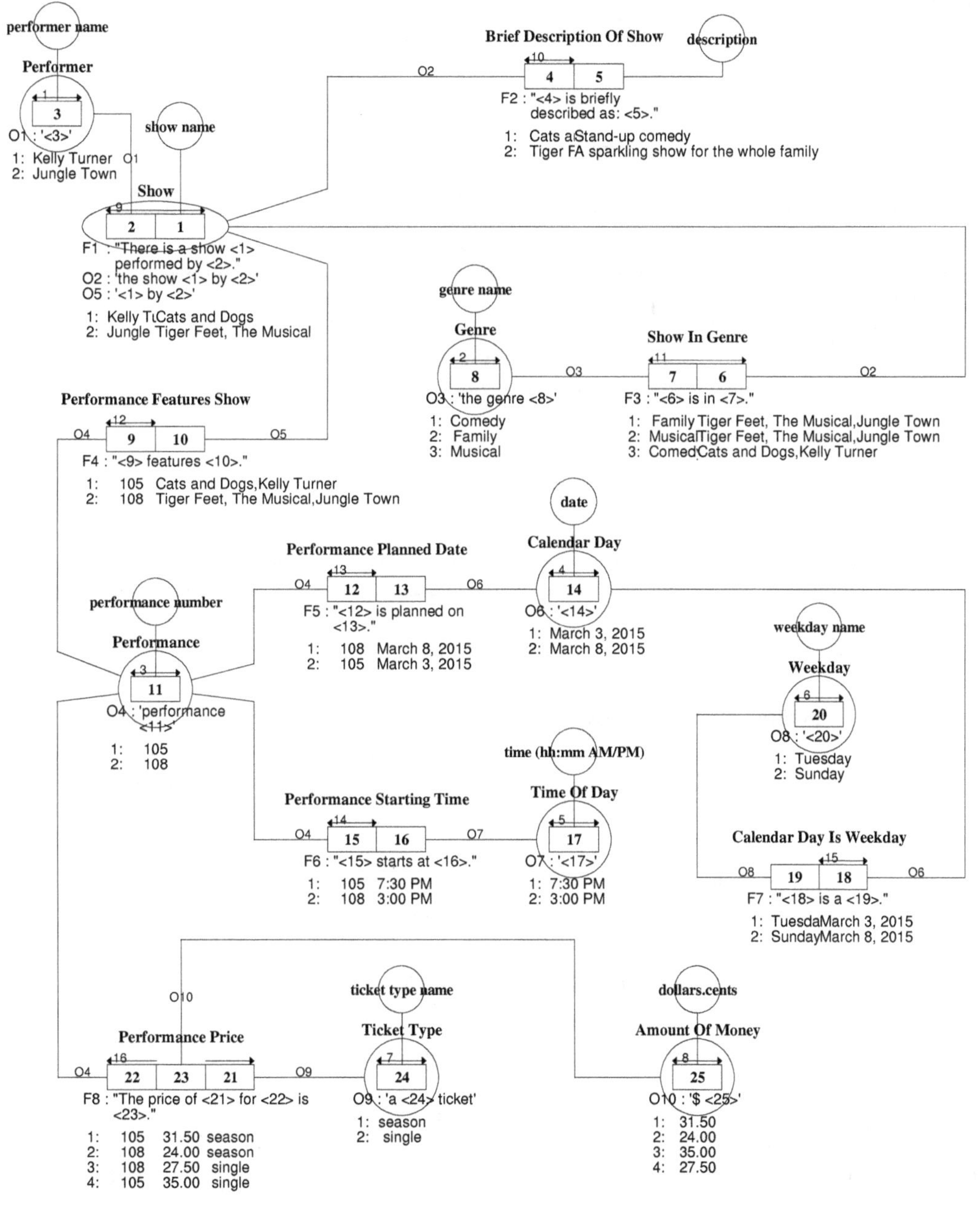

Figure 4.14 FCO-IM diagram for the performance schedule; UCs added

Fact Type Performance Price: "The price of a <21> ticket for performance <22> is $<23>."							
Test UC on:	**Fact**	**Ticket Type**	**Perfor-mance**	**Price ($$.cc)**	**Allowed ?**	**Domain Expert Comment**	**Conclusion**
Roles 21+22	1: 2:	season season	108 108	24.00 ***25.50***	} ✗	No prices 'under the counter'	UC 16 on Roles 21+22
Roles 21+23	3: 4:	season season	108 ***120***	24.00 24.00	} ✓	Yeah, sure	No UC on Roles 21+23
Roles 22+23	5: 6:	season ***promo***	108 108	24.00 24.00	} ✓	No limits on price policy please	No UC on Roles 22+23
Only one UC on combinations of two Roles found: no checks necessary. Done!							
Statements in Model Style: "A combination of a ticket type and a performance can have at most one price." "A combination of a ticket type and a price can apply to several performances." "A combination of a performance and a price can apply to several ticket types."							

Table 4.15 Summary of procedure applied to Fact Type 'Performance Price'

4.3 Totality Constraints (TCs)

Key Points

- **Totality Constraints (TCs) can apply to Roles played by Object Types.**
- **Technically, a Totality Constraint (TC) on one Role means that the *total* Population of the Object Type must also be in the Population of that Role.**
- **Semantically, a Totality Constraint on one Role means that a Fact of this type must be known for *every* Object (like a NOT NULL column in a table).**
- **There is a procedure with useful guidelines to find all TCs for an Object Type, but it does not claim completeness.**

Business Rules like "Every show must have a brief description." or "A reservation request part must refer to a particular performance." occur very often. They translate in FCO-IM into Totality Constraints. (Other information modeling techniques have different concepts for the same thing. Relational databases (see Appendix B, [14]): NOT NULL columns; ERM (see Appendix B, [12]): mandatory attributes or minimal cardinalities of '1', etc.). The corresponding Statements in Model Style (see Section 4.1.1) are "A show must have at least one description." and "A reservation request part must concern at least one performance."

Totality Constraints (TCs for brevity; the term Totality Constraint is abbreviated from here on as TC) are the second most important type of Constraint in an FCO-IM information model. In the FCO-IM procedure to draw up a conceptual information model (see Section 3.1), they are determined in step 7. Uniqueness Constraints are determined in step 5, and the intermediate step 6 (Checking) is treated later, in Chapter 5. We prefer to discuss all the basic constraints in this chapter first, and so deviate here a little from the order in which the steps are carried out in practice.

Totality Constraints (TCs) can only be placed on Roles played by an Object Type. If a TC is placed on one Role, it means that *all* Objects from this Object Type must play this Role. In other words, the *total* Population of the Object Type must play this Role, hence the name for this type of Constraint. In still other words, for *every* recorded Object a Fact must be known in this Fact Type. If a TC is placed on a combination of roles, it means that *all* Objects from this Object Type must play *at least one* of these Roles. In other words, for *every* recorded Object at least one Fact must be known in one of these Fact Types.

In an FCO-IM diagram like the one in Figure 4.18, a TC is shown as a big dot (•). The dot of a TC on one Role is placed on the line that connects the Role with the Object Type on the edge of the Object Type. A TC on several Roles is placed in a small medallion that is connected to the Roles it concerns (see TC 12 in Figure 4.38).

There is no short and sure, complete procedure to find all the TCs in an information model as was given for Uniqueness Constraints in Section 4.2.2. Still, there is a good procedure to find almost all TCs systematically, given below in Section 4.3.2.

Each TC found should be Stated in Model Style (see the examples in Sections 4.3.1 and Appendix A2.2), which allows the modeler to easily compare the presence of a TC with Business Rules Stated in Domain Style (see Section 4.1.1), and also to compare them with Constraints in other modeling techniques like ERM (see Appendix B, [12]), if desired. In this book, an informal way of Stating the presence (or absence) of a TC in Model Style is used. Each such Statement concerns the presence of absence of exactly one TC. However, in an FCO-IM diagram, only the actually existing TCs are entered as big dots connected to the Roles they concern.

Section 4.3.1 below illustrates how TCs are determined in dialogues between the modeler and the domain expert and what other decisions are considered in the process. Section 4.3.2 gives the general procedure, which is illustrated in a few typical cases in Section 4.3.3. Section 4.3.4 gives a summary of the rest of the TC-determination for the performance schedule part of the information model of Serviceton Music Theater and for a special case from another part as well.

4.3.1 ILLUSTRATIONS OF HOW TOTALITY CONSTRAINTS ARE DETERMINED

To determine Totality Constraints (TCs) in an FCO-IM information model, the modeler considers every Object Type in turn. He starts with Object Type 'Show' (see Figure 4.18) and has the dialogue in Textbox 4.16 with the domain expert.

In this dialogue, he tests for all the TCs on just one Role played by Object Type 'Show'. So he first tests for a TC on Role 4 (must every show have at least one brief description?), then for a TC on Role 6 (must every show be in at least one genre?) and finally for a TC on Role 10 (must every show be featured in at least one performance?).

Please note that the modeler can usually ask the domain expert abstract questions like "Must every show be in at least one genre?". This is contrary to how Uniqueness Constraints (UCs) are determined, namely always using concrete examples of Facts (see Sections 4.2.2 and 4.2.3), because abstract questions about UCs are almost always too difficult to state or understand. But such questions about TCs can usually be well understood by domain experts. Of course, if there is any doubt, a quickly made concrete example will clarify things immediately (as is shown in Textbox 4.16).

Modeler:	I see there are several kinds of facts to be recorded about shows. Could there be a show without a brief description?
Domain expert:	I'm not sure I understand your question completely.
Modeler:	Well, you record facts like this one (draws the table below): "The show Cats and Dogs by Kelly turner is briefly described as: Stand-up comedy.".

Fact	Show Show name	 Performer	Description
1	Cats and Dogs	Kelly Turner	Stand-up comedy
2	Tiger Feet, The Musical	Jungle Town	--

Could we have a show recorded in the database like this one: "There is a show Tiger Feet, The Musical performed by Jungle Town.", for which you don't have such a brief description?

Domain expert: Ah, I see. No, we always give every show a brief description for the program (whether online or in the folders) so the customers get a better idea what they can expect.

Modeler: OK. You can also specify one or more genres a show is in. Must every show be in at least one genre, or could you have a show without any genre specified?

Domain expert: No, at least one genre is required.

Modeler: OK, fine. And we already know that a show can be featured in several performances. So I guess there's no point in having a show in the database without any performance it's featured in?

Domain expert: Well, actually we do often record shows before we know when they will be performed exactly. We work a few years ahead, and of course we do know all the performances for the coming season, but usually we already know many shows before the schedule is completed for later seasons.

Textbox 4.16 Dialogue to determine the TCs for Object Type 'Show'

The modeler makes the following summary of the dialogue in Textbox 4.16 in a table on his laptop during the dialogue itself. Of course he also enters the date and the name of the domain expert interviewed, and so the documentation of the TC-determination arises simultaneously with the interview and requires no extra effort later. The TCs are entered into the model (see Figure 4.18).

OT: Show			
Test TC on Role(s):	**Question**	**Answer (Y/N), Comment**	**Conclusion**
4	Can there be a show without a brief description?	N	TC 1 on Role 4

6	Must every show be in at least one genre?	Y	TC 2 on Role 6
10	Can there be a show without a performance?	Y: for later seasons shows are known before the schedule is completed.	No TC on Role 10
Statements in Model Style: "A show must be briefly described by at least one description." "A show must be in at least one genre." "A show does not need to be featured in a performance."			

Table 4.17 TC-documentation arising from the dialogue in Textbox 4.16

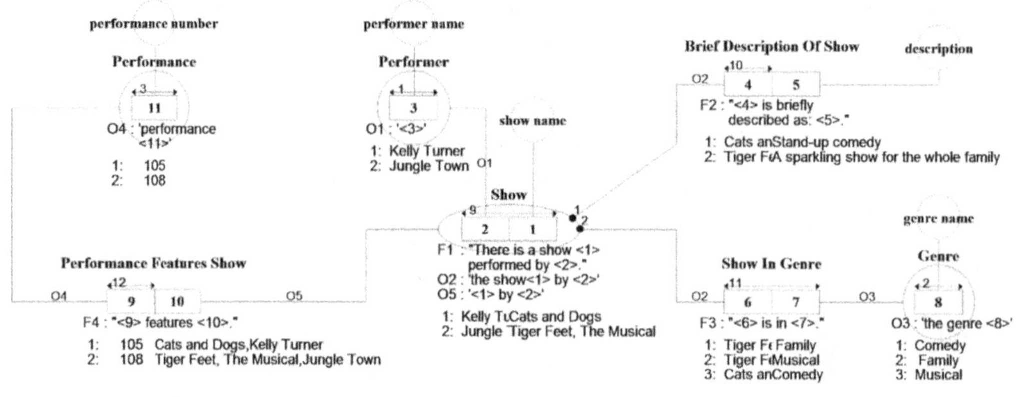

Figure 4.18 TCs on Roles played by Object Type 'Show'

Next, the modeler turns to Object Types 'Performer' and 'Genre'. The modeler and domain expert have the dialogue shown in Textbox 4.19. Please note that the modeler uses a different kind of questions here. This is because both these Object Types only play a Role in Fact Types that do *not* have a Uniqueness Constraint (UC) on just this one Role. This contrasts with Object Type 'Show', which *does* play a Role with a UC on just this Role (Role 4, with UC 10 on it). See the procedure in Section 4.3.3 for further explanation and details. The dialogue leads to the following two conclusions about TCs.

Modeler:	The same performer can star in several different shows. Would you like to have a list of possible performers to choose from? That would prevent typos or different ways to identify the same performer (as in 'Kelly Turner' or 'K. Turner') in your information system.
Domain expert:	Not a bad idea, I guess, but there are so many performers it would make a HUGE list, and we haven't had many problems

	like that. Performers are always clear about their stage name, and I can't recall any spelling problems there.
Modeler:	OK. Then how about the genres you assign to shows? Same thing here: Would you like a list of genres to choose from, or just type them in on the fly?
Domain expert:	Ah, yes that would be nice to have. That's a smaller list, and we did have problems with our annual monitoring report when we failed to count the two entries 'Stand-up comedy' and 'Stand up comedy' (an understandable typo) as the same genre. So yeah, if you can make a pick list for genres, please do!

Textbox 4.19 Dialogue to determine the TCs for Fact Types 'Performer' and 'Genre'

The first conclusion is that there is a TC on Role 2. The reason is that the domain expert does not want a list of all possible performers. This means all performers that are actually recorded in the database must indeed perform in at least one show. In other words, there can be no performers in the Population of Object Type 'Performer' that are missing in the Population of Role 2 from Fact Type 'Show'. In still other words, the *total* Population of Object Type Performer must be present in the Population of Role 2. Therefore the modeler concludes there must be a TC on Role 2.

The second conclusion is there can be no TC on Role 7, and we must yet add a Fact Expression Type to the model. The reason is that the domain expert does indeed want a stored list of all possible genres. Such a *domain list* can be implemented later easily as a one-column table (known as a *domain table*) that contains all the genres. This means that there can be genres actually recorded in the database, like 'Punk' or 'Techno' or 'Experimental theater', although no show has been recorded in these genres for Serviceton Music Theater yet. So how can those genres be entered into the Population of Object Type 'Genre' at all if they have not been added to the Population of Fact Type 'Show In Genre' yet? Fully Communication Oriented means we must have a Fact Expression Type to enter such genres. This can be easily supplied using expressions like "There is a genre Techno.". So the desire of the domain expert to have a pick list of genres leads to this pair of modeling decisions:

- There is no TC on Role 7 since there can be genres in the Population of Object Type 'Genre' that are not (yet) used to put shows in.

- A Fact Expression Type for Fact Type 'Genre' must be added because otherwise it is impossible to enter genres that are not (yet) used. Here, F9 follows from Analyzing Fact Expressions like "There is a genre Techno." or "There is a genre Experimental theater." (See Section 3.6.2).

The modeler makes the following summaries of the dialogue in Textbox 4.19 in a table on his laptop during the dialogue itself. See Figure 4.22 for the corresponding FCO-IM diagram.

OT: Performer			
Test TC on Role(s):	Question	Answer (Y/N), Comment	Conclusion
2	Would you like a list of possible performers?	N, too big, no problems with performer names.	TC 3 on Role 2
Statements in Model Style: "No domain list is needed for performers." "A performer must perform in at least one show."			

Table 4.20 TC-documentation arising from the dialogue in Textbox 4.19 for Object Type 'Performer'

OT: Genre			
Test TC on Role(s):	Question	Answer (Y/N), Comment	Conclusion
7	Would you like a list of possible genres?	Y	No TC on Role 7, and Fact Expression Type added for Genre
Statements in Model Style: "A domain list is desired for genres." "A genre does not need to contain a show."			

Table 4.21 TC-documentation arising from the dialogue in Textbox 4.19 for Object Type 'Genre'

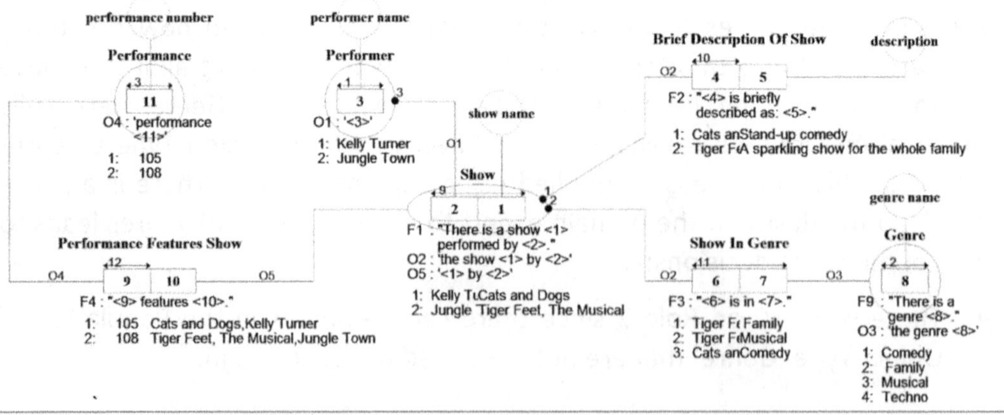

Table 4.22 TC and/or Fact Expression Type added to Object Types 'Performer' and 'Genre'

4.3.2 PROCEDURE TO FIND ALL TCS IN AN INFORMATION MODEL

Unlike the procedure to determine all Uniqueness Constraints (see Section 4.2.2), which will find all UCs with a minimum of effort, the procedure to find all Totality Constraints (TCs) is not quite so airtight. This is even worse for all other kinds of Constraints, for which nothing even remotely like a clear cookbook is available. It is still an unsolved problem how to find all the Business Rules; requirement analysis is more an art than a science, and your skills at it will improve with experience. Still, many practical guidelines can be given, and the procedure below supplies some.

The procedure to find all TCs also tries to minimize the amount of work to be done. For this purpose, we have built in a few guidelines from our experience in practice. The advantage is less work in carrying out the procedure, but on the downside it makes the procedure harder to read. We hope to have struck a balance so you will be able to cut a few corners without finding the procedure too much of a maze.

To minimize effort, the procedure below distinguishes between two kinds of Object Types: those that have *Own Attribute Fact Types* and those that don´t have such Fact Types (see Definition 4.23). Those two kinds of Object Types can be treated quite differently to find their TCs fast. In addition, a few typical cases (see Definition 4.24) that occur in (almost) every information model are given; recognizing those at first sight will help as well.

The name 'Attribute Fact Type' arises because such Fact Types translate into attributes in various non-elementary information modeling techniques like ERM (see Appendix B, [12], UML (see Appendix B, [13]) and Relational databases (see Appendix B, [14]). Some Object Types in an FCO-IM information model have Own Attribute Fact Types, such as Object Type Show; it plays Role 4 in Fact Type 'Brief Description Of Show', which has UC 10 on Role 4 only (see Figure 4.22). Such Object Types should be tested for TCs as described in Textbox 4.25, lines 22-25, and illustrated in the dialogue in Textbox 4.16 and Table 4.17.

Other Object Types in an FCO-IM information model do not have Own Attribute Fact Types, like Object Types 'Performer' and 'Genre' (see Figure 4.22), and they should be tested in the way described in Textbox 4.25, lines 5-20, and illustrated in the dialogue in Textbox 4.19 and Tables 4.20 and 4.21.

4.3.2.1 Attribute Fact Type and Own Attribute Fact Type

A Fact Type is an ***Attribute Fact Type*** if it has the following two properties:

- the Fact Type has only two Roles and
- there is only one Uniqueness Constraint (UC) on just one of the Roles.

If an Object Type plays a Role in an Attribute Fact Type, then this Fact Type is an ***Own Attribute Fact Type*** of this Object Type if the UC is on the Role played by the Object Type.

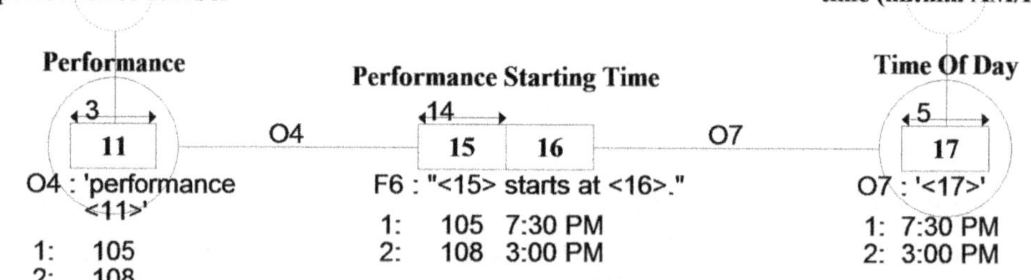

In this figure, Fact Type 'Performance Starting Time' is an Attribute Fact Type.

It is an Own Attribute Fact Type of Object Type 'Performance'; the UC is at its own side.

It is not an Own Attribute Fact Type of Object Type 'Time Of Day'; the UC is on the other side.

Definition 4.23 Attribute Fact Type, Own Attribute Fact Type

4.3.2.2 Typical Cases

There are a few frequently occurring typical cases of Object Types for which the major part of the 'ordinary' procedure can be safely skipped. These cases are specified in Definition 4.24 below. All such Object Types usually play Roles in many Fact Types that are *not* Own Attribute Fact Types (see Definition 4.23). Checking for a Totality Constraint (TC) on any one Role or combination of Roles they play would be a big waste of time and effort because they almost always will turn out to have only one TC—namely, on the combination of *all* the Roles they play.

The following typical cases are considered in the procedure in Textbox 4.25:

- Object Types that represent physical quantities like 'Length', 'Area', 'Volume', 'Weight', 'Voltage', etc. (see also Figure 3.43).
- An Object Type for a number of countable things/concepts/people, usually modeled as an Object Type 'Number' with Label Type 'integral number' (see Figure 3.45).
- An Object Type for sums of money, usually modeled as an Object Type 'Amount of Money' with Label Type 'dollars.cents' (see the model in Figure 4.32).
- An Object Type for calendar days, usually modeled as an Object Type 'Calendar Day' with Label Type 'date' (see the model in Figure 4.32).
- Other similar Object Types (for a timestamp, time of day, weekday, geographical coordinates, bit rate, etc.).

Definition 4.24 Typical cases

Actually, in the Serviceton Music Theater case, there is an exception to the typical cases stated in Definition 4.24: Object Type 'Calendar Day' *does* have an Own Attribute Fact Type here. This shows these 'typical cases' are not infallible laws, only hopefully useful rules of thumb that work very often, but not always, to make shortcuts. But if you are ever in doubt, put the nose to the grindstone and drudge through the systematic part of the procedure (given in Textbox 4.25).

The procedure in Textbox 4.25 is given in two parts. The first part starts in lines 1-21 with the shortcuts for the Object Types without an Own Attribute Fact Type (including the typical cases). In the second part, lines 22-42, the systematic approach is given for other Object Types (or if the shortcuts fail).

The procedure does not cover every theoretically possible case, but we think it does cover over 99% of all cases in practice. Please let us know if you encounter practical situations that do not fall under this procedure.

Procedure to find all TCs in an information model

Note: Lines 5-21 concern some common typical cases, to minimize the work to be done. We do not claim completeness here. If in doubt, proceed using lines 22-42.

1 For each Object Type in the model do the following steps
2 IF the Object Type has at least one Own Attribute Fact Type
(see Definition 4.23)
3 THEN continue with line 22
4 ELSE continue with line 5 below

Part 1: Object Type without an Own Attribute Fact Types

Pick list?

5 Determine whether a pick list for all Objects of this Object Type is desired
6 Use questions like:
a Would you like a list of all possible <Object Type name>s
to avoid a lot of typing, typos or
entering different ways to name the same things/persons?
b Do you have a predefined list of <Object Type name>
names/numbers/codes to be used by everyone, or do you just type
new ones on the fly?

Yes, Pick list

7 IF the answer to the questions in line 6 is 'Yes'
8 THEN no TC is present on any of its Roles,
and it should have a Fact Expression Type
9 State this result in (abbreviated) Model Style using a sentence like:
"A domain list is desired for <Object Type name>s."

Add Fact Expression type?

10 Check whether the Fact Type inside the Object Type already has a
Fact Expression Type
11 IF there is no Fact Expression Type
12 THEN add one
Use expressions like "There is a(n) <Object Type name>...."
13 Done!

No Pick list. Typical case?

14 ELSE the answer to the questions in line 6 is 'No'
15 THEN determine whether this Object Type is a typical case
(see Definition 4.24)

Yes, typical case

```
16   IF      this Object Type is a typical case
17   THEN    add one TC on the combination of all the Roles
             played by the Object Type
18           State this result in (abbreviated) Model Style using a sentence
             like: "No domain list is desired for <Object Type name>s."
19           Add the TC to the model
20           Done!
```

No typical case

```
21   ELSE    continue with line 22
```

Part 2: Object Type with at least one Own Attribute Fact Type

Note: lines 22-42 describe the (incomplete) systematic way to find the TCs on Roles played by one Object Type. Lines 27-32 are meant as shortcut.

TCs on only one Role

```
22   For each Role played by this Object Type
23       Test for a TC on only this Role. Use questions like:
             a   Can there be a(n) <Object Type name> without a ....?
             b   Must every <Object Type name> have at least one ....?
24   State the results of all tests in Model Style (see Section 4.1.1)
25   Add all the found TCs (if any) to the model
```

TCs on combinations of Roles

```
26   For all the Roles without a TC yet (if any):
```

Possible shortcut

```
27   IF      all of these Roles without a TC
             are not in any Own Attribute Fact Type
28   THEN    test for a TC on the combination of all of these Roles without a TC
29           Hint: It might be fruitful here to ask whether a pick list is desired
             (see lines 5-6)
30           IF      such a TC is present
31           THEN    State the result in Model Style
32                   Add the TC to the model
33                   Done!
```

Shortcut is not applicable

34 ELSE Look for TCs on any combination of Roles
Remark: This is impossible to do completely in practice if there are many Roles. Instead, look for Business Rules stated elsewhere, and use your common sense and experience

35 If you have done any tests here, state the results in Model Style

36 Add any found TCs to the model

Add Fact Expression type?

37 IF at least one TC was found in lines 22-36

38 THEN Done!

39 ELSE Check whether the Fact Type inside the Object Type has a Fact Expression Type

40 IF there is no Fact Expression Type

41 THEN add one
Use expressions like "There is a(n) <Object Type name>...."

42 Done!

Textbox 4.25 Procedure to determine TCs

4.3.3 SUMMARY OF DETERMINING TCS FOR THE REMAINING FTS OF THE PERFORMANCE SCHEDULE

See Figure 4.32 below, which contains the results of determining the TCs for the performance schedule part of Serviceton Music Theater. Object Types 'Performer', 'Show' and 'Genre' were done in Section 4.3.2 already. Line numbers below refer to the procedure to determine TCs given in Textbox 4.25.

Object Type 'Performance'

Lines 1-4: This is an Object Type with Own Attribute Fact Types, so line 3 applies.

Lines 22-25: See Table 4.26, the entries for a TC on one Role only.

Lines 26-27: The condition fails (Role 15 without a TC *is* in an Own Attribute Fact Type).

Lines 34-36: To make sure, the modeler does check for a TC on roles 15+22. See Table 4.26.

Lines 37-38: Two TCs were found, so the procedure ends here for this Object Type.

OT: Performance			
Test TC on Role(s):	**Question**	**Answer (Y/N), Comment**	**Conclusion**
9	Is the show known for every planned performance?	Y: we can't plan a performance without a show.	TC 4 on Role 9
12	Does every performance have a planned date?	Y	TC 5 on Role 12
15	Does every performance have a planned starting time?	N: this can be fixed later.	No TC on Role 15
22	Are prices known for every performance?	N: we often plan the show and the date, and settle other things later.	No TC on Role 22
15+22	Is either a time or a price is always recorded?	N, not necessarily.	No TC on Roles 15+22
Statements in Model Style: "A performance must feature in at least one show." "A performance must be planned on at least one calendar day." "A performance does not need to have a starting time." "A performance does not need to have prices." "A performance does not need to have either a starting time or prices."			

Table 4.26 TC-documentation for Object Type 'Performance'

Object Type 'Calendar Day'

Lines 1-4: The modeler knows from experience that an Object Type like 'Calendar Day' is one of the typical cases specified in Definition 4.23. Such Object Types almost always do not play a Role in an Own Attribute Fact Type and have only one TC on the combination of all the Roles they play (as the procedure states in line 17). However, here this Object type *does* have an Own Attribute Fact Type. So line 3 applies, but the modeler keeps in mind that it is 'almost' a typical case.

Lines 22-25: See Table 4.27, the entries for a TC on one Role only. Apart from Roles 13 and 18, shown in Figure 4.32, this Object Type also plays Role 57 in Fact Type 'Reservation Request Registration Date' (See IGD 'Reservation Request' in Section Appendix A1.3.) This Role must be considered too.

Role 18. The modeler starts with Role 18, rather than with the other Roles, because it is in an Own Attribute Fact Type of this Object type (see Definition 4.23). That usually makes it easy to phrase a meaningful question, whereas such questions are often difficult or awkward to phrase for Roles in other Fact Types. See the summary in Table 4.27.

Roles 13 and 57. The modeler now wants to establish whether the *total* Population of 'Calendar Day' is in the Population of Role 13 or in that of Role 57. But he knows from experience that this is as good as never the case: Why should *all* the recorded dates in the database have a performance planned? There could be dates on which no performance is planned but a reservation request was registered, or vice versa. Therefore he considers these two roles more or less together. See the summary in Table 4.27.

Lines 26-33: The condition in line 27 is satisfied. Line 29: The modeler also knows from experience it is often desired to have a calendar implemented in the information system. Users can then easily pick a date without thinking how they should spell it ('March 8, 2015', '3/8/2015' (USA), '8/3/2015' (Europe), '20150308', etc.) and the big risk of typing it wrongly is also avoided. The domain expert would indeed welcome this, so *all* the dates in the coming years will be in the Population of Object Type 'Calendar Day'. There might well be dates that are *not* in the Population of Role 13 or Role 57, so there is no TC on the combination of these Roles. See Table 4.27.

Lines 37-38: One TC was found, so the procedure ends here for this Object Type.

OT: Calendar Day			
Test TC on Role(s):	**Question**	**Answer (Y/N), Comment**	**Conclusion**
18	Must the weekday be known for every calendar day?	Y	TC 6 on Role 18
13, 57	I suppose it's possible for a date to have a performance planned but no reservation registered, and vice versa?	Y	No TC on Role 13 No TC on Role 57
13+57	Would you like to have a calendar implemented?	Y!	No TC on 13+57
Statements in Model Style: "A calendar day must be at least one weekday." "A calendar day does not need to have a performance planned." "A calendar day does not need to have a reservation request registered." "A calendar day does not need to have a performance planned or a reservation request registered." "A domain list is desired for calendar days."			

Table 4.27 TC-documentation for Object Type 'Calendar Day'

Object Type 'Time Of Day'

Lines 1-4: This is an Object Type without Own Attribute Fact Types, so line 4 applies.

Lines 5-6: See the summary in Table 4.28.

Lines 7-9: No TC.

Lines 10-13: No Fact Expression Type is present yet, so one is added (see Figure 4.32).

OT: Time Of Day			
Test TC on Role(s):	**Question**	**Answer (Y/N), Comment**	**Conclusion**
16+60	Would you like a pick list of all possible times of day a performance can start?	Y: we want only certain starting times: every 15 minutes, not in between.	No TC on Roles 16+60, and a Fact Expression Type added
Statements in Model Style: "A domain list is desired for times of day." "A time of day does not need to be the day on which a performance is planned." "A time of day does not need to be the day on which a reservation request was registered."			

Table 4.28 TC-documentation for Object Type 'Time Of Day'

Object Type 'Weekday'

Lines 1-4: This is an Object Type without Own Attribute Fact Types, so line 4 applies.

Lines 5-6: See the summary in Table 4.29. Actually, the modeler is surprised by the answer, but he knows this issue will be addressed again when Value Constraints are considered (see Section 4.5), so he accepts the refusal for the time being.

Line 14: No pick list.

Lines 15-20: Yes, typical case. A TC on all Roles (that is only Role 19) is added.

OT: Weekday			
Test TC on Role(s):	**Question**	**Answer (Y/N), Comment**	**Conclusion**
19	Would you like a pick list of all possible weekdays?	N: don't bother.	TC 7 on Role 19
Statements in Model Style: "No domain list is desired for weekdays." "A weekday does not need to be the weekday of a calendar day."			

Table 4.29 TC-documentation for Object Type 'Weekday'

Object Type 'Ticket Type'

Lines 1-4: This is an Object Type without Own Attribute Fact Types, so line 4 applies.

Lines 5-6: See the summary in Table 4.30. Once more (see Table 4.29) the modeler is surprised but knows this issue will be addressed again when Value Constraints are considered (see Section 4.5), so he accepts the decision for the time being.

Lines 7-9: No TC.

Lines 10-13: No Fact Expression Type is present yet, so one is added (see Figure 4.32).

OT: Ticket Type			
Test TC on Role(s):	**Question**	**Answer (Y/N), Comment**	**Conclusion**
21	Would you like a pick list of all possible ticket types?	Y	No TC on Role 21, and a Fact Expression Type added
Statement in Model Style: "A domain list is desired for ticket types." "A ticket type does not need to have a price for a performance."			

Table 4.30 TC-documentation for Object Type 'Ticket type'

Object Type 'Amount of Money'

Lines 1-4: This is an Object Type without Own Attribute Fact Types, so line 4 applies.

Lines 5-6: See the summary in Table 4.31. The modeler agrees it is a bad idea to make a list of all possible amounts of money.

Line 14: No pick list.

Lines 15-20: Yes, typical case. A TC on all Roles is added (here, only Role 23). Please note that in general an Object Type like 'Amount Of Money' can play hundreds of Roles, and there probably still will be only one TC on the combination of all of them.

OT: Amount Of Money			
Test TC on Role(s):	**Question**	**Answer (Y/N), Comment**	**Conclusion**
23	Would you like a pick list of all possible amounts of money?	N. That would really be over the top.	TC 8 on Role 23.
Statement in Model Style: "No domain list is desired for amounts of money." "An amount of money must be the price of a ticket type for a performance."			

Table 4.31 TC-documentation for Object Type 'Amount of Money'

For an example of a TC on a combination of Roles, see the complete information model for Serviceton Music Theater in Appendix A. In the diagram for the customer part of the model, there is a TC on the combination of Roles 37 and 40. The reason is that Serviceton must be able to contact a customer, so either a phone number or an email address (or both) must be recorded for every customer. This was Stated as Business Rule BR 24 (see Section Appendix A3.2) in Domain Style as "To be able to contact a customer, an email address and/or a phone number must be known for each customer." and is Stated in Model Style as "A customer must have at least one email address and/or be phoned at a telephone." (see Appendix A2.2, Object Type 'Customer').

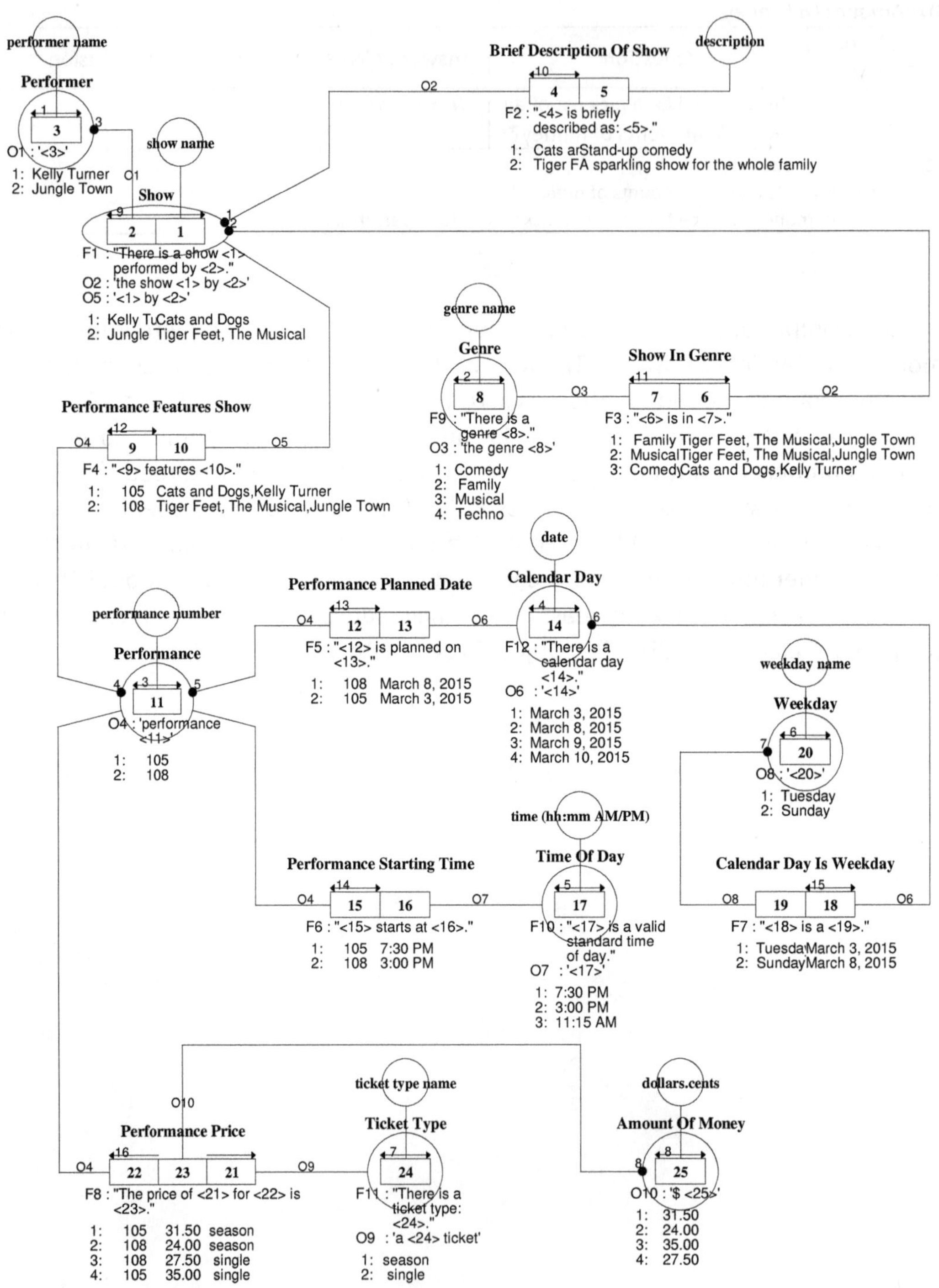

Figure 4.32 FCO-IM diagram for the performance schedule; TCs added

4.4 Value Constraints (VCs)

Key Points

- **Value Constraints (VCs) can apply to Label Types.**
- **If there is a choice between modeling a Business Rule as a VC or as a domain list, it is strongly recommended to use a domain list.**

A Label is a name, code, number or anything else you can type in on a keyboard. Labels of the same kind are modeled as a Label Type. A Label Type can be seen as a source from which any Label of this kind can be drawn as you please. But sometimes there are Business Rules that place restrictions on the labels that can be drawn from such a source. A few examples (not from Serviceton Music Theater) Stated in Domain Style (see Section 4.1.1):

BR a: "Weekdays are written out in full: Sunday, Monday, Tuesday, etc."

BR b: "Genders are given as 'M' and 'F' for male and female respectively."

BR c: "The status of a task can only be 'accepted', 'queued', 'active' or 'completed'."

BR d: "Months are indicated by their month number."

BR e: "A percentage is a number between 0.0 and 100.0."

Such Business Rules can be modeled in FCO-IM using a Value Constraint. A Value Constraint (VC) belongs to a Label Type and specifies what the allowed values are. Typically a VC gives a list of all allowed values or a range of allowed numbers. A few examples (LT stands for Label Type):

VC 1 on LT 'weekday name': {Monday, Tuesday, Wednesday, Thursday, Friday, Saturday, Sunday}

VC 2 on LT 'gender code': {M, F}

VC 3 on LT 'status name': {accepted, queued, active, completed}

VC 4 on LT 'month code': {1 ... 12}

VC 5 on LT 'percentage': {0.0 ... 100.0}

Examples of Statements of these VCs in Model Style:

VC 1: "The only allowed weekday names are: Monday, Tuesday, Wednesday, Thursday, Friday, Saturday, Sunday."

VC 2: "The only allowed gender codes are: M, F."

VC 3: "The only allowed status names are: accepted, queued, active, completed."

VC 4: "The only allowed month codes are integral numbers from 1 through 12.'

VC 5: "The only allowed percentages are real numbers between 0.0 and 100.0."

4.4.1 VALUE CONSTRAINT OR DOMAIN LIST?

A Business Rule that specifies a list of allowed values can be modeled as a Value Constraint (VC) but also as a *domain list* (see Section 4.3.1, the discussion about Object Type 'Genre'). Instead of giving the allowed values in a VC that concerns a Label Type, the list could be entered as the population of a Fact Type with one Role played by this Label Type. Figures 4.33 and 4.34 give these two possibilities for Business Rule BR a. In Figure 4.33, VC 1 was added to Label Type 'weekday name' without any changes to the rest of the model. In Figure 4.34, the list of weekday names is now in the Population of Object Type 'Weekday', and some other things were changed accordingly. TC 7 in Figure 4.33 was removed in Figure 4.34 because it is now no longer required that the *total* Population of Object Type 'Weekday' be in the Population of Role 19 (even if it usually would be; for instance, the possibility that no calendar days that fall on a Monday are recorded should not be ruled out). But then a Fact Expression Type is required for Fact type 'Weekday' because otherwise it would not be possible to enter 'Monday' into the population of Fact Type 'Weekday' at all (see also lines 37-42 in the procedure to find TCs in Textbox 4.25 and the discussion in Section 4.3.1 for Object Type 'Genre').

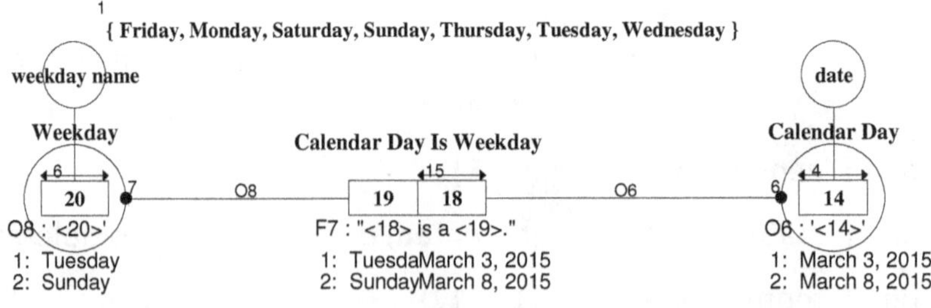

Figure 4.33 Business Rule BR a modeled as Value Constraint VC 1

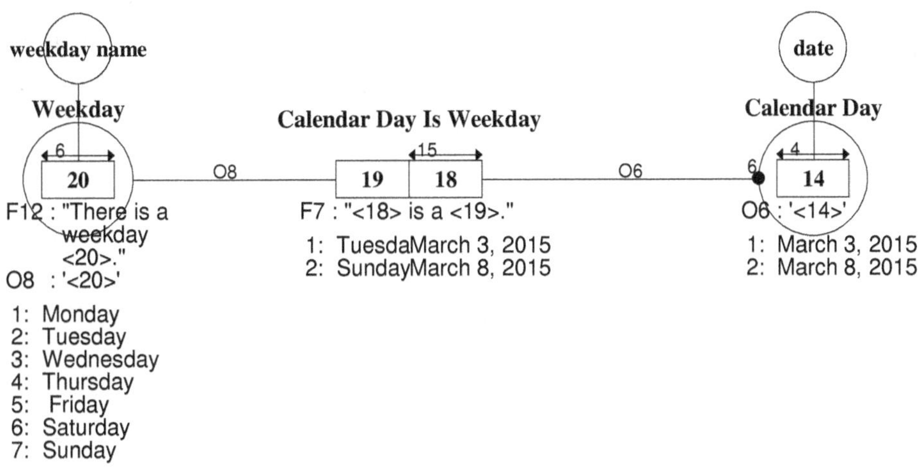

Figure 4.34 Business Rule BR a modeled as domain list

Both ways of modeling are valid, but nevertheless we strongly advise to use domain lists in cases like this. Arguments for this are:

- A domain list contains *ordinary data*. In a Relational database (see Appendix B, [14]), for instance, the list will be implemented as a *domain table*: an ordinary table that contains the seven weekdays, one in each row. A VC, however, is *metadata* (see Section 6.1.2): it is stored in a special way, like a check constraint on all the table columns into which weekdays can be entered. If a change would have to be made in the names of the weekdays, then ordinary data can be changed easily using the standard update mechanisms of the database management system, but metadata can usually only be changed with a lot more time, effort and costs.
- The list of seven weekdays has to be typed in anyway, whether as VC or as domain list. The advantage of using a domain table is that you only have to do this once: all other tables can use a drop down list to pick one of its allowed values even if they have changed recently (*single point of definition*). In contrast, with a VC you probably have to type the list in several times (check constraints on all the table columns that contain weekdays), and any change must be repeated for all of these check constraints as well.
- Such changes to things people think are very constant do in fact happen! BR b: Recently (2014), the German government has added a third gender to the

usual 'M' and 'F', namely 'X', to allow intersex children (babies born without clear gender body parts, more yearly than you might hope) to postpone their gender identification until they can decide on this themselves (many transgender cases spring from a gender classification that was made too early). BR a: Weekday names are probably fairly safe, although during the French Revolution (1792) there was a serious attempt to start using weeks of ten days, with names like 'primidi', 'duodi', etc. BR c: Status names are much more prone to change; if the procedures in an organization change (and they change a *lot* faster than the data they operate on), then a few more and/or different status names are very likely. Still, if you're reasonably sure that such changes will not take place (after all, there have been no attempts to change weekdays since 1792), a VC is a valid way to model them.

- A list of allowed values can concern more than one Label Type. For instance, day numbers can vary between 1 and 31, and month numbers between 1 and 12. Still, no date with month '2' and day '30' exists. So it is not possible to specify all possible calendar days in one year with VCs on separate Label Types for 'month number' and 'day number', and a domain list would be a better choice.

The above considerations lead us to advise:

- If a Business Rule specifies a concrete list of allowed names/numbers/codes, model it as a domain list (i.e. as an Object Type with all allowed values in its Population). This Object Type has no TC, but it does have a Fact Expression Type like "There is a … .".
- If a Business Rule specifies a range of values that cannot be given one by one, like BR e above, then model it as a VC.

It is because of this advice that we have included questions like "Would you like a list of all possible <Object Type name>s …?" in the procedure to determine TCs (see Textbox 4.25). They diminish the need for VCs where a domain list suffices.

4.4.2 PROCEDURE TO FIND ALL VCS IN AN INFORMATION MODEL

The modeler should check for each Label Type whether a VC applies for it. This concerns of course only Label Types for which no domain list (pick list) has already been modeled. The modeler can use questions like:

- Is there a list of possible/allowed values for <Label Type name>s?

- Are there any limits on the possible/allowed values for <Label Type Name>s?

If a VC is found, it should be added to the model and Stated in Model Style (see examples below). Checking each Label Type also provides an opportunity to verify that a Label Type without an Object Type is modeled correctly. If a domain list would be desired after all, an Object Type must be added.

4.4.3 SUMMARY OF DETERMINING VCS FOR THE REMAINING FTS OF THE PERFORMANCE SCHEDULE

Label Type 'performer name'

The modeler has already asked the domain expert about a possible list of performer names (see Table 4.20) and wasn't surprised by the answer because he knows from experience there are very many performers. There can be no such thing as a list of all performers. Still, it is good to verify such hunches because in the context of an organization like Serviceton, he might be in for a surprise.

Label Type 'show name'

The same considerations as for 'performer name' above were given by the domain expert.

Label Type 'description'

A description is an unstructured text, so no standard list is wanted, no form requirements apply (but it should not be too long). No Object Type for 'description': OK.

Label Type 'genre name'

A domain list was already desired (see Table 4.21).

Label Type 'performance number'

The modeler and domain expert might have a dialogue as shown in Textbox 4.35. The modeler makes a note to ensure the system will automatically generate performance numbers but adds no VC to Label Type 'performance number'.

Modeler:	Is there a list of possible or allowed performance numbers? Or is there is a rule they should satisfy, like bank numbers have?

Domain expert:	No, we just number performances consecutively. By the way, we would appreciate it if the new information system could generate those numbers automatically; it's a hassle to have to invent them ourselves.

Textbox 4.35 Dialogue to determine a VC for Label Type 'performance number'

Label Type 'date'

A domain list was already desired (see Table 4.27).

Label Type 'time (hh:mm AM/PM)'

A domain list was already desired (see Table 4.28).

Label Type 'weekday name'

A domain list was not desired when TCs were determined (see Table 4.29), but there *is* a small list of allowed weekday names and the modeler knows why a domain list would be advantageous here. So he repeats the arguments given above: choosing from a drop-down list is user-friendly, saves a lot of typing, prevents typos, allows for easy changes in the future that are not foreseen yet (like changing to other weekday names like 'Mon', 'Tue', 'Wed' etc.) and satisfies the principle of 'single point of definition'. Eventually he convinces the domain expert to settle for a domain list instead. The model is changed accordingly by deleting TC 7 and adding a Fact Expression Type to Fact Type 'Weekday' (see the model in Figure 4.37).

Label Type 'ticket type name'

A domain list was already desired (see Table 4.30). However, the modeler double-checks with the domain expert because it surprised him that the domain expert had earlier accepted a domain list here but refused one for weekdays (see Tables 4.30 and 4.31). They might have the dialogue in Textbox 4.36.

Modeler:	Do you have a fixed set of possible ticket types, or could you create new ticket types in the future?
Domain expert:	At the moment, yes, we have only single tickets and season tickets. But of course I can't rule out our manager will think of other ticket types in the future. We have actually discussed offering cheaper last-minute tickets lately, but have not decided to introduce them yet.
Modeler:	OK, then a domain list is a good choice, it allows you to add last-minute tickets later easily if you want to.

Textbox 4.36 Dialogue to determine a VCs for Label Type 'ticket type name'

Label Type 'dollars.cents'

No domain list was desired (see Table 4.31), and the modeler knows from experience that a list of possible amounts of money (from $0.00 to maybe over a billion dollars) would not help users in any way, so he simply concludes not to have a VC here.

Final FCO-IM diagram

The diagram in Figure 4.37 shows the information model after determining VCs. No VCs were found, but changes were made in the modeling of Object Type 'Weekday'. The TC on Role 19 was deleted and a Fact Expression Type was added. A VC was found later in another Fact Type, however (see IGD 'Reservation Request' in Appendix A1.3.).

The Population in the diagram in Figure 4.37 satisfies all the Constraints as an example of an allowed Population. Please note, though, that in general this is not required. It is usually very difficult to make such a Population, and it isn't necessary in an information model on the conceptual level to have one. Of course, in the finally implemented information system at the physical level, the Population must indeed always satisfy all the Constraints! For this reason, the process part of the information system, which allows the users to add, edit or delete Facts, will contain many checking procedures derived from the Constraints (with error messages like "This field is required." etc.). In an FCO-IM model however, one or two Facts per Fact Type as a small example of its Population will suffice. The conceptual model specifies all the Fact Types, Object Types and Constraints, and it is from these that a model at the logical level (Relational database schema; see Appendix B, [14]) and the physical level (actual implementation) can be automatically derived (see Chapter 7). For that purpose, the Population in the information model is not needed and so does not need to satisfy all Constraints. It does serve as illustration of the concrete Facts from which the model was built in the first place and remains important for verification and validation of the model (see Chapter 5).

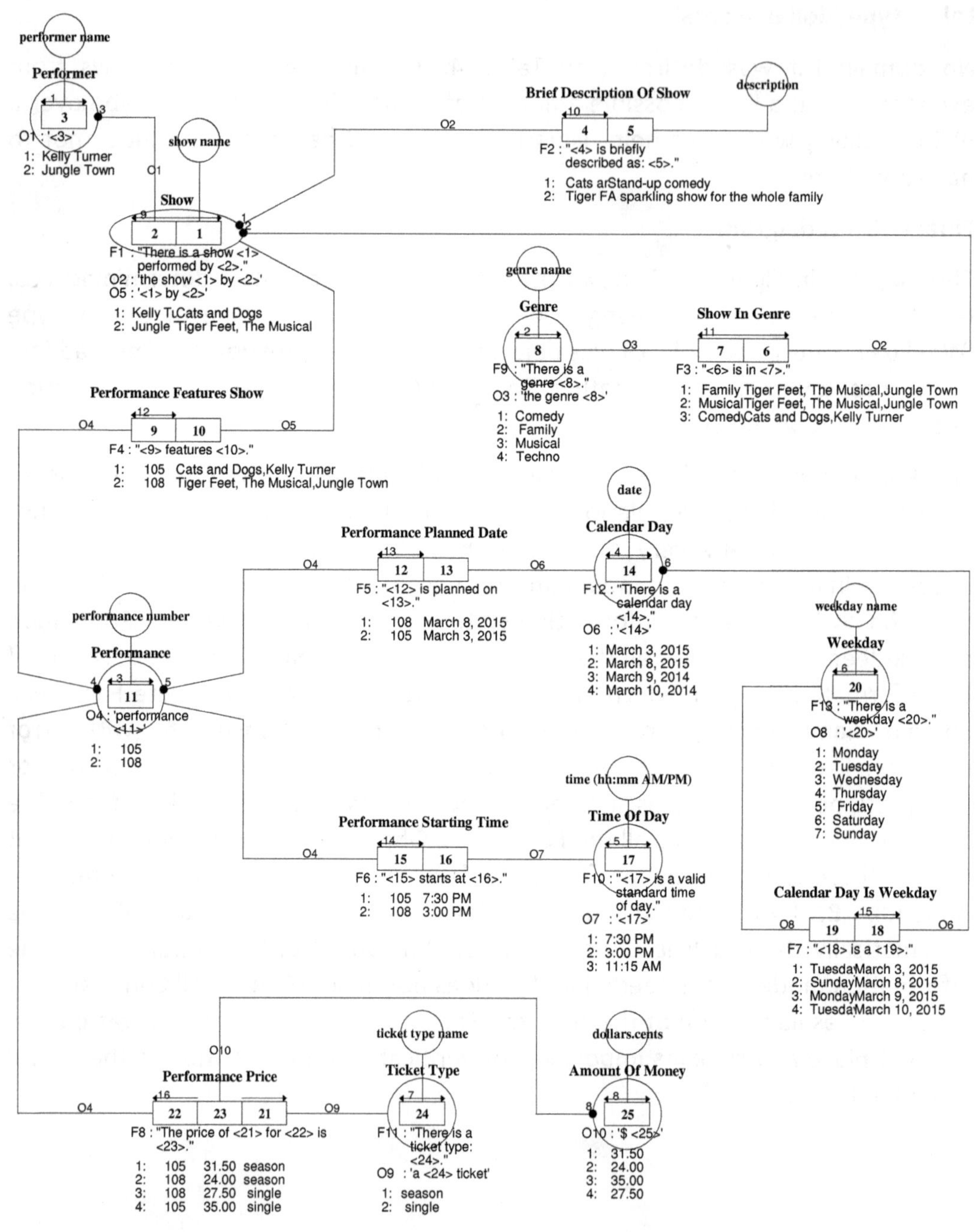
performer name
Performer
1
3
3
O1 : '<3>'
1: Kelly Turner
2: Jungle Town
O1
show name
Show
9
2
1
1
2
F1 : "There is a show <1> performed by <2>."
O2 : 'the show <1> by <2>'
O5 : '<1> by <2>'
1: Kelly TuCats and Dogs
2: Jungle Tiger Feet, The Musical
O2
Brief Description Of Show
description
10
4
5
F2 : "<4> is briefly described as: <5>."
1: Cats arStand-up comedy
2: Tiger FA sparkling show for the whole family
genre name
Genre
2
8
F9 : "There is a genre <8>."
O3 : 'the genre <8>'
1: Comedy
2: Family
3: Musical
4: Techno
O3
Show In Genre
11
7
6
O2
F3 : "<6> is in <7>."
1: Family Tiger Feet, The Musical,Jungle Town
2: MusicalTiger Feet, The Musical,Jungle Town
3: ComedyCats and Dogs,Kelly Turner
Performance Features Show
12
O4
9
10
O5
F4 : "<9> features <10>."
1: 105 Cats and Dogs,Kelly Turner
2: 108 Tiger Feet, The Musical,Jungle Town
date
Calendar Day
Performance Planned Date
13
O4
12
13
O6
4
14
6
F5 : "<12> is planned on <13>."
1: 108 March 8, 2015
2: 105 March 3, 2015
F12 : "There is a calendar day <14>."
O6 : '<14>'
1: March 3, 2015
2: March 8, 2015
3: March 9, 2014
4: March 10, 2014
performance number
Performance
3
4
5
11
O4 : 'performance <11>'
1: 105
2: 108
weekday name
Weekday
6
20
F13 : "There is a weekday <20>."
O8 : '<20>'
1: Monday
2: Tuesday
3: Wednesday
4: Thursday
5: Friday
6: Saturday
7: Sunday
time (hh:mm AM/PM)
Time Of Day
Performance Starting Time
14
O4
15
16
O7
5
17
F6 : "<15> starts at <16>."
1: 105 7:30 PM
2: 108 3:00 PM
F10 : "<17> is a valid standard time of day."
O7 : '<17>'
1: 7:30 PM
2: 3:00 PM
3: 11:15 AM
Calendar Day Is Weekday
15
O8
19
18
O6
F7 : "<18> is a <19>."
1: TuesdaMarch 3, 2015
2: SundayMarch 8, 2015
3: MondayMarch 9, 2015
4: TuesdaMarch 10, 2015
O10
ticket type name
Ticket Type
dollars.cents
Amount Of Money
Performance Price
16
O4
22
23
21
O9
7
24
8
8
25
F8 : "The price of <21> for <22> is <23>."
1: 105 31.50 season
2: 108 24.00 season
3: 108 27.50 single
4: 105 35.00 single
F11 : "There is a ticket type: <24>."
O9 : 'a <24> ticket'
1: season
2: single
O10 : '$ <25>'
1: 31.50
2: 24.00
3: 35.00
4: 27.50

Figure 4.37 FCO-IM diagram for the performance schedule; after VC-determination

4.5 Other Constraints

Key Points

- **There are many other kinds of Constraints.**
- **There is no standard procedure to find all Constraints.**
- **Examples of Business Rules (in Domain Style) and Constraints (in Model Style) are given, together with an example of a Population that *violates* them.**

In previous sections, the most important kinds of Constraints were discussed: Uniqueness Constraints, Totality Constraints and Value Constraints. For each, written Statements were given as well: as Business Rules in Domain Style and as Constraints in Model Style (see Section 4.1.1). Since this is a book that tells you not only *what* information modeling is, but also *how* you should do it, more or less complete procedures have been given: a complete procedure for Uniqueness Constraints in Section 4.2.2, a partial but detailed procedure for Totality Constraints in Section 4.3.2, and a short procedure for Value Constraints in Section 4.4.2. But there are many other kinds of Constraints, and each information modeling technique has its own zoo of standard kinds of Constraints. Object Role Modeling (ORM), with its modeling tool Norma (see Appendix B, [10]), offers an especially wide range of Constraints, each verbalized automatically in Model Style. However, there is no good procedure to determine any of those other types of Constraints that we know of. They usually follow from Business Rules or from questions asked by an experienced modeler during interviews with domain experts.

This closing section offers an anthology of several other kinds of Constraints that often occur, without attempting to find them in a systematic way. For each, a Business Rule is Stated in Domain Style and the corresponding Constraint in Model Style. In addition, an example of combinations of Facts that *violate* the Constraint is given to show what should *not* be allowed. Such violations are a good way to make clear what the Business Rules mean, how they are modeled and what the information system should prevent from happening in the Population. All examples are taken from the Serviceton Music Theater case study, which is described in Chapter 2. The complete information model for this context is given in Appendix A.

4.5.1 TOTALITY CONSTRAINT ON TWO OUT OF MANY ROLES

BR 24: To be able to contact a customer, an email address and/or a phone number must be known for each customer.

TC 12: A customer must have at least one email address and/or be phoned at a telephone.

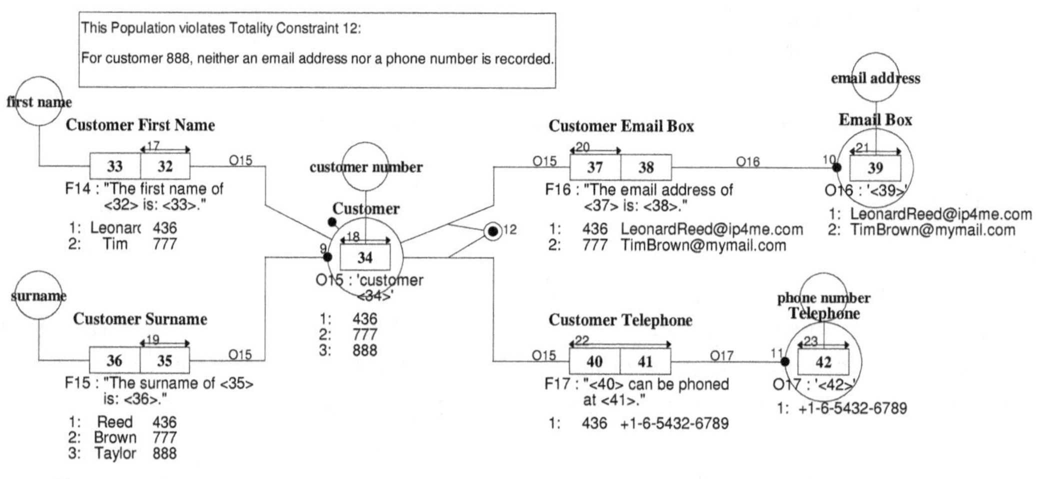

Figure 4.38 Population violating TC 12

4.5.2 SUBSET CONSTRAINT BETWEEN TWO ROLES

BR 26: For a customer address, address line 2 is optional and should only be entered if address line 1 is also used.

SC 1: The customers in the Population of 'Customer Address Line 2'(Role 45) must be a part of the customers in the Population of 'Customer Address Line 1'(Role 43).

If the Population of a certain Role (here, Role 45) must be a part of the Population of another Role (here, Role 43), then there is a Subset Constraint from 45 to 43. Notation: 45 -->-- 43.

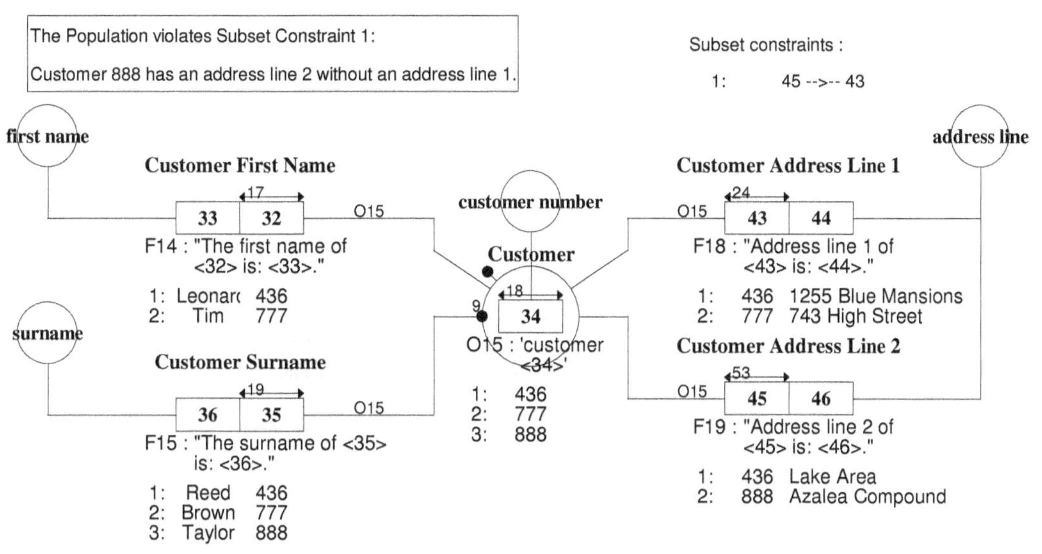

Figure 4.39 Population violating SC 1

Please note that many Subset Constraints follow from Roles with a Totality Constraint and Roles without one. In Figure 4.39 there is also a Subset Constraint 32 -->-- 35, because Role 35 has a TC, and Role 32 doesn't (the dot attached to the Object Type near the connecting line to Role 32 doesn't belong to this Role; it means Object Type 'Customer' plays other Roles that are not shown in this diagram, which do have a TC somewhere (see IGD Customer in Appendix A1.2)). A first name is not recorded for *all* customers, whereas a surname is, so the population of Role 32 is a part of that of Role 35. But this is already implied by Role 35 having a Totality Constraint, and Role 32 not having one. Therefore only Subset Constraints that do *not* follow from TCs have to be specified. This is the case with SC 1, since neither Role 43 nor Role 45 has a TC. Further reading on Subset Constraints: see Appendix B, [1, Section 3.5].

4.5.3 EQUALITY CONSTRAINT BETWEEN TWO OR MORE ROLES

BR 25: Reservation requests (whether on paper or on the website) must always contain the complete address of a customer: address line(s), town, state, ZIP code and country.

This Business Rule concerns three Fact Types: ´Customer Address Line 1´, ´Customer Town´ and ´Customer ZIP code´. These must all be filled in for each customer. That means the populations of roles 43, 45 and 54 must contain exactly the same customers. This leads to two Equality Constraints:

EC 1: The customers in the Population of 'Customer Address Line 1'(Role 43) must be the same as the customers in the Population of 'Customer Town'(Role 47).

EC 2: The customers in the Population of 'Customer Town'(Role 47) must be the same as the customers in the Population of 'Customer ZIP Code'(Role 54).

If the Population of a certain Role (e.g. Role 43) must be equal to the Population of another Role (e.g. Role 47), then there is an Equality Constraint between 43 and 47. Notation: 43 --<>-- 47. As the notation already tries to show, an Equality Constraint 43 --<>--47 is an abbreviation for two Subset Constraints 43 -->--47 and 43 --<-- 47. So EC 1 and EC 2 can be modeled as four Subset Constraints, as CaseTalk (see Appendix B, [2]) does. See Figure 4.40, which shows a violation of EC 2.

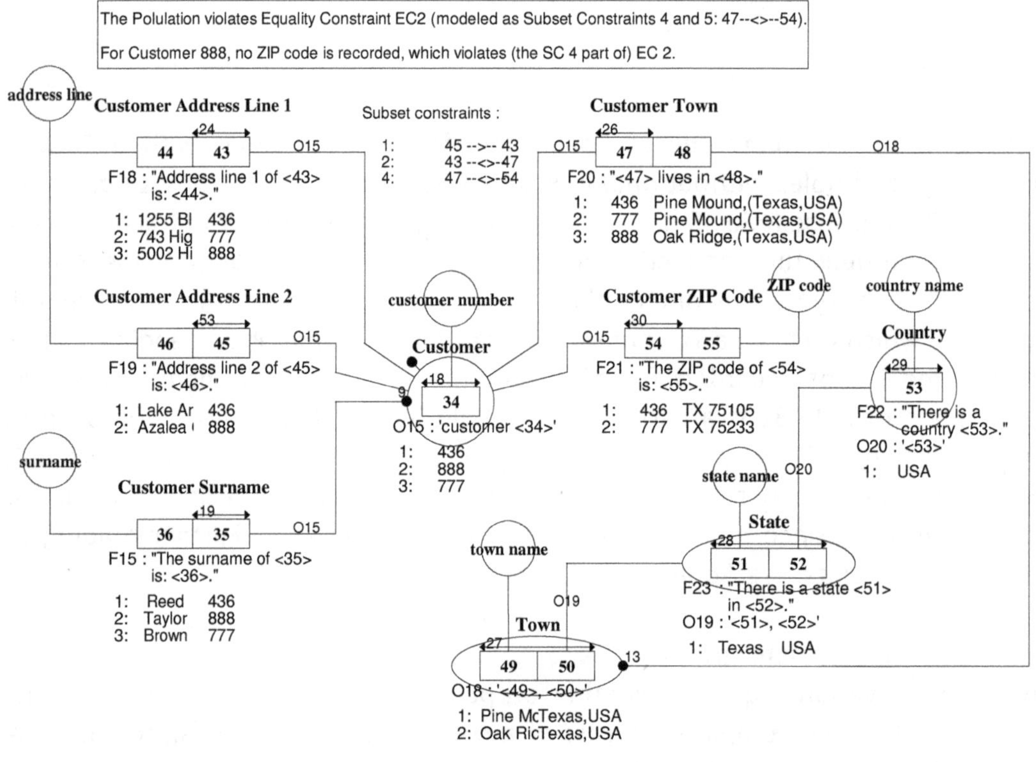

Figure 4.40 Population violating (SC 4 part of) EC 2

It follows from 43 --<>--47 and 47 --<>--54 that also 54 --<>--43 must always be true, so it is not necessary to specify that last Equality Constraint separately. For further reading on Equality Constraints, see Appendix B, [1, Section 3.5].

4.5.4 CARDINALITY CONSTRAINT WITH VALUE REQUIREMENT

BR 07: Each performance has a single ticket price and a season ticket price.

This Business Rule leads to a complicated Cardinality Constraint. A Cardinality Constraint specifies *how many times* the same value should occur in the Population of a Role. All performances must have both a single and a season ticket price, but may have prices for other kinds of tickets in the future as well (see Section 4.4.3, Label Type 'ticket type name'). So every performance should occur in the Population of Role 22 *at least two times*. If only season and single tickets would be allowed, there would be a "pure" Cardinality Constraint on Role 22: '=2', meaning every value occurring in Role 22 must be there exactly two times. Since other kinds of tickets might be allowed as well, this would have to be modified. But changing '=2' into '>=2' for 'at least two' is not enough; it is also necessary to specify that both 'season' and 'single' must occur as ticket types in each performance. Hence the following Constraint C 1:

C 1: FOR ANY x IN 'Performance Price'(22):
ALL VALUES y IN {'season', 'single'}
MUST EXIST IN (x, y) IN 'Performance Price'(22, 21)

An example of a Population that violates C 1 is shown in Figure 4.41.

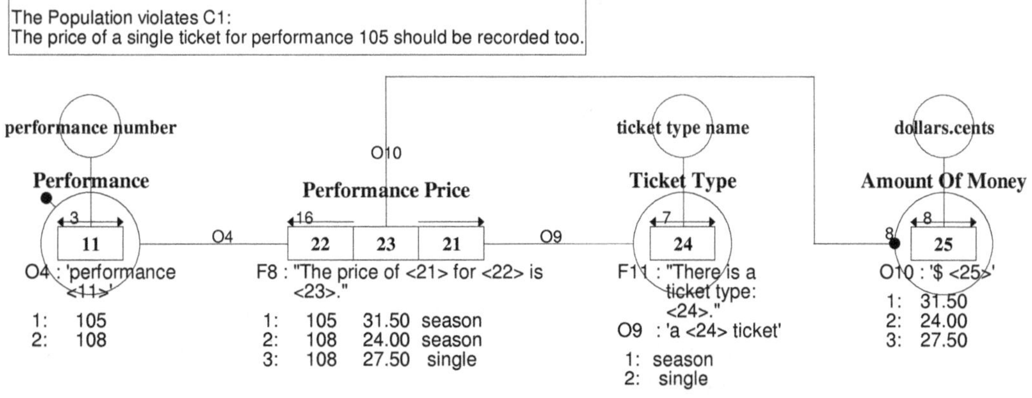

Figure 4.41 Population violating C 1

For further reading on Cardinality Constraints, see Appendix B, [1, Section 3.7].

4.5.5 UNIQUENESS CONSTRAINT BETWEEN TWO FACT TYPES

BR 30: Tickets for the same performance must all be for different seats (no two tickets for the same seat in the same performance).

This Business Rule concerns Fact Types 'Ticket For Performance' and 'Ticket For Seat'. Figure 4.42 shows an example of violating this Rule: There are two tickets for performance 104 and seat 25 in row 13. Please note that this wrong Population does satisfy all other Constraints in the model. BR 30 can be modeled by a new kind of Uniqueness Constraint UC 55 as explained below:

UC 55: Inter Fact Type Uniqueness Constraint on Roles 84+86.

Such a UC is not shown as a double-pointed arrow in CaseTalk (see Appendix B, [2]), but as a 'U' in a small medallion with lines connecting the medallion to the relevant Roles (see Figure 4.42).

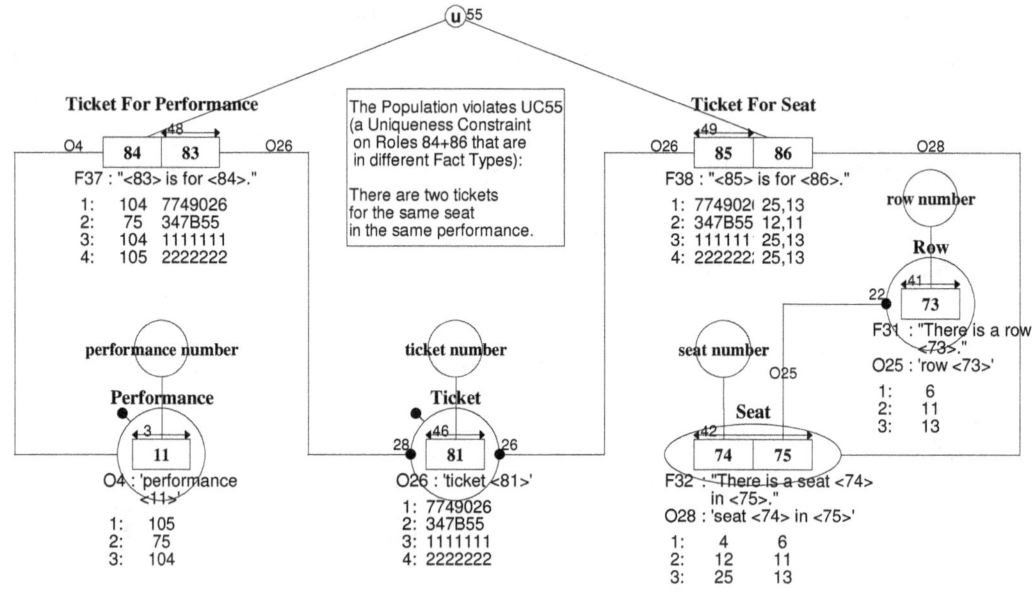

Figure 4.42 Population violating UC 55

An Inter Fact Type Uniqueness Constraint is like an ordinary UC but acts on Roles in different Fact Types. Its meaning becomes clear if those Fact Types are *joined*: combined into one compound Fact Type. This join yields a non-elementary Fact Type, which violates the N Rule (see Section 5.3.1), and for that reason is not suitable to use in an elementary information model. It is only used to illustrate the meaning of UC 55 as shown in Figure 4.43, in which UC 55 is now visible as an 'ordinary' UC. Please compare Figures 4.43 and 4.44 carefully (Roles 84 and 86 in Figure 4.42 correspond with Roles 92 and 93 in Figure 4.43) to be able to interpret the Inter Fact Type UC in Figure 4.42 more easily.

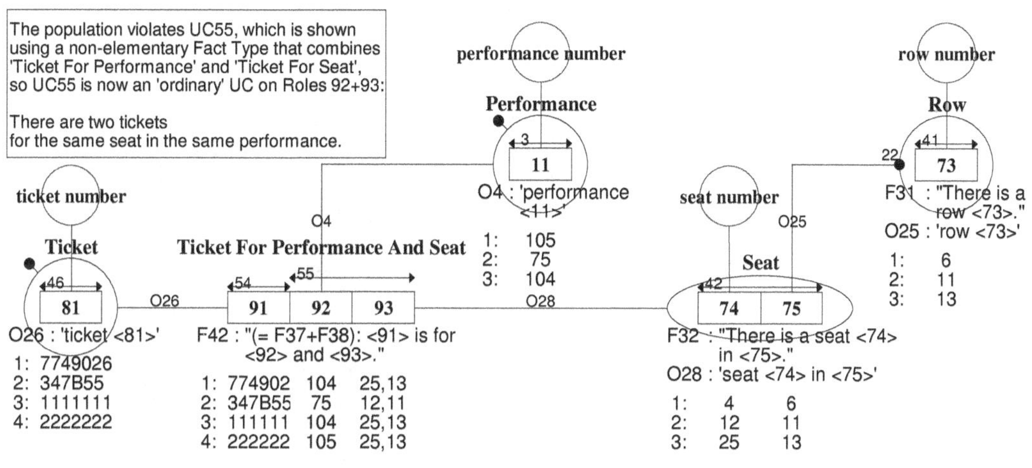

Figure 4.43 Population violating UC 55, shown by a non-elementary Fact Type

For further reading on Inter Fact Type UCs, see Appendix B, [1, Section 3.2.3].

4.5.6 CIRCULAR CONSTRAINT

BR 31: Any ticket for an approved reservation request part must be for the same performance that is stated in the reservation request part.

In IGD 'Tickets' (see Section A1.4), a number of Fact Types form a closed loop; see Figure 4.44 below that highlights this loop. Such loops often have a *circular constraint* that ensures the Population in the loop closes in a correct way. This loop indeed needs one: Starting at Object Type Ticket, you can see that a ticket is for a performance (FT 'Ticket For Performance') but also that a ticket can be for an approved reservation request part (follow the FTs from OT 'Ticket for reservation' to OT 'Reservation Request Part') that is also for a performance (FT 'Reservation Request Part For Performance'). For the same ticket, these performances must be the same. This is not automatically the case, as Figure 4.44 shows. Its Population satisfies all Constraints (except C 2, see below) but still violates BR 31, so a new Constraint is needed to prevent that. A way to express such a circular constraint in Model Style (see Section 4.1.1) is:

C 2: For all values P1, P2, Q and R with the properties

1) Ticket Q is for performance P1

2) Ticket Q is for the approved reservation request part R that concerns performance P2

the following must hold as well: performances P1 and P2 are the same.

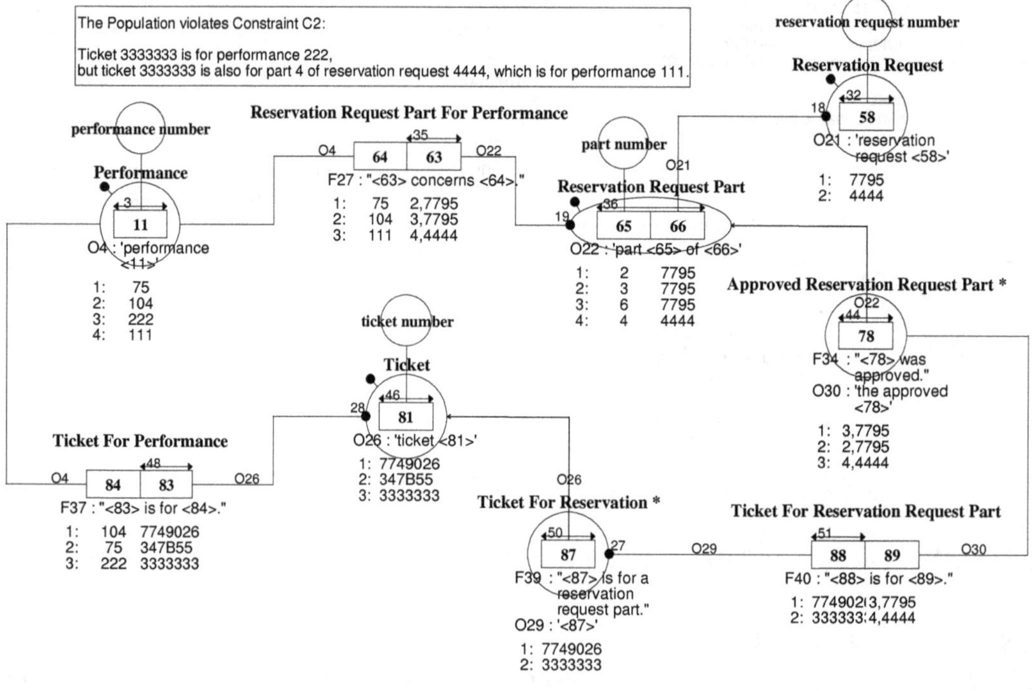

Figure 4.44 Population violating C 2

For further reading on Circular Constraints: the modeling technique Object Role Modeling (ORM) and its tool Norma (see Appendix B, [10]) offer a good way to specify circular constraints.

4.5.7 DYNAMIC CONSTRAINT

BR 28: The status of a reservation request always starts as 'registered' and can only change in the following ways:

a 'registered' → 'rejected'
(if the reservation request part cannot be satisfied).

b 'registered'→ 'approved'
(if the reservation request part has been satisfied).

c 'approved → 'assigned'
(when the seats have been assigned).

d 'assigned' → 'completed'
(when the tickets have been printed and sent to the customer).

This is an example of a dynamic rule. It doesn't specify what the population should be at one moment in time, like all other Business Rules and Constraints discussed so far, but how the Population can *change* from one moment to the next. A formulation in Model Style could be:

C 3: FOR ANY UPDATE in Fact Type 'Status Of Reservation Request Part':
IF x IS NOT IN 'Status Of Reservation Request Part'(70)
THEN (x, 'registered') can be added
ELSE IF a Fact (x, 'registered') IS IN (70, 71)
THEN it can change to (x, 'rejected');
IF a Fact (x, 'registered') IS IN (70, 71)
THEN it can change to (x, 'approved');
IF a Fact (x, 'approved') IS IN (70, 71)
THEN it can change to (x, 'assigned');
IF a Fact (x, 'assigned') IS IN (70, 71)
THEN it can change to (x, 'completed').

No example of a violation of this Constraint is given in the form of an IGD with a Population; it couldn't actually show a wrong update happening. Database programmers should implement C 3 somehow so every attempted update on Fact Type 'Status Of Reservation Request Part' is checked.

4.5.8 DEONTIC TOTALITY CONSTRAINT ON A ROLE

BR 14: For each approved reservation request part, seats are assigned to customers.

BR 15: For each approved reservation request part, tickets for these seats (see BR 14) are printed.

These two Business Rules both specify that something is to be done for *all* approved reservation request parts, but there might be a time delay between approving a reservation request part and assigning seats and also between assigning seats and printing tickets. This means that *eventually* every approved reservation request part must have tickets for it but not *immediately*. Figure 4.45 shows the relevant part from IGD 'Tickets' (see Section A1.4).

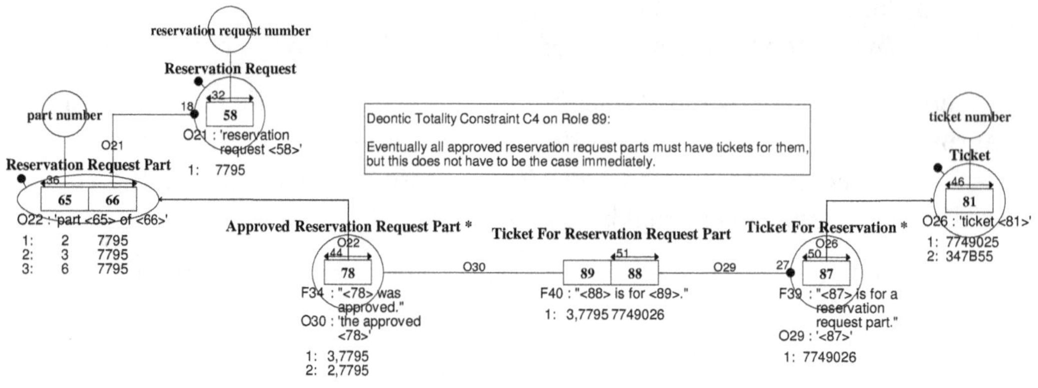

Figure 4.45 Role 89 has a Deontic Totality Constraint

Role 89 cannot have an ordinary Totality Constraint (TC) because that means all approved reservation request parts must have tickets immediately. So a sort of 'soft' version of a TC is needed that allows the constraint to be broken for a short while. Such soft versions of Constraints are known as *Deontic Constraints*: Constraints that apply in principle but allow some slack (exceptions, delays etc.). The 'strict' Constraints that do not allow any deviation are known as *Alethic Constraints*. All other Constraints in this book are Alethic.

Business Rules BR 14 and BR 15 can be modeled by placing a Deontic Totality Constraint C 4 on Role 89. A working database will have to do something with this Deontic Constraint (give a reminder after 24 hours or a week, or do something else?), but this is not explored further here. No example of a violation of C 4 can therefore be given yet.

C 4: Eventually an approved reservation request part must have at least one ticket for it.

FCO-IM and CaseTalk (see Appendix B, [2]) have no standard symbol for Deontic Constraints yet. Object Role Modeling (ORM, see Appendix B, [10]) and its software tool Norma, however, offer many Deontic Constraints.

Chapter 5
How to Check your Model and get it Approved

Key Points

- **An information model should be verified (is the model correct?) and validated (does the domain expert approve?).**
- **Verbalizations are crucial for validation.**
- **The modeler should regularly perform several tests to verify the model:**
    - **Does the model satisfy FCO-IM form rules?**
    - **Are all Fact Types indeed elementary?**
    - **Is there any hidden redundancy in the model?**

How can a modeler make sure his model is correct (*verify* it) and obtain the approval of the domain experts (*validate* it)?

The most important way in which the domain expert can verify the model, and in which the domain expert can validate it, is using the verbalizations from which the model was built in the first place (see Section 5.1 below).

Apart from this evaluation by the domain expert (*external* review), there are also a few checks the modeler should apply to the model himself (*internal* review). These are discussed in the other sections of this chapter: well-formedness rules (Section 5.2), tests for elementariness (Section 5.3) and a test for hidden redundancy (Section 5.4).

5.1 Verbalizations are Crucial to Verify and Validate the Model

Information models are meant for ICT experts but not for the management that decided to spend a lot of money on building an information system, nor for the employees who will use it in their everyday work nor for other stakeholders in the organization. All of these people are experts in their own field but usually cannot read arcane abstract models of information structures. On the other hand, these information models were built by ICT experts, who usually don't know much about the organization or the ins and outs of all sorts of specialized daily tasks that the information system should support. So how can the modeler be sure his model does indeed capture the information correctly, and how can the domain expert evaluate the quality of the information model? This is difficult, even if several other common problems in the communication between the modeler and the domain expert are left aside like users who are notoriously bad at making clear what they actually want or modelers who in their ivory tower think they have just found a much smarter way to do things than the organization employs.

It is here that the *Verbalizations* of the concrete examples of the Facts can be used with good effect once again. Since natural language is the only effective way of communication we all share, modelers and domain experts can use it as common ground for mutual understanding. Show any domain expert a set of examples (in table form, in a graph like a pie chart or in any other visual form familiar to the domain expert) *together with the Verbalizations* and ask him whether these Verbalizations correctly express the meaning of the Facts (see, for example, Figure 3.3 for the concrete examples and Table 3.4 for the Verbalizations). If they don't, adjust them until they do (and adapt the information model accordingly). If two domain experts disagree, the modeler will require them to come to a joint decision before he can continue. If all Verbalizations have been approved, then this is an important demonstration of the correctness of the model.

A good FCO-IM modeling tool like CaseTalk (see Appendix B, [2]) allows the modeler to regenerate the Verbalizations from any part of the model (in the way shown in Section 3.5) and print them for the domain experts for verification and validation.

5.2 FORM RULES FOR AN FCO-IM DIAGRAM

There are several form rules an FCO-IM diagram should satisfy. If a diagram does not comply with these rules, it is not well-formed and should be corrected. Here, only the most important ones that a modeler should keep an open eye for are mentioned. For a further discussion, see Appendix B, [1, Section 2.5.2].

5.2.1 NAMING CONVENTIONS

The naming conventions below are used in this book and in the modeling tool CaseTalk (see Appendix B, [2]) that implements almost everything discussed in this book (and also does a lot more). Other choices could have been made, but we have settled on these.

- **Names for Fact Types (Object Types) and Label Types.** In FCO-IM, every Fact Type (it doesn't matter whether it is inside an Object Type or not) and Label Type must have a unique name. A Label Type cannot have the same name as a Fact Type, either. An Object Type always has the same name as the Fact Type that's inside it.

    Incidentally, this last point is unique in FCO-IM and emphasizes that it is actually *not* the real world that is being modeled but only the *communication about* the real world. For further discussion, see Appendix B, [1, Section 1.3].

  This rule forces both modeler and domain expert to be creative in finding clear and meaningful names. Avoid codebook-like or unclear names like 'FactType35' or 'Thingy3'. Don't be afraid of rather long names as long as they make clear what kind of Fact Type (or Object Type) or Label Type it is. Brevity is not a virtue here; better 'Approved Reservation Request Part' than 'AppResReqPar' or even worse, 'ARRP'. All names should be clear at first glance; see all the examples in this book. No modeling tool can help you here. It is up to you to find good names.

- **Role numbers.** In FCO-IM, every Role has a unique role number. A good modeling tool like CaseTalk (see Appendix B, [2]) can generate these automatically.

- **Fact Expression Type and Object Expression Type numbers.** In FCO-IM, every Fact Expression Type has a unique number that starts with 'F', and every Object Type Expression has a unique number that starts with 'O'. A good modeling tool like CaseTalk (see Appendix B, [2]) can generate these automatically.

5.2.2 REQUIREMENTS FOR FACT EXPRESSION TYPES AND OBJECT EXPRESSION TYPES

The modeler should check the rules below himself, especially the last two cases. A good modeling tool like CaseTalk (see Appendix B, [2]) can check these rules on demand and so help the modeler verify his model.

- **Object Type.** Every Object Type must have at least one Object Expression Type, and can have several. For every Role played by an Object Type, the number of the Object Expression Type that applies for this Role is written next to the line connecting the Role to the Object Type. Incidentally, FCO-IM allows several Object Expression Types for one Role (all from the same Object Type). See Appendix B, [1, Sections 2.10 and 6.2] for cases where this is convenient or even mandatory.
- **Fact Type outside an Object Type.** Every Fact Type that is not inside an Object Type must have a Fact Expression Type. Incidentally, more than one Fact Expression Type per Fact Type is allowed, but in an elementary information model there is usually only one Fact Expression Type for each such Fact Type. When a model in another modeling technique is derived (see Chapter 7), like a Relational database schema (see Appendix B, [14]) or an ERM model (see Appendix B, [12]), then several Fact Expression Types per Fact Type are quite common. This is because such models are not elementary (see also Chapter 7).
- **Fact Type inside an Object Type.** Here, there are two cases, depending on whether or not there is at least one Totality Constraint (see Section 4.3) on any of the Roles played by the Object Type. Of course, you can't check this before you have actually determined all the Totality Constraints for this Object Type (see Section 4.3.2).
    - **Case 1**: There is no Totality Constraint on any of the Roles played by the Object Type. Then the Fact Type inside the Object Type *must* have a Fact Expression Type (it is explained in the discussion of Textbox 4.19 why this must be so). More than one is also allowed but quite rare in an elementary information model.
    - **Case 2:** There is at least one Totality Constraint on at least one Role played by the Object Type. Then it is not required that the Fact Type

inside the Object Type should have a Fact Expression Type, though it is always allowed.

See several examples of both cases in Figure 4.37: 'Genre', 'Weekday', 'Time Of Day' and 'Ticket Type' have no Totality Constraint (TC) and so must have a Fact Expression Type. All other Object Types do have at least one TC and so are free to have a Fact Expression Type or not (both possibilities occur several times).

5.3 IS THE MODEL REALLY ELEMENTARY?

A basic purpose of an FCO-IM information model is that every Fact Type represents an *indivisible* chunk of information; leave out any one part and you lose information (see Figure 3.12 for an example of information loss by incompleteness of Facts). Other Fact Oriented Modeling techniques like Object Role Modeling (ORM) (see Appendix B, [10]) and, to a lesser extent, CogNIAM (see Appendix B, [11]) also model *elementary* (i.e. non-divisible) Fact Types. Other information modeling techniques like Entity Relationship Modeling (ERM) (see Appendix B, [12]), Unified Modeling Language (UML) (see Appendix B, [13]) and the Relational model (for relational databases, see Appendix B, [14]) have drawbacks in working with either *half Fact Types* (an attribute or table column is only half a Fact Type at best) and with *prematurely clustered Fact Types* (an entity type or a table with attributes is usually a collection of several Fact Types). We advocate the viewpoint that a *conceptual information model* should contain only elementary Fact Types, because:

- There are thousands of ways to cluster Fact Types, but there is only one unclustered version.
- With the basic indivisible building blocks known, any compound structure can be easily built (take a user interface screen, for instance: every elementary Fact Type is either completely on it or not at all. You don't have to consider only parts of entity types etc.).
- Thinking in terms of *complete elementary Facts* makes the communication between modelers and domain experts a lot easier because verbalizations of these elementary Facts that everyone understands can be used instead of arcane diagrams.

- Non-elementary modeling is often a cause of redundancy in the model (see the examples in Figure 5.3 and the explanation given there).

Therefore, the model should be tested to make sure there are no non-elementary Fact Types. There are two very easy tests for this, known as the N Rule and the N-1 Rule. A third test (the Projection-Join Test) is rarely needed and difficult to perform, and therefore outside the scope of this book, but see Appendix B, [1, Section 3.3.1.3 and references therein] for a further discussion. However, if a model passes all these tests, it is certainly elementary.

5.3.1 N RULE

The N Rule concerns only Fact Types inside Object Types.

> **N Rule**
>
> Consider a Fact Type with N Roles (N=1, 2, 3, ...) inside an Object Type.
>
> Such a Fact Type can have only one Uniqueness Constraint, namely on all its N Roles.

Textbox 5.1 N Rule

So Object Types can only contain Fact Types with a Uniqueness Constraint (UC) on all their Roles. It is for this reason that a modeler should always determine the UCs on such Fact Types carefully, too, and cannot assign one automatically (see Section 4.2.4, the first sentence in the part that determines UCs for Fact Type 'Show'). Otherwise a possible modeling error would be overlooked.

See Figure 5.2 for examples of Fact Types that satisfy the N Rule and therefore are OK. Figure 5.3 shows examples of Fact Types that do not satisfy the N Rule and therefore must be remodeled.

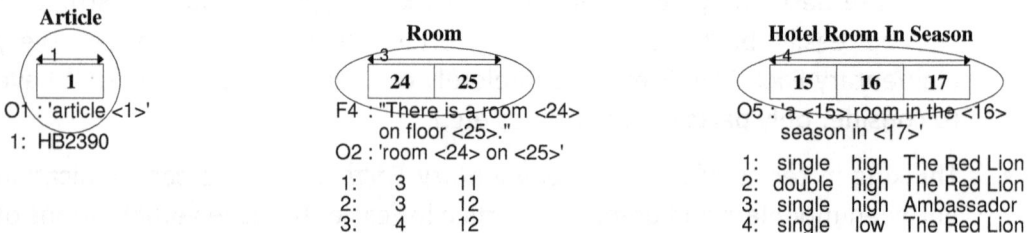

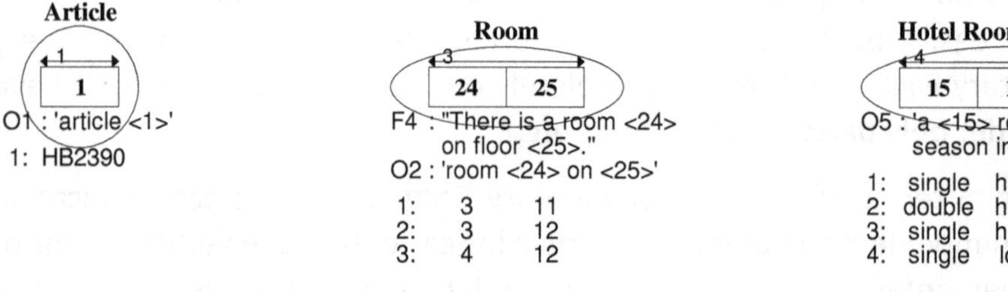

Figure 5.2 Fact Types that satisfy the N Rule

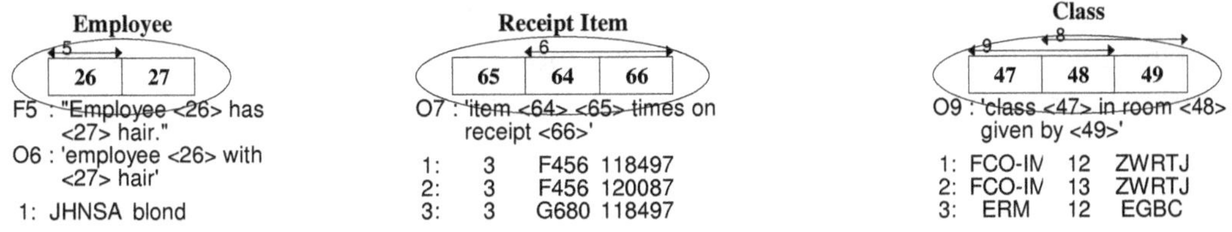

Figure 5.3 Fact Types that violate the N Rule and should be remodeled

To explain why modeling as in Figure 5.3 causes non-elementary Fact Types, consider Object Type Employee in Figure 5.3. In every Fact Type played by this Object Type (not shown in Figure 5.3), Object Expression Type O6 will be used like in the following two concrete Fact Expressions:

FE 1: "*Employee JHNSA with blond hair* was born in 1980."

FE 2: "*Employee JHNSA with blond hair* wears shoes of size 9."

Both these Fact Expressions can be split into other ones, each with fewer components, without loss of information, so they are not elementary (see also Section 3.3.3.2), namely:

FE 1a: "*Employee JHNSA has blond hair.*"

FE 1b: "Employee JHNSA was born in 1980."

FE 2a: "*Employee JHNSA has blond hair.*"

FE 2b: "Employee JHNSA wears shoes of size 9."

Please note as well that FE 1a and FE 2a are identical, so this same elementary Fact is actually present several times in the information model. This is an example of *redundancy*: modeling the same elementary Fact more than once (see Section 4.2.1, the third conclusion drawn from Textbox 4.4). The conclusions are therefore:

- FE 1 and FE 2 are not elementary (splitting without losing information is possible).
- There is redundancy in the modeling (one composing Fact is modeled twice: FE 1a and FE 2a).

These errors of non-elementariness and redundant modeling indeed occur together very often. Both should be avoided; therefore, all the examples in Figure 5.3 should be remodeled. They all require better verbalizations.

A good modeling tool like CaseTalk (see Appendix B, [2]) can check the N Rule on demand and so help the modeler verify his model (although a short glance at the diagram is enough to determine whether all Object Types satisfy the N Rule).

5.3.2 N-1 RULE

The N-1 Rule concerns only Fact Types outside Object Types. It can detect one important type of non-elementariness in such Fact Types, but not all. For the other cases (see the 'ELSE'-component in Textbox 5.4), there is another test (the Projection-Join test), but that is difficult to perform, and seldom needed in practice. It is therefore outside the scope of this book (see Appendix B, [1, Section 3.3.1.3 and references therein] for a further discussion).

N-1 Rule

Consider a Fact Type with N Roles (N=1, 2, 3, ...), *not* inside an Object Type.

IF	such a Fact Type has a Uniqueness Constraint on *less than N-1 Roles,*
THEN	it is not elementary and must be split into Fact Types with fewer components
ELSE	the N-1 Rule doesn't show whether it is elementary or not.

Textbox 5.4 N-1 Rule

See Figure 5.5 for examples of Fact Types that violate the N-1 Rule (all Uniqueness Constraints have been determined correctly) and therefore should be split into Fact Types with fewer components.

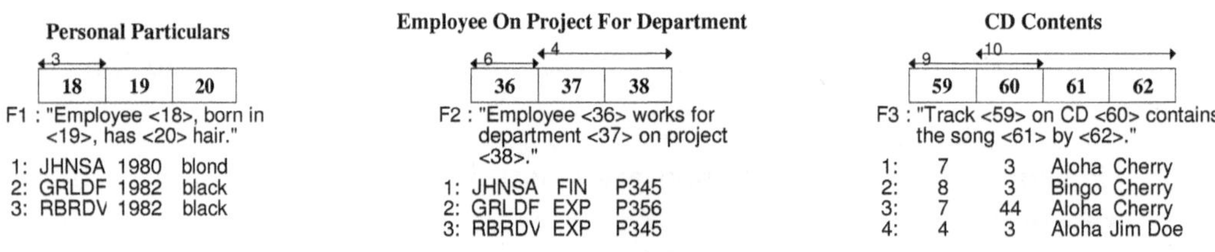

Figure 5.5 Fact Types that violate the N-1 Rule and should be remodeled

In Figure 5.5, all Fact Types are non-elementary (assuming the Uniqueness Constraints are correct). They should therefore all be split into Fact Types with fewer components. This means that the modeler and domain expert must re-verbalize the example Facts. Sometimes the modeler can guess what the new verbalizations will be, but even then he should verify this guess explicitly with a domain expert. In Figure 5.5, the second and third examples certainly need further investigation before a new and better verbalization can be given (Why is the combination of department and project unique? How is a song identified? etc.). For the first example, the situation is clearer, and improving the verbalization is easy:

Old: `FE 1:` "`Employee JHNSA, born in 1980, has blond hair.`"

New: `FE 1a:` "`Employee JHNSA was born in 1980.`"
`FE 1b:` "`Employee JHNSA has blond hair.`"

Note that the old expression FE 1 has three components (employee, birth year and hair color), whereas the new expressions FE 1a and FE 1b have only two components each. This is true in general: if the N-1 Rule shows that a Fact Type with N Roles is not elementary, then it must be split into at least two new Fact Types, each with at most N-1 Roles.

In Section 4.2.3, (the second example, Table 4.10) the modeler found a Uniqueness Constraint on just one Role in a Fact Type with three Roles: UC 16 on Role 61 of Fact Type 'Employee Office'. This Fact Type must therefore be split. The result is:

Old: `FE 2:` "`Employee 237 works for department ExPro in office room C55.`"

New: `FE 2a:` "`Employee 237 works for department ExPro.`"
`FE 2b:` "`Employee 237 works in office room C55.`"

This yields two new Fact types, each with two Roles.

Figure 5.6 shows examples of Fact Types that do not violate the N-1 Rule. For such Fact Types, we advise to double-check the verbalizations by asking yourself and the domain expert: "Can the same examples be verbalized using expressions with less components without loss of information?" and to leave it at that. If this is not enough to remedy any doubts, the Projection-Join test (see Appendix B, [1, Section 3.3.1.3]) can be invoked, but we have had to apply it in practice only rarely. (Said aside: this test finds cases that are in 3rd Normal Form or 4th Normal Form but not in 5th Normal Form (see any textbook on Normal Forms), but using verbalizations of concrete examples of elementary Facts seems to greatly reduce the possibility of making such errors.)

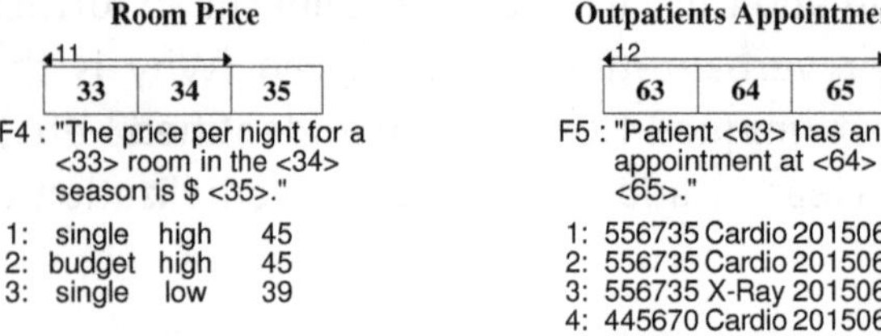

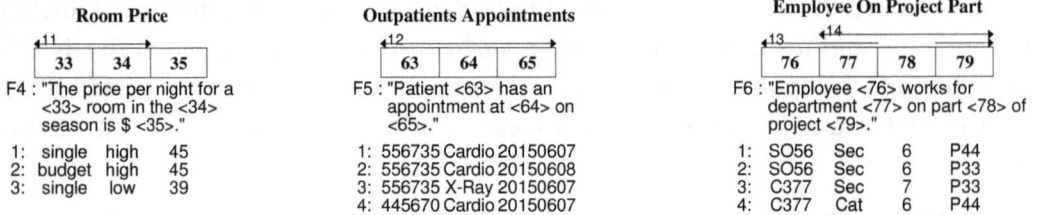

Figure 5.6 Fact Types that do not violate the N-1 Rule

A good modeling tool like CaseTalk (see Appendix B, [2]) can check the N-1 Rule on demand and so help the modeler verify his model (although a short glance at the diagram is enough to determine whether any Fact Type violates the N-1 Rule).

5.3.3 WHEN TO PERFORM THE N RULE AND N-1 RULE TESTS

Both the N Rule and the N-1 Rule use Uniqueness Constraints (UCs), so the model can only be tested using these Rules after the UCs have been determined. Indeed, in the FCO-IM procedure to draw up a conceptual Information Model (see Section 3.1), UCs are determined in step 5 and these tests are carried out immediately after in step 6, even before Totality Constraints (TCs) are determined (in step 7) or anything else is done. In this book, we have discussed some of these later steps previously in Sections 4.3 (TCs) and 4.4 (Value Constraints) and so have deviated from the order in the procedure for didactical reasons.

It is best to do these tests immediately after the UCs have been determined. The reason is: it might be necessary to correct a few modeling errors, which would change some Fact Types and possibly some Object Types as well, so any work on TCs would have to be redone for those changes.

5.4 WAS ANY OBJECT TYPE OVERLOOKED?

Another possible source of redundancy in the model is if an Object Type should have been modeled but was accidentally overlooked. This possible error should always be tested for; indeed, we have not yet encountered a modeling case in practice where the model has passed the Overlooked Object Type Test for this more 'hidden' form of redundancy in one go. An experienced modeler can spot it easily in any given FCO-IM information model although it is harder to see than violations of the N Rule and the N-1 Rule. Fortunately, a good modeling tool like

CaseTalk (see Appendix B, [2]) can check this on demand as well and so help the modeler verify his model.

5.4.1 EXAMPLE OF OVERLOOKED OBJECT TYPE IN SERVICETON THEATER

To make the problem clear, let's look at a few verbalizations from the Reservation Request part of the Serviceton Theater model. As explained in more detail in Section 2.1, a customer can send in a reservation request for several performances, each of which is termed a 'reservation request part'. For each performance in the reservation request (i.e. each reservation request part), the customer states the number of desired seats. The normal procedure then is as follows. When Serviceton receives the request, it registers every reservation request part. At a later stage, the reservation manager tries to satisfy as many reservation requests as possible. If this succeeds for a particular reservation request part, its status is changed from 'registered' to 'approved'. In a still later stage, the exact seats are assigned to the reservation request, and the status changes again from 'approved' to 'assigned'. These later steps can be performed independently for each reservation request part.

Verbalizations of example Facts (see Section 2.1 for concrete examples) are given in Textbox 5.7. Now suppose that the modeler and domain expert Sort and Analyze these Fact Expressions (see Sections 3.4 and 3.6) and come up with the result also shown in Textbox 5.7. The corresponding FCO-IM diagram is shown in Figure 5.8, with all Uniqueness Constraints correctly determined as well (see Section 4.2). Although this looks fine, and indeed passes both the N Rule and N-1 Rule tests, still there are some problems with this model, which is why the word 'WRONG' has been added to three Fact Type names.

What's wrong is that the Fact Types with Fact Expression Types F41, F42 and F43 are clearly stating some things about a *reservation request part* (the performance it concerns, the number of seats it claims and the status it has). A *reservation request part* is therefore an obviously important type of Object in Serviceton Theater, which is distinct from a *reservation request* (of which it is only a part). Yet there is no corresponding Object Type for it in the information model. Apparently this Object Type was overlooked by the modeler and the domain expert.

```
Reservation Request By Customer:
   "Reservation request 7795 was made by customer 436."
   Reservation Request:021             Customer:015
                F26: "<61> was made by <62>."
```

```
  'reservation request 7795'               'customer 436'
         reservation request number             customer number

    O21: 'reservation request <58>'       O15: customer <34>'


Reservation Request Part For Performance WRONG:
  "Part 2 of reservation request 7795 concerns performance  75."
  "  "  3  "        "         "     7795     "          "      104."
  "  "  6  "        "         "     7795     "          "      138."
  part number Reservation Request:O21         Performance:O4
                    MATCH                              MATCH

          F41: "Part <651> of <661> concerns <64>."


Number Of Seats In Reservation Request Part WRONG:
  "Part 2 of reservation request 7795 claims 2 seats."
  "  "  3 of       "         "     7795    "   4   "  ."
  "  "  6 of       "         "     7795    "   2   "  ."
  part number Reservation Request:O21     Number:O23
                    MATCH                    MATCH

          F42: "Part <652> of <662> claims <68> seats."


Status Of Reservation Request Part WRONG:
  "The status of part 2 of reservation request 7795
                                                 is 'assigned'."
  "  "     "    "   "  3  "       "          "    7795
                                                  "  'approved'."
  "  "     "    "   "  6  "       "          "    7795
                                                  "  'registered'."
            part number Reservation Request:O21  Status:O24
                                 MATCH

        F43: "The status of part <653> of <663> is <71>."
                                                 'assigned'
                                                 'approved'
                                                 'registered'
                                                  status name

                                                  O24: ''<72>''
```

Textbox 5.7: Wrong Analysis of several Fact Types concerning reservation request parts

Overlooking an Object Type for a reservation request part not only fails to model all the important kinds of objects, but it also causes the information model to have redundancy in the modeling. In Figure 5.8, the three wrong Fact Types all contain a combination of two Roles played by 'part number' and 'Reservation Request'. But this combination is just what identifies a reservation request part. So each of these Fact Types actually does contain a reservation request part, but in a non-explicit hidden way. Still, in this non-explicit hidden way, a reservation request part is actually modeled three separate times where only once would be enough.

Therefore it is better to model a reservation request part as an Object Type, explicitly and only once. This is shown in the FCO-IM diagram in Figure 5.9. Please note all the differences and similarities between Figures 5.8 (implicit and redundant modeling) and 5.9 (explicit and non-redundant modeling).

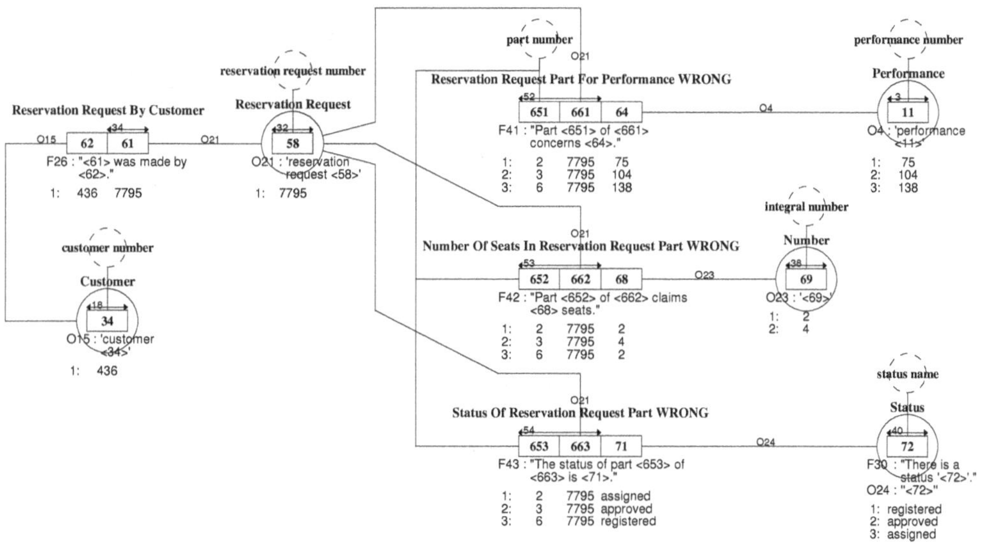

Figure 5.8 FCO-IM diagram in which an Object type is overlooked

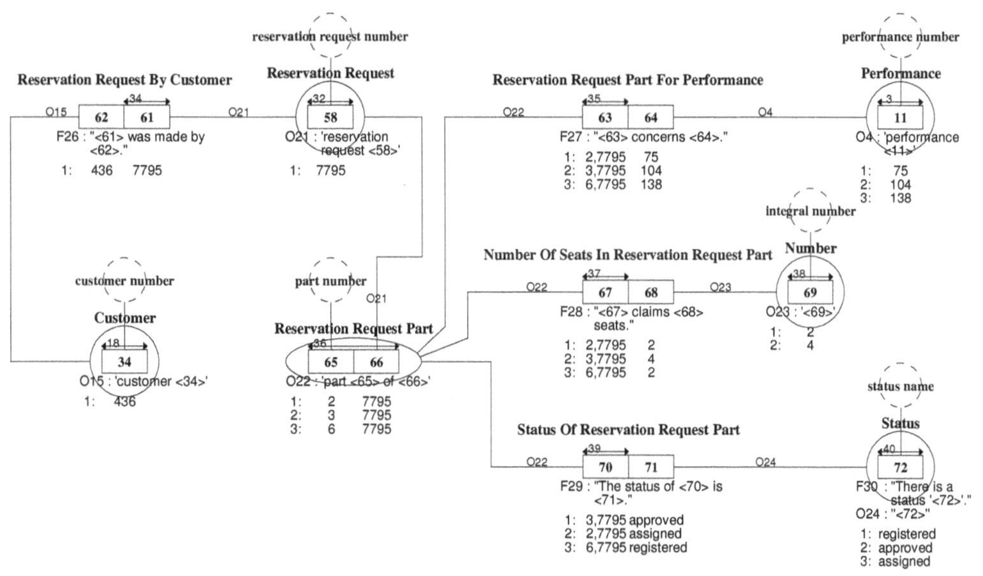

Figure 5.9 FCO-IM diagram with the previously overlooked Object Type added

Textbox 5.10 contains the corrected Sorting and Analyzing of the same Fact Expressions as in Textbox 5.7, resulting in the diagram in Figure 5.9. Please compare Textboxes 5.7 and 5.10 carefully as well, and notice the extra layer in Textbox 5.10.

```
Reservation Request By Customer:
  "Reservation request 7795 was made by customer 436."
   Reservation Request:O21                Customer:O15

                    F26: "<61> was made by <62>."

  'reservation request 7795'             'customer 436'
         reservation request number          customer number

   O21: 'reservation request <58>'    O15: customer <34>'


Reservation Request Part For Performance:
  "Part 2 of reservation request 7795 concerns performance  75."
  "  "  3  "       "         "   7795     "          "     104."
  "  "  6  "       "         "   7795     "          "     138."
     Reservation Request Part:O22                Performance:O4
                                                     MATCH

                              F27: "<63> concerns <64>."

  'Part 2 of reservation request 7795'
  '  "  3  "        "         "  7795'
  '  "  6  "        "         "  7795'
  part number Reservation Request:O21
                        MATCH

   'O22: 'part <65> of <66>'


Number Of Seats In Reservation Request Part:
  "Part 2 of reservation request 7795 claims 2 seats."
  "  "  3 of       "         "   7795    "   4   "   ."
  "  "  6 of       "         "   7795    "   2   "   ."
     Reservation Request Part:O22       Number:O23
                   MATCH                     MATCH

                              F28: "<67> claims <68> seats."


Status Of Reservation Request Part:
  "The status of part 2 of reservation request 7795
                                                 is 'assigned'."
  " "      "    "   "  3  "       "          "  7795
                                                  " 'approved'."
  " "      "    "   "  6  "       "          "  7795
                                                  " 'registered'."
                 Reservation Request Part:O22     Status:O24
                                 MATCH
```

F29: “The status of <70> is <71>.”
‘assigned’
‘approved’
‘registered’
status name
O24: ‘‘<72>’’

Textbox 5.10: Correct Analysis of the Fact Types concerning reservation request parts

5.4.2 GENERAL PATTERN REVEALING AN OVERLOOKED OBJECT TYPE

Figure 5.11 shows the general pattern that should alert the modeler to a possibly overlooked Object Type.

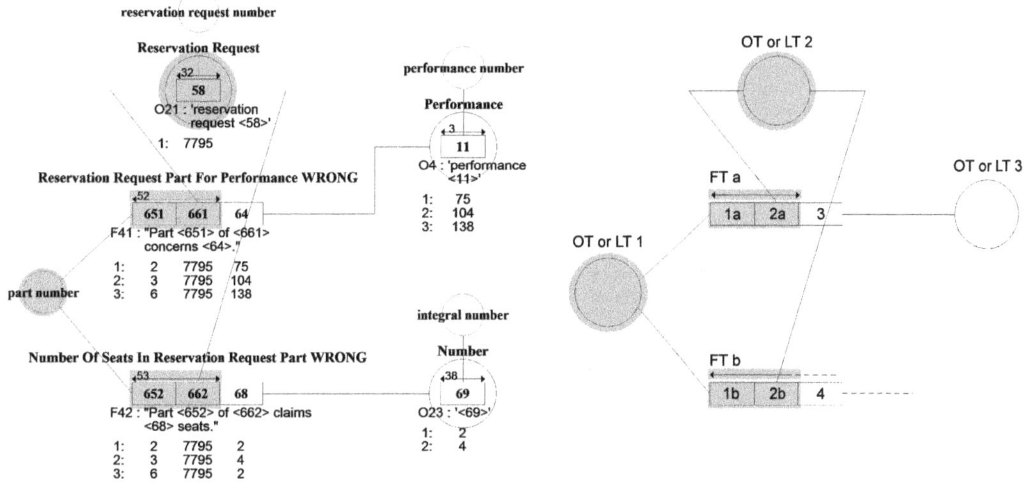

Figure 5.11 Pattern signaling an overlooked Object Type

In Figure 5.12 this Object Type has been brought out. Both figures show this pattern highlighted in two of the three Fact Types from the Serviceton Music Theater model (see also Figures 5.8 and 5.9) on the left hand side and in an abstraction with only the essential parts on the right hand side. The significant parts of this pattern are:

- In at least two Fact Types, there is a combination of Roles played by the same combination of Object Type(s) and/or Label Types. Here, the combination ‘OT or LT 1’+’OT or LT 2’ plays the combination of Roles 1a+2a in FT a and 1b+2b in FT b. In general, there can be more Fact Types with this combination (as in the example in Figure 5.8), and the combination can consist of three or more Roles. For more complex examples, see Appendix B, [1, Section 3.3.2].

- These combinations of Roles mentioned above are each completely under a Uniqueness Constraint (UC). Please note that this UC can be *longer* than the combination of Roles (indicated in Figure 5.11 by the dashed line extending over Role 4) but not shorter.
- The same combination of values can be present in the population of all of these combinations of Roles, and they represent the *exact same* Object in all cases.

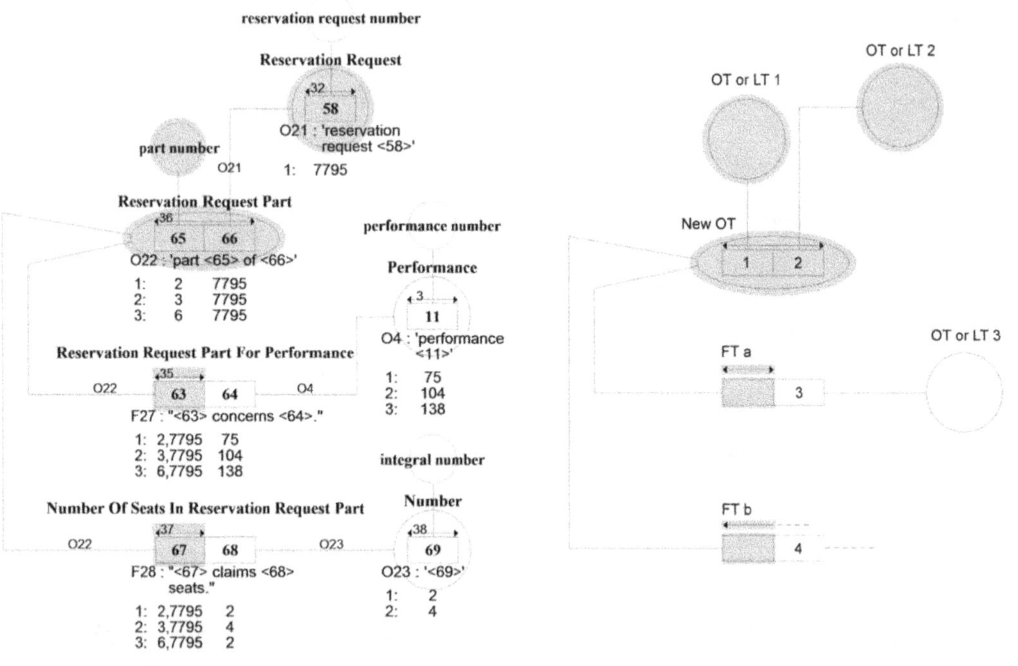

Figure 5.12 Pattern after bringing out the overlooked Object Type

If this pattern is found, an Object Type should almost always be added. This overlooked Object Type will have a Fact Type inside with the same combination of Roles as in the pattern; in the other Fact Types, this combination is replaced by one new Role (see Figure 5.12).

If an overlooked Object Type is found, the corresponding Fact Expressions must be re-Analyzed to include the new Object type. This might compel the modeler and domain expert to rephrase the Verbalizations a little if the Object Expressions for the new Object Type happen to be disconnected sentence parts (see Section

3.4.7). For example, if the Verbalization for Fact Type 'Status of Reservation Request Part' would be FE 1a, then it should be rephrased into FE 1b (Object Expression parts double underlined):

```
FE 1a: "In reservation request 7795, the status of part 2 is
       'assigned'."
FE 1b: "The status of part 2 of reservation request 7795 is
       'assigned''."
                              Reservation Request Part:022
```

5.4.3 WHEN TO PERFORM THE OVERLOOKED OBJECT TYPE TEST AND ADD A NEW OBJECT TYPE

The pattern in Figure 5.11 can only be spotted after the Uniqueness Constraints (UCs) have been determined. Indeed, in the FCO-IM procedure to draw up a conceptual information model (see Section 3.1), UCs are determined in step 5, and this check is carried out immediately after this in step 6, even before Totality Constraints (TCs) are determined (in step 7) or anything else is done. In this book, we have discussed some of these later steps previously in Sections 4.3 (TCs) and 4.4 (Value Constraints) and so have deviated from the order in the procedure for didactical reasons.

It is best to do this test immediately after the UCs have been determined. The reason is: it might be necessary to add a new Object Type, which would affect Roles played by other Object Types, so any work on TCs would have to be redone for these changes. See Figure 5.8, in which Object Type 'Reservation Request' plays four Roles before the overlooked Object Type is brought out, and Figure 5.9, in which it plays only two Roles afterwards.

In rare cases the pattern is found but the modeler and domain expert decide not to add an Object Type after all (usually the condition specified in the third bullet above is not satisfied). Therefore, a good modeling tool like CaseTalk (see Appendix B, [2]) will spot the pattern but issue only a warning, not an error, allowing the modeler to override the warning. However, in over 99% of cases the 'hidden' Object Type should certainly be brought out.

The importance of performing this test in practice can hardly be overrated; in our experience it has surfaced overlooked Object Types in every modeling case.

Chapter 6
Advanced Topics

6.1 Freedom of Choice: Alternative Ways to Model the Same Fact Expressions

Key Points

- **Alternative ways of modeling might be possible:**
    - **During Sorting, if different Fact Types can be formed**
        - **This leads to different Relational database structures**
        - **Pros and cons are discussed, and a general modeling advice is given.**
    - **During Analyzing, if an 'extra' Object Type can be formed or not**
        - **This does not lead to different Relational database structures**
        - **Such an 'extra' Object Type sometimes *must* be formed (see also Section 5.4).**

6.1.1 DIFFERENT WAY OF SORTING: DIFFERENT TABLE STRUCTURES

6.1.1.1 Different Fact Types if Only a Few Fixed Values Exist

As already pointed out in Section 3.4.2, there can be some freedom of choice in Sorting Fact Expressions in certain cases. For example, in Textbox 6.1 all Fact Expressions that refer to a price of a ticket have been assigned to a single Fact Type named 'Performance Price'. But it is also possible to assign these Fact

Expressions to two different Fact Types, one for single tickets and one for season tickets, as is shown in Textbox 6.2.

```
Performance Price:
  "The price of a single ticket for performance 105 is $35.00."
  "The price of a season ticket for performance 105 is $31.50."
  "The price of a single ticket for performance 108 is $27.50."
  "The price of a season ticket for performance 108 is $24.00."
```

Textbox 6.1 All Fact Expressions assigned to a single Fact Type

```
Performance Price Single Ticket:
  "The price of a single ticket for performance 105 is $35.00."
  "The price of a single ticket for performance 108 is $27.50."

Performance Price Season Ticket:
  "The price of a season ticket for performance 105 is $31.50."
  "The price of a season ticket for performance 108 is $24.00."
```

Textbox 6.2 The same Fact Expressions assigned to two different Fact Types

The consequences for the further information modeling and the Relational table structures that follow from these alternatives are illustrated in Figures 6.3, 6.4 and 6.5, which will be discussed below.

The second way, shown in Textbox 6.2, is only possible if there is a small and fixed number of types of ticket. For the sake of this example, let's suppose the domain expert has insisted (contrary to the discussion in Textbox 4.36) that only single tickets and season tickets are offered by Serviceton Music Theater. In other words, there is now a Business Rule "Only single and season tickets are offered." In the information model, this Business Rule translates into a Value Constraint (see Section 4.4) on Label Type 'ticket type name': VC 2: {season, single} (see Figure 6.3). So the alternative way of Typing and Naming shown in Textbox 6.2 is possible here. There are good reasons to prefer the first way of modeling in this case (see the pros and cons discussed below), but in general these two ways can both be considered by the modeler and domain expert.

Other examples where such alternatives are possible:

- Facts including gender: {M, F} or {male, female}
- Facts including a type of season: {high season, low season}

- Facts including a class of passenger: {economy class, business class, first class}
- Facts including a type of customer: {regular, frequent, special, VIP}
- Facts including a day of the week: {Mon, Tue, Wed, Thu, Fri, Sat, Sun}
- Facts including a month of the year: {Jan, Feb, Mar, Apr, May, Jun, Jul, Aug, Sep, Oct, Nov, Dec}

In general, if there is a small fixed number of values for a component of certain Facts, then these Facts can either be assigned to just one Fact Type or be divided into as many different Fact Types as there are values for this component. Let's call these two ways the 'Single Fact Type Way' and the 'Multiple Fact Type Way'.

6.1.1.2 Consequences for the Information Model and Table Structure

Figures 6.3 and 6.4 give the result of Analyzing the Facts, sorted in one Fact Type and in two Fact Types respectively. Only the top level of Analyzing the Fact Types is shown (for the further Analysis of the Object Expressions, see Section 3.6.4). There is an extra Object Type 'Ticket Type' in the Single Fact Type Way, which is absent in the Multiple Fact Type Way. The reason for this absence is that the sentence part 'a single ticket' *does not change* in any of the Facts assigned to Fact Type 'Performance Price Single Ticket'. Neither does the sentence part 'a season ticket' change in 'Performance Price Season Ticket', so these parts are fixed text in both Fact Types and therefore remain in the corresponding Fact Type Expressions.

Figure 6.3 and 6.4 also give the relevant parts of both FCO-IM information models. The Totality Constraint dots attached to Object Types 'Performance' and 'Calendar Day' indicate that these Object Types play other Roles, not shown here, which have a TC on them somewhere (see the complete information model in Appendix A). In the Single Fact Type Way of modeling, there is only one Fact Type for the prices, which has three Roles, and an extra Object Type 'Ticket Type' that plays one of these Roles in this Fact Type. In the Multiple Fact Type Way of modeling, there are as many Fact Types as there are ticket types, each with only two Roles, and no Object Type for ticket types.

```
Performance Price:
  "The price of a single ticket for performance 105 is $35.00."
  " "     "    " " season    "     "        "     105  " "31.50."
  " "     "    " " single    "     "        "     108  " "27.50."
  " "     "    " " season    "     "        "     108  "  24.00."
              Ticket Type:O9       Performance:O4      Amount Of
                                                       Money:O10

          F8: "The price of <21> for <22> is <23>."
```

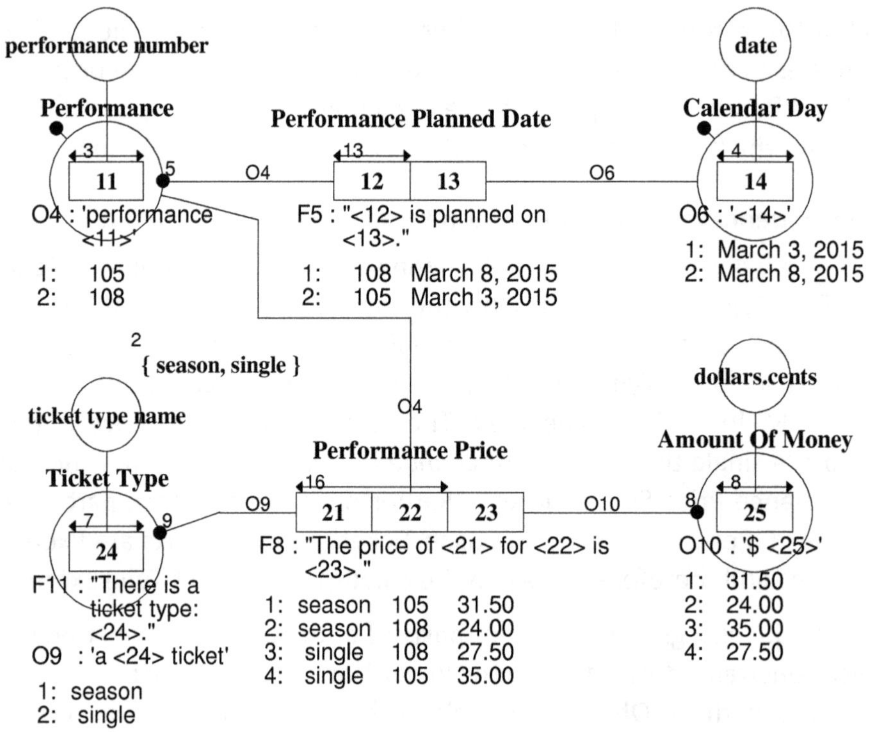

Figure 6.3 All Facts in the same Fact Type: information model

```
Performance Price Single Ticket:
  "The price of a single ticket for performance 105 is $35.00."
   "  "    "    "  "    "      "   "       "       108   "  "27.50."
                                  Performance:O4     Amount Of
                                                     Money:O10

      F12: "The price of a single ticket for <221> is <231>."

Performance Price Season Ticket:
  "The price of a season ticket for performance 105 is $31.50."
   "  "    "    "  "    "      "   "       "       108   "  "24.00."
                                  Performance:O4     Amount Of
                                                     Money:O10

      F13: "The price of a season ticket for <222> is <232>."
```

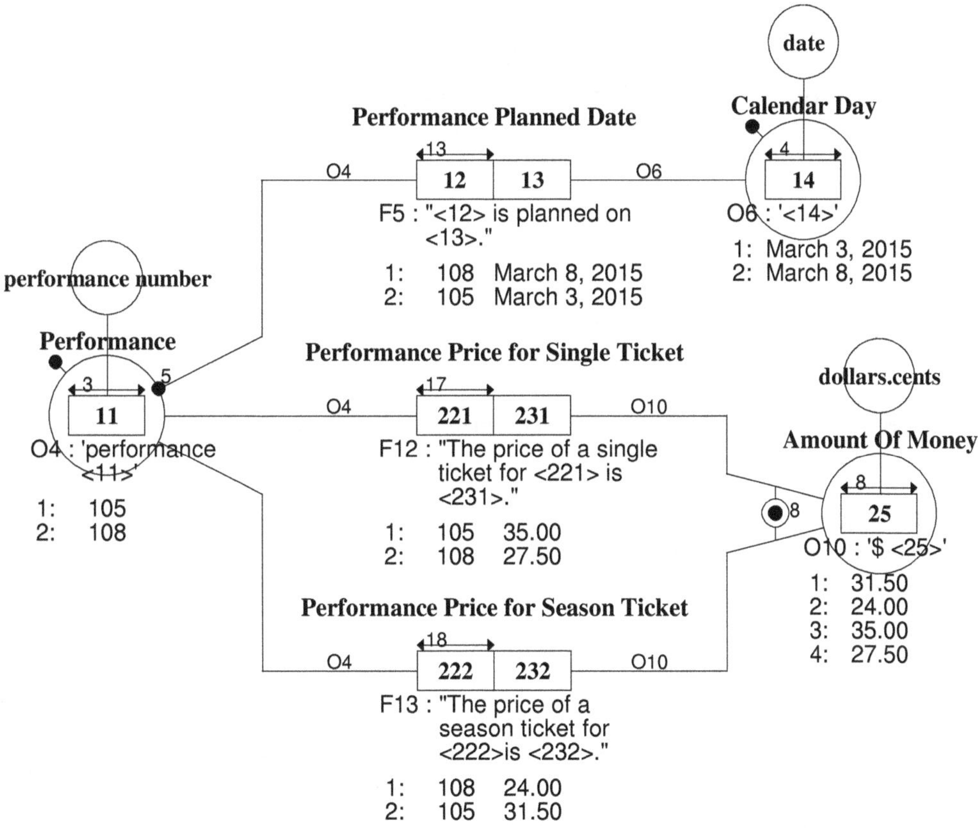

Figure 6.4 Facts in different Fact Types: information model

Please note the Uniqueness Constraints and Totality Constraints. (See Sections 4.2.3, 4.3.4 and 4.4.3 for most details.) Because the domain expert in this example insists that single tickets and season tickets are the only kinds ever to be offered in Serviceton Music Theater (see Textbox 4.36, where the domain expert actually decided otherwise), Object Type 'Ticket Type' in Figure 6.3 has Totality Constraint 9 on Role 21, and Label Type 'ticket type name' has Value Constraint 2: {single, season}. TC 8 in Figure 6.4 means that all amounts of money in the Population of Role 25 must occur in at least one of the Populations of Roles 231 and 232; no list of possible amounts of money is desired. Also please note that both models in Figures 6.3 and 6.4 contain *exactly the same* Fact Expressions.

Figure 6.5 illustrates the consequences of the Single Fact Type Way and the Multiple Fact Type Way for the structure of the tables that are derived from the information models in Figures 6.3 and 6.4. See Chapter 7 for how a Relational database (see Appendix B, [14]) is derived from an information model.

Tables resulting from the model in Figure 6.3

Table Performance

performance number NN	planned date NN	...
105	March 3, 2015	...
108	March 8, 2015	...
...	...	...

F5: "Performance <performance number> is planned on <planned date>."

FKref 1

Table Performance Price

performance number NN	ticket type NN	price NN
105	single	35.00
105	season	31.50
108	single	27.50
108	season	24.00
...	...	...

F8: "The price of a <ticket type> ticket for performance <performance number> is $<price>."

FKref 1: Performance Price (performance number) → Performance (performance number)

IR 2: Column Performance Price(ticket type) can only contain the values 'single' or 'season'.

Table resulting from the model in Figure 6.4

Table Performance

<u>performance number</u> NN	planned date NN	price single ticket OP	price season ticket OP	...
105	March 3, 2015	35.00	31.50	...
108	March 8, 2015	27.50	24.00	...
...	...	...	...	...

F5: "Performance <performance number> is planned on <planned date>."

F12: "The price of a single ticket for performance <performance number> is $<price single ticket>."

F13: "The price of a season ticket for performance <performance number> is $<price season ticket>."

Figure 6.5 Database structures resulting from the models in Figures 6.3. and 6.4

The tables in Figure 6.5 are presented with table and column names (the Primary Key (PK) columns are underlined; table 'Performance Price' has a PK over two columns), and OP (for optional) or NN (for not null). The model in Figure 6.4 leads to only one table, whereas the model in Figure 6.3 leads to two tables, with a foreign key reference from table 'Performance Price' (column 'performance number') to table 'Performance' (column 'performance number'). This reference means that every value in column Performance Price(performance number) must also occur in column Performance(performance number). In other words, there can be no entry in table Performance Price for a performance that is absent in table Performance. The Fact Expression Types are given as well, adapted to the table structure: all Object Expression Types filled in, and column names in the blanks (see Chapter 7 and Appendix B, [1, Chapter 4] for details). Any concrete Fact Expression can be regenerated by choosing a Fact Expression Type and then filling in the appropriate Labels from a row in the table. Please check that both table structures indeed contain exactly the same Facts. Finally, in Figure 6.5 there is an Integrity Rule IR 2 on column Performance Price(ticket type), which is the translation of Value Constraint 2 in the FCO-IM diagram.

6.1.1.3 Pros and Cons of These Two Alternatives

There are two main differences between these two alternative ways of modeling. The Single Fact Type Way compared to the Multiple Fact Type Way:

- **Is more robust against possible future changes.** Suppose Serviceton Theater would like to introduce new ticket types in the future such as 'discount ticket' or 'promotion ticket'. In the Single Fact Type Way, this would be easy to do. Both in the FCO-IM model and in the table structure, just add the new values 'discount' and 'promotion' to the Value Constraint (or even better: use a *domain list* implemented as a *domain table* instead of the Value Constraint (see Section 4.4.1) and simply update this table). In the Multiple Fact Type Way, this is more difficult to do. In the FCO-IM model, two new Fact Types 'Performance Price for Discount Ticket' and 'Performance Price for Promotion Ticket' must be added and their UCs and other constraints determined. The will result in changes in the structure of table 'Performance': two extra columns 'price discount ticket' and 'price promotion ticket' must be added with OP or NN following from the constraints in the FCO-IM model. Clearly, these changes are more complex in the second way of modeling.

- **Leads to a more complex table structure.** The Single Fact Type Way leads to a table structure with two tables 'Performance' and 'Performance Price', the second one with a compound primary key, and with a foreign key reference between the tables. In contrast, the Multiple Fact Type Way leads to a table structure with only one table 'Performance', which is the same as in the other way of modeling except it has some extra columns: one column for each type of ticket. Clearly, the first structure is more complex, with an extra foreign key constraint and value constraint to be monitored by the system. In addition, most people find the second table structure more convenient to read, with all the prices for a particular performance in the same row, instead of spread over several rows in another table. However, all the Facts can be presented in any desired form from either table structure in a view on screen or in a report on paper. Therefore this preference carries little weight since end users hardly ever have access to the core database tables directly.

6.1.1.4 Advice to Choose Between These Two Ways of Modeling

We advise to use the Single Fact Type Way unless there are good reasons not to do so. The robustness against future changes generally outweighs the greater complexity. You should consider the Multiple Fact Type Way of modeling only if you are *very* sure the number of possible values will not change. As a caveat: in 2013 the German government extended the two possible genders, 'M' and 'F', to include 'X' for babies born without "clear gender-determining physical characteristics". So if you thought it was a safe bet that the number of gender values will never change, think again!

6.1.2 GENERAL ADVICE ON MODELING: AS DATA INSTEAD OF METADATA

The advice given in Section 6.1.1.4 above is a special case of a more general information modeling advice, presented in Textbox 6.6 and discussed below:

General Advice on Modeling Information

IF	there is a choice between modeling information as *data* or as *metadata*
THEN	model it as data
UNLESS	there is a good reason not to do so

Textbox 6.6 General advice on modeling

Data and Metadata

It is often useful to distinguish between *data* and *metadata*. Loosely speaking, *data* are the 'ordinary' Facts, like all the examples from Serviceton Music Theater, and *metadata* is information *about* these 'ordinary' Facts, like which values are allowed as ticket types or where on the computer screen and in what color the performances are to be placed. In short: data are Facts, and metadata are Facts about Facts. Since both data and metadata are Facts, but with a different focus, the distinction sometimes tends to get blurred. Here is a rather loose definition of data and metadata in an FCO-IM model or in a Relational table structure, which will do for this section:

- In an FCO-IM model, the *Population* (the concrete Facts) is data; everything else (Fact Types, Object Types, Constraints, etc.) is metadata.
- In the Relational database tables that are derived from an FCO-IM model, the values in the table cells are data; all the rest (tables, columns, integrity rules, etc.) is metadata.

In Figure 6.3, the ticket types are chiefly modeled as data: The values 'single' and 'season' are in the Population of the FCO-IM model (Object Type 'Ticket Type' and Fact Type 'Performance Price') and of the Relational table 'Performance Price' (column 'ticket type'). In Figure 6.4 however, the ticket types are only modeled as metadata: The words 'single' and 'season' occur only in the Fact Expression Types

F12 and F13 in both the FCO-IM model and the Relational database schema, not in the Population.

Modeling things as data versus as metadata usually has the following trade-offs:

As data:

- more flexible information modeling (it is easy to add a new ticket type or delete an obsolete one by simply updating the Populations)
- more complex database structure (extra table and foreign key reference)

As metadata:

- more rigid information modeling (adding or deleting a ticket type requires adding or deleting Fact Types and table columns)
- more simple database structure (less tables and integrity rules to manage)

As a second illustration of this data/metadata trade-off, the ticket types example can be carried even further. Suppose that only two ticket types are used at Serviceton Theater, and the domain expert has declared that 'single' tickets and 'season' tickets are the only kinds ever to be offered in Serviceton Theater (see Section 4.4.3 where the domain expert actually decided otherwise). This Business Rule can also be modeled as data or as metadata. Both versions are shown in Figures 6.7 and 6.8.

As metadata, this Business Rule could be modeled in the FCO-IM model by adding a Value Constraint (see Section 4.4) to Label Type 'ticket type name'. In a Relational database (see Appendix B, [14]), this constraint would translate into a similar integrity rule IR 2 on column 'ticket type' in table 'Performance Price' (see Section 7.1). This is shown in Figure 6.8.

As data, this Business Rule could be modeled in the FCO-IM model by explicitly declaring the allowed ticket types in Fact Expressions like "There is a ticket type: single." and "There is a ticket type: season.". This is actually a *domain list* for ticket types (see the discussion in Sections 4.3.4 and 4.4.1), modeled in the FCO-IM model by Fact Expression Type F11 for 'Ticket Type'. This domain list would be implemented in a Relational database (see Appendix B, [14]) as a separate table for possible ticket types. This is shown in Figure 6.7.

Allowed ticket type names modeled as data (Population of F11 and table 'Ticket Type')

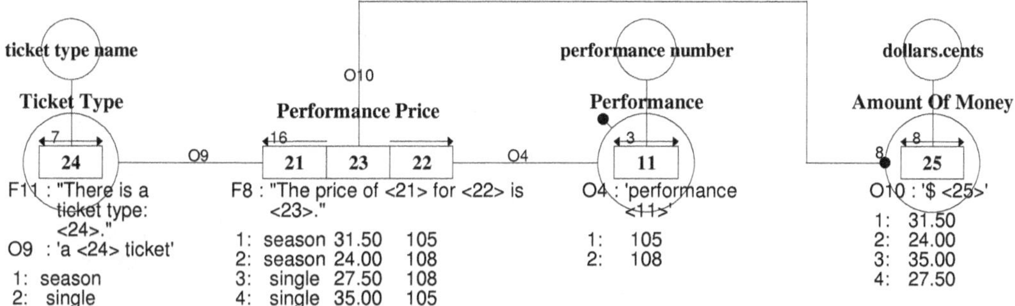

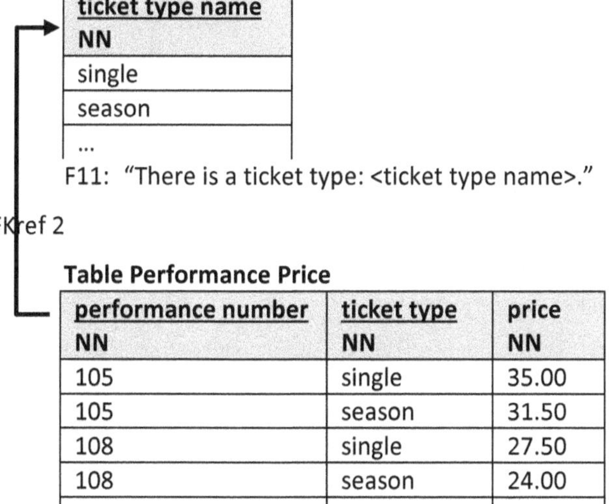

Table Ticket Type

ticket type name NN
single
season
...

F11: "There is a ticket type: <ticket type name>."

FKref 2

Table Performance Price

performance number NN	ticket type NN	price NN
105	single	35.00
105	season	31.50
108	single	27.50
108	season	24.00
...	...	...

F8: "The price of a <ticket type> ticket for performance <performance number> is $<price>."

FKref 2: Performance Price (ticket type) → Ticket Type (ticket type name)

Figure 6.7 Allowed ticket types modeled as data

Allowed ticket type names modeled as metadata (VC 2 in the model, and IC 2 on column 'ticket type'

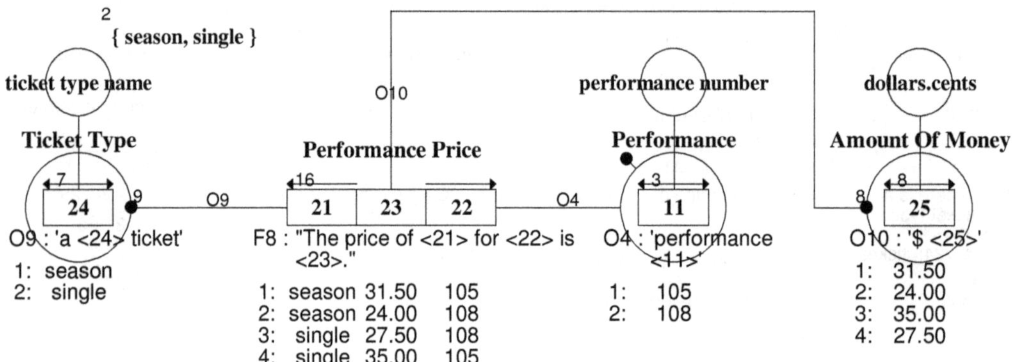

Table Performance Price

performance number NN	ticket type NN	price NN
105	single	35.00
105	season	31.50
108	single	27.50
108	season	24.00
...	...	...

F8: "The price of a <ticket type> ticket for performance <performance number> is $<price>."

IC 2: Column Performance Price(ticket type) can only contain the values 'single' or 'season'.

Figure 6.8 Allowed ticket types modeled as metadata

The same trade-offs can be seen in Figures 6.7 and 6.8 as in Figures 6.3 and 6.4. When modeled as data, the information model is more flexible (simply add or delete an allowed ticket type in the FCO-IM model by adding or deleting a Fact from Fact Type 'Ticket Type' or, in the Relational database, by a simple update on table 'Ticket Type'). But the database is also more complex (an extra table and foreign key reference). When modeled as metadata, the information model is more rigid (to add or delete an allowed ticket requires changing VC 2 in the FCO-IM model and IR 2 in the database implementation, which needs special programming activities instead of simply updating a table), but the database is simpler (one table and foreign key reference less to manage).

Our advice is to model things where possible as data unless there are good reasons not to do so. In our experience the increased flexibility usually outweighs having to manage the extra tables and foreign key references. Moreover, domain lists (pick lists) are very handy for things like ticket types, calendar days, countries, and many other things that have names you don't want spelling variants or errors in, especially if they might be updated sometimes even if that happens only very rarely. If implemented as data, a simple update (by a user authorized to change this kind of Facts) suffices without requiring any programming effort.

This general advice lies behind the discussion of determining Totality Constraints (Section 4.3, "Would you like a pick list ...?") and Value Constraints (Section 4.4.1: VC or domain list?).

6.1.3 DIFFERENT WAY OF ANALYZING: EXTRA OBJECT TYPE

6.1.3.1 Recognizing an Extra Object Type

During the Analyzing step in the FCO-IM procedure (see Section 3.1), the information modeler and domain expert look at places where sentence parts vary and try to find out whether these parts are Object Expressions or Labels (see Section 3.6). For Object Expressions, this can sometimes be done in different ways if there are more than two varying parts in the sentences. An example is shown in Figures 6.9 and 6.10. Figure 6.9 repeats the Analysis of Fact Type 'Performance Price', done in Section 3.6.4, and Figure 6.10 shows a different way that leads to an extra Object Type 'Ticket Type for Performance'.

```
Performance Price:
  "The price of a single ticket for performance 105 is $35.00."
  "  "     "   " " season    "    "      "      105  " "31.50."
  "  "     "   " " single    "    "      "      108  " "27.50."
  "  "     "   " " season    "    "      "      108  " "24.00."
                 Ticket Type:09      Performance:04    Amount Of
                                                       Money:010
            F8: "The price of <21> for <22> is <23>."
```

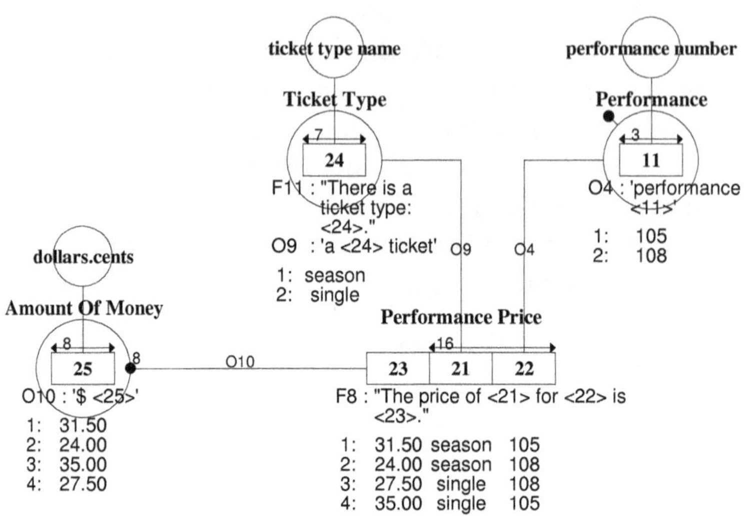

Figure 6.9 Analysis of Fact Type 'Performance Price': no extra Object Type

In this example, it depends on the view of the domain expert whether or not the sentence part 'a single ticket for performance 105' is regarded as a phrase that identifies a meaningful Object. Is 'Ticket Type for Performance' an important Object Type in Serviceton Music Theater? As was the case in Section 6.1.1, this choice makes no difference for the *data* (exactly the same Fact Expressions are modeled in both ways), only for the *metadata* (see Section 6.1.2), which would contain an extra Object Type. Please note Totality Constraint 9 on role 32 in Figure 6.10, without which the two models would not be equivalent: An extra Fact Expression Type would then be needed for the new Object Type (see Textbox 4.25, lines 37-42). Both ways of modeling in Figures 6.9 and 6.10 lead to the same Relational database table (see Appendix B, [14]); it is the same table 'Performance Price' as is shown in Figures 6.5, 6.7 and 6.8.

As long as Object Expressions like 'a season ticket for performance 108' occur only in this one Fact Type 'Performance Price', we have no advice to choose between the two ways of modeling shown in Figures 6.9 and 6.10. The information model might be slightly more complicated but might show an important Object Type, and there is no difference in the Relational database that can be derived from the models. However, if the same Object Expressions occur in sentences of more than one Fact Type, then there is no longer a free choice between these ways of modeling, and the extra Object Type *must* be modeled. The next section shows why.

```
Performance Price:
   "The price of a single ticket for performance 105 is $35.00."
   "  "     "    " " season    "    "       "    105  " "31.50."
   "  "     "    " " single    "    "       "    108  " "27.50."
   "  "     "    " " season    "    "       "    108  " "24.00."
                   Ticket Type for Performance:O15    Amount Of
                                                      Money:O10

                          F12: "The price of <32> is <23>."

                'a single ticket for performance 105'
                '" season    "    "       "      105'
                '" single    "    "       "      108'
                '" season    "    "       "      108'
                   Ticket Type:O9     Performance:O4

                     O15: '<21> for <22>."
```

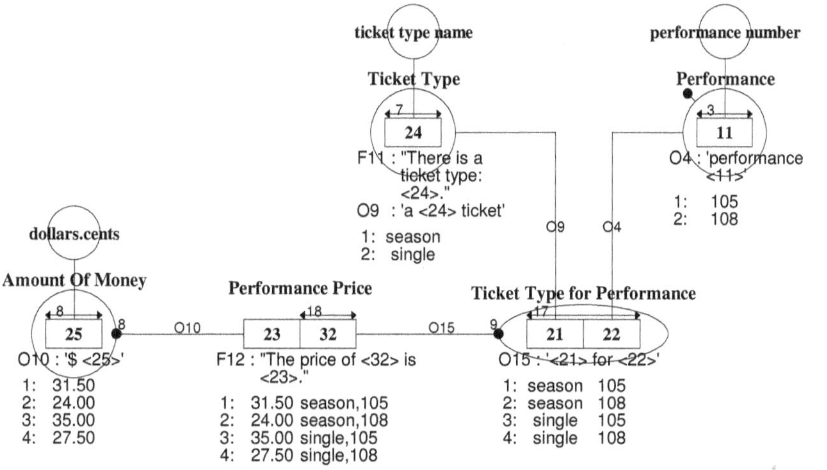

Figure 6.10 Analysis of Fact Type 'Performance Price': extra Object Type 'Ticket For Performance'

6.1.3.2 Two 'Extra' Object Types That are the Same Must be United

Suppose that the following two Fact Types have to be modeled for Serviceton Music Theater: 'Performance Price' is already familiar, and 'Ticket Availability' has been added for the discussion in this section. Here is the Analysis of both Fact Types without recognizing an extra Object Type. The corresponding FCO-IM diagram with two Fact Types containing three Roles each is given in Figure 6.11, part a.

```
Performance Price:
   "The price of a single ticket for performance 105 is $35.00."
   "  "     "    " " season    "    "       "    105  " "31.50."
```

```
  " "     "     " " single     "    "          "        108   " "27.50."
  " "     "     " " season     "    "          "        108   " "24.00."
                  Ticket Type:O9        Performance:O4       Amount Of
                                                             Money:O10

                                  F12: "The price of <32> is <23>."
```

```
Ticket Availability:
 "A season ticket for performance 105 will be available from
                                                   December 1, 2014."
 "" season     "     "        "        108      "  "     "        "
                                                   December 1, 2014."
 "" single     "     "        "        105      "  "     "        "
                                                   February 1, 2015."
  Ticket Type:O9       Performance:O4                Calendar Day:O6

                       F12: "<41> for <42> will be available from <43>."
```

In an alternative Analysis, an extra Object Type can be recognized in both Fact Types. This is completely analogous to what is shown in Figures 6.9 and 6.10, but now in two separate Fact Types. For the sake of the discussion, suppose that these two Object Types are given different names at first: 'Ticket Type for Performance 1' and 'Ticket Type for Performance 2'. The corresponding FCO-IM diagram with the two extra Object Types is given in Figure 6.11, part b.

```
Performance Price:
  "The price of a single ticket for performance 105 is $35.00."
  " "     "     " " season     "    "          "        105   " "31.50."
  " "     "     " " single     "    "          "        108   " "27.50."
  " "     "     " " season     "    "          "        108   " "24.00."
                    Ticket Type for Performance 1:O15        Amount Of
                                                             Money:O10

                                  F12: "The price of <32> is <23>."


                   'a single ticket for performance 105'
                   '" season     "    "          "   105'
                   '" single     "    "          "   108'
                   '" season     "    "          "   108'
                   Ticket Type:O9        Performance:O4

                        O15: '<21> for <22>."


Ticket Availability:
 "A season ticket for performance 105 will be available from
                                                   December 1, 2014."
 "" season     "     "        "        108      "  "     "        "
                                                   December 1, 2014."
 "" single     "     "        "        105      "  "     "        "
                                                   February 1, 2015."
   Ticket Type For Performance 2:O16                 Calendar Day:O6
```

```
F12: "<41> for <42> will be available from <43>."

'a season ticket for performance 105'
'" season    "     "        "     108'
'" single    "     "        "     105'
 Ticket Type:O9       Performance:O4

     O16: '<41> for <42>."
```

a) Two Fact Types with 3 Roles

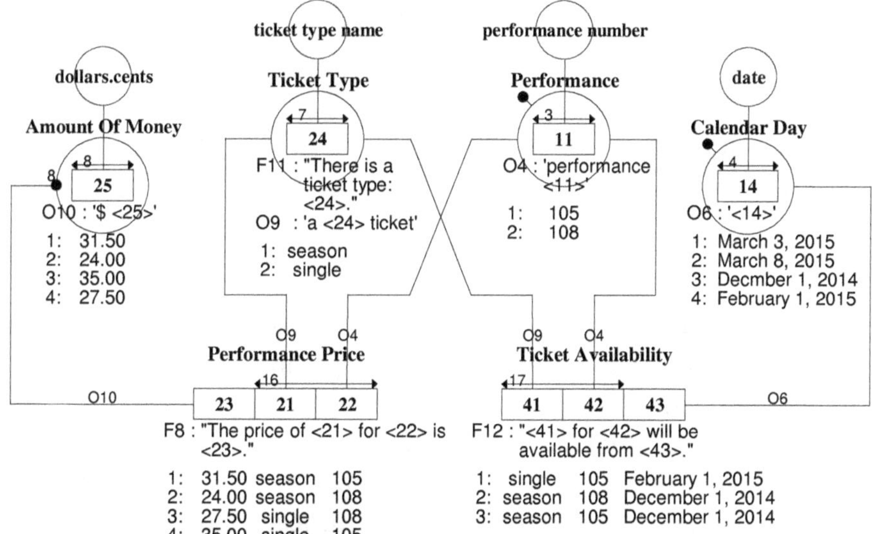

b) Two 'extra' Object Types modeled: they are actually the same

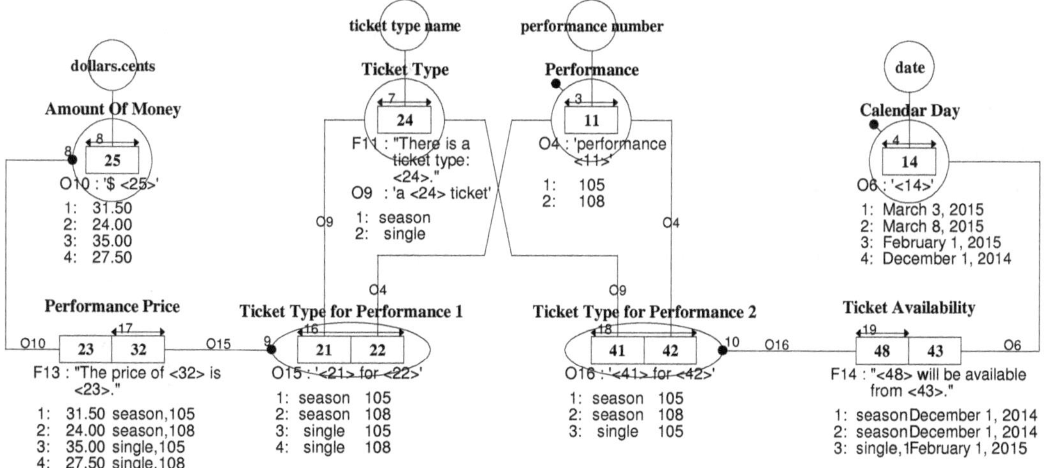

c) The two Object Types united

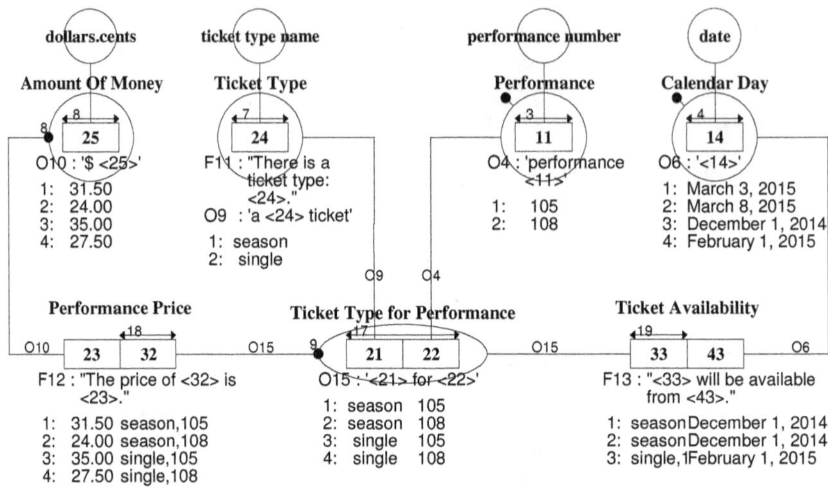

Figure 6.11 The same 'extra' Object Type in several Fact Types should be brought out and united

But obviously the two 'extra' Object Types in Figure 6.11, part b are really the same: they are both a combination of a ticket type and a performance, and some Objects in their Populations are exactly the same (for instance, 'a season ticket for performance 105' is present in both Populations, clearly concerning the same Object in both cases). These Populations don't have to be exactly identical (they're not) because Facts in 'Ticket Availability' might concern a different set of Objects than Facts in 'Performance Price'. However, if the same Object *can* be in both Populations, then the Object Types must be the same because each Object should belong to only one Object Type (unless Subtypes are involved; see Section 6.2 for Subtypes). So the Analysis should recognize only one extra Object Type, the same in both Fact Types (note the word 'MATCH' in the Analysis of 'Ticket Availability' now). The corresponding FCO-IM diagram with this single extra Object Type is given in Figure 6.11, part c.

```
Performance Price:
  "The price of a single ticket for performance 105 is $35.00."
  "  "       "  " season     "     "          "  105  " "31.50."
  "  "       "  " single     "     "          "  108  " "27.50."
  "  "       "  " season     "     "          "  108  " "24.00."
                 Ticket Type for Performance:O15      Amount Of
                                                      Money:O10

                                 F12: "The price of <32> is <23>."
```

```
'a single ticket for performance 105'
'" season    "      "        "      105'
'" single    "      "        "      108'
'" season    "      "        "      108'
 Ticket Type:09        Performance:04

        O15: '<21> for <22>."
```

```
Ticket Availability:
 "A season ticket for performance 105 will be available from
                                             December 1, 2014."
 "" season   "    "      "     108     "  "      "       "
                                             December 1, 2014."
 "" single   "    "      "     105     "  "      "       "
                                             February 1, 2015."
   Ticket Type For Performance:O15               Calendar Day:O6
              MATCH

             F12: "<41> for <42> will be available from <43>."
```

In summary, the main points in this section are:

- During Analyzing, sometimes an 'extra' Object Type can be modeled.
- If such an extra Object Type occurs in only one Fact Type, there is a free choice in modeling it or not.
- However, if the *same* Object Type can be modeled in more than one Fact Type, it should be brought out explicitly.

The reason for the last rule is that if such an Object Type is not brought out, it is modeled implicitly more than once. This causes (hidden) redundancy in the metadata. This redundancy can be made visible by modeling the Object Type explicitly, which is then present more than once in the model. This redundancy must be removed by uniting the two Object Types.

The points above are the reason behind the test for 'overlooked Object Types' in Section 5.4.

6.2 Some Things are Special: Introduction to Subtypes

Key Points

- **A common kind of Business Rule is: "We record [...] *only for* [...]".**
- **Such rules can be modeled using Subtypes.**
- **A Subtype is an Object Type that is a part of another Object Type, called its Supertype.**
- **A Subtype consists of the same Objects as the Supertype but only those with a special property.**
- **There are two kinds of Subtypes:**
  - **Declarative Subtypes, for which this special property is stated explicitly.**
  - **Derivable Subtypes, for which this special property is derived from other Fact Types.**
- **The difference is discussed between Fact Types with one Role that model an 'ordinary' Object Type, a Declarative Subtype and a Derivable Subtype.**

Business Rules that Concern Subtypes

Here are a few examples of a kind of Business Rule that often occurs, taken from various contexts:

BR 1: Only students with a minimum GPA of 3.0 can enroll in the honors program.

BR 2 The driving range is recorded only for electric and hybrid vehicles.

BR 3 An indoor parking space can only be assigned to executive employees.

BR 4 Measurements of PSA-levels can be recorded only for male patients.

BR 5 The number of pregnancies is recorded only for female patients.

BR 6 A discount percentage applies only to orders placed by regular customers.

In all of these examples, there are groups of persons/things/concepts (Object Types) and smaller groups belonging to these larger groups that have a special property. Such a smaller group is called a *Subtype* of the larger group, which in turn is called the *Supertype*. In addition, in all of these examples there is a kind of Facts (Fact Type) to be recorded only for the Subtype but not for the whole Supertype.

	Supertype	**Subtype**	**Fact Type**
BR 1	Student	Student with GPA >= 3.0	Enrollment in honors program
BR 2	Vehicle	Electric or hybrid vehicle	Driving range
BR 3	Employee	Executive employee	Assigned indoor parking space
BR 4	Patient	Male patient	PSA-level measured
BR 5	Patient	Female patient	Number of pregnancies
BR 6	Order	Order by regular customer	Discount percentage

BR 6 might also hint at another Supertype/Subtype combination: customer/regular customer. If that combination really exists, there must be another Business Rule to say what kind of Facts are to be recorded for regular customers only.

Most information modeling techniques include a way to model such Business Rules in the form of Supertypes that have Subtypes. An introduction to how this can be done in FCO-IM is given below.

6.2.1 DECLARATIVE AND DERIVABLE SUBTYPES

To introduce Subtypes the example below is used, this time from a different context than Serviceton Music Theater. Let's suppose a car rental company records several Facts about the cars they rent. Cars are identified by their license plate number (the company operates nation-wide). The type of vehicle is recorded: gasoline, diesel, electric, or hybrid. Some cars have a tow hitch, and for such cars the maximum load they can pull is recorded. For electric and hybrid cars, the maximum driving range before the batteries must be recharged is recorded if it is known.

The information modeling was carried out according to all the rules and procedures stated earlier in this book: Collecting concrete examples, Verbalizing,

Sorting, Analyzing, etc. Only the final result is given in Figure 6.12. Everything that has to do with Subtypes will be discussed below. Please take a few minutes to study the rest first (everything except the textboxes and Fact Type 'Car with Tow Hitch').

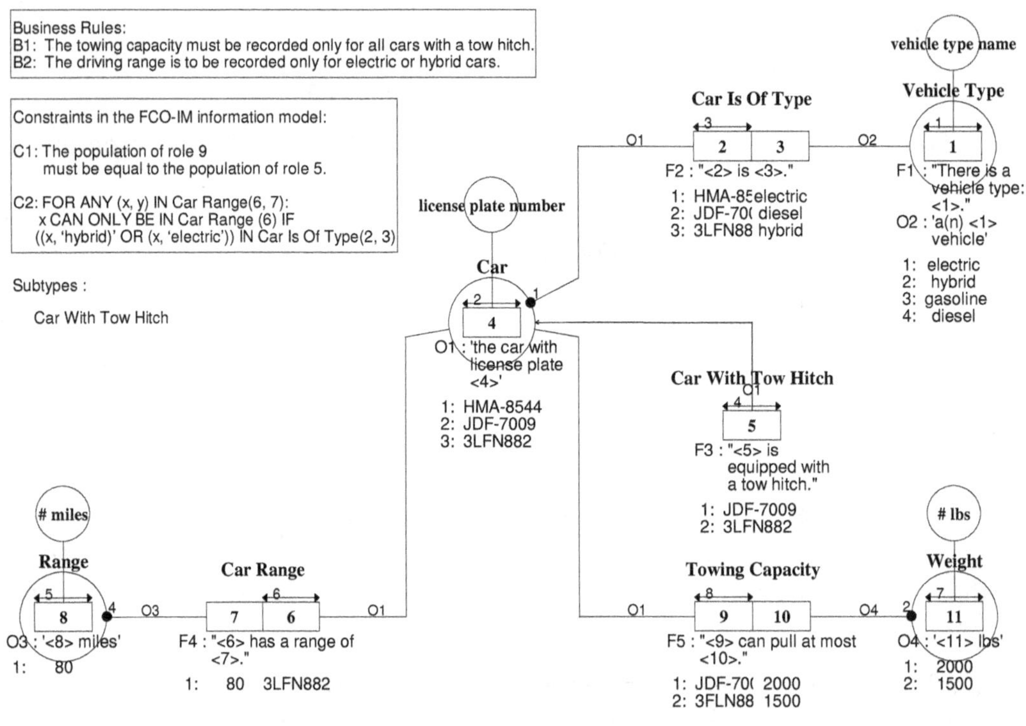

Figure 6.12 Declarative Subtype 'Car With Tow Hitch'

6.2.1.1 Declarative Subtype

Fact Type 'Car With Tow Hitch' models Facts like "The car with license plate JDF-7009 is equipped with a tow hitch.". Comparing the Populations of Fact Types 'Car' and 'Car With Tow Hitch', it is clear that *all* the cars are in the Population of 'Car', whereas only those cars that have a tow hitch are in the Population of 'Car With Tow Hitch'. The Population of the latter Fact Type therefore defines a *special kind of car* in which only the cars are found with the property that they have a tow hitch. Not every car has this property (otherwise it wouldn't be worth recording it), so the number of cars with this property is *smaller* than the total number of cars. The Population of Role 5 is therefore a *part* (or *subset*) of the Population of Role 4. Therefore Object Type 'Car With Tow Hitch' can be seen as a *Subtype* of Object Type 'Car'. As was explained in Section 3.5.3, all cars are sorted into an

Object Type 'Car'. Likewise, all cars with a tow hitch are sorted into Fact Type 'Car With Tow Hitch', which can therefore also be seen as an Object Type, even though it is not enclosed in a circle (or ellipse). This is shown explicitly in Figure 6.12: below the two textboxes is a list of Subtypes, which contains 'Car With Tow Hitch'. Since a Fact Type is used to explicitly declare which cars have a tow hitch, this is a *Declarative Subtype*.

Two Business Rules are shown in the top textbox in Figure 6.12 that follow from the description given above. Please note that Business Rules are not a part of a conceptual information model and are shown in Figures 6.12–6.15 for convenience only. These Business Rules have been translated into Constraints on the Populations of the Fact Types, shown in the second textbox in Figure 6.12. Please note that Constraints are indeed a part of a conceptual information model and should always be shown. The Constraints are Stated informally, using a kind of pseudo-code. Constraint C1 demands that the Populations of Roles 5 and 9 are equal, which guarantees that only all the cars with a tow hitch have their towing capacity recorded. C1 is an example of an Equality Constraint, and could also be given as two Subset Constraints 5 --<>-- 9 (see Section 4.5.3). Constraint C2 effectively says that for any Tuple of Fact Type 'Car Range' the following must be true: the same car that is recorded in Role 6 must also occur in role 2, together with either the value 'hybrid' or 'electric' in Role 3 of the same Tuple of Fact Type 'Car Is Of Type'. So the driving range can only be recorded for electric or hybrid cars, in accordance with Business Rule B2.

Since Subtype 'Car With Tow Hitch' exists, there is a simpler way to realize Business Rule B1 that doesn't need an Equality Constraint on roles 5 and 9. Simply let Role 9 be played by Subtype 'Car With Tow Hitch' instead of by its Supertype 'Car' (these two different ways of Analyzing the same sentences is left as an exercise for the reader). Figure 6.13 shows this way of modeling: Role 9 played by the Subtype ensures that the towing capacity is recorded *only* for cars with a tow hitch, and Totality Constraint 3 on Role 9 ensures that it is recorded for *all* such cars. This realizes Business Rule B1 without needing an Equality Constraint, so now only C2 is left in the lower textbox.

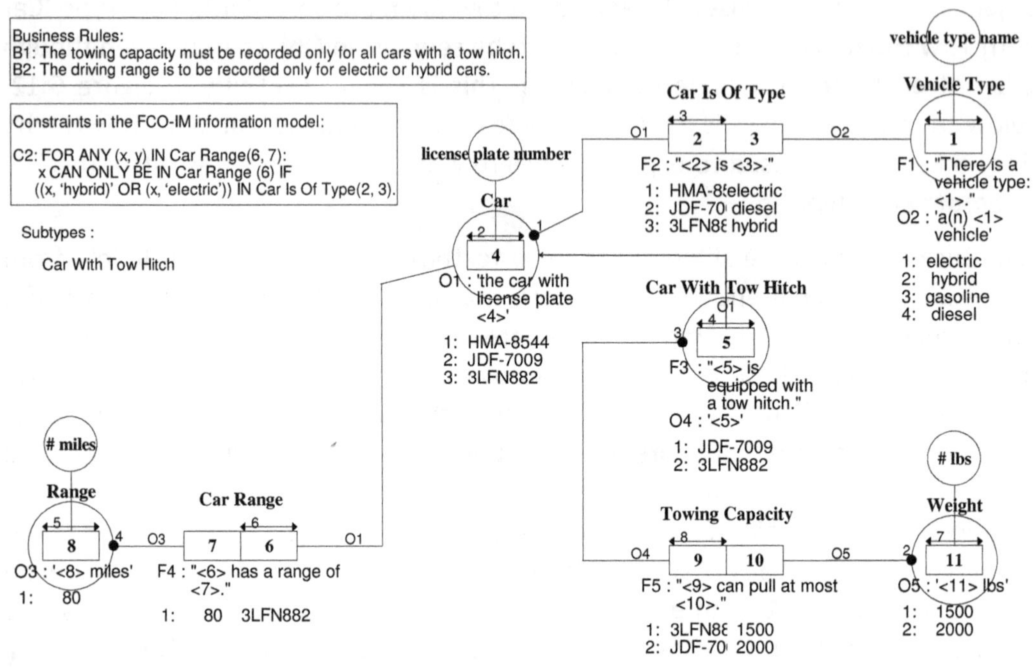

Figure 6.13 Subtype 'Car With Tow Hitch' plays a Role in Fact Type 'Towing Capacity'

This way of using Subtypes to model Business Rules like B1 yields diagrams that are much easier to read and requires less complex constraints, so we strongly recommend this way of modeling.

6.2.1.2 Derivable Subtype

Would it be possible to model Business Rule B2 in a similar way as B1? Let's try and see what happens. A subtype 'Electric Or Hybrid Cars' can be made using sentences like "The car with license plate 3LFN882 is an electric or hybrid car.". But this information is already present in Fact Type 'Car Is Of Type', which contains sentences like "The car with license plate 3LFN882 is a(n) hybrid vehicle.", from which the subtype-sentences can be easily derived (they're almost but not quite the same). Adding such derivable Subtype-sentences therefore also introduces a form of redundancy: The new Facts can be derived from existing Facts, so they add nothing really new. This will result in data pollution in no time if users are allowed to enter, update or delete such derived Facts (you'll be amazed to see how fast and in how many cases this would indeed happen), unless the system prevents all possible errors. Therefore, such *Derivable Fact Types* must have a *Derivation Rule*, which will specify its Population so the system can update these

Fact Types instead of the user. In FCO-IM, a Derivable Fact Type is marked with an asterisk (*) to signal the redundancy, and every Derivable Fact Type must have a Derivation Rule. Figure 6.14 shows the Derivable Fact Type 'Electric Or Hybrid Car' with its Derivation Rule D2 added to the second textbox. D2 states effectively that all cars that occur in the Population of Fact Type 'Car Is Of Type' together with either 'hybrid' or 'electric' in the same Tuple, are in the Population of 'Electric Or Hybrid Car'. Constraint C2 has been adapted a little, using the new Subtype instead of the original Fact Type 'Car Is Of Type'.

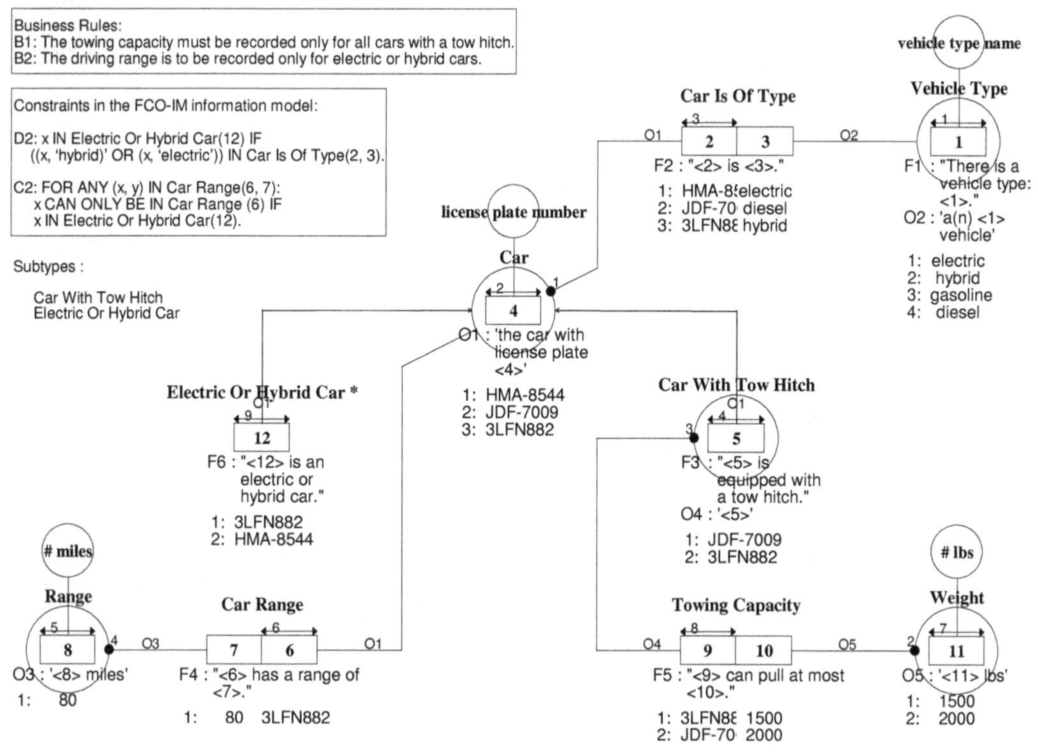

Figure 6.14 Derivable Subtype 'Electric Or Hybrid Car' with Derivation Rule

Since the Fact Type that models the new Subtype 'Electric Or Hybrid Car' is a Derivable Fact Type, this Subtype is not a Declarative Subtype but a Derivable Subtype. This new Subtype is now also present in the list of Subtypes given below the two textboxes in Figure 6.14.

With the new Derivable Subtype in place, it is possible to model Business Rule B2 in a similar way as was done with Business Rule B1. The result is shown in Figure 6.15. Role 6 is now played by Subtype 'Electric Or Hybrid Car' instead of by its

Supertype 'Car'. Role 6 now played by the Subtype ensures that the driving range is recorded *only* for electric or hybrid cars, and the absence of a Totality Constraint on Role 6 means that it does not have to be recorded for *all* such cars (B2 doesn't require this, whereas B1 does require the towing capacity to be recorded for *all* cars with a tow hitch). This realizes Business Rule B2 without needing C2, but here Derivation Rule D2 is needed to ensure the introduced redundancy cannot cause data pollution.

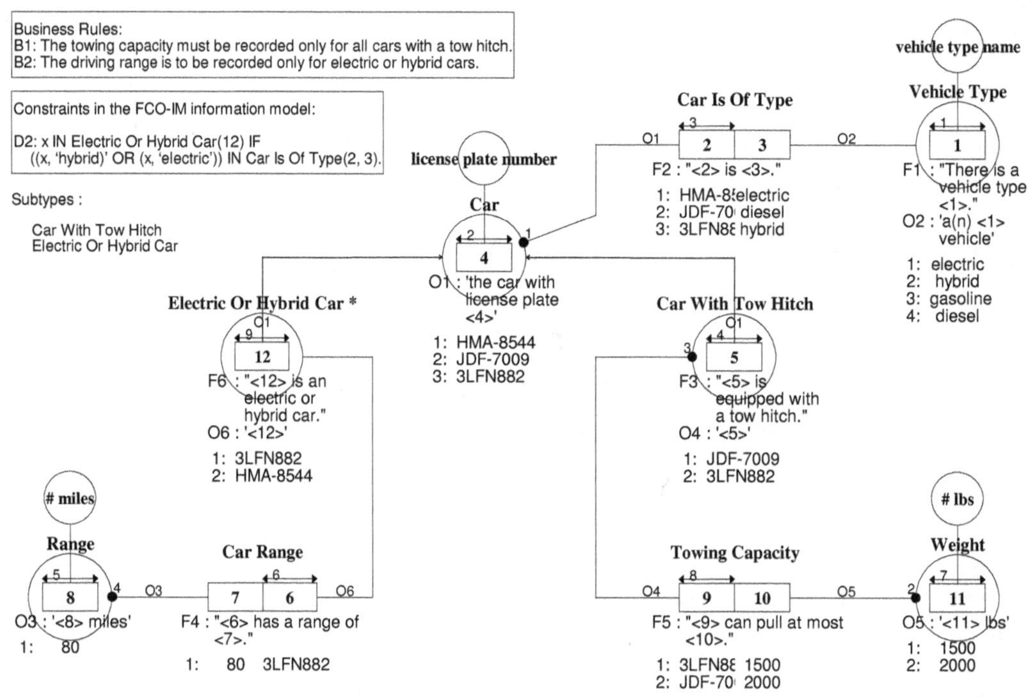

Figure 6.15 Subtype 'Electric Or Hybrid Car' plays a Role in Fact Type 'Car Range'

So a Derivable Subtype comes at the cost of having to specify a Derivation Rule for it. But then this way of using Subtypes to model Business Rules like B2 still yields diagrams that are much easier to read and requires less complex constraints, so in practice the trade-off is still a positive one. We strongly recommend this way of modeling for Derivable Subtypes.

Requirement for Derivation Rules of Derivable Subtypes

There is one hard requirement that every Derivation Rule for a Subtype must satisfy (see Textbox 6.16): any Fact Type mentioned after the word 'IF' in the Derivation Rule must be played by the Supertype, *not* by the Subtype itself.

Violating this requirement would lead to circular reasoning, a serious logical error (also known as 'begging the question'). The requirement in Textbox 6.16 covers the simple Subtypes discussed in this book and can be easily extended for more complex cases (multi-layered networks of Supertypes and Subtypes); for further reading, see Appendix B, [1, Section 6.1].

Requirement for Derivation Rules of Derivable Subtypes

A Derivation Rule for a Declarative Subtype has the general form:

> **x IN <Subtype>**
> **IF <condition using values in the Population of other Fact Types>**

All Fact Types used in the condition after the word 'IF' must be played by the Supertype, not by the Subtype itself.

Textbox 6.16 Requirement for Derivation Rules of Derivable Subtypes

Indeed, if it would not be possible to find a Derivation Rule that satisfies this requirement, then no Derivable Subtype should be made. Please check that all Derivation Rules for Subtypes in this book satisfy this requirement.

Although Business Rules are not a part of a conceptual information model, whereas Constraints are, there should be a clear and explicitly documented correspondence between the two. This should state for each Business Rule how it is modeled; for instance:

B1: Modeled by Declarative Subtype 'Car With Tow Hitch' playing Role 9 in Fact Type 'Towing Capacity', and Totality Constraint 3 on Role 9.

B2: Modeled by Derivable Subtype 'Electric Or Hybrid Car' playing Role 6 in Fact Type 'Car Range' with Derivation Rule D2.

See Appendix A3 for the complete list of Business Rules and how they are modeled in the Serviceton Music Theater case study.

6.2.2 DIFFERENCE BETWEEN SUBTYPES AND 'ORDINARY' OBJECT TYPES

There are differences between Fact Types that are Subtypes and Fact Types that are not Subtypes. At the conceptual level of an FCO-IM information model, there is a difference in what is being modeled. At the logical level of a derived Relational database, for example (see Chapter 7), there is a difference in which Fact Types can be seen as an attribute of a Subtype or of a non-Subtype. Both aspects are discussed below.

6.2.2.1 Conceptual Level: Difference in What Is Modeled by a Subtype or a Non-Subtype

Figure 6.17 illustrates these differences. It shows a correct information model, with a few Fact Types containing a small sample Population. These Fact Types are taken from a context with the following properties:

P1 The mean global temperature is recorded for every year. See Object Type 'Year', Fact Type 'Mean Global Temperature' and Totality Constraint 1 on Role 1.

P2 If there was a severe El Niño (also known as a warm El Niño Southern Oscillation (ENSO) phase, i.e. the ocean water near the west coast of Peru is much warmer than usual) in the first three months of a year, then such a year is marked as an 'El Niño Year'. See Fact Type 'El Niño Year'.

P3 Object Type 'El Niño Year' is a Subtype of Object Type 'Year', because it contains a subset of all the years with the special property that there was a severe El Niño in those years. See the list of Subtypes shown just above the Supertype 'Year'.

P4 A severe El Niño causes several abnormal climate conditions globally such as droughts in some areas and heavy rainfall in others. The estimated economic damage in Peru due to such an ENSO effect is recorded only for El Niño years. See Fact Type 'Economic Losses Peru', in which Role 6 is played by Subtype 'El Niño Year'.

P5 In the USA, presidential elections are held every four years. The presidential candidates in every election are recorded. See Fact Type 'Candidate In Election'.

P6 A particular election is identified by the AD-date of the year in which the election is held. See Object Expressions like 'the presidential election of 2012' used in Facts in the Population of Fact Type 'Candidate In Election'.

P7 Object Type 'Election' is *not* a Subtype of Object Type 'Year' because it *does not model any years*. It models elections, not election years. It is therefore not in the list of Subtypes shown just above Object Type 'Year'.

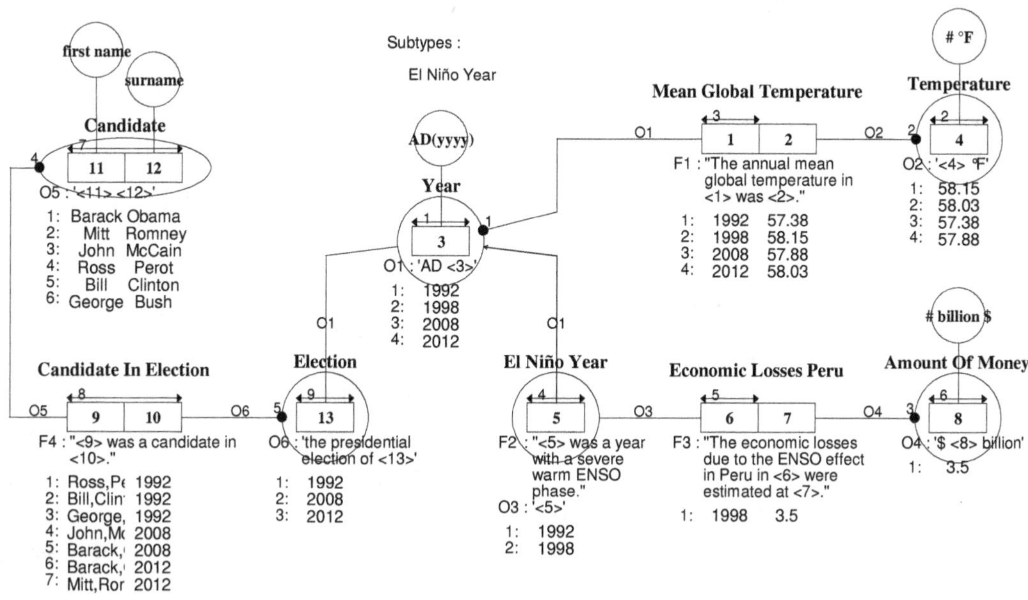

Figure 6.17 Difference between Subtypes and non-Subtypes

Properties P3 and P7 above highlight the difference between Subtype and non-Subtype Object Types. Although both 'Election' and 'El Niño Year' are identified by an AD date, elections are not years whereas El Niño years are indeed years. There is nothing in the structure of the information model from which this difference can be seen.

- Both 'Election' and 'El Niño Year' are Fact Types with one Role, played by 'Year'.
- In this example, 'El Niño Year' happens to have a Fact Expression Type, whereas 'Election' doesn't, but this difference is accidental and cannot be used to distinguish between Subtypes and non-Subtypes. A Fact Expression for 'Election' can be easily added with sentences like "There was a presidential election in AD 2008.".
- The Population of 'Election' can also be considered to be derivable: Elections are only held in a year with an AD date of 1788 or greater, which is divisible by 4 and is not later than the present year. But this Derivation Rule could apply equally well to Subtypes and non-Subtypes.

So the only way to make a distinction between Subtypes and non-Subtypes is by explicitly stating which Object Types are Subtypes. Therefore the list of Subtypes is an indispensable part of an information model and should always be shown in diagrams. The FCO-IM modeling tool CaseTalk (see Appendix B, [2]) provides a special notation for Subtypes: the line connecting a Role of a Subtype to its Supertype is thicker than other Role connections and is shaped like an arrow. Other information modeling techniques like ORM (see Appendix B, [10]), ERM (see Appendix B, [12]) and UML (see Appendix B, [13]) also contain special constructs to model subtypes.

6.2.2.2 Logical Level: Difference in Which Fact Types are Attributes of a Subtype or a Non-Subtype

The term 'attribute' is used in several non-elementary information modeling techniques like ERM, UML and Relational databases (see any textbook on those techniques) and refers to only a *part* of a complete elementary Fact. This term therefore rather belongs to the logical level, not the conceptual level. Fact Oriented Modeling methods are also called *'attribute-free'* to highlight they work only with complete elementary Fact Types and therefore do not need attributes. However, when deriving a logical data model from a conceptual information model (see Chapter 7 for details) it is important to use this term. In such derivations, many attributes come from Own Attribute Fact Types in the conceptual model (see Section 4.3.2). Subtypes and non-Subtypes are treated differently with respect to Own Attribute Fact Types.

Own Attribute Fact Types can be seen as attributes of the Object Type that plays the Role with the Uniqueness Constraint on it. So in Figure 6.17, Fact Type 'Mean Global Temperature' is an attribute of Object Type 'Year'. Likewise, 'Economic Losses Peru' is an attribute of 'El Niño Year'. But if Subtypes and Supertypes are involved, an Object Type may have more attributes than that. The following definition holds:

> The attributes of any Object Type are:
>
> - all its Own Attribute Fact Types, plus
> - if it has at least one Supertype: all the Own Attribute Fact Types of all its Supertypes.

So Fact Type 'Mean Global Temperature' is also an attribute of 'El Niño Year' but not of 'Election'.

This has consequences for Relational table structures that can be derived from the diagram in Figure 6.17. It is possible to generate a separate table for El Niño years that has a column 'Mean Global Temperature', but it is not possible to generate a separate table for elections that has a column 'Mean Global Temperature'. For further details, see Chapter 7 and Appendix B, [1, Section 7.1].

6.3 A Window on Further Modeling Power

This is an introductory book on Fact Oriented Modeling (FOM) in Fully Communication Oriented Information Modeling (FCO-IM). Nevertheless, many subjects are treated in depth and detail such as Verbalizing, Analyzing, and determining Uniqueness and Totality Constraints. Other subjects are discussed less profoundly like Constraints, Subtypes and transformations to other modeling techniques. Still other topics are only mentioned in passing—or not at all. This chapter closes with a short list of subjects that are outside the scope of this book, but do belong to the world of FOM and FCO-IM, just to show that beyond the hills lie fascinating mountains:

- **Constraints**. Many types of Constraints have been defined and can be specified in FOM, especially in Object Oriented Modeling (ORM) and its modeling tool Norma (see Appendix B, [10]): for instance, circular constraints and constraints on homogeneous Fact Types (Fact Types with two or more Roles played by the same Object Type). However, at present there is no overarching practical general technique of specifying Constraints available that does not require the arcane mathematical skills to use First Order Predicate Logic.
- **Subtypes**. Only Subtypes that have one Supertype are mentioned in this book. In practice, however, extensive networks of Subtypes can exist in which a Subtype can have several direct Supertypes and many layers of Supertypes of Supertypes, etc. There is also a good formal procedure to determine this network of Supertypes, called the Subtype Matrix Method. Further reading about this can be found in Appendix B, [1, Section 6.1.2].
- **Generalization**. This is a concept in which two or more Object Types are united into a more abstract 'generalized' higher-order Object Type without losing their own identity. In FCO-IM this concept even enables modelers to deal with recursive identification structures (like the hierarchy of directories and files on your computer, which can have paths of arbitrary depth) without introducing dummy numbers. FCO-IM is the *only* modeling

technique that can do this. Further reading about this can be found in Appendix B, [1, Section 6.2] and [9].

- **Metamodeling**. All information can be modeled in FCO-IM. The metadata (see Section 6.1.2) of any specific FCO-IM model (Fact Types, Object Types, Fact Expression Types, Constraints etc.) can also be seen as an example of information to be modeled. Modeling metadata produces an information *metamodel.* Designing CASE tools, or building algorithms to transform an FCO-IM model into a Data Vault model, is all about metamodeling. Creating a good information metamodel is one of the most challenging and interesting aspects in the field of information modeling and part of current research in FCO-IM (see for instance Appendix B, [4] and [7]).

- **Transactions**. A transaction is a series of updates in the Population of a database. An *elementary transaction* contains the smallest number of updates necessary to change the Population so it will still satisfy all the Constraints. From an elementary FCO-IM data model, a set of elementary transactions can be derived. This approach in which the building blocks of processes are generated automatically from the data model is also a current line of research in FCO-IM (see Appendix B, [4]).

Chapter 7
Model Transformations

Chapters 3 through 6 show how to create an FCO-IM information model by Collecting concrete examples, Verbalizing Facts, Sorting and Analyzing Fact Expressions, drawing a diagram and adding Constraints. We will refer to an FCO-IM diagram in this chapter as an IGD, from its technical name Information Grammar Diagram, which is also used in CaseTalk (see Appendix B, [2]). The subject of this chapter is how to derive other models from an elementary IGD such as a Relational database schema (see Appendix B, [14]) and an Entity-Relationship Model diagram (see Appendix B, [12]). For these transformations from an IGD to other models, only the most common cases that might occur in an IGD will be illustrated. Subtypes, for example, are not taken into account (for this, see Appendix B, [1, Section 7.1]).

When data modelers carry out such transformations in practice, they use software tools to get the job done almost completely automatically. Therefore, not all of the intricate details of the transformations will be discussed in this chapter, but enough to understand the essence and possibilities of the model transformations. The main idea behind these transformations holds not only for these, but also for transformations to other modeling techniques. This is because a conceptual information model in terms of elementary Facts can be relatively easily translated into a model of another technique by updating the *metadata* while preserving the Verbalizations, the structure of the elementary Fact Types, and the Constraints.

7.1 Transformation of an FCO-IM IGD Into a Relational Database Schema

This section treats the transformation from an elementary FCO-IM IGD to a Relational database schema, i.e., a database schema with which a Relational database can be created, to store and maintain the modeled information in a redundancy-free way. The reader is expected to be familiar with the concepts and the terminology of the Relational model (see any textbook on Relational databases).

7.1.1 WHAT IS A RELATIONAL DATABASE, REALLY?

Key Point

- **A Relational database is really a storage medium for Facts.**

A Relational database is more than a collection of tables in which rows with data values are kept. What kinds of things are actually stored in a Relational database? An example will be used to answer this question and to link databases with the rest of the subjects in this book. Consider the Relational database schema below. It describes a collection of tables for storing a part of the customer related data for Serviceton Music Theater (addresses are omitted for brevity, as are some other metadata (see Section 6.1.2) for reservation requests).

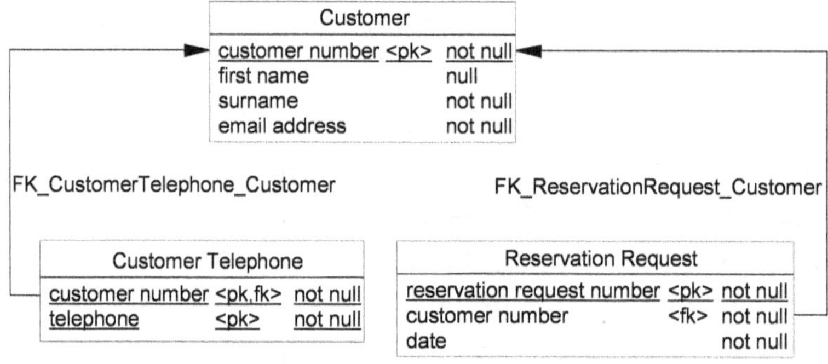

Figure 7.1 Database schema with customer related metadata

In Figure 7.1, tables are shown as rectangles containing a list of their columns (or attributes); '<pk>' stands for Primary Key and '<fk>' for Foreign Key. The primary key columns are underlined as well (redundantly, since the '<pk>'s indicate the same thing, but whereas redundancy is to be avoided or strictly controlled in digital systems, it is nice for us visually inclined humans). The foreign key references, named FK_..., are shown as arrows pointing from the child table column to the parent table column. Each column has a 'null' or 'not null' indicator telling whether or not it is allowed that there is a row in the table without a value entered into this column. In Figure 7.2, the three tables are presented with an example Population in a different layout with the columns listed horizontally, enabling the Population to be entered as rows. The foreign key references and 'not null' indicators are omitted here, but the primary key is still visible by the underlining of its column name(s) to help visualize the point to be made below.

Table Customer

customer number	first name	surname	email address
436	Leonard	Reed	LeonardReed@ip4me.com
512	Jim	Jones	JJones@planet.com

Table Customer Telephone

customer number	telephone
436	+1-6-5432-6789
512	831-969-7531
512	06-3535-9811

Table Reservation Request

reservation request number	customer number	date
587	436	January 12, 2015
588	512	January 12, 2015

Figure 7.2 Database tables with Population

Table 'Customer'

The meaning of the data in the first row of the table 'Customer' can be expressed in natural language by Verbalizing Facts (see Section 3.3). For each value in a non-primary key column, an elementary Fact Expression is created by verbalizing this value in relation to the value in the primary key column of the same row: 436, in this case.

customer number	first name	surname	email address
436	Leonard	Reed	LeonardReed@ip4me.com

Figure 7.3 Elementary Facts in table 'Customer'

This results in the following three Fact Expressions:

```
"The first name of customer 436 is: Leonard."
"The surname of customer 436 is: Reed."
```

"The email address of customer 436 is: LeonardReed@ip4me.com."

Verbalizing the Facts stored in the second row of the table Customer in Figure 7.2 yields:

"The first name of customer 512 is: Jim."
"The surname of customer 512 is: Jones."
"The email address of customer 512 is: JJones@planet.com."

So table 'Customer' holds the Population of three Fact Types. The semantics of this table can be expressed by using the corresponding Fact Expression Types (see Section 3.5.1):

"The first name of customer <customer number> is: <first name>."
"The surname of customer <customer number> is: <surname>."
"The email address of customer <customer number> is: <email address>."

Table 'Reservation Request'

Similarly, the table 'Reservation Request' holds Facts. The Facts in this table, grouped by row, can be verbalized like this:

"Reservation request 587 was made by customer 436."
"Reservation request 587 was registered on January 12, 2015."

"Reservation request 588 was made by customer 512."
"Reservation request 588 was registered on January 13, 2015."

The corresponding Fact Expression Types, which describe the semantics of this table, are:

"Reservation request <reservation request number> was made by customer <customer number>."
"Reservation request <reservation request number> was registered on <date>."

Table 'Customer Telephone'

All columns of the table 'Customer Telephone' are part of the primary key. In such a case, each row contains one Fact. The table holds the following Facts:

"Customer 436 can be phoned at +1-6-5432-6789."
"Customer 512 can be phoned at 831-969-7531."
"Customer 512 can be phoned at 06-3535-9811."

The corresponding Fact Expression Type, which describes the semantics of this table, is:

"Customer <customer number> can be phoned at <telephone>."

The examples above illustrate that each table of a Relational database holds Facts about the domain in question. A database table is equivalent to a set of one or more elementary Fact Types. Therefore, a Relational database is really a *'Fact Base'*: a storage medium for Facts.

In our experience, database users can benefit greatly from regarding the contents of tables as collections of several *elementary Facts*, as illustrated explicitly in Figure 7.3. In other words, a table does not consist of a bunch of separate columns, but of a bunch of small *clusters of columns* in which each cluster contains one elementary Fact Type (see also Sections 3.3.3.2 and 1.3.1).

7.1.2 DERIVATION OF A RELATIONAL SCHEMA: INDICATING TABLES IN THE IGD

The previous Section 7.1.1 shows that a table in a Relational database can hold Facts from different elementary Fact Types. Therefore, if a Relational database schema is to be derived from an IGD, the aim is to combine as many Fact Types as possible in the same table without introducing redundancy (i.e. without ever having to store the same Fact more than once). The resulting number of tables is then as small as possible.

The procedure to identify the tables that can be derived from an elementary IGD is described in this section. This procedure is illustrated with the IGD in Figure 7.4. This IGD relates to the performance schedule of the Serviceton Music Theater case (see Chapter 2 and Chapters 3 through 6, which concern the same context). However, please note that the model in Figure 7.4 contains a few differences compared with the 'real' model for the performance schedule developed in Chapters 3 through 6 and Appendix A, which we introduced for didactical reasons. The most striking difference is the Uniqueness Constraint (UC; see Section 4.2) on Fact Type 'Show In Genre'. In this section it is assumed that each show is in exactly one genre, so there is a UC 17 on only Role 6 here, whereas in the 'real' model there is a UC 11 on the combination of Roles 6+7. Furthermore, the Fact Expression Types for 'Calendar Day' and 'Time Of Day' are dropped, and the words 'date', 'time' and 'price' are written inside Roles 13, 16 and 23, respectively. These words will be used to derive clearer column names (see Section 7.1.3.4).

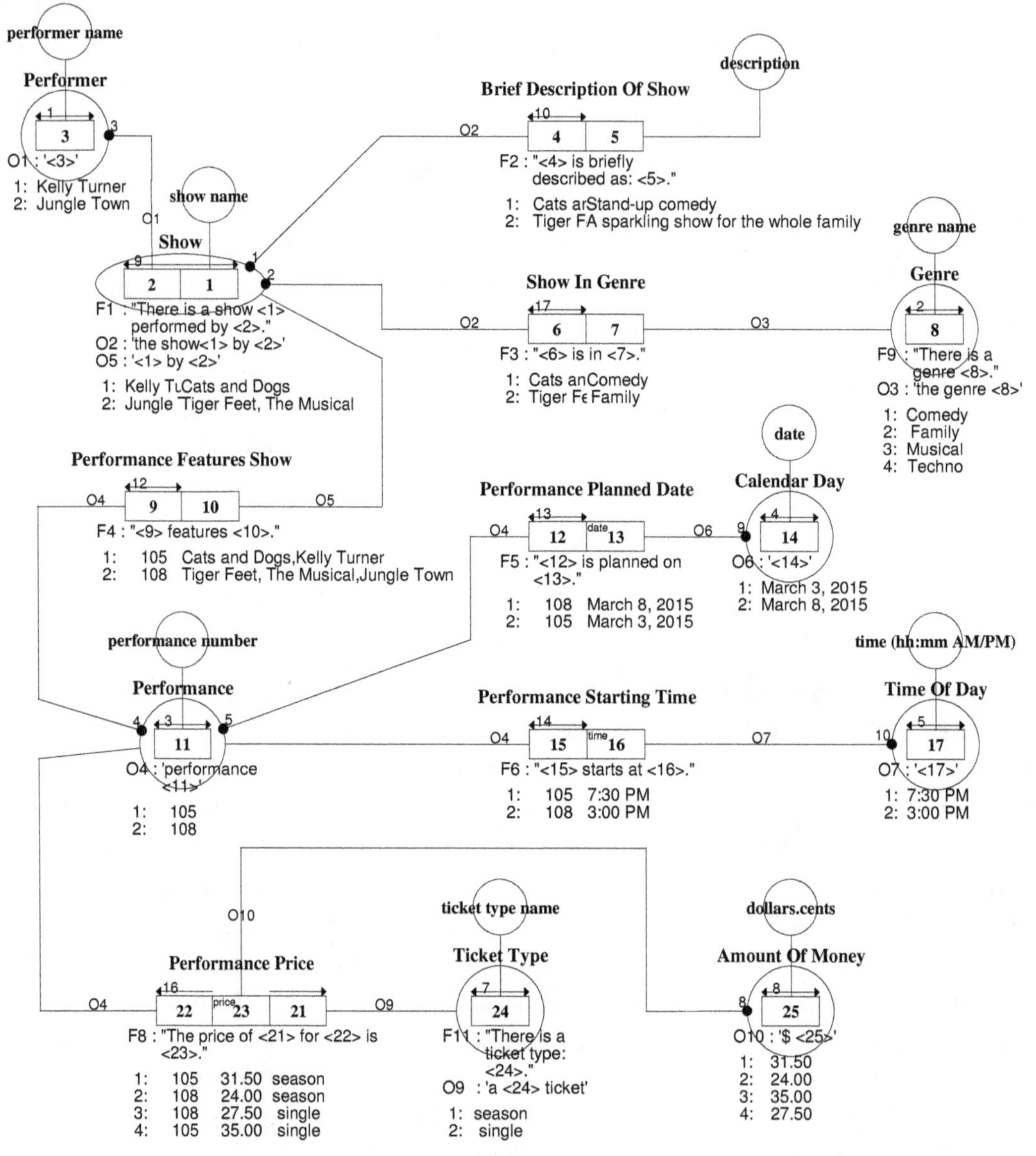

Figure 7.4 Elementary IGD for the performance schedule (slightly modified)

7.1.2.1 Placing Fact Types Together in one Table

When transforming an elementary IGD to a Relational database schema, Facts from different Fact Types might be placed together in one database table. Indeed, the aim is to combine as many Fact Types as possible (see Section 7.1.2). So the following question arises: Which Fact Types from the IGD in Figure 7.4 can be grouped into the same table? The key to its answer lies in Object Types that have Own Attribute Fact Types (see Definition 4.23), as is illustrated in the examples below.

Object Type 'Show'

In Figure 7.4, consider Object Type 'Show' and its Own Attribute Fact Types: 'Brief Description Of Show' and 'Show In Genre'. *Each show* has *one brief description* (Uniqueness Constraint 10 on Role 4) and is in *one genre* (Uniqueness Constraint 17 on Role 6). Therefore, the following Facts can be combined in one row of the database table 'Show':

```
"There is a show Cats and Dogs performed by Kelly Turner."
"The show Cats and Dogs by Kelly Turner is briefly described as:
  Stand-up comedy."
"The show Cats and Dogs by Kelly Turner is in the genre Comedy."
```

Another row of the same table will contain the following Facts:

```
"There is a show Tiger Feet, The Musical performed by Jungle
  Town."
"The show Tiger Feet, The Musical by Jungle Town is briefly
  described as: A sparkling show for the whole family."
"The show Tiger Feet, The Musical by Jungle Town is in the genre
  Family."
```

The table 'Show' with its Population then looks like this (the primary key is underlined):

Table Show

<u>show name</u> (Role 1)	**<u>Performer</u>** (Role 2)	**description** (Role 5)	**Genre** (Role 7)
Cats and Dogs	Kelly Turner	Stand-up comedy	Comedy
Tiger Feet, The Musical	Jungle Town	A sparkling show for the whole family	Family

Note that Roles 1, 2, 5 and 7 correspond with columns of the table. The primary key of this table matches Uniqueness Constraint 9 on Roles 1 and 2, the identifying Roles of Object Type Show. The Fact Expressions Types, stating the table's semantics, are:

```
"There is a show <show name> performed by <Performer>."
"The show <show name> by <Performer> is briefly described as:
  <description>."
"The show <show name> by <Performer> is in the genre <Genre>."
```

Object Type 'Performance'

Object Type 'Performance' has Own Attribute Fact Types (see Definition 4.23) as well, namely 'Performance Features Show', 'Performance Planned Date' and 'Performance Starting Time'. *Each performance* features *one show* (Uniqueness Constraint 12 on Role 9), is planned on *one date* (Uniqueness Constraint 13 on Role 12) and is planned at *one time* (Uniqueness Constraint 14 on Role 15). So the following Facts from these Own Attribute Fact Types can be combined in one row of the database table 'Performance':

"Performance 105 features Cats and Dogs by Kelly Turner."
"Performance 105 is planned on March 3, 2015."
"Performance 105 starts at 7:30 PM."

Another row of the same table will contain the following Facts:

"Performance 108 features Tiger Feet, The Musical by Jungle Town."
"Performance 108 is planned on March 8, 2015."
"Performance 108 starts at 3:00 PM."

The resulting table is shown below:

Table Performance

<u>performance number</u> (Role 11)	**Show** (Role 10)		**date** (Role 13)	**time** (Role 16)
	show name	**Performer**		
105	Cats and Dogs	Kelly Turner	March 3, 2015	7:30 PM
108	Tiger Feet, The Musical	Jungle Town	March 8, 2015	3:00 PM

Please note that each of the Roles 11, 10, 13 and 16 corresponds with a (combination of) column(s) of the table. The primary key of this table matches Uniqueness Constraint 3 on Role 11, the identifying Role of Object Type 'Performance'. The Fact Expressions Types that belong to the table 'Performance' are:

"Performance <performance number> features <show name> by <performer>."
"Performance <performance number> is planned on <date>."
"Performance <performance number> starts at <time>."

The conclusion of this section is therefore that an Object Type that has Own Attribute Fact Types can be grouped into one database table together with these Fact Types. In the IGD in Figure 7.4, this applies to Object Types 'Show' and

'Performance'. When a database schema from this IGD is derived, tables containing several Fact Types will be created for 'Show' and 'Performance'.

7.1.2.2 Visualizing Tables in an IGD

It is quite easy to spot at a glance which tables will result from an FCO-IM IGD. Therefore, in this section the findings of the previous Section 7.1.2.1 will be visualized in the IGD. For each table a polygon will be drawn covering the corresponding Fact Type(s) (see Figure 7.7 for the result). The working method to identify the tables consists of four steps, which are given in Textbox 7.5 and discussed one by one below.

Step 1

See the procedure in Textbox 7.5 that summarizes the following explanation. In the IGD in Figure 7.6, one polygon covers Object Type 'Performance' and its Own Attribute Fact Types 'Performance Features Show', 'Performance Planned Date' and 'Performance Starting Time' (step 1A). This polygon expresses that these Fact Types can be grouped into the table 'Performance'. The Role of an Own Attribute Fact Type that is not covered by a Uniqueness Constraint is called an *Attribute Role*. Role 11 and the Attribute Roles 10, 13 and 16 are marked to indicate that these Roles correspond with columns in the table 'Performance' (step 1B). Uniqueness Constraint 3 on Role 11, the identifying Role of Object Type 'Performance', corresponds with the primary key of table 'Performance' (step 1C).

Similarly, another polygon covers Object Type 'Show' and its Own Attribute Fact Types 'Brief Description Of Show' and 'Show In Genre' to indicate that these can all be grouped into the table 'Show' (step 1A). Roles 1, 2, 5 and 7 correspond with columns of this table (step 1B). The primary key of the table matches Uniqueness Constraint 9 on Roles 1 and 2 (step 1C).

Step 1: Group Object Types with their Own Attribute Fact Types.

Definition of *Attribute Role*:

> The Role of an Own Attribute Fact Type (see Definition 4.23) that is not covered by a Uniqueness Constraint is called an Attribute Role.

For each Object Type that has Own Attribute Fact Types:

A Draw a polygon that covers the Object Type and its Own Attribute Fact Types to visualize the table.

B Mark the Roles of the Object Type and the Attribute Roles of the Own Attribute Fact Types in the polygon to indicate that these Roles will be transformed to columns of the table.

C Designate as primary key the Uniqueness Constraint that is inside the Object Type (and so expresses how it is identified).

Step 2: Indicate other Fact Types as tables.

For each remaining Fact Type that is not inside an Object Type, a separate table will be created:

A Draw a polygon around this Fact Type to visualize the table.

B Mark the Roles of this Fact Type to indicate that these Roles will be transformed to columns of the table.

Step 3: Indicate other Object Types as tables or cross them out.

For each remaining Object Type with a Fact Expression Type (for such Object Types, a separate domain table will be created):

A Draw a polygon around this Object Type to visualize the table.

B Mark the Role(s) of this Object Type to mark they will become columns.

For each remaining Object Type (it doesn't have a Fact Expression Type, and for such Object Types, no table will be created):

C Cross out this Object Type.

Step 4: Add references between tables.

Definition of *Connector*:

A connector is the line that indicates that a Role is played by an Object Type.

For each connector between polygons:

A Turn the connector into an arrow, pointing

- from the role in one polygon
- to the Object Type within the other polygon with the arrow's point at the border of the other polygon.

These arrows indicate foreign key to primary key references.

Textbox 7.5 Procedure to visualize tables in an FCO-IM IGD

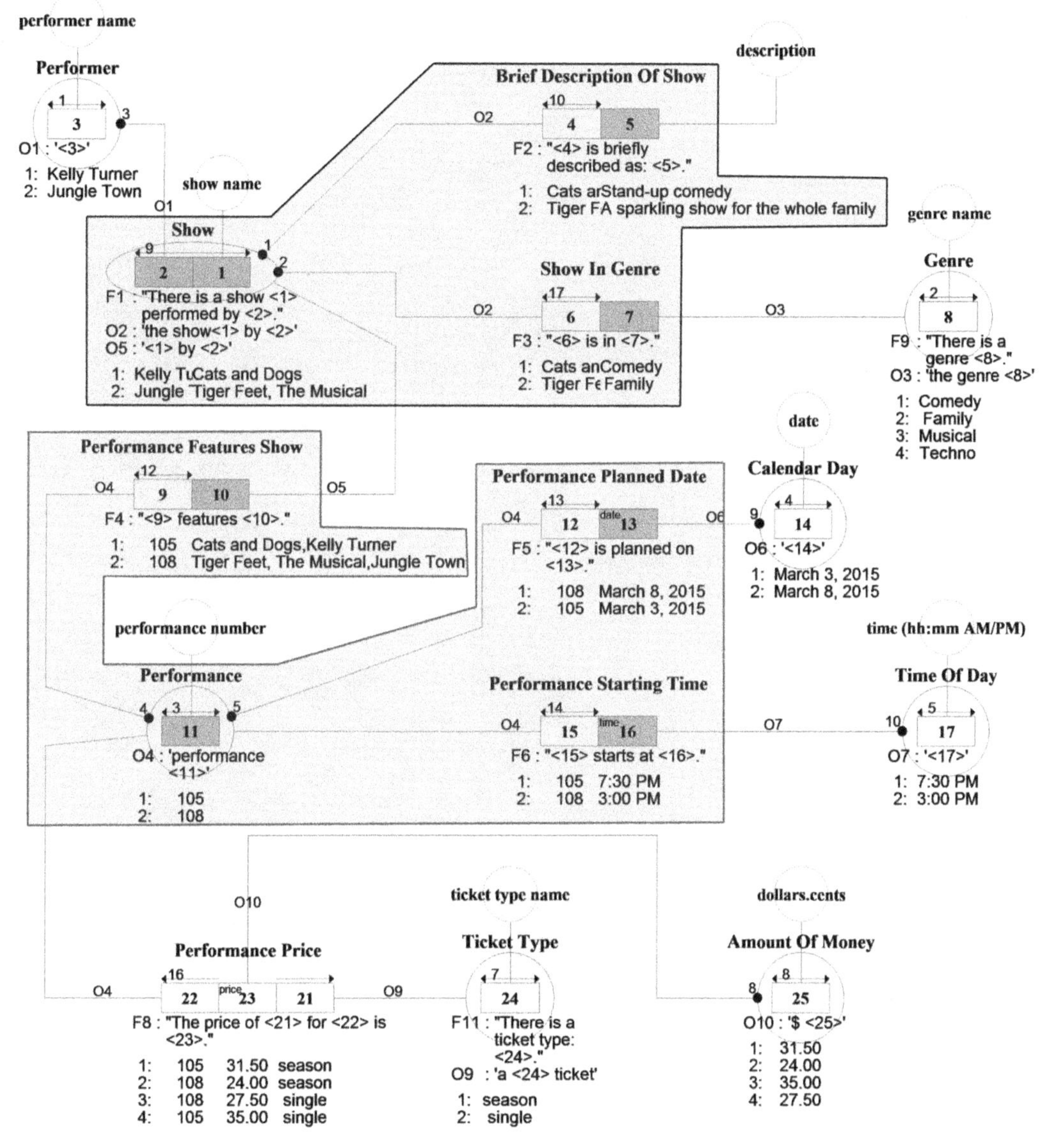

Figure 7.6 Elementary IGD with polygons for Object Types with Own Attribute Fact Types

Step 2

Step 2 in the procedure in Textbox 7.5 applies to Fact Type 'Performance Price' in the example IGD; see the result in Figure 7.7. A polygon that encloses 'Performance Price' is drawn to indicate it as a table (step 2A), and its Roles are marked to indicate that they correspond with columns (step 2B).

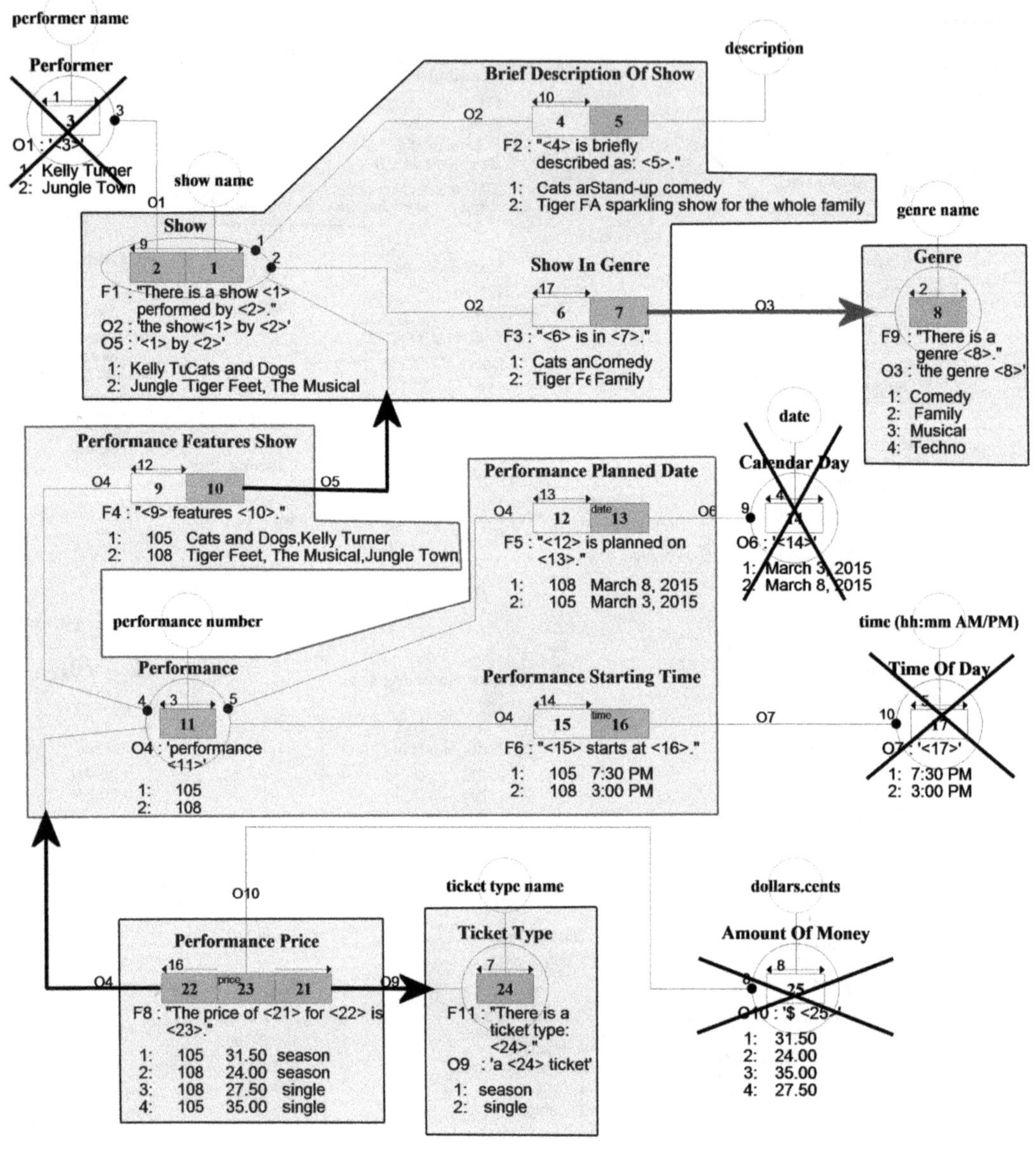

Figure 7.7 Elementary IGD with polygons to indicate tables and arrows to indicate FK → PK references

Step 3

Step 3 in the procedure in Textbox 7.5 applies to the remaining (i.e. not yet covered by a polygon) Object Types 'Genre' and 'Ticket Type' since they have Fact Expression Types. For these Object Types, a domain list is desired. This means that there will be a domain table, i.e., a table to hold domain values, in the database.

For example, table 'Ticket Type' will hold the values 'season' and 'single'. Therefore, in Figure 7.7 polygons covering these Object Types are drawn (step 3A). Their Roles are marked to indicate that they correspond with columns (step 3B).

The remaining (i.e. not yet covered by a polygon) Object Types ′Performer′, ′Calendar Day′, ′Time Of Day′ and ′Amount Of Money′ are crossed out (i.e. marked with a big X to show they do not lead to a separate table) in step 3C. See the result in Figure 7.7.

Step 4

In the IGD in Figure 7.7, four foreign key to primary key references are determined because four connectors between polygons exist (see step 4 in Textbox 7.5): from Show (Role 7) to Genre, from Performance (Role 10) to Show, from Performance Price (Role 21) to Ticket Type and from Performance Price (Role 22) to Performance.

So after applying steps 1 to 4 from the procedure in Textbox 7.5, it can be seen at a glance that the database derived from the IGD in Figure 7.4 consists of the five tables 'Show', 'Performance', 'Performance Price', 'Genre' and 'Ticket Type'. Furthermore, there is a first indication about the columns, primary keys and foreign keys of these tables. In the next section, this will be worked out in more detail.

7.1.3 DERIVATION OF A RELATIONAL SCHEMA: GROUP, LEXICALIZE, REDUCE AND CONVERT

In this section four operations on the IGD are discussed, which will lead to a Relational database schema. The approach is to change the IGD in steps so it will be transformed into a Relational schema in disguise using the FCO-IM diagramming technique. Some of the steps can be used to transform an IGD to other modeling techniques as well (see Section 7.2). These steps are:

- Group: Combine Fact Types and Object Types that will fit in the same table.
- Lexicalize: Remove Object Types so only Fact Types and Label Types are left.
- Reduce: Remove superfluous tables (if any).
- Convert: Generate meaningful table and column names.

Each step is illustrated in a separate section below.

7.1.3.1 Group

The background for the first step 'Group' is explained in the previous Section 7.1.2. To Group means to combine Object Types and their Own Attribute Fact Types (see Definition 4.23). The two big polygons in Figure 7.7 express that the Fact Types 'Brief Description Of Show' and 'Show In Genre' can be grouped with Object Type 'Show' and that Fact Types 'Performance Features Show', 'Performance Planned Date' and 'Performance Starting Time' can be grouped with Object Type 'Performance'.

The result of this grouping is shown in the G-IGD (Grouped-IGD) in Figure 7.8. The most important changes made to Object Type 'Show' and its Own Attribute Fact Types, compared to the elementary IGD in Figure 7.7, are:

- The Attribute Roles (see the definition in Textbox 7.5) Role 5 from Fact Type 'Brief Description Of Show' and Role 7 from 'Show In Genre' (highlighted in Figure 7.7) were moved into the Fact Type inside Object Type 'Show'.
- The Fact Expression Types from 'Brief Description Of Show' and 'Show In Genre', F2 and F3, were moved into 'Show' as well and adjusted (Object Expression Type O2 was substituted).
- The Tuples from the Populations of 'Brief Description Of Show' and 'Show In Genre' were joined with the Population of 'Show'.
- The Fact Types 'Brief Description Of Show' and 'Show In Genre' were removed.

Object Type 'Performance' and its Own Attribute Fact Types 'Performance Features Show', 'Performance Planned Date' and 'Performance Starting Time' were changed likewise, see the result in Figure 7.8. There is an important extra remark to make about Role 16. In the elementary IGD (see Figure 7.7), there was no Totality Constraint on Role 15 of Fact Type ´Performance Starting Time´, so the starting time is not mandatory for a performance. *After grouping*, null values might therefore appear in the Population of Role 16 (usually indicated by a dash: '-'), for each performance without a starting time (in the example Population, no null values happen to exist). Therefore Role 16 has become optional after grouping (marked 'OP' in Figure 7.8).

Figure 7.8 shows the IGD after Grouping. This is called a G-IGD. Please note that this is no longer an elementary IGD. Object Types 'Show' and 'Performance' are now clusters of three elementary Fact Types each (three Fact Expression Types for one Fact Type; see Section 5.2). These Object Types now violate the N Rule (see Section 5.3.1) and Role 16 is now optional. All of these things are impossible in an elementary IGD. Still, exactly the same Fact Expressions are modeled in Figures 7.8 and 7.9; you can easily verify this using the procedure in Section 3.5. A G-IGD is a transformed IGD, about halfway between an elementary information model and a Relational schema, with optimal clusters of Fact Types without redundancy.

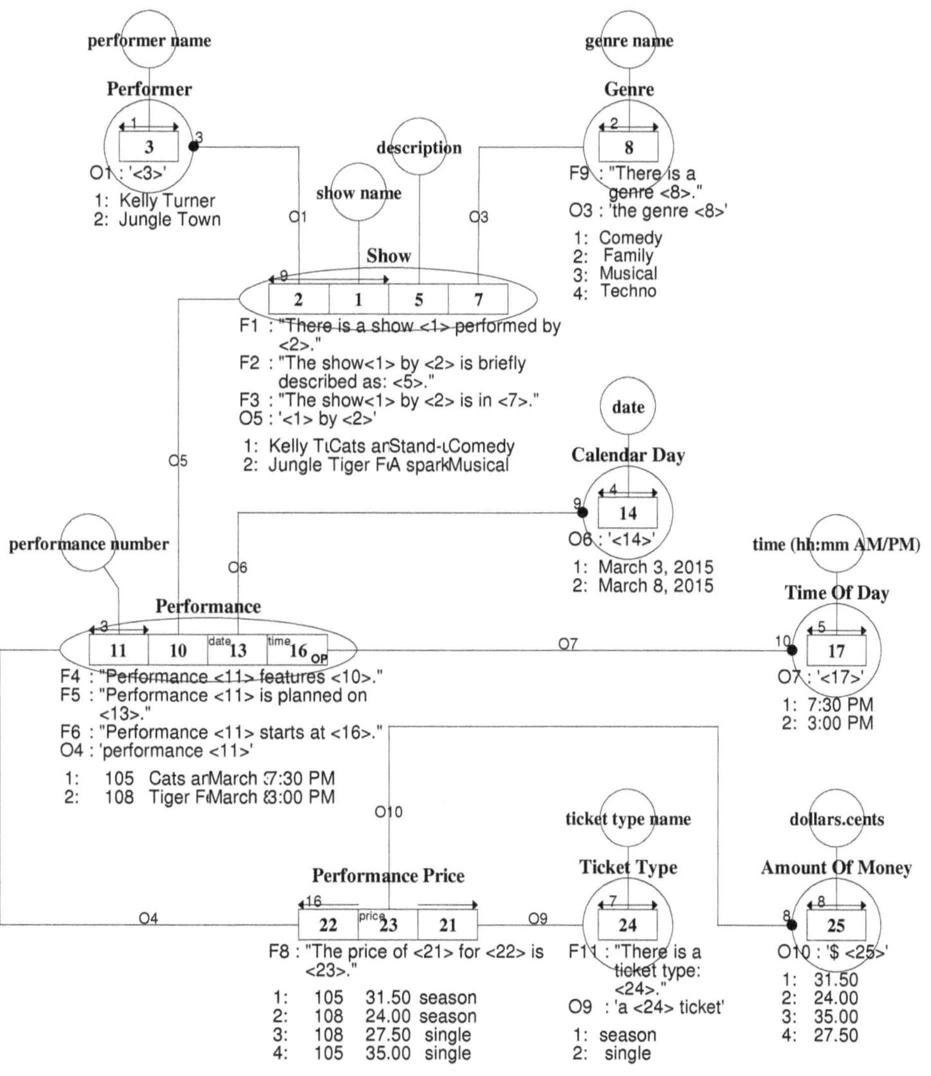

Figure 7.8: IGD after the step Group: G-IGD

Constraints that might be lost

If an elementary IGD is grouped, it should be checked that no constraints are lost in the process. Consider, for example, the elementary IGD for customer information in Figure 7.9 (again, this deviates for didactical reasons in a few respects from the 'real' information model for Serviceton Music Theater in Appendix A). In this IGD there is a Uniqueness Constraint (UC 66) on Role 38, expressing that each customer has at most one phone number, and a Totality Constraint (TC 15) on the combination of Roles 35 and 38, meaning that a customer must have a phone number and/or an email address.

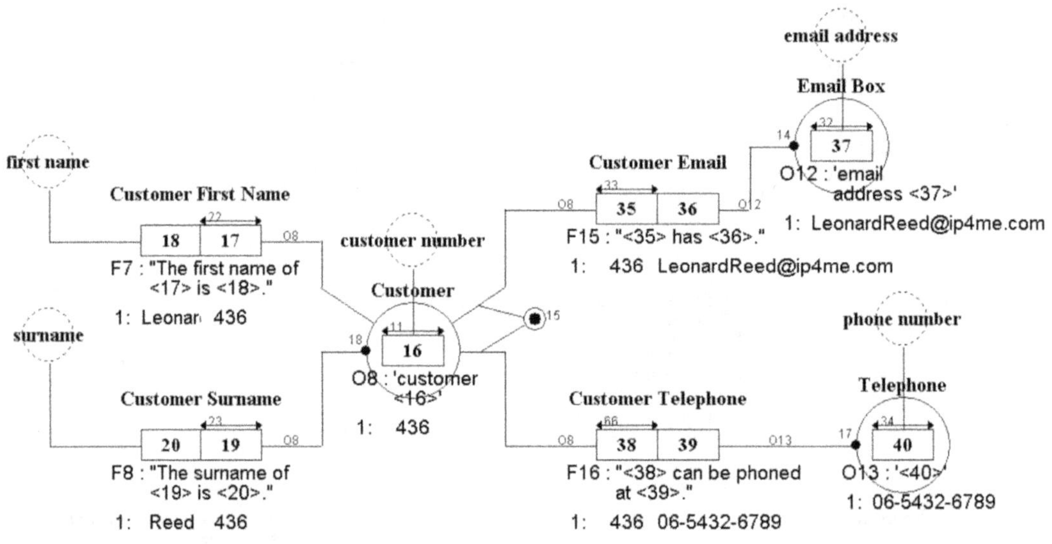

Figure 7.9 Elementary IGD for customer information, version 1

After grouping (see Figure 7.10), Roles 36 and 39 are moved to Fact Type 'Customer'. Both Roles have become optional because a null value in either Role is allowed in each Tuple. But TC 15 expresses that it is *not* allowed to have a null value in *both* Roles in the same Tuple. This is not covered by making both Roles optional, which means that TC 15 was lost in the process. So an extra Constraint has to be supplied to the grouped model: "A customer must have a phone number and/or email address." added as Textbox in the IGD in Figure 7.10. In a later stage this Constraint will be translated to an integrity rule in the logical Relational schema.

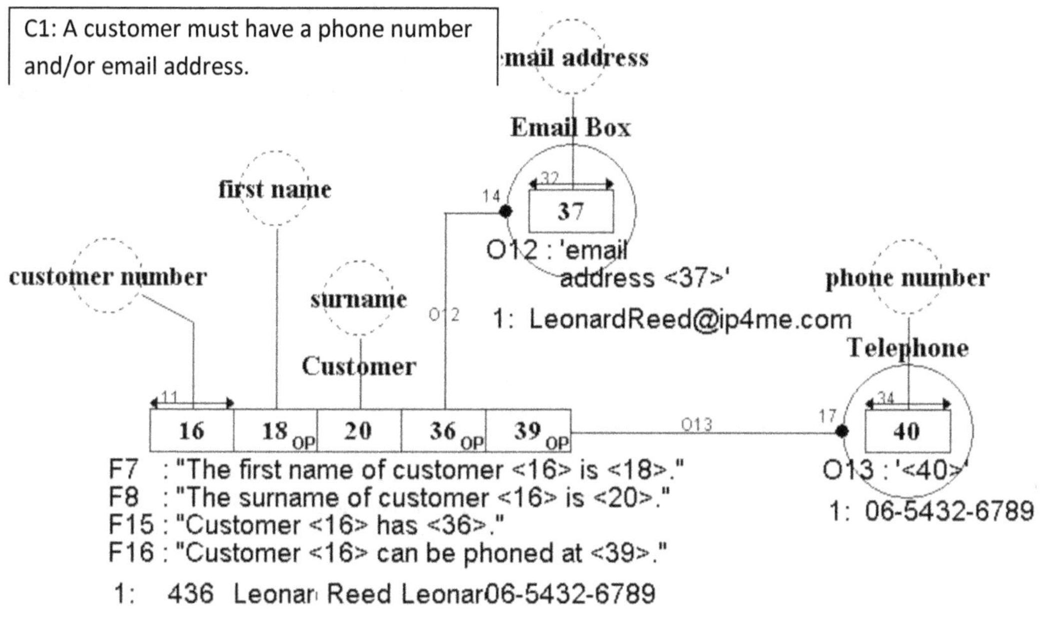

Figure 7.10 G-IGD with constraint C1 to replace TC 15

Group Fact Types with Two Single Role Uniqueness Constraints

A case that occurs quite often is when a Fact Type with two Roles has two Uniqueness Constraints, one on each Role (see Section 4.2.1). Consider the IGD in Figure 7.11. Fact Type 'Invoice For Reservation Request' has two Single Role Uniqueness Constraints. According to Definition 4.23, a Fact Type with two Single Role Uniqueness Constraints is not an Attribute Fact Type.

Nevertheless, a Fact Type with two Single Role Uniqueness Constraints can be grouped. To which Object Type it will be grouped depends on the Totality Constraints on the Roles of this Fact Type. If only one of the Roles has a Totality Constraint and the other one does not, then the Fact Type can be considered as an Own Attribute Fact Type of the Object Type that plays the mandatory Role and be grouped accordingly. In the IGD in Figure 7.11, there is a Totality Constraint 4 on Role 12 and no Totality Constraint on Role 13. Therefore the Fact Type 'Invoice For Reservation Request' will be considered as an Own Attribute Fact Type of Object Type 'Invoice' and it will be grouped to 'Invoice'. Role 13 did not become optional after grouping because of TC 4; every invoice must be for a reservation request, so there can be no null value in the Population of Role 13 even after grouping. The result of grouping in this way is displayed in Figure 7.12.

If you would have grouped the other way around, then Role 12 would be moved to Object Type 'Reservation Request' and would have become optional (because Role 13 does not have a TC). If possible, it is better to avoid optional Roles (handling null values in a database is awkward at best, and not all database management systems process them properly).

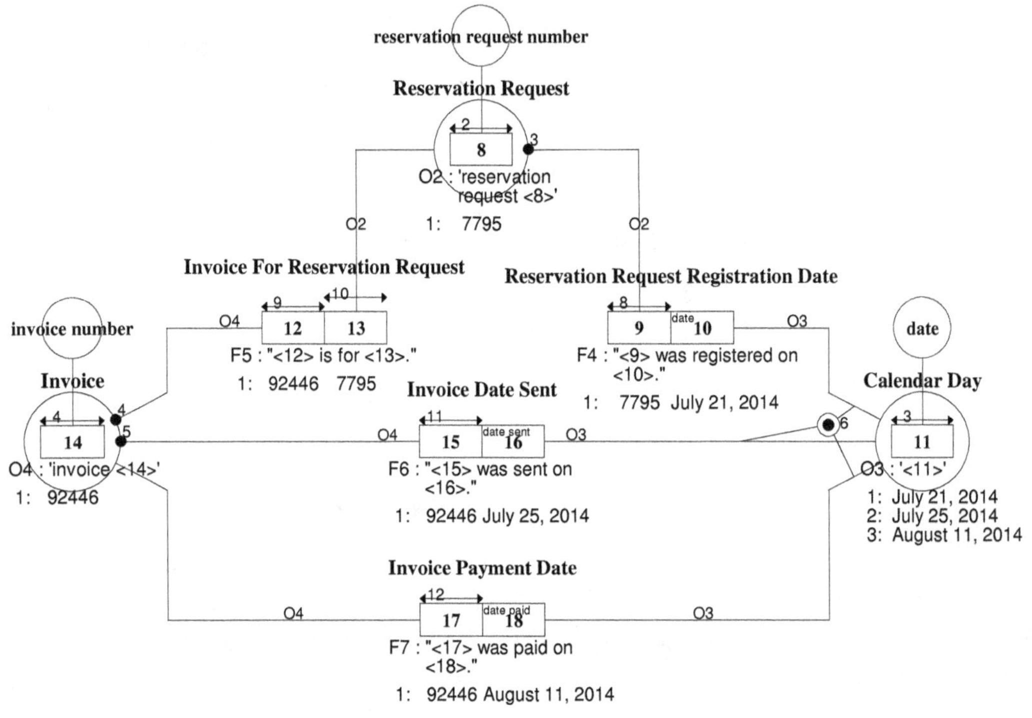

Figure 7.11 IGD with Fact Type with two Single Role UCs, before grouping

If both Roles have a Totality Constraint, or if neither Role has one, then the modeler can choose to consider the Fact Type as Own Attribute Fact Type of either one of the Object Types. In these cases there is no preference, and one can be chosen arbitrarily. For further details, see Appendix B, [1, Section 4.1].

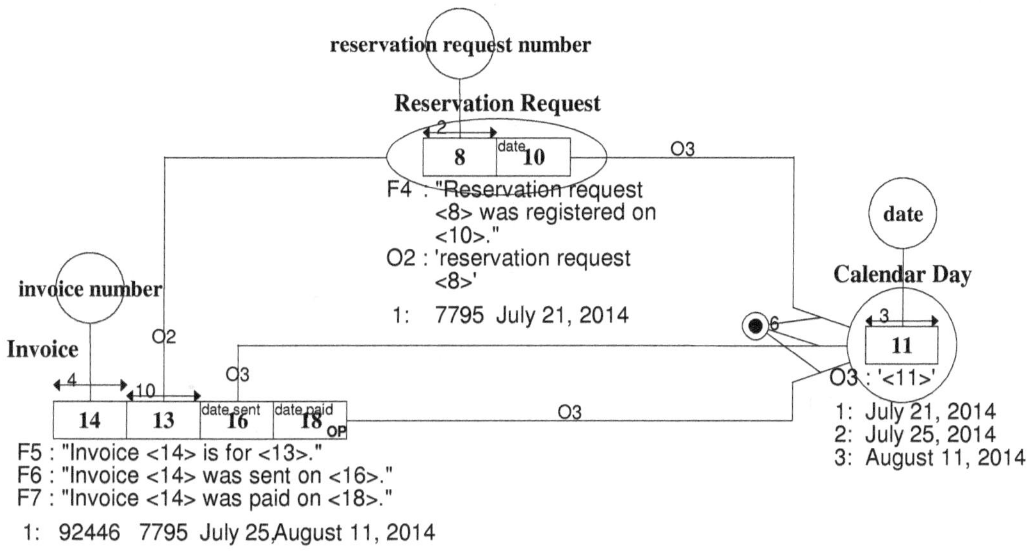

Figure 7.12 IGD with Fact Type with two Single Role UCs, after grouping

Summary of how to Group

For each Own Attribute Fact Type:

1 Move the Attribute Role to the Fact Type inside the Object Type played by the other Role.

2 Move the Fact Expression Type to the Object Type played by the other Role. Adjust the expressions to the new situation (substitute the Object Expression Type(s)).

3 Join the Population with the Population of the Object Type played by the other Role.

4 The moved Attribute Role will become optional
UNLESS there was a Single Role Totality Constraint on the other Role.

5 Remove the Own Attribute Fact Type.

6 Check whether any Constraints were lost in the process.
If so, add new constraints to replace them.

Textbox 7.13 Summary of how to Group

7.1.3.2 Lexicalize

In the Group step of the transformation of an elementary FCO-IM IGD into a Relational schema, all elementary Fact Types are maximally clustered without introducing any redundancy so the number of tables will be as small as possible (see Section 7.1.3.1). What's next? In a Relational schema, each column of a table has a domain. If every Role after the Group step would be played by a Label Type, then the transformation would be almost done because each Role would map to a table column and each Label Type to a domain. But in a G-IGD there are probably still many Roles played by an Object Type instead of a Label Type, and such Roles cannot be mapped to the Relational model directly. Therefore the next step is to transform the G-IGD to a new IGD in which each Role (equivalent to a column) is played by a Label Type (equivalent to a domain). This step is called Lexicalize.

The IGD in Figure 7.8 has eight Roles that are played by an Object Type: Roles 2 and 7 from Object Type 'Show', Roles 10, 13 and 16 from 'Performance' and Roles 21, 22 and 23 from 'Performance Price'. All of these Roles have to be Lexicalized, i.e., should be played by a Label Type.

Let's first consider Roles 2 and 7 from Object Type 'Show'. Role 7 is cut off from Object Type 'Genre' and connected to Label Type 'genre name' instead. Fact Expression Type F3 is adjusted (substitution of Object Expression Type O3) to fit the new situation. This cutting and reconnecting comes at a cost; it should remain to be ensured that each value in the Population of Role 7 is also present in the Population of Role 8, because in FCO-IM the Population of a Role played by an Object Type is always 'taken from' that of the Object Type itself (there can be no value in the Population of such a Role that is missing in that of the Object Type itself). Before lexicalizing, this was automatically the case, but now a Subset Constraint (see Section 4.5.2) has to be added to enforce this: Show(7) -->-- Genre(8). This Subset Constraint corresponds with the foreign key reference from the table Show to the table Genre (see also the arrow from Role 7 to the polygon around 'Genre' in Figure 7.7).

Similarly, Role 2 is cut off from Object Type 'Performance' and connected to Label Type 'performer name'. Now Object Type 'Performer' will disappear because it does not have a Fact Expression Type and does not play a Role anymore.

Figure 7.14 displays the result of lexicalizing Roles 2 and 7 from Object Type 'Show'.

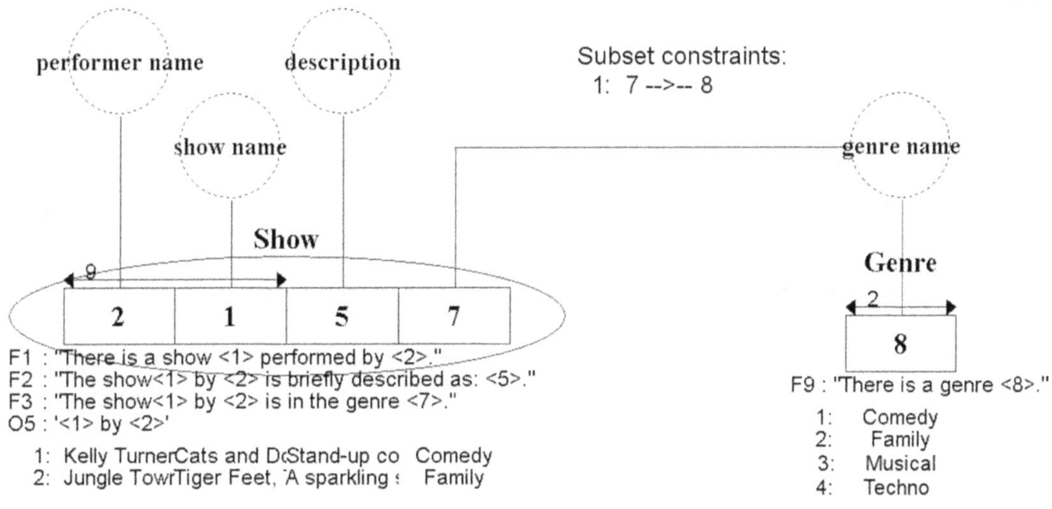

Figure 7.14 Part of IGD after lexicalizing roles in Object Type Show

Other Roles in the IGD in Figure 7.8 that have to be Lexicalized are Roles 10, 13 and 16 (Fact Type 'Performance') and Roles 21, 22 and 23 (Fact Type 'Performance Price'). For Roles 13, 16, 21 and 23, the Lexicalization process is straightforward. These Roles will be connected to respectively Label Types 'date', 'time (hh:mm AM/PM)', 'ticket type name' and 'dollars.cents'. Object Types 'Calendar Day', 'Time Of Day' and 'Amount Of Money' disappear (no more Roles played, no Fact Expression Type), but 'Ticket Type' remains (it has a Fact Expression Type) and one Subset Constraint is added: Performance Price(21) -->-- Ticket Type(24).

The remaining two Roles (22 and 10) need special attention.

Role 22

To which label type should Role 22 be connected? Role 22 is played by Object Type 'Performance', and the Object Expression Type for this Role (O4: 'performance <11>') is the guide here. It points to Role 11, which is played by Label Type 'performance number'. Moreover, Role 11 is covered by a Single Role Uniqueness Constraint, and so it serves as the identifying part (primary 'key'). In other words, it can still be seen after grouping that a performance is identified by its performance number. Therefore, after lexicalizing Role 22 is played by Label Type 'performance number'. To compensate for this cutting and reconnecting, the following Subset Constraint (see Section 4.5.2) has to be added: Performance Price(22) -->-- Performance(11).

Role 10

How to Lexicalize Role 10? Role 10 is played by Object Type 'Show', which is identified by the *combination* of 'show name' and 'Performer', see Uniqueness Constraint 9 on Roles 1 and 2. Because the identifier of 'Show' consists of two components, Role 10 will be split in two parts: Role 10.1, which will be played by Label Type 'show name', and Role 10.2, which will be played by Label Type 'performer name' (see the already Lexicalized Fact Type 'Show' in Figure 7.14). The following Subset Constraint has to be added: Performance(10.1, 10.2) -->-- Show(1, 2).

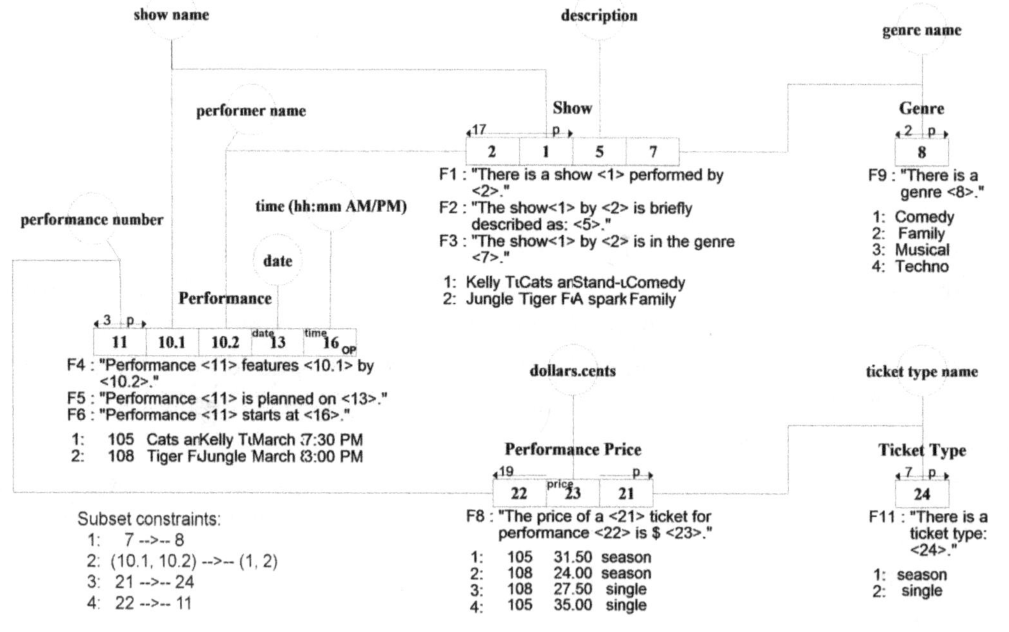

Figure 7.15 IGD after the step Lexicalize: GL-IGD

During Lexicalization all Object Types and Object Expression Types will disappear because the whole point of Lexicalizing is to have no more Roles played by an Object Type anymore. In particular, Object Types without Own Attribute Fact Types that do not have a Fact Expression Type will be simply deleted (they were not combined with Fact Types in the Group step and are not needed as domain lists). In the example IGD, this applies to Object Types 'Performer', 'Calendar Day', 'Time of Day' and 'Amount of Money', exactly the Object Types that are crossed out in Figure 7.7.

So finally the Lexicalize step results in the IGD displayed in Figure 7.15. Such an IGD is called a GL-IGD. The Uniqueness Constraint of each Fact Type is marked with 'p', meaning 'primary'. A Fact Type might have several UCs, and one is to be chosen as the primary UC. A primary Uniqueness Constraint will be translated into a primary key, others to alternative keys.

Mandatory children

If a Relational table has a foreign key, it is called a *child* of the table with the corresponding primary key, which is called the *parent*. Between these two child/parent tables, there is always an 'ordinary' FK-reference from the child to the parent, which means that all values in the foreign key must 'come from' the values in the primary key. But sometimes there is also another reference in the opposite direction, from the parent to the child. This means that *all* values in the primary key must appear in the foreign key. In other words, every parent record *must* have a child. Such a child table is called a *mandatory child*. This section shows where those mandatory child references come from.

Consider a second version of the IGD for customer information in Figure 7.16 (again, this deviates in a few respects from the 'real' information model for Serviceton Music Theater in Appendix A). There also are some differences with the first version in Section 7.1.3.1 (see Figure 7.9). In Figure 7.16 there is a Uniqueness Constraint 35 on the combination of Roles 38+39 instead of one on only Role 38, and there are Single Role Totality Constraints 36 and 37 on Roles 35 and 38 instead of one on the combination. So here each customer has exactly one email address and one or more telephone numbers.

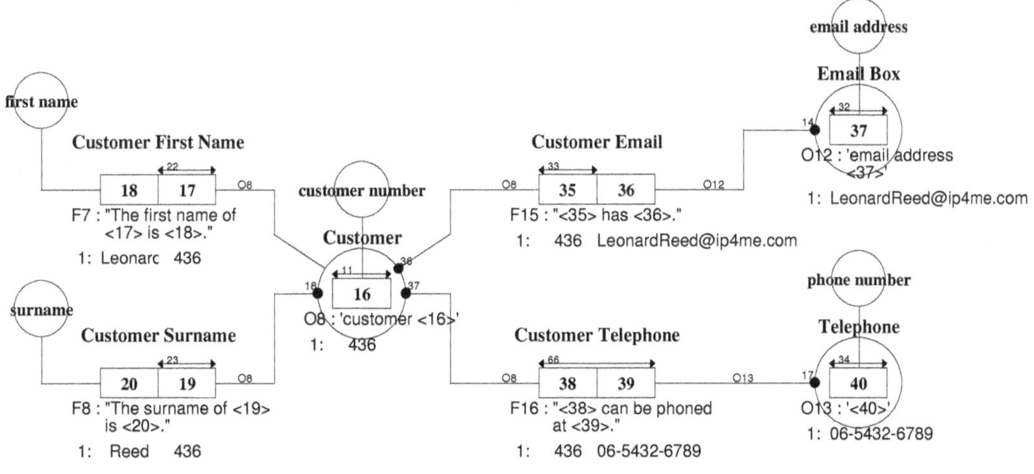

Figure 7.16 Elementary IGD for customer information, version 2

The IGD after the Group step is presented in Figure 7.17. In this case no Totality Constraint was lost.

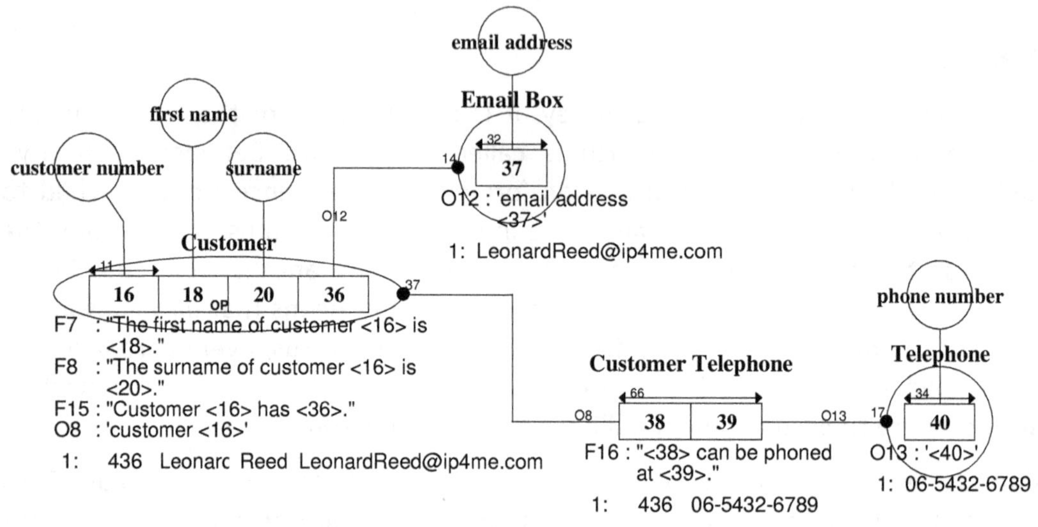

Figure 7.17 G-IGD for customer information, version 2

After performing the Lexicalize step, Role 38 is played by Label Type 'customer number' and the following Subset Constraint was added: SC 1: Customer Telephone(38) -->-- Customer(16). In addition, because of Totality Constraint 37 on Role 38, this Subset Constraint in the other direction has to be added as well: SC 2: Customer(16) -->-- Customer Telephone(38). Both Subset Constraints together form an Equality Constraint (see Section 4.5.3). The result is shown in Figure 7.18.

When this GL-IGD is transformed to a database schema, SC 1 is mapped to a foreign key reference: table 'Customer Telephone' is a child of table 'Customer'. SC 2, pointing the other way from the 'Customer' to the 'Customer Telephone' table, means that for each customer row in the table Customer there is at least one related row in the table 'Customer Telephone'. So 'Customer Telephone' is a *mandatory child* of 'Customer'. This shows that mandatory children stem from Totality Constraints when a Role is Lexicalized.

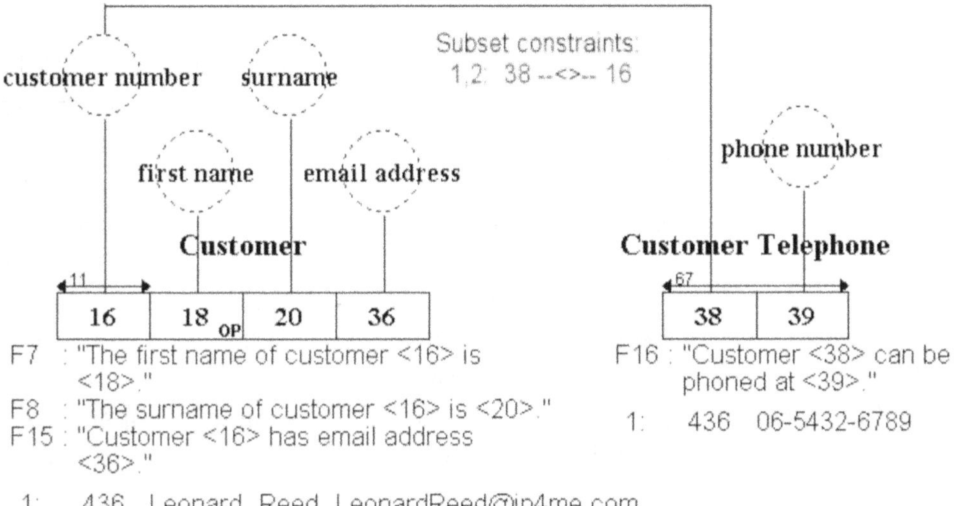

Figure 7.18 GL-IGD for Customer Information with two Subset Constraints

---

Summary of how to Lexicalize

For each Role played by an Object Type:

1. Cut the Role off from the Object Type and connect it to the corresponding Label Type.

   If the Object Type has a compound identifier, the Role should be split into the same number of parts as the identifier consists of and connected to the corresponding Label Types.

   If the Object Type does not have a Fact Expression Type and does not play a Role anymore, then remove it from the model.

2. Adjust the Expression Types that refer to the Lexicalized Role (substitute the Object Expression Type(s)).

3. Add a Subset Constraint from the Lexicalized Role to the Object Type that played this role.

   If there was a Totality Constraint on the Lexicalized Role, then also add a Subset Constraint in the reverse direction.

Textbox 7.19 Summary of how to Lexicalize

7.1.3.3 Reduce

In the Group and Lexicalize steps of the transformation of an elementary FCO-IM IGD into a Relational schema, all elementary Fact Types are maximally clustered and all Object Types are removed. However, the GL-IGD still contains exactly the same Fact Expressions as the elementary IGD, and all Constraints from the elementary IGD are accounted for in the GL-IGD as well (see Sections 7.1.3.1 and 7.1.3.2). What more is there to do? The small third step of the transformation is called Reduce because it aims to reduce the number of tables; there might be superfluous tables that can be missed without loss of information. The IGD in Figure 7.20 illustrates this third step (again, the IGD deviates in a few respects from the 'real' information model for Serviceton Music Theater in Appendix A). Fact Expression Type F12 "There is a performer <3>." has now been added to Object Type 'Performer'.

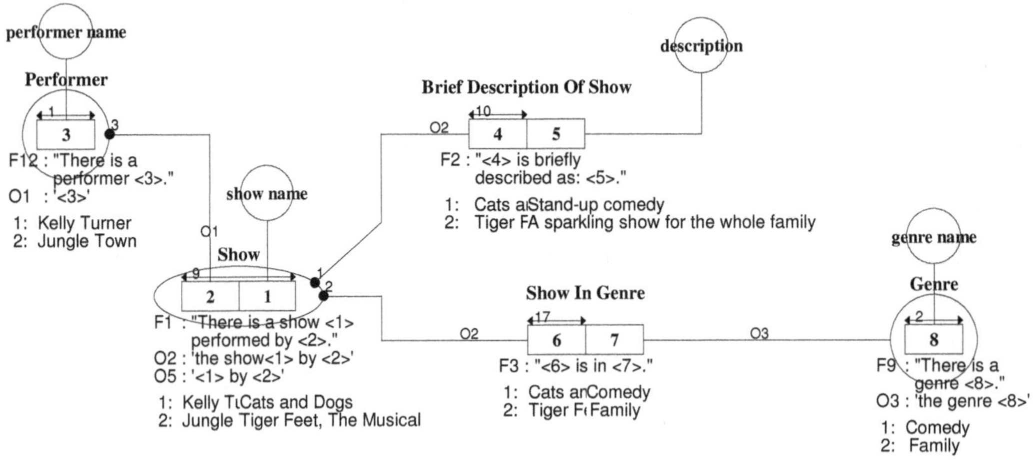

Figure 7.20 El-IGD with Fact Expression Type for Object Type 'Performer'

The IGD after Grouping and Lexicalizing is shown in Figure 7.21.

During the Lexicalization of Role 2, Subset Constraint 1: Show(2) -->-- Performer(3) was added. The consequence of Totality Constraint 3 in the elementary IGD is that the Subset Constraint in the reverse direction is also needed: SC 2: Performer(3) -->-- Show(2) (see Section 7.1.3.2). Together SCs 1 and 2 form an Equality Constraint (see Section 4.5.3). During the Lexicalization of Role 7, Subset Constraint 3: Show(7) -->-- Genre(8) was added.

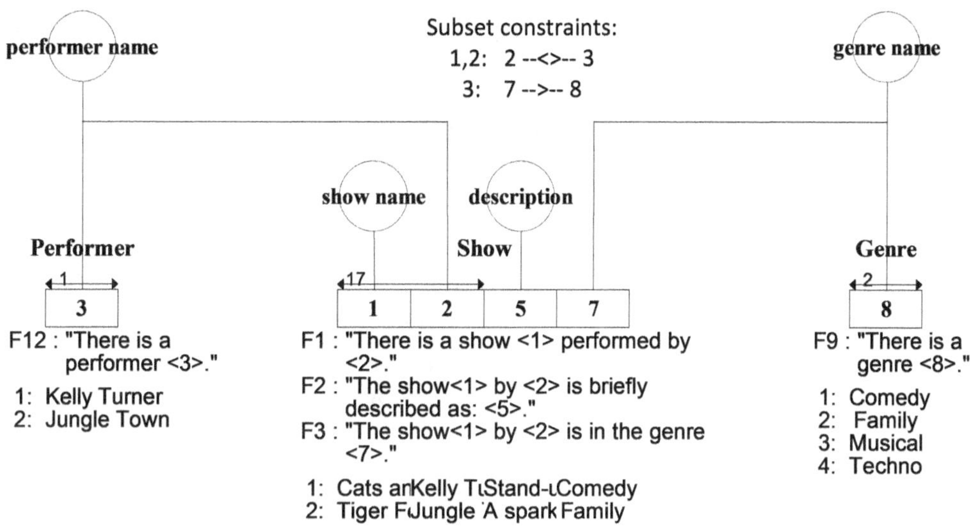

Figure 7.21 GL-IGD for 'Show' with Fact Expression Type for 'Performer'

The Equality Constraint 2 --<>-- 3 means that the Population of Role 2 is exactly the same as the Population of Role 3. So all relevant performers are in the Population of Role 2 as well as in that of Role 3. Therefore a separate table for performers is not needed. Fact Type 'Performer' can be deleted without loss of information, so the number of tables will be smaller (in other words, reduced). The result of the Reduce step is the GLR-IGD shown in Figure 7.22.

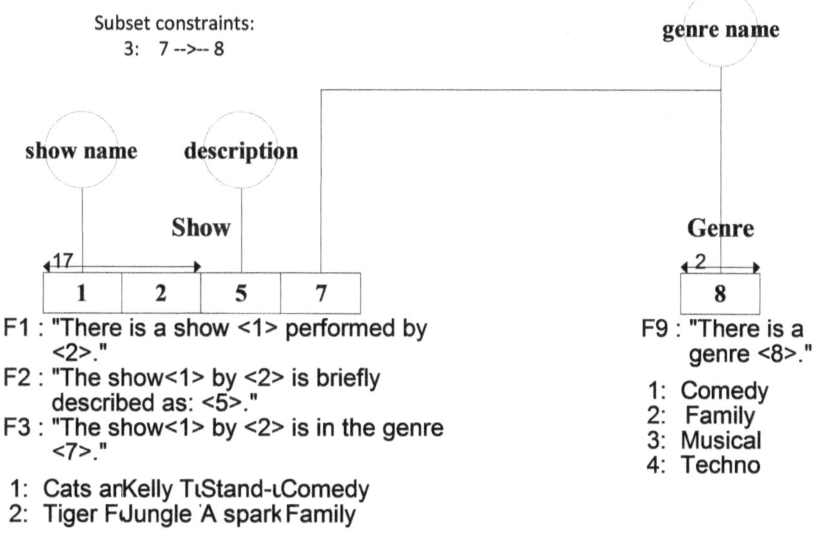

Figure 7.22 GLR-IGD for Show

Summary of how to Reduce

If, after Grouping and Lexicalizing, there is a Fact Type with an Equality Constraint on *all* its Roles, then this Fact Type can be deleted without loss of information.

Textbox 7.23 Summary of how to Reduce

It is not likely that the Reduce step will yield many Fact Types that can be deleted. The questions the modeler asks the domain expert when Totality Constraints are determined (see Textbox 4.25, especially the questions about a pick list) should seldom lead to a model like the one in Figure 7.20. Still, such cases cannot be ruled out, and it is easy to check for them. A good modeling tool like CaseTalk (see appendix B, [2]) will find them automatically. Deleting Fact Types that might be reduced is not mandatory, though, and there might be reasons to keep the 'superfluous' table anyway (a pick list can still be handy in such cases) at the cost of having an extra table and an Equality Constraint to maintain.

7.1.3.4 Convert: The Resulting Relational Database Schema

Convert, the last step of the transformation of an elementary FCO-IM IGD into a Relational schema, involves translating the GLR-IGD into a Relational database schema. A GLR-IGD is already almost a Relational schema: every Fact Type becomes a table, every Role a column, every Label Type a domain and most of the Subset Constraints a FK-reference (other SCs possibly a mandatory child).

The only matter that deserves a little attention is generating meaningful table names and column names, which ideally should be generated automatically. The most important actions in this step are summarized in Textbox 7.24.

Summary of how to Convert

1. For each Fact Type in the GLR-IGD, create a table. The table gets the name of the corresponding Fact Type. In CaseTalk (see Appendix B, [2]) the modeler can specify an alias to replace this name if desired.
2. For each Role the following steps have to be performed:
   - Create a column. By default the name of the column is the name of the Object Type or Label Type that originally played the Role. In CaseTalk

(see Appendix B, [2]) the modeler can specify an alias to replace this name if desired.

- If the Role is covered by (a part of) a primary Uniqueness Constraint, then the column is part of the primary key of the table and marked with <pk>.
- If the Role is optional, then the column is marked with <null>, else with <not null>.
- The Label Type of the Role will be transformed to the domain of the column.

3 Create a foreign key reference for each Subset Constraint pointing to the identifying Role(s) of a Fact Type.

4 For each Constraint that doesn't have an equivalent integrity rule yet (like the second Subset Constraint in mandatory child references), translate it into one or more integrity rules to be implemented later by database programmers.

Textbox 7.24 Summary of how to Convert

This step applied to the GLR-IGD in Figure 7.15 (the Reduce step yields no reducible tables) results in five tables: 'Genre', 'Show', 'Performance', 'Ticket Type' and 'Performance Price' (see Figures 7.26 and 7.27). How the column names of the table 'Performance' are derived is discussed in detail below (see Figure 7.25).

The Roles numbers of Fact Type 'Performance' are replaced by the column names 'performance number', 'show name', 'Performer', 'date' and 'time'. The column names 'date' and 'time' are derived from the alias names assigned to Roles 13 and 16 (see Figure 7.15). The column 'performance number' is marked with <pk> because the corresponding Role 11 is covered by the primary Uniqueness Constraint. All columns of the table Performance are 'not null' except column 'time' because Role 16 is optional. For each Role, the Label Type it plays is translated into a domain for the corresponding column. A data type can be assigned to each domain; for example, NUMERIC(3) to domain 'performance number' and VARCHAR(40) to domain 'show name' (not shown in Figure 7.25).

Finally, Subset Constraint 2 (10.1, 10.2) -->-- (1, 2) is translated into a foreign key reference from the columns 'show name' and 'Performer' of table 'Performance' to the primary key of table 'Show'.

The schema for the table 'Performance' is displayed in Figure 7.25.

Performance			
performance number	performance number	<pk>	not null
show name	show name	<fk>	not null
Performer	performer name	<fk>	not null
date	date		not null
time	time (hh:mm AM/PM)		null

Figure 7.25 Table 'Performance'

The other Fact Types and Subset Constraints are transformed in a similar way. The result of converting the complete GLR-IGD in Figure 7.15 to a Relational schema is presented in Figure 7.26. The domains are not displayed for brevity.

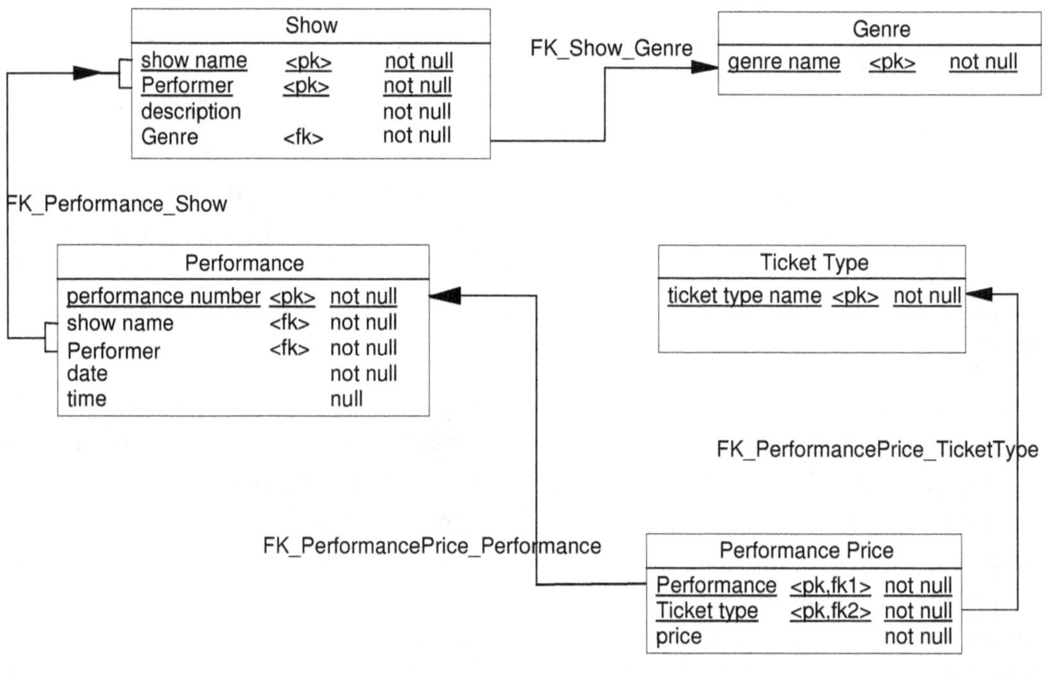

Figure 7.26 Logical Relational schema for the performance schedule part

Finally, Figure 7.27 shows a second version of the Relational schema in which the Fact Expression Types for each table are displayed as well. By incorporating these expressions in the Relational schema, the meaning and the structure of the elementary Facts in the tables is documented explicitly. We strongly recommend to always supply such Fact Expression Types with the tables.

Genre		
genre name	<pk>	<not null>
F9: "There is genre <genre name>."		

Show		
show name	<pk>	<not null>
Performer	<pk>	<not null>
description		<not null>
Genre	<fk>	<not null>
F1: "There is a show <show name> performed by <Performer>." F2: "The show <show name> by <Performer> is shortly described as: <description>." F3: "The show <show name> by <Performer> is in the genre <Genre>."		

FK_Show_Genre: Show(Genre) → Genre(genre name)

Performance		
performance number	<pk>	<not null>
show name	<fk>	<not null>
Performer	<fk>	<not null>
date		<not null>
time		<null>
F4: "Performance <performance number> features <show name> by <Performer>." F5: "Performance <performance number> is planned on <date>." F6: "Performance <performance number> starts at <time>."		

FK_Performance_Show:
Performance(show name, Performer) → Show(show name, Performer)

Performance Price		
Performance	<pk,fk1>	<not null>
Ticket Type	<pk,fk2>	<not null>
Price		<not null>
F8: "The price for a <Ticket Type> for performance <Performance> is $<price>."		

FK_PerformancePrice_Performance:
    Performance Price(Performance) → Performance(performance number)

FK_PerformancePrice_TicketType:
    Performance Price(Ticket Type) → Ticket Type(ticket type name)

Ticket Type		
ticket type name	<pk>	<not null>
F11: "There is a ticket type <ticket type name>."		

Figure 7.27 Logical Relational schema with Fact Expression Types

7.2 Transformation of an FCO-IM IGD Into an Entity Relationship Diagram

Because many data modelers use data modeling techniques other than FCO-IM, it is desirable to be able to generate other types of data models from an FCO-IM IGD. This section discusses the transformation to an Entity Relationship Diagram (ERD) (see Appendix B, [12]). There are several diagramming styles for Entity Relationship Modeling. In this book the Information Engineering notation will be used.

The starting point of the transformation towards an ERD is the elementary IGD in Figure 7.28 (once more, for didactical reasons, this deviates slightly from the 'real' information model for Serviceton Music Theater in Appendix A).

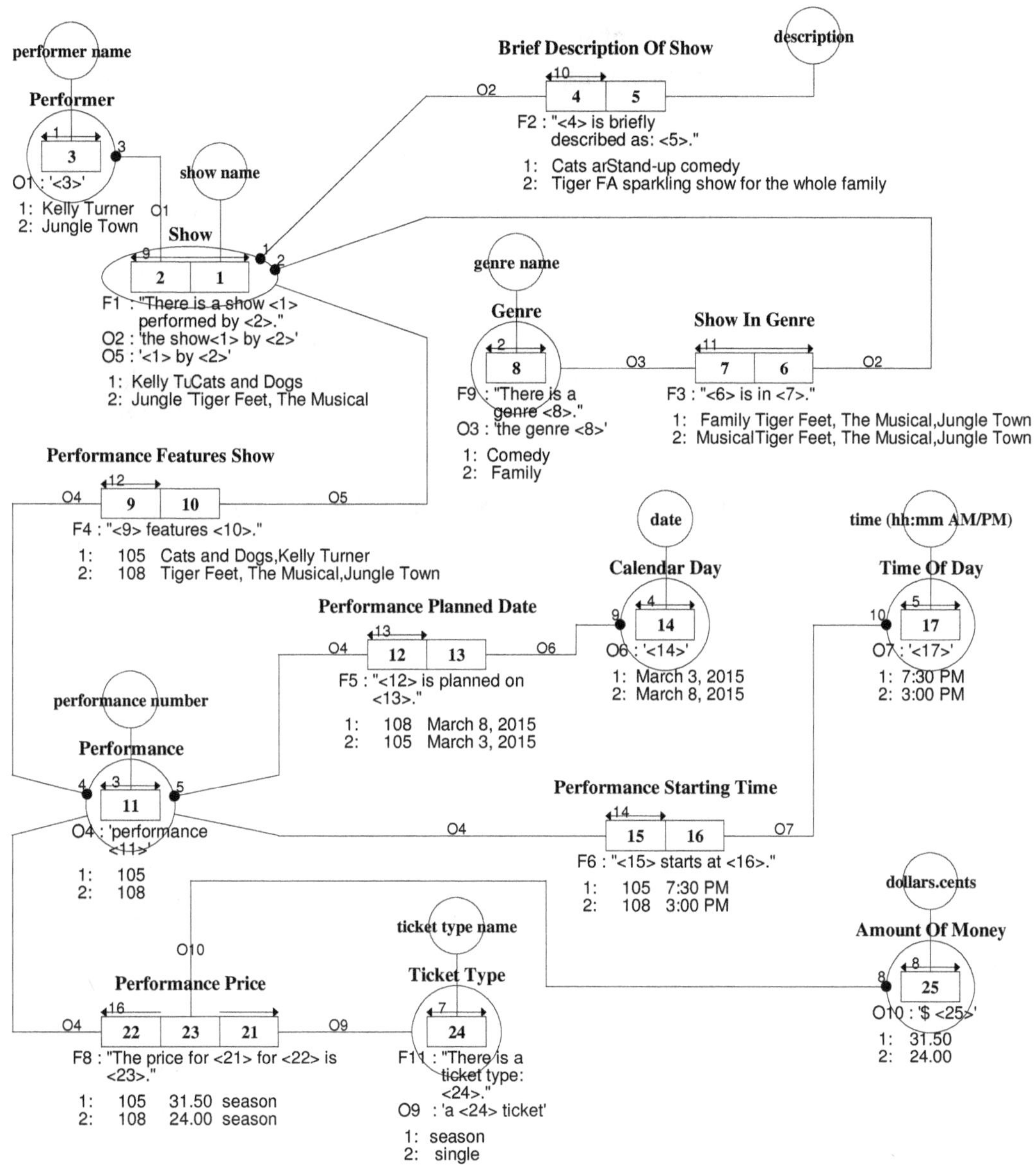

Figure 7.28 Elementary IGD for the performance schedule (slightly modified)

The transformation from an IGD to an ERD consists of two steps. The first step is creating an 'ERD in disguise'. The second step is converting the 'ERD in disguise' to a real ERD.

7.2.1 STEP 1

Step 1 Transform the elementary IGD to an 'ERD in disguise', still using the FCO-IM diagram technique.

A Perform the Group step as discussed in Section 7.1.3.1, but with one exception. Fact Types with two Roles, with two Single Role Uniqueness Constraints and with both Roles played by Object Types, should not be grouped; such a Fact Type will be transformed into a one-to-one relationship in step 2B.

B Remove all Object Types that have no Own Attribute Fact Types (see definition 4.23) and no Fact Expression Type. Connect their identifying Label Types to the Roles they play instead.

The result of performing step 1 on the IGD in Figure 7.28 is shown in Figure 7.29.

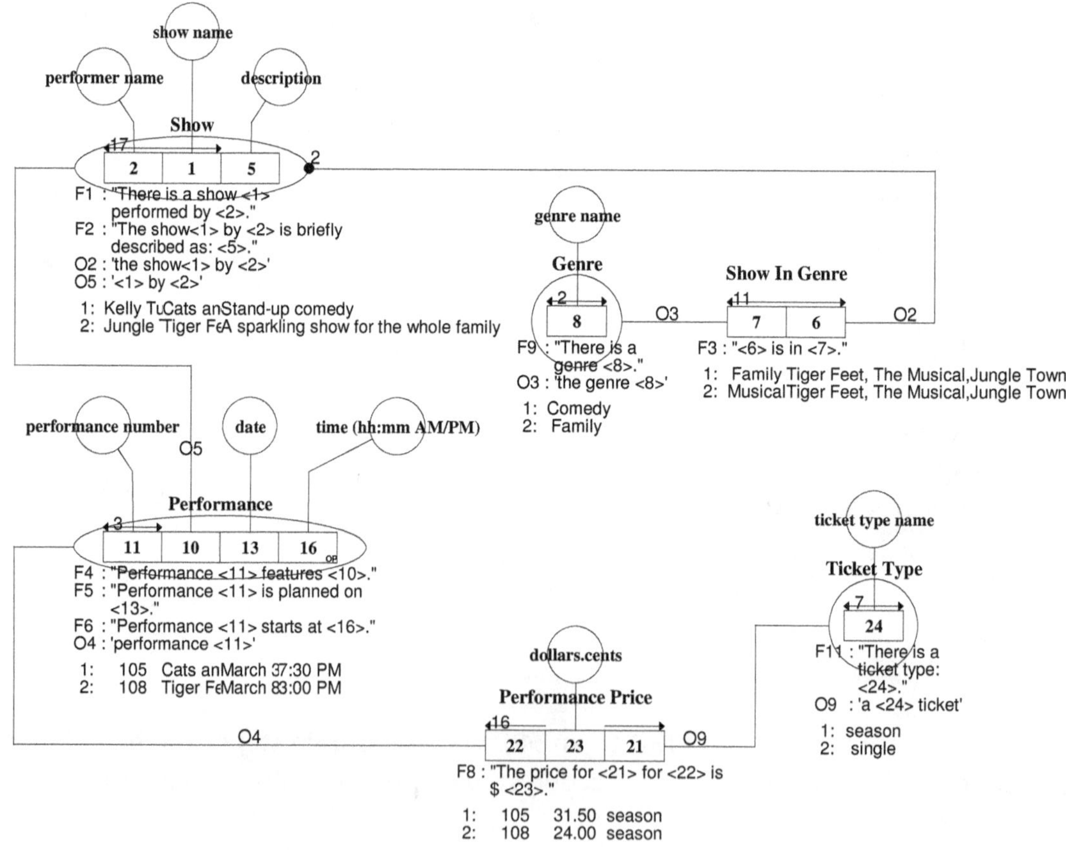

Figure 7.29 IGD for performance schedule after step 1

The exception mentioned in step 1A does not occur. Object Types 'Performer', 'Calendar Day', 'Time of Day' and 'Amount of Money' are removed in step 1B, and their identifying Label Types 'performer name', 'date', 'time (hh:mm AM/PM)' and 'dollars.cents' are connected to the Roles they played instead.

7.2.2 STEP 2

This step consists of four substeps.

Step 2A	Create an entity type for each Object Type and for each Fact Type with more than two Roles.

From the IGD in Figure 7.29, entity types are created for the Object Types and Fact Types 'Show', 'Genre', 'Performance', 'Performance Price' and 'Ticket Type' (see Figure 7.30).

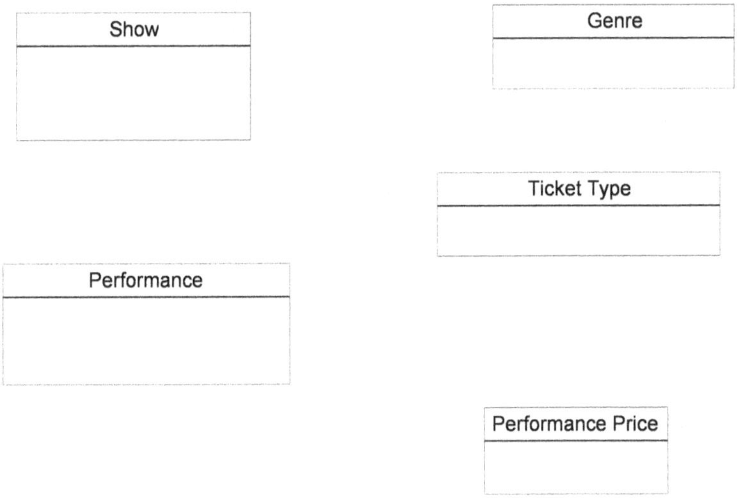

Figure 7.30 ERD after performing step 2A

Step 2B	Create a relationship for each Fact Type with two Roles and determine its cardinalities.

There is one Fact Type with two Roles left in the IGD in Figure 7.29: 'Show In Genre'. This Fact Type is transformed to a relationship between entities 'Genre' and 'Show'. Cardinalities of the relationship are derived from Uniqueness Constraints and Totality Constraints. A Totality Constraint determines the minimum cardinality; a Uniqueness Constraint the maximum cardinality. Please note the Statements of such Uniqueness Constraints and Totality Constraints in

Model Style (see Section 4.1.1 and Appendix A), already given for the FCO-IM model, can be carried over directly into ERM!

Figure 7.31 contains a schematic overview of the transformation of Fact Types with two Roles to a relationship including their cardinalities.

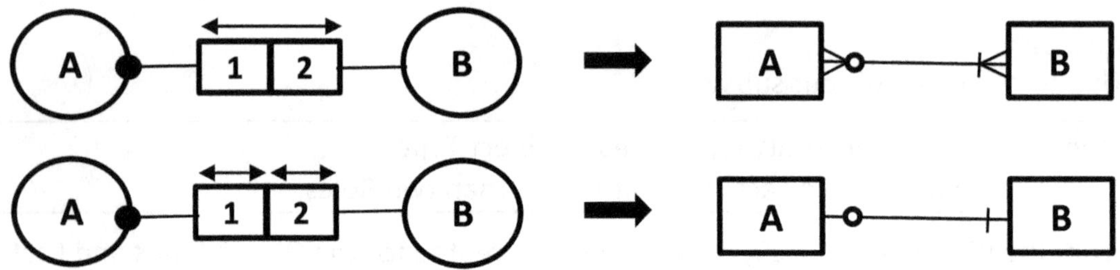

Figure 7.31 Transformation of Fact Types with two Roles

The Fact Type 'Show In Genre' is of the type shown at the top of Figure 7.31: There is a Uniqueness Constraint on both Roles, Role 6 has a Totality Constraint, and Role 7 does not. This corresponds with four Statements of Constraints in Model Style. All four Statements are given in Appendix A and are repeated here, together with the corresponding Constraints in the FCO-IM IGD and cardinalities of the relationship in ERM (please check this thoroughly; it is a central point of this book):

"A show can be in several genres."
UC 11 on Roles 6+7 Maximum cardinality 'many' near 'Genre'

"A genre can contain several shows."
UC 11 on Roles 6+7 Maximum cardinality 'many' near 'Show'

"A show must be in at least one genre."
TC 2 on Role 6 Minimum cardinality '1' near 'Genre'

"A genre does not need to contain a show."
No TC on Role 7 Minimum cardinality '0' near 'Show'

Please note how these Statements in Model Style map to Constraints in the FCO-IM IGD and to cardinalities in the ERM diagram. We advocate to always state every Constraint in a similar way to emphasize that there is a common meaning behind the different forms they may assume in different modeling techniques and to show the correspondence between such different techniques.

So a many-to-many relationship 'Show In Genre' is added to the ERD with appropriate minimum cardinalities (see Figure 7.32).

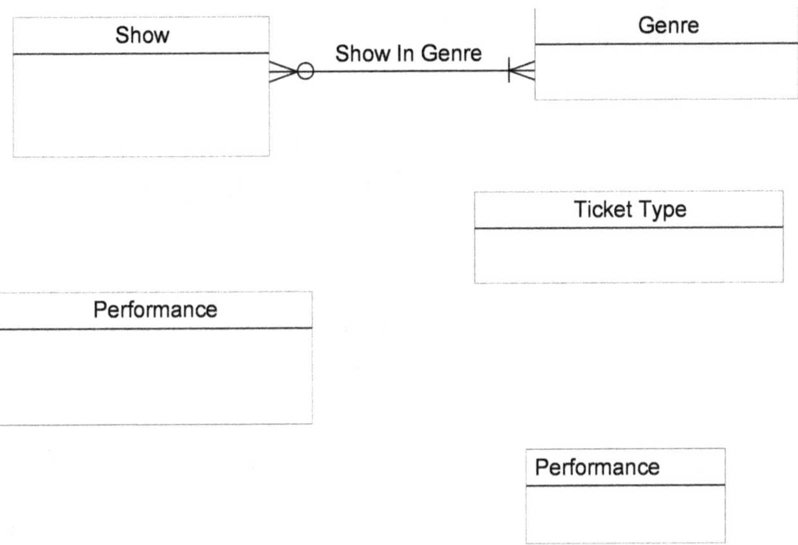

Figure 7.32 ERD after performing step 2B

Step 2C	Create an attribute for each Role played by a Label Type. The attribute is mandatory unless the Role is optional. The attribute is marked with <pi> (for 'primary identifier') if the Role is covered by the primary Uniqueness Constraint.

This step, applied to the IGD in Figure 7.29, gives the result shown in Figure 7.33.

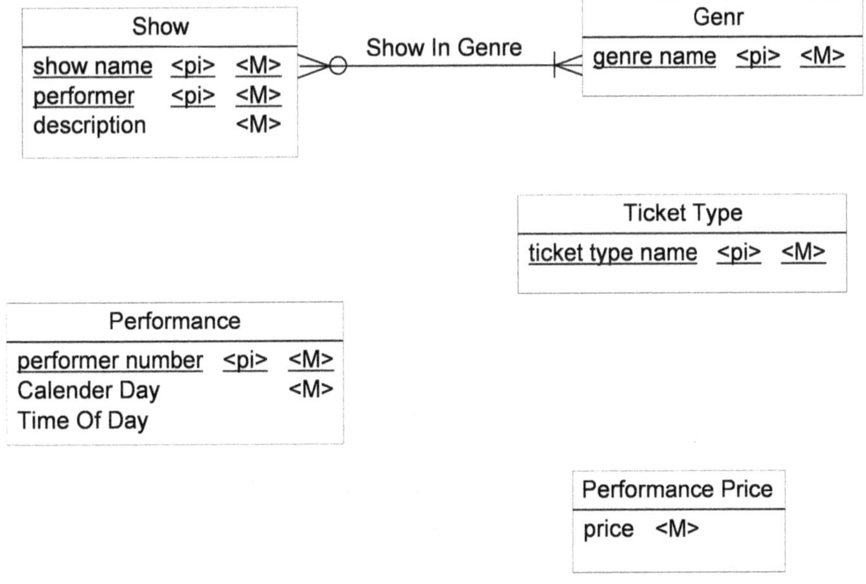

Figure 7.33 ERD after performing step 2C

Step 2D	For each Role played by an Object Type:
	Create a 1-to-many relationship.
	This relationship has cardinality 1 at the side of the entity type that corresponds with the Object Type that plays this Role.
	This relationship has cardinality 'many' at the side of the entity type that contains this Role.
	This relationship has a *dependency* (see any textbook on ERM) at its 'many' side if this Role is an identifying Role.

In the example IGD in Figure 7.29, this substep applies to Roles 10, 21 and 22. Roles 21 and 22 are identifying Roles, therefore the relationships created for these Roles are dependent at the side of entity type 'Performance Price'. The final ERD is displayed in Figure 7.34.

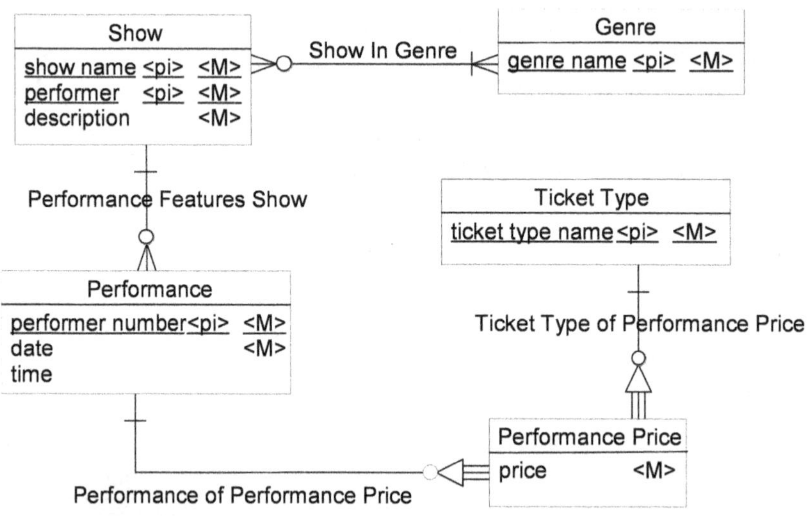

Figure 7.34 ERD after performing step 2D

7.3 Transformation of an FCO-IM IGD Into Other Modeling Techniques

In the previous sections of this chapter, transformations from an FCO-IM information model to a Relational Schema and to an Entity Relationship Model are described. The same principles used there can be applied to transformations to other models. Please note that these principles include:

- Whatever modeling technique is used, the same elementary Facts are being modeled.
- Whatever modeling technique is used, the same Business Rules are being modeled.
- Whatever form of *representing* these Facts and Rules is used (ranging from a low-level representation like a Relational database schema to a high-level management dashboard that shows vastly aggregated data the Board of Directors is interested in), it is crucial to accurately and fully model the basic Facts from which this information can be computed.
- Models in all modeling techniques can be transformed into each other using transformation algorithms at the level of their *metadata,* which is illustrated extensively in this chapter. The metadata of a model, i.e. data about the structure of the model, is stored in a *repository.* A transformation algorithm takes the metadata in the repository of the source model, performs well-defined operations on it and stores the result in the repository of the target model. So if you want to learn more about model transformations, take a dive into the world of metadata and repositories (see for instance Appendix B, [8]).

We particularly hope to have illustrated that although different modeling techniques may put a different emphasis on their 'native' Constraints, essentially every Constraint owes its existence to a (part of a) Business Rule that specifies something about the data to be recorded. These Business Rules are *independent* from the modeling technique of choice.

Generating models and scripts from conceptual information models can be very helpful to information systems developers. Recurring tasks, like deriving a Relational schema and DDL script, are in practice performed with support by software tools (like CaseTalk; see Appendix B, [2]) in which transformation algorithms at the metadata level are implemented.

Many enterprises and organizations build *data warehouses* and use Business Intelligence (see Appendix B, 29]) for decision-making. So frequently used models and structures for data warehouses, like a dimensional model (see Appendix B, [15]), a Data Vault model (see Appendix B, [16]) or an Anchor Modeling model (see Appendix B, [17]), are obvious targets for model transformations. Indeed, the research group Model-Based Information Systems of HAN University of Applied Sciences is developing transformation algorithms from an FCO-IM model into all of these techniques.

For example, the transformation to a Data Vault model requires mapping FCO-IM elements to concepts like hubs, links and satellites, the three core components of a Data Vault model (see Appendix B, [16]). Once again, the steps Reduce, Group and Lexicalize (see Section 7.1) are part of the transformation from an FCO-IM IGD to a Data Vault model (one of the authors of this book, Marco Engelbart, is actively involved in designing a transformation algorithm for this transformation).

More experience was gained with the transformation from an FCO-IM IGD to a *dimensional model* (a star-like schema with a central 'fact table' surrounded by satellite 'dimension tables'; see appendix B, [15]). This starts with the Group and Reduce steps (see Section 7.1.3), after which the typical dimensional modeling concepts measures, fact tables and dimension tables have to be identified. The working method and supporting FCO-IM-based tool for deriving a dimensional model from an elementary FCO-IM IGD (the FCO-IM Bridge Tools) have been successfully applied in practice (see Appendix B, [3] and [15]) in large scale data warehouse projects for a world-wide operating bank and a major Dutch hospital.

The concept of model transformations at the metadata level (the core business of the research group Model-Based Information Systems at HAN University of Applied Sciences) has proven its value in practice more than once.

Chapter 8
Perspectives on Information Modeling

This closing chapter takes a brief but broad look at innovative and future directions in information systems and the digital world, looking in particular at those topics and aspects that have a clear relation to Fact Oriented Modeling (FOM), concretely or potentially, and positioning FOM in all this.

8.1 Business Support

Information systems have become what they are primarily because they help businesses and organizations by efficiently expressing, structuring, storing, processing and reporting all sorts of information. Language (words but also numbers) was initially the main carrier of information, and databases, whether or not designed using FOM, reflect language patterns and expressions in a heavily structured way. Apart from data/information processing (with its computational character), it is not unreasonable to say that information systems are devices that support structured communication that in turn is vital in running business processes. This core aspect is extensively covered throughout the book, so we do not have much more to say about it here. However, many additional aspects link in with the core, and we will briefly discuss a number of them below.

8.2 Business Processes, Business Rules

The support, design and improvement of business processes, often involving some sort of business process modeling (e.g., through languages like BPMN (see Appendix B, [18]) or UML Activity Diagrams (see Appendix B. [13]), has perhaps superseded or enveloped the core art and science of data modeling in the last decade. As briefly discussed in Chapter 1 and illustrated in Chapter 2, such modeling goes pretty much hand in hand with information modeling or data modeling. However, well-designed databases are still key in any digital or automated business process support setup.

A strongly related approach, business rules (also mentioned in Chapters 1 and 2), blends in well with both business processes and databases and is now part and parcel of the field of business information systems. From a technology point of view, business rules apply logic-based artificial intelligence techniques to reason about data, and trigger responses to certain situations (patterns, states) reflected in this data. This is key in many systems that automate operational decision taking in the business, including quite complex cases. For example, calculating the mortgage that someone can get (output) given information on the status and situation of that person (input) has now been fully automated by many financial service providers, allowing potential clients to find out their personalized mortgage options online from home very quickly and without much effort. Business rules are executed by rule engines, and these require well-structured, machine readable rules (embodying the decision making) as well as properly structured, high quality input from databases.

Interestingly, FOM has played a substantial part in shaping ideas about the structure and formulation of business rules. For example, it was one of the pillars of the OMG SBVR standard (Semantics of Business Vocabulary and Rules, see Appendix B, [20]), which has been a major step in furthering the large-scale industrial formulation and use of business rules, and which has been incorporated in many tools aiding analysis, design and development of rule-based information systems. The inherent FOM practice of verbalizing facts in a well-structured, logical way has been a crucial factor in this. There is a widely acknowledged need to express business rules not (only) as programming code, but in a more natural yet controlled language that can be expressed, validated and used by business people. It is to be expected that FOM, possibly in an evolved form integrated in a wider rule setup, will continue to play its part in this respect.

8.3 Semantic Web (Machine Readability, AI, Rules, Ontology)

The link between business rules and Artificial Intelligence provides a good bridge to a related area in information and web systems: the Semantic Web (see Appendix B, [24]). This is an effort to make web content machine readable (to a certain extent), thus making it possible to apply AI techniques in web activities like intelligent searching, use of rules for reasoning, active combination and re-use of on-line information from various sources, and so on. Though the semantic web community does not generally use FOM related representations, a group led by Robert Meersman at the Free University of Brussels (see Appendix B, [25]) has carried out large projects using FOM in the context of knowledge representation on the web. In that area of research and enterprise, *ontologies* (see Appendix B, [25]) have been at the center of interest for more than a decade. Ontologies are conceptual schemas of a sort, usually with hyperonymic ('is-a') relations at the core, which help define concepts for knowledge domains and therefore can be used to bridge semantic gaps (i.e. translate) between domains.

Scholarly discussions aside, there are strong similarities in both use and structure between ontologies and FOM information models (ontologies are networks of supertype-subtype relationships; see Section 6.2 and Appendix B, [1, Chapter 6]). Indeed, the Brussels group mentioned above have used their approach in various ways, complementary to but also as an alternative to the use of standard hyperonym-based ontologies. Their results have carried over to industry and are now used in Data Governance approaches (Collibra; see Appendix B, [26]).

8.4 Interoperability (Ontologies, Standards, Diversity)

This brings us from the World Wide Web to a related but broader issue: interoperability. Information modeling has been used extensively to bring together, centralize, and standardize information structures across large domains, often with the goal to create an integrated information system or at least effectively link a number of such systems. A similar goal is pursued by many efforts in view of the Semantic Web. Large ontologies have been created in numerous domains to get a grip on semantics and have created data bridges between domains. Clearly, FOM is potentially in the middle of this.

Standardization is often mentioned as a main goal for which data modeling in large domains is used. However, standardization is often a hard, time consuming process that requires a number of parties to mutually *understand, agree on* and *commit to* information structures. This is not so much a technical or even a linguistic challenge as a practical and socio-psychological one. People, in particular groups of people, are generally unwilling to give up or change 'their' language and the conceptual frameworks they work with, as these are deeply embedded in operations in the domain as well as the psyche of the people working in it. This fundamental issue lies behind many huge problems faced when dealing with efforts like system integration, data quality improvement (see Appendix B, [21]), interoperability (see Appendix B, [27]), business process re-engineering (see Appendix B, [28]) and even simply the introduction of a new system.

While information modeling excels as a tool in integration and standardization efforts, it can also be used very effectively when embracing diversity, helping to cope with the identification and analysis of conceptual differences between domains. Such differences are generally not just there because they have grown historically. Specific concepts used in domains reflect the specifics of work and communication in that domain; natural language as used by humans has the tendency to adapt to its context of use. In many cases, Business-IT alignment and user friendliness of systems in fact require considerable respect for the conceptual specificities and quirks of the domains in question. Information modeling can help making conceptual differences between domains crystal clear. Whether or not standardization efforts ensue is another matter, but creating interoperability links between domains should start with a clear understanding and description of the domains as such. FOM, with its strong natural language element and its built-in respect for facts (instance level), and also its well-developed validation capacity using natural language verbalizations, is particularly well suited for use in such situations.

8.5 Quality of Data, Quality of Information, Data Governance

Quality of data (see Appendix B, [21]) for a large part hinges on a good, widely shared and operationalized understanding of what particular data and metadata mean. Only then is it possible to determine how high or low the data quality is. FOM has two roles to play here. As a technique it can help to analyze, describe and exchange information about the semantics and structure of domains and their data. The second, related aspect does not concern FOM as a technique per se, but rather as a means to communicate about data, meaning, and data quality. From a quality management perspective, a communication-intensive process of 'talking about data' is a crucial part of any approach to data and information quality. Once again, FOM's explicit way of working and its natural language analysis and verbalization capacity make it a particularly powerful tool for talking about language, information and data in a precise way. In this respect, the Collibra (see Appendix B, [26]) approach mentioned earlier is a stock example of how FOM can be used in this context.

8.6 Business Intelligence, Data Warehousing

Quality of data is a quite generic principle and goal, but its origins lie largely in the need for accurate management information. FOM has been extensively used in the field of business intelligence (see Appendix B, [29]). Very often, this involves the design and use of Data Warehouses (see Appendix B, [15]), databases especially designed and structured to support complex queries (often predesigned) that go beyond what a regular operations-related database can deliver. FOM has been proven to be a valuable tool in this area too, in particular when it is combined with modeling techniques more specifically aimed at the design and management of Data Warehouses (e.g., Data Vault (see Appendix B, [16]) or Star Schemas (see Appendix B, [15])). It is possible to use transformation algorithms generating such models from a FOM model (see Section 7.3).

8.7 Big Data, NoSQL, Analytics

Recently, the world has embraced 'Big Data' as a promising trend. Indeed, the ever increasing availability of huge amounts of data with at its source many kinds of operational processes (professional and industrial as well as private), in combination with powerful analytical methods and techniques, creates massive opportunities for up-scaled, pervasive business intelligence with a very wide, integrated coverage (i.e. combining very different sorts of data from many different sources). Interestingly, the Big Data movement also involves the rise of 'no-SQL' databases (see Appendix B, [30]). This approach is moving away from the relational database paradigm that has been so familiar for decades and that is so closely linked with the FOM approaches. It is not clear yet how FOM might be used outside the logical, well-structured world of relational databases, e.g. for the generation of no-SQL instead of good old SQL databases. However, viewing FOM not as a design tool but as an analysis-and-communication tool, it may well turn out extremely useful for getting a grip on unstructured, organic domains even if it is not used to generate actual databases.

8.8 Links with Other Modeling Schools

FOM is part of a larger world of data and process modeling and analysis. Links with UML, in particular Class Diagrams (see Appendix B, [13]), and ERM (see Appendix B, [12]) have been well explored, particularly by Terry Halpin, the main man behind the Object Role Modeling (ORM) flavor of FOM (see Appendix B, [10]). Many academic publications exist about comparison of FOM with other modeling techniques and also on transformations/translations between models in various languages. The link with process models (e.g. BPMN; see Appendix B, [18]) has also been well explored. Worth mentioning is work by Sjir Nijssen and his company (PNA) on his CogNIAM approach (see appendix B, [11]), embedding the arch-form of FOM, NIAM, in a wider set of modeling techniques. In software engineering, links with FOM have been explored from a Functional Programming point of view, relating basic FOM structures with the iTasks cooperative information system developed at Radboud University Nijmegen (see Appendix B, [31]). At the same university, links have been explored between ORM and System Dynamics (see Appendix B, [32]).

8.9 System Generation, Model-Based Development, and Evolutionary Systems

The use of FOM, and in particular FCO-IM, in mainstream information system analysis and design has been discussed throughout the book, but now we would like to take a wider, future-oriented perspective by linking this to evolutionary approaches to system development.

For decades, the dream of many system developers has been to be able to master the step-by-step change of information systems to the point of realizing systems that are so well aligned with business operations that they do not just support operations perfectly, but also smoothly and quickly move with every change in business operations. The envisioned ideal is systems that respond immediately to small changes in needs and requests without having to go through a laborious and slow development cycle rendering new 'releases of the system'. Agile development, typically using Scrum (see Appendix B, [33]), has perhaps brought us closer to this, but many people in both industry and science have a somewhat different vision: model-based development. Many different versions of this vision exist, and quite a few of them have been implemented industrially with varying success.

The gist of model-based development is that exact descriptions of the system, expressed in models wielding concepts related to business, communication, processes, information, business rules, etc., are used to (semi-)automatically *generate* operational systems. Sometimes, the use of 'engines' is involved here (as an alternative to code generation). The key idea is, then, that by changing the models, the operational system can also be changed very quickly with a minimum of effort and without software errors. For example, a small Arnhem-based company named Gorilla IT, set up by alumni of the Academy of Communication and Information Technology (ICA) of HAN University of Applied Sciences, Arnhem, the Netherlands (the home base of the authors of this book) successfully practice such a FOM-based/Model-Based generation approach. Also, the information systems supporting educational operations at ICA (2400 students, 150 staff) have for many years been run and maintained through a similar setup. The name of the research group that the authors of this book belong to (Model-Based Information Systems) makes no secret of this frame of mind.

8.10 Alternative Uses of FOM

Once people have learned how to do FOM, they show a tendency to use it in unexpected ways. To conclude, we consider a few examples of the use of FOM outside the realm of information systems modeling and design. They mostly illustrate how fundamental the principles of FOM are with respect to conceptual structure, therefore lending itself for use in many areas and activities.

There is some similarity, for example, between FOM and the educational, brainstorm-like technique called Concept Mapping (see Appendix B, [34]), which is not to be confused with Mind Mapping. Any activity that requires good insight into concepts within a domain and relations between them (by some called 'semantic networks') can potentially benefit from Concept Mapping, and if more in-depth, formal analysis is required, FOM. The resulting conceptual models have been used for example in:

- creative conceptual design and co-design (innovative systems and applications);
- the design of conceptual research models and databases for qualitative and quantitative research design (i.e., structuring research projects);
- meta-modeling, i.e. the modeling of modeling languages. This is part of *Method Engineering*, a branch of the field of information systems focusing on rational, well-founded engineering of methods and techniques for the analysis, design and production of information systems.

APPENDIX A
Serviceton Music Theater Complete FCO-IM Information Model

The complete FCO-IM information model for the Serviceton Music Theater case study used throughout the book is presented here.

Section A1 presents the FCO-IM Information Grammar Diagrams (IGD) with the Verbalizations.

A1.1 IGD Schedule

A1.2 IGD Customer

A1.3 IGD Reservation Request

A1.4 IGD Tickets

Please note that the Population in the diagrams does not satisfy all the Constraints. This is no problem in an FCO-IM Information Model; such a model is made to accurately specify the *metadata* (Fact Types and Object Types with their Expression Types, and Constraints, see Section 6.1.2). In contrast, the Population ('ordinary' data) in such a model only serves as concrete examples of the Facts in each Fact Type. Of course, in an operational database the population must always satisfy all of these Constraints. It is indeed also possible to populate the diagrams completely correctly, but this would require a lot of time and effort for a result that is irrelevant at this level.

Section A2 lists all the Constraints and accounts for each of them.

A2.1 Uniqueness Constraints

A2.2 Totality Constraints

A2.3 Value Constraints

A2.4 Subtypes

A2.5 Other Constraints

Perhaps you are surprised at the many pages that account for all the Uniqueness Constraints and Totality Constraints. This is not a drawback of FCO-IM, however. All of these constraints are present in one form or another in all other information modeling techniques as well: cardinalities for relationship types in ERM, NOT NULL columns in Relational tables, etc. So they all have to be determined anyway, and FCO-IM provides a thorough way to do so during interviews with domain experts. This enables the modeler to make the documentation on the fly instead of afterwards (if still made at all).

Section A3 finally gives the complete list of Business Rules and specifies with which Constraints they correspond if they were included in the Information Model.

A3.1 Business Rules from the description

A3.2 Business Rules from interviews

A1 IGDs

A1.1 IGD SCHEDULE

```
Brief Description Of Show:
   "The show Cats and Dogs by Kelly Turner is briefly described as:
    Stand-up comedy."
   "The show Tiger Feet, The Musical by Jungle Town is briefly
    described as: A sparkling show for the whole family."

Calendar Day:
   "There is a calendar day July 21, 2014."
   "There is a calendar day March 10, 2015."
   "There is a calendar day March 3, 2015."
   "There is a calendar day March 8, 2015."
   "There is a calendar day March 9, 2015."

Calendar Day Is Weekday:
   "March 10, 2015 is a Tuesday."
   "March 3, 2015 is a Tuesday."
   "March 8, 2015 is a Sunday."
   "March 9, 2015 is a Monday."

Genre:
   "There is a genre Comedy."
   "There is a genre Family."
   "There is a genre Musical."
   "There is a genre Techno."

Performance Features Show:
   "Performance 105 features Cats and Dogs by Kelly Turner."
   "Performance 108 features Tiger Feet, The Musical by Jungle
    Town."

Performance Planned Date:
```

```
  "Performance 105 is planned on March 3, 2015."
  "Performance 108 is planned on March 8, 2015."
```

Performance Price:

```
  "The price of a season ticket for performance 105 is $31.50."
  "The price of a season ticket for performance 108 is $24.00."
  "The price of a single ticket for performance 105 is $35.00."
  "The price of a single ticket for performance 108 is $27.50."
```

Performance Starting Time:

```
 "Performance 105 starts at 7:30 PM."
 "Performance 108 starts at 3:00 PM."
```

Show:

```
  "There is a show Cats and Dogs performed by Kelly Turner."
  "There is a show Tiger Feet, The Musical performed by Jungle
   Town."
```

Show In Genre:

```
  "The show Cats and Dogs by Kelly Turner is in the genre Comedy."
  "The show Tiger Feet, The Musical by Jungle Town is in the genre
   Family."
  "The show Tiger Feet, The Musical by Jungle Town is in the genre
   Musical."
```

Ticket Type:

```
  "There is a ticket type: season."
  "There is a ticket type: single."
```

Time Of Day:

```
  "10:15 AM is a valid standard time of day."
  "11:15 AM is a valid standard time of day."
  "3:00 PM is a valid standard time of day."
  "7:30 PM is a valid standard time of day."
```

Weekday:

```
  "There is a weekday Friday."
  "There is a weekday Monday."
  "There is a weekday Saturday."
  "There is a weekday Sunday."
  "There is a weekday Thursday."
  "There is a weekday Tuesday."
  "There is a weekday Wednesday."
```

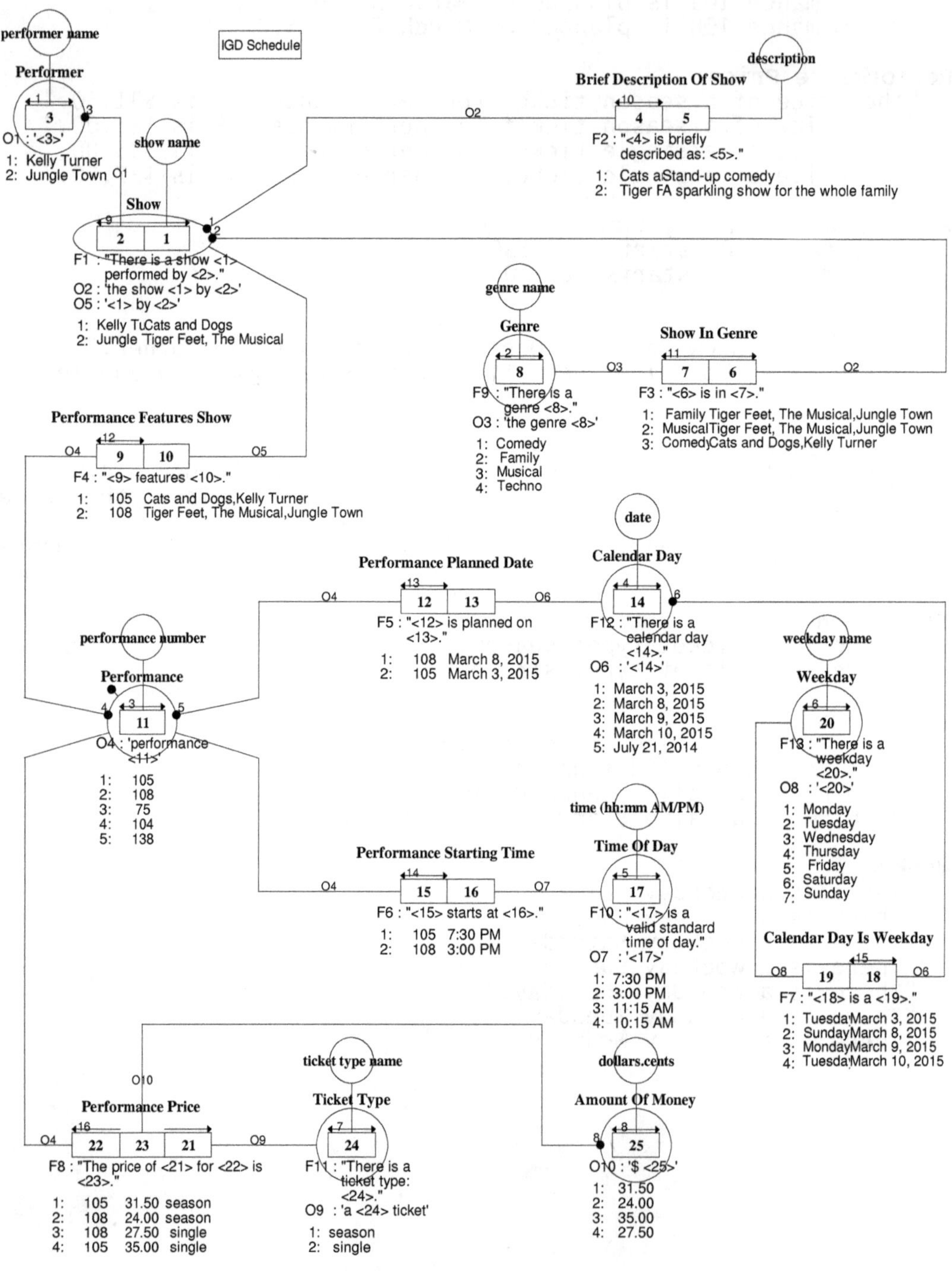
IGD Schedule
performer name
Performer
3
O1 : '<3>'
1: Kelly Turner
2: Jungle Town
show name
Show
2 1
F1 : "There is a show <1> performed by <2>."
O2 : 'the show <1> by <2>'
O5 : '<1> by <2>'
1: Kelly TuCats and Dogs
2: Jungle Tiger Feet, The Musical
description
Brief Description Of Show
4 5
F2 : "<4> is briefly described as: <5>."
1: Cats aStand-up comedy
2: Tiger FA sparkling show for the whole family
genre name
Genre
8
F9 : "There is a genre <8>."
O3 : 'the genre <8>'
1: Comedy
2: Family
3: Musical
4: Techno
Show In Genre
7 6
F3 : "<6> is in <7>."
1: Family Tiger Feet, The Musical,Jungle Town
2: MusicalTiger Feet, The Musical,Jungle Town
3: ComedyCats and Dogs,Kelly Turner
Performance Features Show
9 10
F4 : "<9> features <10>."
1: 105 Cats and Dogs,Kelly Turner
2: 108 Tiger Feet, The Musical,Jungle Town
date
Calendar Day
14
F12 : "There is a calendar day <14>."
O6 : '<14>'
1: March 3, 2015
2: March 8, 2015
3: March 9, 2015
4: March 10, 2015
5: July 21, 2014
Performance Planned Date
12 13
F5 : "<12> is planned on <13>."
1: 108 March 8, 2015
2: 105 March 3, 2015
performance number
Performance
11
O4 : 'performance <11>'
1: 105
2: 108
3: 75
4: 104
5: 138
weekday name
Weekday
20
F13 : "There is a weekday <20>."
O8 : '<20>'
1: Monday
2: Tuesday
3: Wednesday
4: Thursday
5: Friday
6: Saturday
7: Sunday
time (hh:mm AM/PM)
Time Of Day
17
F10 : "<17> is a valid standard time of day."
O7 : '<17>'
1: 7:30 PM
2: 3:00 PM
3: 11:15 AM
4: 10:15 AM
Performance Starting Time
15 16
F6 : "<15> starts at <16>."
1: 105 7:30 PM
2: 108 3:00 PM
Calendar Day Is Weekday
19 18
F7 : "<18> is a <19>."
1: TuesdaMarch 3, 2015
2: SundayMarch 8, 2015
3: MondayMarch 9, 2015
4: TuesdaMarch 10, 2015
Performance Price
22 23 21
F8 : "The price of <21> for <22> is <23>."
1: 105 31.50 season
2: 108 24.00 season
3: 108 27.50 single
4: 105 35.00 single
ticket type name
Ticket Type
24
F11 : "There is a ticket type: <24>."
O9 : 'a <24> ticket'
1: season
2: single
dollars.cents
Amount Of Money
25
O10 : '$ <25>'
1: 31.50
2: 24.00
3: 35.00
4: 27.50

A1.2 IGD CUSTOMER

Country:
"There is a country USA."

Customer Address Line 1:
"Address line 1 of customer 436 is: 1255 Blue Mansions."

Customer Address Line 2:
"Address line 2 of customer 436 is: Lake Area."

Customer Email Box:
"The email address of customer 436 is: LeonardReed@ip4me.com."

Customer First Name:
"The first name of customer 436 is: Leonard."

Customer Surname:
"The surname of customer 436 is: Reed."

Customer Telephone:
"Customer 436 can be phoned at +1-6-5432-6789."

Customer Town:
"Customer 436 lives in Pine Mound, Texas, USA."

Customer With Postal Address:
"The postal address of customer 436 is known."

Customer ZIP Code:
"The ZIP code of customer 436 is: TX 75105."

Reservation Request By Customer:
"Reservation request 7795 was made by customer 436."

State:
"There is a state Texas in USA."

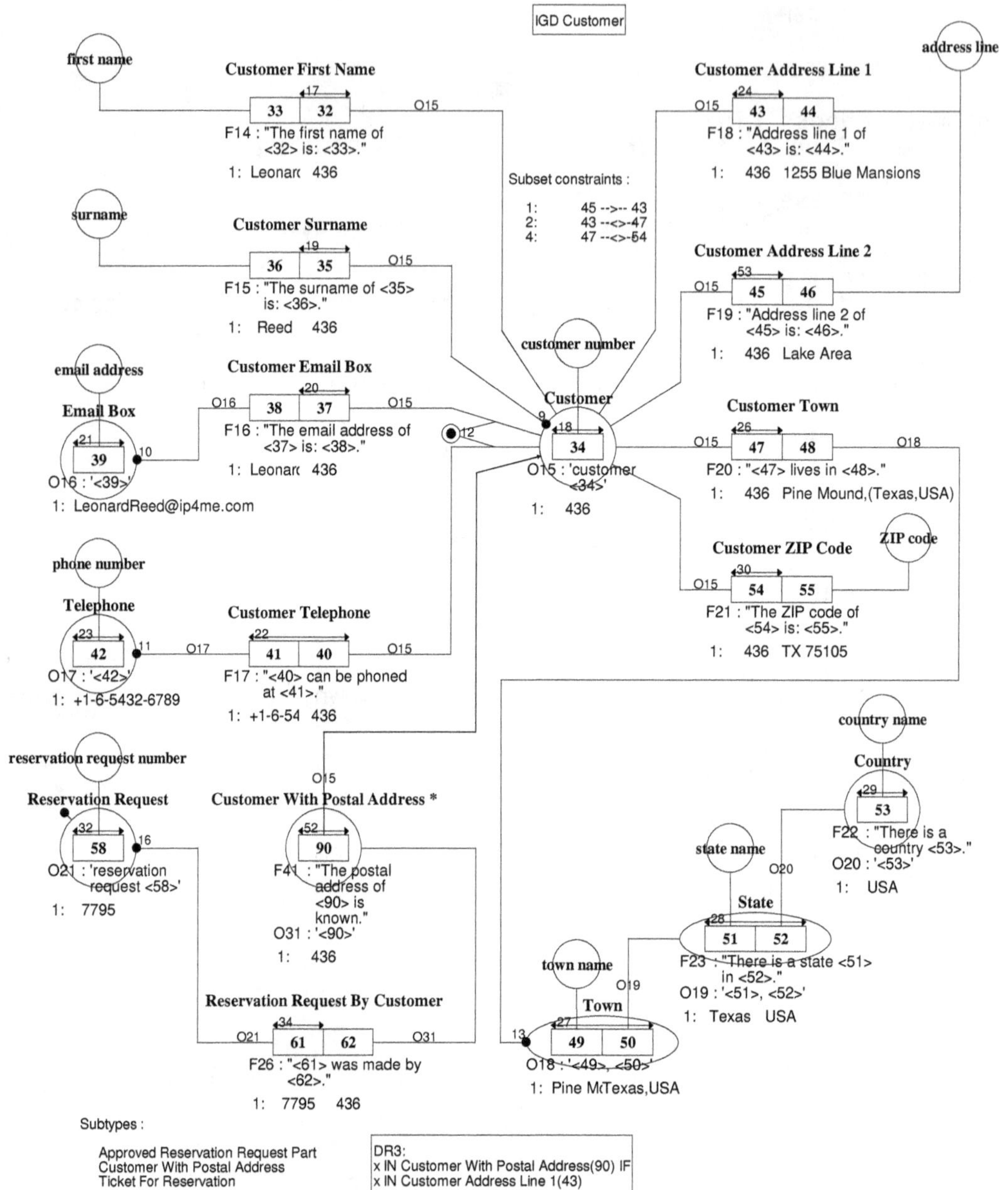
IGD Customer
first name
Customer First Name
F14 : "The first name of <32> is: <33>."
1: Leonar 436
surname
Customer Surname
F15 : "The surname of <35> is: <36>."
1: Reed 436
email address
Email Box
O16 : '<39>'
1: LeonardReed@ip4me.com
Customer Email Box
F16 : "The email address of <37> is: <38>."
1: Leonar 436
phone number
Telephone
O17 : '<42>'
1: +1-6-5432-6789
Customer Telephone
F17 : "<40> can be phoned at <41>."
1: +1-6-54 436
Subset constraints :
1: 45 -->-- 43
2: 43 --<>-47
4: 47 --<>-54
customer number
Customer
O15 : 'customer <34>'
1: 436
address line
Customer Address Line 1
F18 : "Address line 1 of <43> is: <44>."
1: 436 1255 Blue Mansions
Customer Address Line 2
F19 : "Address line 2 of <45> is: <46>."
1: 436 Lake Area
Customer Town
F20 : "<47> lives in <48>."
1: 436 Pine Mound,(Texas,USA)
Customer ZIP Code
ZIP code
F21 : "The ZIP code of <54> is: <55>."
1: 436 TX 75105
reservation request number
Reservation Request
O21 : 'reservation request <58>'
1: 7795
Customer With Postal Address *
F41 : "The postal address of <90> is known."
O31 : '<90>'
1: 436
Reservation Request By Customer
F26 : "<61> was made by <62>."
1: 7795 436
country name
Country
F22 : "There is a country <53>."
O20 : '<53>'
1: USA
state name
State
F23 : "There is a state <51> in <52>."
O19 : '<51>, <52>'
1: Texas USA
town name
Town
O18 : '<49>, <50>'
1: Pine M Texas,USA
Subtypes :
Approved Reservation Request Part
Customer With Postal Address
Ticket For Reservation
DR3:
x IN Customer With Postal Address(90) IF
x IN Customer Address Line 1(43)

A1.3 IGD RESERVATION REQUEST

Calendar Day:

"There is a calendar day July 21, 2014."
"There is a calendar day March 10, 2015."
"There is a calendar day March 3, 2015."
"There is a calendar day March 8, 2015."
"There is a calendar day March 9, 2015."

Customer With Postal Address:

"The postal address of customer 436 is known."

Number Of Seats In Reservation Request Part:

"Part 2 of reservation request 7795 claims 2 seats."
"Part 3 of reservation request 7795 claims 4 seats."
"Part 6 of reservation request 7795 claims 2 seats."

Reservation Request By Customer:

"Reservation request 7795 was made by customer 436."

Reservation Request Part For Performance:

"Part 2 of reservation request 7795 concerns performance 75."
"Part 3 of reservation request 7795 concerns performance 104."
"Part 6 of reservation request 7795 concerns performance 138."

Reservation Request Registration Date:

"Reservation request 7795 was registered on July 21, 2014."

Reservation Request Registration Time:

"Reservation request 7795 was registered at 10:15 AM."

Status:

"There is a status 'approved'."
"There is a status 'assigned'."
"There is a status 'registered'."

Status Of Reservation Request Part:

"The status of part 2 of reservation request 7795 is 'assigned'."
"The status of part 3 of reservation request 7795 is 'approved'."
"The status of part 6 of reservation request 7795 is 'registered'."

Time Of Day:

"10:15 AM is a valid standard time of day."
"11:15 AM is a valid standard time of day."
"3:00 PM is a valid standard time of day."
"7:30 PM is a valid standard time of day."

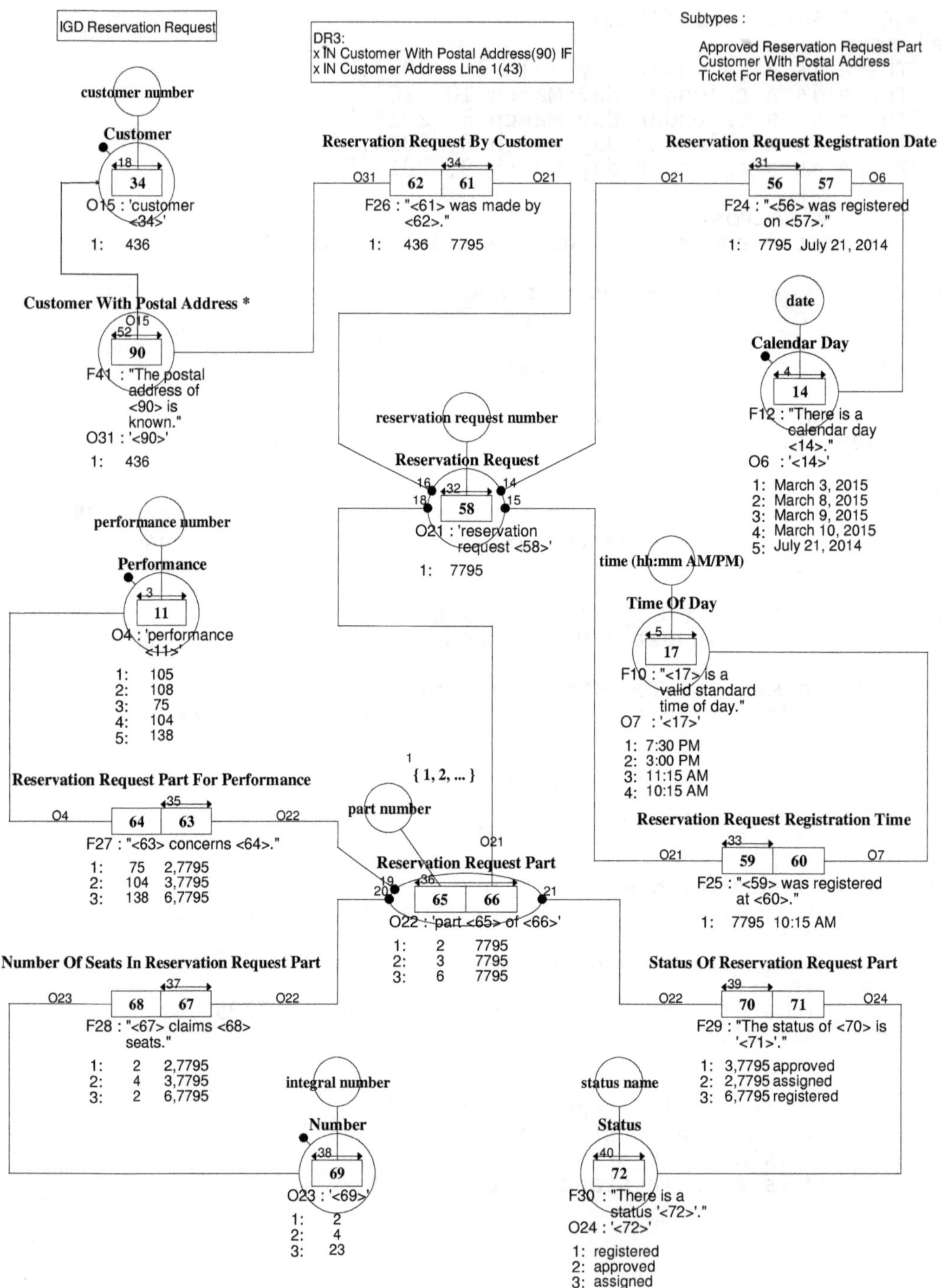
IGD Reservation Request
DR3:
x IN Customer With Postal Address(90) IF
x IN Customer Address Line 1(43)
Subtypes :
Approved Reservation Request Part
Customer With Postal Address
Ticket For Reservation
customer number
Customer
18
34
O15 : 'customer <34>'
1: 436
Reservation Request By Customer
O31
34
62
61
O21
F26 : "<61> was made by <62>."
1: 436 7795
Reservation Request Registration Date
O21
31
56
57
O6
F24 : "<56> was registered on <57>."
1: 7795 July 21, 2014
Customer With Postal Address *
O15
52
90
F41 : "The postal address of <90> is known."
O31 : '<90>'
1: 436
date
Calendar Day
4
14
F12 : "There is a calendar day <14>."
O6 : '<14>'
1: March 3, 2015
2: March 8, 2015
3: March 9, 2015
4: March 10, 2015
5: July 21, 2014
reservation request number
Reservation Request
16
14
18
32
15
58
O21 : 'reservation request <58>'
1: 7795
performance number
Performance
3
11
O4 : 'performance <11>'
1: 105
2: 108
3: 75
4: 104
5: 138
time (hh:mm AM/PM)
Time Of Day
5
17
F10 : "<17> is a valid standard time of day."
O7 : '<17>'
1: 7:30 PM
2: 3:00 PM
3: 11:15 AM
4: 10:15 AM
1
{ 1, 2, ... }
part number
Reservation Request Part For Performance
O4
35
64
63
O22
F27 : "<63> concerns <64>."
1: 75 2,7795
2: 104 3,7795
3: 138 6,7795
Reservation Request Registration Time
O21
33
59
60
O7
F25 : "<59> was registered at <60>."
1: 7795 10:15 AM
O21
Reservation Request Part
19
36
20
65
66
21
O22 : 'part <65> of <66>'
1: 2 7795
2: 3 7795
3: 6 7795
Number Of Seats In Reservation Request Part
O23
37
68
67
O22
F28 : "<67> claims <68> seats."
1: 2 2,7795
2: 4 3,7795
3: 2 6,7795
Status Of Reservation Request Part
O22
39
70
71
O24
F29 : "The status of <70> is '<71>'."
1: 3,7795 approved
2: 2,7795 assigned
3: 6,7795 registered
integral number
Number
38
69
O23 : '<69>'
1: 2
2: 4
3: 23
status name
Status
40
72
F30 : "There is a status '<72>'."
O24 : '<72>'
1: registered
2: approved
3: assigned

A1.4 IGD TICKETS

Approved Reservation Request Part:
"Part 2 of reservation request 7795 was approved."
"Part 3 of reservation request 7795 was approved."

Free Seats For Performance:
"There are still 23 seats free for performance 104."

Number Of Seats In Reservation Request Part:
"Part 2 of reservation request 7795 claims 2 seats."
"Part 3 of reservation request 7795 claims 4 seats."
"Part 6 of reservation request 7795 claims 2 seats."

Reservation Request Part For Performance:
"Part 2 of reservation request 7795 concerns performance 75."
"Part 3 of reservation request 7795 concerns performance 104."
"Part 6 of reservation request 7795 concerns performance 138."

Row:
"There is a row 11."
"There is a row 13."
"There is a row 6."

Seat:
"There is a seat 12 in row 11."
"There is a seat 25 in row 13."
"There is a seat 4 in row 6."

Seat Assigner:
"There is a seat assigner: box office."
"There is a seat assigner: reservation manager."

Status:
"There is a status 'approved'."
"There is a status 'assigned'."
"There is a status 'registered'."

Status Of Reservation Request Part:
"The status of part 2 of reservation request 7795 is 'assigned'."
"The status of part 3 of reservation request 7795 is 'approved'."
"The status of part 6 of reservation request 7795 is 'registered'."

Ticket For Performance:
"Ticket 347B55 is for performance 75."
"Ticket 7749026 is for performance 104."

Ticket For Reservation:
"Ticket 7749026 is for a reservation request part."

Ticket For Reservation Request Part:
"Ticket 7749026 is for the approved part 3 of reservation request 7795."

Ticket For Seat:
"Ticket 347B55 is for seat 12 in row 11."
"Ticket 7749026 is for seat 25 in row 13."

Ticket Issued By:
"Ticket 347B55 was issued by the box office."
"Ticket 7749026 was issued by the reservation manager."

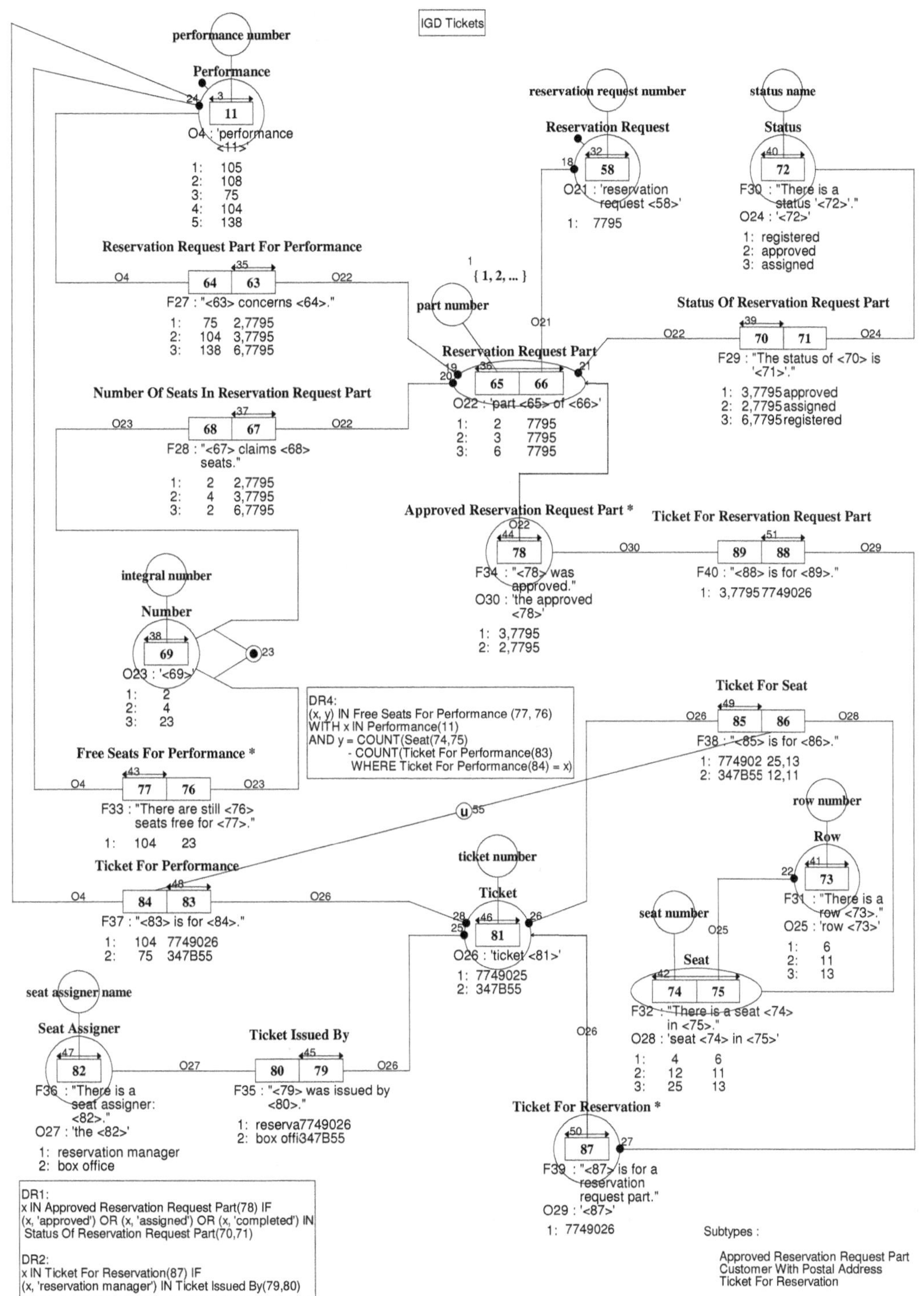
IGD Tickets
performance number
Performance
11
O4 : 'performance <11>'
1: 105
2: 108
3: 75
4: 104
5: 138
reservation request number
Reservation Request
58
O21 : 'reservation request <58>'
1: 7795
status name
Status
72
F30 : "There is a status '<72>'."
O24 : '<72>'
1: registered
2: approved
3: assigned
Reservation Request Part For Performance
64 63
F27 : "<63> concerns <64>."
1: 75 2,7795
2: 104 3,7795
3: 138 6,7795
1
{ 1, 2, ... }
part number
Reservation Request Part
65 66
O22 : 'part <65> of <66>'
1: 2 7795
2: 3 7795
3: 6 7795
Status Of Reservation Request Part
70 71
F29 : "The status of <70> is '<71>'."
1: 3,7795approved
2: 2,7795assigned
3: 6,7795registered
Number Of Seats In Reservation Request Part
68 67
F28 : "<67> claims <68> seats."
1: 2 2,7795
2: 4 3,7795
3: 2 6,7795
Approved Reservation Request Part *
78
F34 : "<78> was approved."
O30 : 'the approved <78>'
1: 3,7795
2: 2,7795
Ticket For Reservation Request Part
89 88
F40 : "<88> is for <89>."
1: 3,7795 7749026
integral number
Number
69
O23 : '<69>'
1: 2
2: 4
3: 23
DR4:
(x, y) IN Free Seats For Performance (77, 76)
WITH x IN Performance(11)
AND y = COUNT(Seat(74,75)
- COUNT(Ticket For Performance(83)
WHERE Ticket For Performance(84) = x)
Ticket For Seat
85 86
F38 : "<85> is for <86>."
1: 774902 25,13
2: 347B55 12,11
Free Seats For Performance *
77 76
F33 : "There are still <76> seats free for <77>."
1: 104 23
row number
Row
73
F31 : "There is a row <73>."
O25 : 'row <73>'
1: 6
2: 11
3: 13
Ticket For Performance
84 83
F37 : "<83> is for <84>."
1: 104 7749026
2: 75 347B55
ticket number
Ticket
81
O26 : 'ticket <81>'
1: 7749025
2: 347B55
seat number
Seat
74 75
F32 : "There is a seat <74> in <75>."
O28 : 'seat <74> in <75>'
1: 4 6
2: 12 11
3: 25 13
seat assigner name
Seat Assigner
82
F36 : "There is a seat assigner: <82>."
O27 : 'the <82>'
1: reservation manager
2: box office
Ticket Issued By
80 79
F35 : "<79> was issued by <80>."
1: reserva7749026
2: box offi347B55
Ticket For Reservation *
87
F39 : "<87> is for a reservation request part."
O29 : '<87>'
1: 7749026
DR1:
x IN Approved Reservation Request Part(78) IF
(x, 'approved') OR (x, 'assigned') OR (x, 'completed') IN
Status Of Reservation Request Part(70,71)
DR2:
x IN Ticket For Reservation(87) IF
(x, 'reservation manager') IN Ticket Issued By(79,80)
Subtypes :
Approved Reservation Request Part
Customer With Postal Address
Ticket For Reservation

A2 Constraints

A2.1 Uniqueness Constraint Determination for All Fact Types with Two or More Roles

For clarity, in many places parts of Object Expression Types were added to the 'bare' Fact Expression Types. In a few cases some extra words were added, inserted between [square brackets].

Fact Types from IGD 'Schedule'

<table>
<tr><th colspan="7">Fact Type 'Show'. F1: "There is a show <1> performed by <2>."</th></tr>
<tr><th>Test UC on:</th><th>Fact</th><th>Show name</th><th>Performer</th><th>Allowed?</th><th>Domain Expert Comment</th><th>Conclusion</th></tr>
<tr><td>Role 1</td><td>1:
2:</td><td>Cats and Dogs
Cats and Dogs</td><td>Kelly Turner
Animals!</td><td>} ✓</td><td>We had 2 shows with the same name once.</td><td>No UC on Role 1 only</td></tr>
<tr><td>Role 2</td><td>3:
4:</td><td>Cats and Dogs
Home Again</td><td>Kelly Turner
Kelly Turner</td><td>} ✓</td><td>Proud to host the same artist again.</td><td>No UC on Role 2 only</td></tr>
<tr><td colspan="7">Because there is no UC on just one Role, UC 9 on the combination of Roles 1+2 was added.</td></tr>
<tr><td colspan="7">"A show is identified by the combination of a show name and a performer."</td></tr>
</table>

<table>
<tr><th colspan="7">Fact Type 'Brief Description Of Show'. F2: "The show <4> is briefly described as: <5>."</th></tr>
<tr><th>Test UC on:</th><th>Fact</th><th>Show</th><th>Description</th><th>Allowed?</th><th>Domain Expert Comment</th><th>Conclusion</th></tr>
<tr><td>Role 4</td><td>1:
2:</td><td>Cats..., Kelly...
Cats..., Kelly...</td><td>Stand-up...
Drama</td><td>} ✗</td><td>Only one description for each show.</td><td>UC 10 on Role 4</td></tr>
<tr><td>Role 5</td><td>3:
4:</td><td>Cats..., Kelly...
Ouch!, Ron...</td><td>Stand-up...
Stand-up...</td><td>} ✓</td><td>We have many stand-up comedy shows.</td><td>No UC on Role 5</td></tr>
<tr><td colspan="7">"A show can be briefly described by at most one description."
"A description can briefly describe several shows."</td></tr>
</table>

Fact Type 'Show In Genre'. F3: "The show <6> is in the genre <7>."						
Test UC on:	**Fact**	**Show**	**Genre**	**Allowed?**	**Domain Expert Comment**	**Conclusion**
Role 6	1: 2:	Cats..., Kelly... Cats..., Kelly...	Musical ***Family***	} ✓	A show can be in several genres.	No UC on Role 6 only
Role 7	3: 4:	Cats..., Kelly... ***Tiger..., Jungle...***	Musical Musical	} ✓	Many shows can be in the same genre.	No UC on Role 7 only
Because there is no UC on just one Role, UC 11 on the combination of Roles 6+7 was added.						
"A show can be in several genres." "A genre can contain several shows."						

Fact Type 'Performance Features Show'. F4: "Performance <9> features <10>."						
Test UC on:	**Fact**	**Perfor-mance**	**Show**	**Allowed?**	**Domain Expert Comment**	**Conclusion**
Role 9	1: 2:	105 105	Cats..., Kelly... ***Tiger..., Jungle...***	} ✗	Only one show in each performance.	UC 12 on Role 9
Role 10	3: 4:	105 ***106***	Cats..., Kelly... Cats..., Kelly...	} ✓	A show can run for weeks if it is successful.	No UC on Role 10
"A performance can feature at most one show." "A show can be featured in several performances."						

Fact Type 'Performance Planned Date'. F5: "Performance <12> features <13>."						
Test UC on:	**Fact**	**Perfor-mance**	**Calendar Day**	**Al-lowed?**	**Domain Expert Comment**	**Conclusion**
Role 12	1: 2:	105 105	March 3, 2015 ***March 4, 2015***	} ✗	Performance starts on only one day even if it lasts till after midnight.	UC 13 on Role 12
Role 13	3: 4:	105 ***106***	March 3, 2015 March 3, 2015	} ✓	One in the afternoon, one in the evening.	No UC on Role 13
"A performance can be planned on at most one calendar day." "A calendar day can be the planned day of several performances."						

Fact Type 'Performance Starting Time'. F6: "Performance <12> starts at <13>."

Test UC on:	Fact	Perfor-mance	Calendar Day	Allowed?	Domain Expert Comment	Conclusion
Role 15	1: 2:	105 105	7:30 PM ***8:00 PM***	} ✗	Performance has one starting time.	UC 14 on Role 15
Role 16	3: 4:	105 ***122***	7:30 PM 7:30 PM	} ✓	Many performances start at 7:30 PM here.	No UC on Role 16

"A performance can start on at most one time of day."
"A time of day can be the starting time of several performances."

Fact Type 'Calendar Day Is Weekday'. F7: "<18> is a <19>."

Test UC on:	Fact	Calendar Day	Weekday	Al-lowed?	Domain Expert Comment	Conclusion
Role 18	1: 2:	March 3, 2015 March 3, 2015	Tuesday ***Friday***	} ✗	The modeler did not bother the Domain Expert with this, the Fact Type and its UC are well-known.	UC 15 on Role 18
Role 19	3: 4:	March 3, 2015 ***March 10, 2015***	Tuesday Tuesday	} ✓		No UC on Role 19

"A calendar day can be at most one weekday."
"A weekday can be the weekday of several calendar days."

Fact Type Performance Price. F8: "The price for a <21> ticket for performance <22> is $<23>."

Test UC on:	Fact	Ticket Type	Perfor-mance	Price ($$.cc)	Allowed?	Domain Expert Comment	Conclusion
Roles 21+22	1: 2:	season season	108 108	24.00 ***25.50***	} ✗	No prices 'under the counter'.	UC 16 on Roles 21+22
Roles 21+23	3: 4:	season season	108 ***120***	24.00 24.00	} ✓	Yeah, sure.	No UC on Roles 21+23
Roles 22+23	5: 6:	season ***promo***	108 108	24.00 24.00	} ✓	No limits on price policy please.	No UC on Roles 22+23

Only one UC on combinations of two Roles found: no checks necessary.

"A combination of a ticket type and a performance can have at most one price."
"A combination of a ticket type and a price can apply to several performances."
"A combination of a performance and a price can apply to several ticket types."

Fact Types from IGD 'Customer'

Fact Type 'Customer First Name'. F14: "The first name of customer <32> is: <33>."

Test UC on:	Fact	Customer	First name	Allowed?	Domain Expert Comment	Conclusion
Role 32	1: 2:	436 436	Leonard ***Steve***	} ✗	Only one given name is to be recorded.	UC 17 on Role 32
Role 33	3: 4:	436 ***555***	Leonard Leonard	} ✓	Obviously.	No UC on Role 33

"A customer can have at most one first name."
"A first name can be the first name of several customers."

Fact Type 'Customer Surname'. F15: "The surname of customer <35> is: <36>."

Test UC on:	Fact	Customer	First name	Allowed?	Domain Expert Comment	Conclusion
Role 35	1: 2:	436 436	Reed ***Jones***	} ✗	The modeler did not bother the Domain Expert with this, the Fact Type and its UC are well-known.	UC 19 on Role 35
Role 36	3: 4:	436 ***555***	Reed Reed	} ✓		No UC on Role 36

"A customer can have at most one first name."
"A first name can be the first name of several customers."

Fact Type 'Customer Email Box'. F16: "The email address of customer <37> is: <38>."

Test UC on:	Fact	Customer	Email Box	Allowed?	Domain Expert Comment	Conclusion
Role 37	1: 2:	436 436	LeonardReed@ip4me.com ***LennysMail@free.com***	} ✗	Only one email address is recorded.	UC 20 on Role 37
Role 38	3: 4:	436 ***555***	LeonardReed@ip4me.com LeonardReed@ip4me.com	} ✓	Even today, people share email.	No UC on Role 38

"A customer can have at most one email address."
"An email address can belong to several customers."

Fact Type 'Customer Telephone'. F17: "Customer <40> can be phoned at <41>."						
Test UC on:	**Fact**	**Custo-mer**	**Telephone**	**Al-lowed?**	**Domain Expert Comment**	**Conclusion**
Role 40	1: 2:	436 436	+1-6-5432-6789 ***831-987-6543***	} ✓	Often cellphone and landline are given.	No UC on Role 40 only
Role 41	3: 4:	436 ***555***	831-987-6543 831-987-6543	} ✓	People can share the same phone number.	No UC on Role 41 only
No detailed structure of phone numbers is required: Serviceton enters the phone numbers as they are stated on the website or on the paper form.						
Because there is no UC on just one Role, UC 22 on the combination of Roles 40+41 was added.						
"A customer can be phoned at several telephones." "A telephone can be used to phone several customers."						

Fact Type 'Address Line 1'. F18: "Address line 1 of customer <43> is: <44>."						
Test UC on:	**Fact**	**Custo-mer**	**Address line 1**	**Al-lowed?**	**Domain Expert Comment**	**Conclu-sion**
Role 43	1: 2:	436 436	1255 Blue Mansions ***62a Main Street***	} ✗	Only one address per customer is recorded.	UC 24 on Role 43
Role 44	3: 4:	436 ***555***	1255 Blue Mansions 1255 Blue Mansions	} ✓	Different customers can be married.	No UC on Role 44
"A customer can have at most one address line 1." "An address line 1 can be the address line 1 of several customers."						

Fact Type 'Address Line 2'. F19: "Address line 2 of customer <45> is: <46>."						
Test UC on:	**Fact**	**Customer**	**Address line 2**	**Al-lowed?**	**Domain Expert Comment**	**Conclu-sion**
Role 45	1: 2:	436 436	Lake Area ***Downtown***	} ✗	Only one address per customer is recorded.	UC 53 on Role 45
Role 46	3: 4:	436 ***555***	Lake Area Lake Area	} ✓	Different customers can be married.	No UC on Role 46
Address line 2 can only be used if address line 1 is used for the same customer as well.						
"A customer can have at most one address line 2." "An address line 2 can be the address line 1 of several customers."						

Fact Type 'Customer Town'. F20: "Customer <47> lives in <48>."

Test UC on:	Fact	Custo-mer	Town	Al-lowed?	Domain Expert Comment	Conclu-sion
Role 47	1: 2:	436 436	Pine Mound Texas USA ***Oakville Ohio USA***	} ✗	Only one address per customer is recorded.	UC 26 on Role 47
Role 48	3: 4:	436 ***555***	Pine Mound Texas USA Pine Mound Texas USA	} ✓	Different customers can be married.	No UC on Role 48

Towns are to be recorded giving town name, state and country. The state and country must be chosen from a standard list (to avoid typos and other ambiguities).

"A customer can live in at most one town."
"A town can be lived in by several customers."

Fact Type 'State'. F23: "There is a state <51> in <52>."

Test UC on:	Fact	State name	Country	Al-lowed?	Domain Expert Comment	Conclusion
Role 51	1: 2:	Northy Northy	Limbabwe ***Latvinia***	} ✓	A state name might occur in different countries.	No UC on Role 51 only
Role 52	3: 4:	Northy ***Southy***	Limbabwe Limbabwe	} ✓	A country (till now, haha) always has several states.	No UC on Role 52 only

A standard list of all (current) countries with their states is to be provided.

Because there is no UC on just one Role, UC 28 on the combination of Roles 51+52 was added.

"A state is identified by the combination of a state name and a country."

Fact Type 'Town'. O18: '<49>, <50>."
NOTE: No Fact Expression Type, still it has 2 Roles so its UC should be checked.

Test UC on:	Fact	Town name	Country	Al-lowed?	Domain Expert Comment	Conclusion
Role 49	1: 2:	Pine Mound Pine Mound	Texas USA ***Idaho USA***	} ✓	A town name might occur in different states.	No UC on Role 49 only
Role 50	3: 4:	Pine Mound ***Oreville***	Texas USA Texas USA	} ✓	A state always contains several towns.	No UC on Role 50 only

Because there is no UC on just one Role, UC 27 on the combination of Roles 49+50 was added.

"A state is identified by the combination of a state name and a country."

Fact Types from IGD 'Reservation Request

Fact Type 'Res. Req. Registration Date'. F24: "Res. Req. <56> was registered on <57>."						
Test UC on:	**Fact**	**Res. Request**	**Calendar Day**	**Allowed?**	**Domain Expert Comment**	**Conclusion**
Role 56	1: 2:	7795 7795	July 21, 2014 ***March 4, 2015***	} ✗	Registering once will do.	UC 31 on Role 56
Role 57	3: 4:	7795 ***7796***	July 21, 2014 July 21, 2014	} ✓	Usually several on the same day.	No UC on Role 57
"A reservation request can be registered on at most one calendar day." "A calendar day can be the registration day of several reservation requests."						

Fact Type 'Res. Req. Registration Time'. F25: "Res. Req. <59> was registered at <60>."						
Test UC on:	**Fact**	**Res. Request**	**Time Of Day**	**Allowed?**	**Domain Expert Comment**	**Conclusion**
Role 59	1: 2:	7795 7795	10:15 AM ***8:00 PM***	} ✗	Registering once will do.	UC 33 on Role 59
Role 60	3: 4:	7795 ***7796***	10:15 AM 10:15 AM	} ✓	Several requests can be registered in the same 15-minute interval.	No UC on Role 60
"A reservation request can be registered on at most one time of day." "A time of day can be the registration time of several reservation requests."						

Fact Type 'Res. Req. By Customer'. F26: "Res. Req. <61> was made by <62>."						
Test UC on:	**Fact**	**Res. Request**	**Customer**	**Allowed?**	**Domain Expert Comment**	**Conclusion**
Role 61	1: 2:	7795 7795	436 ***555***	} ✗	Only one customer can make a res. request.	UC 34 on Role 61
Role 62	3: 4:	7795 ***7796***	436 436	} ✓	Same customer can make several res. requests.	No UC on Role 62
"A reservation request can be made by at most one customer." "A customer can make several reservation requests."						

Fact Type 'Reservation Request Part'. O22: 'part <65> of reservation request <66>'
NOTE : No Fact Expression Type, still it has 2 Roles so its UC should be checked.

Test UC on:	Fact	Part number	Res. Request	Allowed?	Domain Expert Comment	Conclusion
Role 65	1: 2:	2 2	7795 ***<u>7777</u>***	} ✓	The modeler did not bother the Domain Expert with this, the example Facts were easily found.	No UC on Role 65 only
Role 66	3: 4:	2 ***<u>3</u>***	7795 7795	} ✓		No UC on Role 66 only

Because there is no UC on just one Role, UC 36 on the combination of Roles 65+66 was added.

"A reservation request part is identified by the combination of a part number and a reservation request."

Fact Type 'Reservation Request Part For Performance'.
F27: "[Reservation request part] <63> concerns performance <64>."

Test UC on:	Fact	Res. Req. Part	Performance	Allowed?	Domain Expert Comment	Conclusion
Role 63	1: 2:	2, 7795 2, 7795	75 ***<u>88</u>***	} ✗	Only one performance in each res. req. part.	UC 35 on Role 63
Role 64	3: 4:	2, 7795 ***<u>3, 7777</u>***	75 75	} ✓	Yes we do like to have fully booked shows.	No UC on Role 64

"A reservation request part can concern at most one performance."
"A performance can be concerned in several reservation request parts."

Fact Type ´Number Of Seats In Reservation Request Part´.
F28: "[Reservation request part] <67> claims <68> seats."

Test UC on:	Fact	Res. Req. Part	Number	Allowed?	Domain Expert Comment	Conclusion
Role 67	1: 2:	2, 7795 2, 7795	2 ***<u>8</u>***	} ✗	If a customer enters '2+8', we make it '10'.	UC 37 on Role 67
Role 68	3: 4:	2, 7795 ***<u>3, 7777</u>***	2 2	} ✓	Obviously.	No UC on Role 68

"A reservation request part can claim at most one number of seats."
"The same number of seats can be claimed in several reservation request parts."

Fact Type ´Status Of Reservation Request Part´.
F28: "The status of [reservation request part] <70> is <71>."

Test UC on:	Fact	Res. Req. Part	Status	Allowed?	Domain Expert Comment	Conclusion
Role 70	1: 2:	2, 7795 2, 7795	approved ***registered***	} ✗	The status can change, new replaces old.	UC 39 on Role 70
Role 71	3: 4:	2, 7795 ***3, 7777***	approved approved	} ✓	Obviously.	No UC on Role 71

"A reservation request part can have at most one status."
"A status can be the status of several reservation request parts."

Fact Types from IGD 'Tickets'

Fact Type ´Seat´. F32: "There is a seat <74> in row <75>."

Test UC on:	Fact	Seat Number	Row	Allowed?	Domain Expert Comment	Conclusion
Role 74	1: 2:	2 2	6 ***7***	} ✓	The modeler did not bother the Domain Expert with this, the example Facts were easily found.	No UC on Role 74 only
Role 75	3: 4:	2 ***14***	6 6	} ✓		No UC on Role 75 only

Because there is no UC on just one Role, UC 47 on the combination of Roles 74+75 was added.

"A performance can have at most one number of free seats."
"The same number can be the number of free seats in several performances."

Fact Type ´Free Seats For Performance´.
F33: "There are still <76> seats free for performance <77>."

Test UC on:	Fact	Number	Performance	Allowed?	Domain Expert Comment	Conclusion
Role 76	1: 2:	23 23	104 ***99***	} ✓	The modeler did not bother the Domain Expert with this, the UC is obvious.	No UC on Role 76
Role 77	3: 4:	23 ***44***	104 104	} ✗		UC 43 on Role 77

"A performance can have at most one number of free seats."
"The same number can be the number of free seats in several performances."

Fact Type ´Ticket Issued By´. F35: "Ticket <79> was issued by seat assigner <80>."

Test UC on:	Fact	Ticket	Seat assigner	Allowed?	Domain Expert Comment	Conclusion

Role 79	1: 2:	7749025 7749025	box office ***res. manager***	} ✗	Only one assigner is responsible for a ticket.	UC 45 on Role 79
Role 80	3: 4:	7749025 ***4444444***	box office box office	} ✓	Obvious.	No UC on Role 80

"A ticket can be issued by at most one seat assigner."
"A seat assigner can issue several tickets."

Fact Type ´Ticket For Performance´. F37: "Ticket <83> is for performance <84>."

Test UC on:	Fact	Ticket	Perfor-mance	Allowed?	Domain Expert Comment	Conclusion
Role 83	1: 2:	7749025 7749025	104 ***99***	} ✗	Each ticket is for one single performance.	UC 48 on Role 83
Role 84	3: 4:	7749025 ***4444444***	104 104	} ✓	Of course.	No UC on Role 84

"A ticket can be for at most one performance."
"For a performance can be several tickets."

Fact Type ´Ticket For Seat´. F38: "Ticket <85> is for seat <86>."

Test UC on:	Fact	Ticket	Seat	Allowed?	Domain Expert Comment	Conclusion
Role 85	1: 2:	7749025 7749025	25, 13 ***19, 12***	} ✗	Each ticket is for one single seat.	UC 49 on Role 85
Role 86	3: 4:	7749025 ***4444444***	25, 13 25, 13	} ✓	Yes, in different performances.	No UC on Role 86

"A ticket can be for at most one seat."
"For a seat can be several tickets."

Fact Type ´Ticket For Reservation Request Part´.
F40: "Ticket [for reservation] <88> is for the approved [reservation request part] <89>."

Test UC on:	Fact	Ticket	Res. Req. Part	Allowed?	Domain Expert Comment	Conclusion
Role 88	1: 2:	7749025 7749025	3, 7795 ***4, 7890***	} ✗	Each ticket is for one performance, so also for a single res. req. part.	UC 51 on Role 88
Role 89	3: 4:	7749025 ***7749026***	3, 7795 3, 7795	} ✓	Yes, both tickets for the same performance.	No UC on Role 89

"A ticket-for-reservation can be for at most one approved reservation request part."
"For an approved reservation request part can be several tickets-for-reservation."

A2.2 TOTALITY CONSTRAINT DETERMINATION FOR ALL OBJECT TYPES

Object Types from IGD 'Schedule'

<table>
<tr><th colspan="4">OT: Show</th></tr>
<tr><th>Test TC on Role(s):</th><th>Question</th><th>Answer (Y/N), Comment</th><th>Conclusion</th></tr>
<tr><td>4</td><td>Can there be a show without a brief description?</td><td>N</td><td>TC 1 on Role 4</td></tr>
<tr><td>6</td><td>Must every show be in at least one genre?</td><td>Y</td><td>TC 2 on Role 6</td></tr>
<tr><td>10</td><td>Can there be a show without a performance?</td><td>Y: for later seasons shows are known before the schedule is completed.</td><td>No TC on Role 10</td></tr>
<tr><td colspan="4">"A show must be briefly described by at least one description."
"A show must be in at least one genre."
"A show does not need to be featured in a performance."</td></tr>
</table>

<table>
<tr><th colspan="4">OT: Performer</th></tr>
<tr><th>Test TC on Role(s):</th><th>Question</th><th>Answer (Y/N), Comment</th><th>Conclusion</th></tr>
<tr><td>2</td><td>Would you like a list of possible performers?</td><td>N, too big, no problems with performer names.</td><td>TC 3 on Role 2</td></tr>
<tr><td colspan="4">"No domain list is needed for performers."
"A performer must perform in at least one show."</td></tr>
</table>

<table>
<tr><th colspan="4">OT: Performance</th></tr>
<tr><th>Test TC on Role(s):</th><th>Question</th><th>Answer (Y/N), Comment</th><th>Conclusion</th></tr>
<tr><td>9</td><td>Is the show known for every planned performance?</td><td>Y: we can't plan a performance without a show.</td><td>TC 4 on Role 9</td></tr>
<tr><td>12</td><td>Does every performance have a planned date?</td><td>Y</td><td>TC 5 on Role 12</td></tr>
<tr><td>15</td><td>Does every performance have a planned starting time?</td><td>N: this can be fixed later.</td><td>No TC on Role 15</td></tr>
<tr><td>22</td><td>Are prices known for every performance?</td><td>N: we often plan the show and the date, and settle other things later.</td><td>No TC on Role 22</td></tr>
<tr><td>15+22</td><td>Maybe either a time or a price is always recorded?</td><td>N, not necessarily.</td><td>No TC on Roles 15+22</td></tr>
<tr><td colspan="4">"A performance must feature in at least one show."
"A performance must be planned on at least one calendar day."
"A performance does not need to have a starting time."
"A performance does not need to have prices."
"A performance does not need to have either a starting time or prices."</td></tr>
</table>

OT: Genre			
Test TC on Role(s):	**Question**	**Answer (Y/N), Comment**	**Conclusion**
7	Would you like a list of possible genres?	Y	No TC on Role 7, Fact Expression Type added
"A domain list is desired for genres." "A genre does not need to contain a show."			

OT: Calendar Day			
Test TC on Role(s):	**Question**	**Answer (Y/N), Comment**	**Conclusion**
18	Must the weekday be known for every calendar day?	Y	TC 6 on Role 18
13, 57	I suppose it's possible for a date to have a performance planned but no reservation registered, and vice versa?	Y	No TC on Role 13 No TC on Role 57
13+57	Would you like a calendar implemented to pick dates from?	Y!	No TC on Roles 13+57. Fact Expression Type added
"A calendar day must be at least one weekday." "A calendar day does not need to have a performance planned." "A calendar day does not need to have a reservation request registered." "A calendar day does not need to have a performance planned or a reservation request registered." "A domain list is desired for calendar days."			

OT: Time Of Day			
Test TC on Role(s):	**Question**	**Answer (Y/N), Comment**	**Conclusion**
16+60	Would you like a pick list of all possible times of day a performance can start?	Y: we want only certain starting times: every 15 minutes, not in between.	No TC on Roles 16+60. Fact Expression Type added
"A domain list is desired for times of day." "A time of day does not need to be the day on which a performance is planned." "A time of day does not need to be the day on which a reservation request was registered."			

OT: Weekday			
Test TC on Role(s):	**Question**	**Answer (Y/N), Comment**	**Conclusion**
19	Would you like a pick list of all possible weekdays?	On second thoughts: Y	No TC on Role 19. Fact Expression Type added
"A domain list is desired for weekdays." "A weekday does not need to be the weekday of a calendar day."			

OT: Ticket Type			
Test TC on Role(s):	**Question**	**Answer (Y/N), Comment**	**Conclusion**
21	Would you like a pick list of all possible ticket types?	Y	No TC on Role 21. Fact Expression Type added
"A domain list is desired for ticket types." "A ticket type does not need to have a price for a performance."			

OT: Amount Of Money			
Test TC on Role(s):	**Question**	**Answer (Y/N), Comment**	**Conclusion**
23	Would you like a pick list of all possible amounts of money?	N. That would really be over the top.	TC 8 on Role 23.
"No domain list is desired for amounts of money." "An amount of money must be the price of at least one ticket type for a performance."			

Object Types from IGD 'Customer'

OT 'Customer':

During the interview interesting points came up as summarized here:

- To be able to communicate with a customer, an email address and/or phone number is required for every customer (BR 24).
- To be able to send tickets, the full address of a customer must be entered on reservation requests (BR 25). On the website, all address fields are mandatory (except address line 2, BR 26). Incompletely filled out forms are either completed after contacting the customer or cannot be processed and are discarded.
- Other customers can also give their postal address if they register on the website or buy tickets at the box office.

- BR 25 and BR 26 lead to a Subset Constraint (SC) and Equality Constraints (ECs); see Section 4.5.

<table>
<tr><th colspan="4">OT: Customer</th></tr>
<tr><th>Test TC on Role(s):</th><th>Question</th><th>Answer (Y/N), Comment</th><th>Conclusion</th></tr>
<tr><td>32</td><td>Do you record the first name for every customer?</td><td>N: some don't enter one, some only an initial, but we don't use initials.</td><td>No TC on Role 32</td></tr>
<tr><td>35</td><td>Do you record the surname for every customer?</td><td>Y</td><td>TC 9 on Role 35</td></tr>
<tr><td>37</td><td>Do you record the email address for every customer?</td><td>Preferably yes, but some customers only give a phone number.</td><td>No TC on Role 37</td></tr>
<tr><td>40</td><td>Do you record a phone number for every customer?</td><td>Preferably even two, but some only give an email address.</td><td>No TC on Role 40</td></tr>
<tr><td>37+40</td><td>But at least email or phone is required?</td><td>Yes, otherwise we can't communicate with the customer.</td><td>TC 12 on Roles 37+40</td></tr>
<tr><td rowspan="2">43, 45, 47 and 54</td><td>Do you record a postal address for every customer?</td><td>No, some customers buy at the box office or register on the website and leave only their email address for messages.</td><td rowspan="2">No TC on any Role 43, 45, 47 or 54. This leads to a SC and ECs</td></tr>
<tr><td>Can any part of the postal address be missed?</td><td>Yes, but only address line 2 (if address line 1 is present).</td></tr>
<tr><td colspan="4">"A customer does not need to have a first name."
"A customer must have at least one surname."
"A customer does not need to have an email address."
"A customer does not need to be phoned at a telephone."
"A customer must have at least one email address and/or be phoned at a telephone."
"A customer does not need to have an address line 1."
"A customer does not need to have an address line 2."
"A customer does not need to live in a town."
"A customer does not need to have a ZIP code."</td></tr>
</table>

<table>
<tr><th colspan="4">OT: Customer With Postal Address</th></tr>
<tr><th>Test TC on Role(s):</th><th>Question</th><th>Answer (Y/N), Comment</th><th>Conclusion</th></tr>
<tr><td>62</td><td>So only customers with a postal address can make reservation requests, but there are also other customers you register the postal address for?</td><td>Yeah that's it.</td><td>No TC on Role 62</td></tr>
<tr><td colspan="4">"A customer with postal address does not need to have made a reservation request."</td></tr>
</table>

<table>
<tr><th colspan="4">OT: Email Box</th></tr>
<tr><th>Test TC on Role(s):</th><th>Question</th><th>Answer (Y/N), Comment</th><th>Conclusion</th></tr>
</table>

38	Do you only record email addresses for existing customers?	Y	TC 10 on Role 38
"No domain list is desired for email boxes." "An email address must be the email address of at least one customer."			

OT: Telephone			
Test TC on Role(s):	**Question**	**Answer (Y/N), Comment**	**Conclusion**
41	Do you want a pick list for phone numbers or just record those of existing customers?	Just for existing customers.	TC 11 on Role 41
"No domain list is desired for telephones." "A phone number must be a phone number at which at least one customer can be phoned."			

OT: Town			
Test TC on Role(s):	**Question**	**Answer (Y/N), Comment**	**Conclusion**
48	Would you like a pick list for all towns? Avoid typos?	No, too many. But for states and countries: yes!	TC 13 on Role 48
"No domain list is desired for towns." "A town must be a town that at least one customer lives in."			

OT: State			
Test TC on Role(s):	**Question**	**Answer (Y/N), Comment**	**Conclusion**
50	So you'd like a pick list of all states, even if there is no customer who lives there?	Yes, like all Canadian states even if we have customers in but a few.	No TC on Role 50. Fact Expression Type is present
"A domain list is desired for states." "A state does not need to contain a town a customer lives in."			

OT: Country			
Test TC on Role(s):	**Question**	**Answer (Y/N), Comment**	**Conclusion**
52	How about countries? A list as well, and can there be a country without a state?	Yes, a list of all countries would be nice. We'll add states later if we need them.	No TC on Role 52. Fact Expression Type is present
"A domain list is desired for countries." "A country does not need to contain a state."			

Object Types from IGD 'Reservation Request'

<table>
<tr><td colspan="4">OT: Reservation Request</td></tr>
<tr><td>Test TC on Role(s):</td><td>Question</td><td>Answer (Y/N), Comment</td><td>Conclusion</td></tr>
<tr><td>56</td><td>Is the registration date known for every res. request?</td><td>Y</td><td>TC 14 on Role 56</td></tr>
<tr><td>59</td><td>Is the registration time known for every res. request?</td><td>Yes, together with the date.</td><td>TC 15 on Role 59</td></tr>
<tr><td>61</td><td>Is a customer always recorded for every res. request?</td><td>Yes, we have to know whom to send the tickets to.</td><td>TC 16 on Role 61</td></tr>
<tr><td>66</td><td>Does every res. request have at least one res. req. part?</td><td>Of course, otherwise there's nothing to reserve.</td><td>TC 18 on Role 66</td></tr>
<tr><td colspan="4">"A reservation request must be registered on at least one calendar day."
"A reservation request must be registered on at least one time of day."
"A reservation request must be made by at least one customer."
"A reservation request must have at least one reservation request part."</td></tr>
</table>

<table>
<tr><td colspan="4">OT: Reservation Request Part</td></tr>
<tr><td>Test TC on Role(s):</td><td>Question</td><td>Answer (Y/N), Comment</td><td>Conclusion</td></tr>
<tr><td>63</td><td>Does every res. req. part concern a performance?</td><td>Y</td><td>TC 19 on Role 63</td></tr>
<tr><td>67</td><td>Does every res. req. part claim a number of seats?</td><td>Yes, we contact customers if they forget to enter it on the paper form.</td><td>TC 20 on Role 67</td></tr>
<tr><td>70</td><td>Does every res. req. part have a status?</td><td>Yes, the first is always 'registered', and it can change but not be missing.</td><td>TC 21 on Role 70</td></tr>
<tr><td colspan="4">"A reservation request part must concern at least one performance."
"A reservation request part must claim at least one number of seats."
"A reservation request part must have at least one status."</td></tr>
</table>

<table>
<tr><td colspan="4">OT: Number</td></tr>
<tr><td>Test TC on Role(s):</td><td>Question</td><td>Answer (Y/N), Comment</td><td>Conclusion</td></tr>
<tr><td>68+76</td><td>Do you want a pick list for all possible numbers of seats claimed, or still free?</td><td>No, that's not necessary.</td><td>TC 23 on Roles 68+76</td></tr>
<tr><td colspan="4">"No domain list is desired for numbers."
"A number must be the number of seats claimed in a res. req. part and/or the number of seats still free for a performance."</td></tr>
</table>

OT: Status			
Test TC on Role(s):	**Question**	**Answer (Y/N), Comment**	**Conclusion**
71	Do you want a pick list for all possible statuses of a res. req. part?	Yes, that's a lot handier than typing them in every time.	No TC on Role 71. Fact Expression Type added
"A domain list is desired for numbers." "A status does not have to be the status of a reservation request part.			

Object Types from IGD 'Tickets'

OT: Row			
Test TC on Role(s):	**Question**	**Answer (Y/N), Comment**	**Conclusion**
75	Do you want a pick list for all the rows in the theater?	Yes, and for the seats too.	TC 22 on Role 75. Fact Expression Type present
	Can there be a row without seats?	N	
"A domain list is desired for rows." "A row must contain at least one seat."			

OT: Seat			
Test TC on Role(s):	**Question**	**Answer (Y/N), Comment**	**Conclusion**
86	So a list of all seats is desired. Can there be a seat for which there is no ticket?	Yes, we'll expand at the back, might take time before all new seats are sold.	No TC on Role 86. Fact Expression Type present
"A domain list is desired for seats." "A seat does not need to have a ticket for it."			

OT: Ticket			
Test TC on Role(s):	**Question**	**Answer (Y/N), Comment**	**Conclusion**
79	Do you record the seat assigner for every ticket?	Y	TC 25 on Role 79
83	Does every ticket state for which performance it is?	Y	TC 28 on Role 83
85	Does every ticket have an assigned seat?	Y	TC 26 on Role 85
"A ticket must be issued by at least one seat assigner." "A ticket must be for at least one performance." "A ticket must be for at least one seat."			

OT: Seat Assigner			
Test TC on Role(s):	**Question**	**Answer (Y/N), Comment**	**Conclusion**
80	Do you want a pick list for all the seat assigners in the theater?	Yes, we'd like standard names for them.	No TC on Role 80. Fact Expression Type added
	Can there be a seat assigner that hasn't issued any seats?	For a new seat assigner, it might take a while before the first tickets are issued.	
"A domain list is desired for seat assigners." "A seat assigner does not need to issue a ticket."			

OT: Approved Reservation Request Part			
Test TC on Role(s):	**Question**	**Answer (Y/N), Comment**	**Conclusion**
89	Does every approved res. req. part have tickets issued for it?	Yes, but usually a bunch of requests is approved first, and tickets are printed later.	No TC on Role 89
"An approved reservation request part does not need to have a ticket for a reservation."			

OT: Ticket For Reservation			
Test TC on Role(s):	**Question**	**Answer (Y/N), Comment**	**Conclusion**
88	Do you record the approved reservation request part for every ticket for a reservation?	Y	TC 27 on Role 88
"A ticket for a reservation must be for at least one approved reservation request part."			

A2.3 VALUE CONSTRAINT DETERMINATION FOR ALL LABEL TYPES

The table below lists all Label Types and summarizes VC-related modeling decisions. In almost all cases where a VC might have been used, it was decided to use a domain list instead. Only for 'part number' VC 1: {1, 2, …} was specified. For 'integral number' the Label Type name was thought to be clear enough (later to be implemented by a data type like 'small integer'). By the way, Label Types 'part number' and 'integral number' cannot be united; 'integral number' identifies an *amount* of countable things, whereas 'part number' is a sequential label to distinguish parts by, so they are conceptually different.

Label Type	**Domain List?**	**Value Constraint?**	**Remark**
address line	N, just LT is OK	N	No fixed structure
country name	Y	N	
customer number	N	N	System has to generate numbers automatically
date	Y	N	Calendar to be implemented.
description	N, just LT is OK	N	
dollars.cents	N	N	
email address	N	N	
first name	N, just LT is OK	N	
genre name	Y	N	
integral number	N	N	
part number	N	No. A reservation form has at most 10 lines, but some customers just continue on the back, and the site has no limit on the number of parts.	For each reservation request, the numbers should be sequential starting from 1. **Value Constraint 1: {1, 2, ...}**
performance number	N	N	System has to generate numbers automatically
performer name	N, too many	N	
phone number	N	N	
reservation request number	N	N	System has to generate numbers automatically
row number	Y	N	
seat assigner name	Y	N	
seat number	Y, with row	N	
show name	N	N	
state name	Y, with country	N	
status name	Y	N	
surname	N, just LT is OK	N	
ticket number	N	N	System has to generate numbers automatically
ticket type name	Y	N	
time (hh:mm AM/PM)	Y	N	List of points in time with 15-minute intervals is desired.
town name	N	N	
weekday name	Y	N	
ZIP code	N, just LT is OK	N	In different countries different structures; treat as string

A2.4 SUBTYPES

Subtypes 'Approved Reservation Request Part' and 'Ticket for Reservation'

BR 29 Tickets for a reservation request part can only be issued for an *approved* reservation request part.

Clearly, an *approved* reservation request part is a special kind of reservation request part. The Business Rule states that tickets can *only* be issued for such approved parts. The status of a reservation request part tells us which parts are approved, which is in a Fact Type played by the Supertype, so a Derivation Rule can be made that satisfies the requirement in Textbox 6.16. Because of BR 28 (see Section A3.2 below) the condition contains the three statuses 'approved', 'assigned' and 'completed'. The tickets will still be for the same approved reservation request part if the status changes from 'approved' to 'assigned' and from 'assigned' to 'completed'.

Subtype: Approved Reservation Request Part

DR 1: x IN Approved Reservation Request Part(78) IF
(x, 'approved') OR (x, 'assigned') OR (x, 'completed') IN
Status Of Reservation Request Part(70, 71)

The same BR 29 also implies a subtype for Tickets. Tickets can also be bought at the box office, but *only* tickets for a reservation request part can be in the Population of Fact Type 'Ticket For Reservation Request Part'. A Derivation Rule that satisfies the requirement in Textbox 6.16 can be given. The domain expert has checked and approved these Derivation Rules.

Subtype: Ticket For Reservation

DR 2: x IN Ticket For Reservation(87) IF
(x, 'reservation manager') IN Ticket Issued By(79, 80)

Finally, Role 89 in Fact Type 'Ticket For Reservation Request Part' is played by Subtype 'Approved Reservation Request Part' and Role 88 by Subtype 'Ticket For Reservation', thus modeling BR 29.

Subtype 'Customer With Postal Address'

BR 25 Reservation requests (whether on paper or on the website) must always contain the complete address of a customer: address line(s), town, state, ZIP code and country.

This Business Rule leads to other Constraints as well (see Table A.2), but also to a subtype. BR 25 implies that a reservation request can *only* be made by a customer who gives a complete postal address. This subtype can be derived in a number of ways, each using one of the three Fact Types that contain the mandatory parts of a postal address (see the Equality Constraints in IGD 'Customer', Section A1.2).

Subtype: Customer With Postal Address

DR 3: x IN Customer With Postal Address(90) IF
x IN Customer Address Line 1(43)

Please note that the Fact Types that contain the address parts cannot be played by the subtype; this would violate the requirement in Textbox 6.16. Role 62 from Fact Type 'Reservation Request By Customer' can now be played by the Subtype.

A2.5 OTHER CONSTRAINTS

Derivation Rule for Derivable Fact Type 'Free Tickets for Performance'

The domain experts would find it very convenient to see at a glance how many seats are still free for a particular performance. Since the performance is recorded for each issued ticket, this is easy to calculate: subtract the number of issued tickets for that performance from the total number of seats. Therefore, the following Derivation Rule holds for Fact Type 'Free Tickets for Performance':

```
DR 4: (x, y) IN Free Seats For Performance(77, 76)
      WITH x IN Performance(11)
       AND y =  COUNT(Seat(74, 75))
              – COUNT(Ticket For Performance(83)
                      WHERE Ticket For Performance(84) = x)
```

From BR 07:

```
C 1: FOR ANY x IN Performance Price(22):
     ALL VALUES y IN {'season', 'single'}
     MUST EXIST IN (x, y) IN Performance Price(22, 21)
```

From BR 31:

C 2: For all values P1, P2, Q and R with the properties

1) Ticket Q is for performance P1
2) Ticket Q is for the approved reservation request part R that concerns performance P2

the following must hold as well: performances P1 and P2 are the same.

From BR 28:

C 3: FOR ANY UPDATE in Fact Type 'Status Of Reservation Request Part':

```
IF      x IS NOT IN 'Status Of Reservation Request Part'(70)
        THEN  (x, 'registered') can be added
ELSE    IF    a Fact (x, 'registered') IS IN (70, 71)
        THEN  it can change to (x, 'rejected');
        IF    a Fact (x, 'registered') IS IN (70, 71)
        THEN  it can change to (x, 'approved');
        IF    a Fact (x, 'approved') IS IN (70, 71)
        THEN  it can change to (x, 'assigned');
        IF    a Fact (x, 'assigned') IS IN (70, 71)
        THEN  it can change to (x, 'completed').
```

From BR 14 and BR 15:

C 4: Deontic TC on Role 89:
Eventually an approved reservation request part must have at least one ticket for it.

A3: TABLES OF BUSINESS RULES

The following tables of Business Rules were drawn up from the description given above in Section 2.1 and from interviews with domain experts. All Business Rules have been checked and approved by the domain experts. The tables also show which Business Rules have been included in the Information Model, and with which Constraints they correspond.

A3.1 Business Rules from the description (Section 2.1)

All Business Rules found in the description are listed here:

BR #	Business Rule	Modeled as:
BR 01	In May, four months before the start of the next	Not modeled: process rule

	theater season, the program is published in a brochure and on the theater's website.	
BR 02	Each show has a title and a performer.	FT 'Show'
BR 03	A show belongs to one or more genres.	FT 'Show In Genre', TC 2 and UC 11
BR 04	A show can have multiple performances.	FT 'Performance Features Show', no UC on Role 10
BR 05	A performance is identified by a unique performance number.	FT 'Performance' and UC 3
BR 06	Serviceton Theater sells two kinds of ticket: a single ticket (normal price) and a season ticket (reduced price). There are some other types as well (from an interview held later).	FT 'Ticket Type' as domain list (F11 and no TC on OT 'Ticket Type')
BR 07	Each performance has a single ticket price and a season ticket price.	Constraint C 1
BR 08	Customers who order tickets for at least six performances before the start of the theater season get season tickets.	Not modeled: to be implemented in the procedures to calculate prices.
BR 09	In all other cases than mentioned in BR 08, customers have to pay the single ticket price.	See BR 08
BR 10	Customers can send in a request for tickets for several performances by either using the paper reservation form in the brochure or the digital form on the theater's website.	Not modeled: process rule
BR 11	It is also possible to buy tickets at the Serviceton Music Theater Box Office.	Not modeled: process rule
BR 12	Reservation requests are processed every week.	Not modeled: process rule
BR 13	Reservation requests are approved if possible.	Not modeled: process rule that will use FT 'Free Seats For Performance'.
BR 14	For each approved reservation request part, seats are assigned to customers.	FTs 'Ticket For Seat' and 'Ticket For Reservation Request Part'; Subtypes 'Approved Reservation Request Part' and 'Ticket For Reservation'
BR 15	For each approved reservation request part, tickets for these seats (see BR 14) are printed.	Constraint C 4
BR 16	For each approved request part the tickets (see BR 15) are sent to the customer's home address.	Not modeled: process rule
BR 17	Each ticket has a unique ticket number.	FT 'Ticket' and UC 46
BR 18	Each ticket is for one specific seat.	FT 'Ticket For Seat', UC 49 and TC 26
BR 19	The rows of seats in Serviceton Music Theater are numbered from 1 to 30 from the stage side up.	FT 'Row' as domain list; orientation not modeled

BR 20	The seats are numbered from left to right.	FT 'Seat' as domain list; orientation not modeled
BR 21	In every row, seat 1 is located on the left hand side (when you face the stage).	FT 'Seat' as domain list; orientation not modeled

Table A.1 Business Rules from the description

A3.2 Business Rules from interviews between domain experts and modelers

Business Rules about identification of Object Types (like BR 05 above) are not listed here separately. The modeler will always check identifiers with the domain expert (see the dialogues in Textboxes 3.28, 3.30, 3.35, 3.37 etc.), and the diagrams in Section A1 above show clearly how each Object Type is identified.

Business Rules that correspond with Uniqueness Constraints and most Totality Constraints are not mentioned separately here, either; they are determined systematically; see the summaries in Sections A2.1 and A2.2.

Other Business Rules are indeed listed, which came up in other dialogues (not included in this book) sometimes prompted by the modeler, sometimes by the domain expert.

BR #	**Business Rule**	**Modeled as:**
BR 22	Customer numbers (which identify customers) are to be assigned automatically.	Not modeled: process rule
BR 23	A standard list of valid times of day is to be used, with 15-minute intervals.	FT 'Time Of Day' as domain list; intervals not modeled
BR 24	To be able to contact a customer, an email address and/or a phone number must be known for each customer.	TC 12 on Roles 37+40 played by OT 'Customer'
BR 25	Reservation requests (whether on paper or on the website) must always contain the complete address of a customer: address line(s), town, state, ZIP code and country.	SCs 2, 3, 4 and 5 on roles 43, 47 and 54 (same as 2 ECs: 43=47 and 47=54); Subtype 'Customer With Postal Address' playing Role 62 in Fact Type 'Reservation Request By Customer'
BR 26	For a customer address, address line 2 is optional and should only be entered if address line 1 is also used.	SC 1 from Role 45 to 43.
BR 27	A standard list of countries and states in those countries is to be used.	FTs 'State' and 'Country' as domain lists
BR 28	The status of a reservation request always starts as 'registered', and can only change in the following ways: a' registered' → 'rejected' (if the reservation request part cannot be satisfied).	Dynamic Constraint C 3

	b 'registered'→ 'approved' (if the reservation request part can be satisfied). c 'approved → 'assigned' (when the seats have been assigned). d 'assigned' → 'completed' (when the tickets have been printed).	
BR 29	Tickets for a reservation request part can only be issued for an *approved* reservation request part.	Subtype 'Ticket For reservation playing Role 88 in FT 'Ticket For Reservation Request Part', and Role 89 in the same FT played by Subtype 'Approved Reservation Request part'.
BR 30	Tickets for the same performance must all be for different seats (no two tickets for the same seat in the same performance).	UC 55
BR 31	Any ticket for an approved reservation request part must be for the same performance that is stated in the reservation request part (see Section 4.5.6 for an explanation of why this Business Rule is needed).	Constraint C 2

Table A.2 Business Rules from the description

APPENDIX B
Further Reading

B1 On FCO-IM

[1] **Fully Communication Oriented Information Modeling (FCO-IM)**, 2002
Guido Bakema; Jan Pieter Zwart; Harm van der Lek.

This older book contains advanced topics in FCO-IM, such as

* Complex networks of Subtypes and Supertypes
* Subtype Matrix Method to determine all subtypes systematically
* Generalization, solving homonym and synonym modeling problems
* Recursive identification structures
  such as computer file folder structures with paths of arbitrary length
* Detailed transformation algorithm to a Relational Database
  including generalization and recursive structures

The book can be downloaded free of charge from the website of [2]:
http://www.casetalk.com, from 'free downloads' page,
and also from
http://www.fco-im.nl → Publications → Books.

[2] **CaseTalk Modeler** is an excellent modeling tool that implements almost everything in this book and most of what is in [1]. It also performs transformations to Relational schemas and data warehouse structures and generates scripts for various implementation platforms, among other things. Its development started at HAN University and was taken over by commercial companies. Presently, it is being maintained by BCP Software with Marco Wobben as the principal developer and architect.
Further information can be found at:
Websites: http://www.casetalk.com
http://www.bcp-software.nl.

[3] **FOM in practice**

Book: **About Facts And Things**, 2014
Peter Alons
Brave New Books, ISBN 9789402114485.

Recent research papers on FCO-IM:

[4] Article: **Elementary Transactions**, 2013
Jan Pieter Zwart, Stijn Hoppenbrouwers
Conference Proceedings OTM2013,
International workshop on Object-Role Modeling (ORM'13),
Springer LNCS 8186, pp 513-523, ISBN 978-3-642-41032-1.
DOI 10.1007/978-3-642-41033-8_65.

[5] Article: **A Dialogue Game Prototype for FCO-IM**, 2011
Stijn Hoppenbrouwers, Albert Pratama Jemmi Oscar,
Dimas Listianto Adisuryo, Jan Pieter Zwart
Conference Proceedings OTM2011,
International workshop on Object-Role Modeling (ORM'11),
Springer LNCS 7046, pp 339-349, ISBN 978-3-642-25125-2,
DOI 10.1007/978-3-642-25126-9_45.

[6] Article: **Advances in FCO-IM (2): A shorter Algorithm for determining Intra Fact Type Uniqueness Constraints**, 2007.
Jan Pieter Zwart, Guido Bakema
Conference Proceedings OTM2007,
International workshop on Object-Role Modeling (ORM'07),
Springer LNCS 4805, pp 719-728, ISSN 0302-9743.

[7] Article: **Advances in FCO-IM (1); Classification and Qualification: Disconnected and Overlapping Object Type Expressions**, 2008
Jan Pieter Zwart, Guido Bakema
Conference Proceedings
of the Second Libyan International Symposium on
Information Systems Modeling and Development, Tripoli Libya.
Downloadable from:
http://www.fco-im.nl → Publications → Articles.

[8] Article: **A fact approach to automatic application development**, 2006
Elton Manoku, Jan Pieter Zwart, Guido Bakema
JCM 36, September 2006.

[9] Article: **A Case Study of Recursive Data Modeling**, 2006
Fazat Nur Azizah, Guido Bakema, Jan Pieter Zwart
First Libyan International Symposium on
Information Systems Modeling and Development,
Tripoli, Lybia, June 2006
Downloadable from:
http://www.fco-im.nl → Publications → Articles.

B2 On Other Fact Oriented Modeling Techniques

[10] **Object Role Modeling (ORM):**

Book: **Information Modeling and relational Databases**, 2008
Terry Halpin, Tony Morgan
Morgan Kaufmann Publishers, ISBN 978-0-12-373568-3

Modeling tool: **Norma**
Excellent modeling tool. Among its features: many constraint types, automated verbalizations of all metadata, mappings to other modeling techniques like ERM, UML and Relational

Websites: http://www.orm.net
https://www.ormfoundation.org

Book: **Object-Role Modeling Fundamentals**, 2015
Terry Halpin
Technics Publications, ISBN 978-1-63462-074-1.

[11] **Cognition enhanced Natural language Information Analysis Method (CogNIAM)**

NIAM was developed by Sjir Nijssen and Terry Halpin in the eighties in Australia.

Book: **Conceptual Schema and Relational Database Design**, 1989
Prentice Hall, ISBN 0-7248-0151-0

FCO-IM, ORM and CogNIAM are all branches from this original tree.
CogNIAM:

Book: Several books in Dutch available at PNA Publishing bv

Websites: http://www.cogniam.eu
http://www.pna-group.com.

B3 On Other Information Modeling Techniques

[12] **Entity-Relationship Modeling (ERM)**

Data modeling technique, originally developed by Peter Chen in the seventies. It does not work with elementary Fact Types. There are many varieties and many different styles of notation like Bachmann, Barker, Crow's Foot, Information Engineering, etc. It is still widely used and supported by many software tools. See any textbook on ERM for details.

[13] **Unified Modeling Language (UML)**

A collection of techniques developed by Grady Booch, Ivar Jacobson and James Rumbaugh in the nineties. Originally intended for object-oriented software engineering; used in other fields including database design as well. It does not work with elementary Fact Types.

Its Class Diagrams are only partially suitable for relational database design. See any textbook on UML for details.

[14] **Relational model**
In the Relational model, information structures consist of tables with columns (attributes). Developed in the sixties by Edgar Codd. Every table has a primary key, and columns can have a NOT NULL constraint. Tables are connected through foreign key references. It is still by far the most used implementation form for databases. Structured Query Language (SQL) is the most used data manipulation language. A Relational database can be automatically derived from any information modeling techniques mentioned in this book (see Chapter 7 for how this is done in FCO-IM). See any textbook on Relational databases and SQL for details.

[15] **Data warehouses**
Dimensional modeling is a set of techniques and concepts used in data warehouse design.
The dimensional model is built on a star-like schema.
Book: **The Data Warehouse Toolkit: The Definitive Guide to Dimensional Modeling** (3rd edition), 2013,
Ralph Kimball, Margy Ross
Wiley, ISBN 978-1118530801
Data warehousing in general:
Book: **Building the Data Warehouse**, 2005
William Inmon
John Wiley and Sons, ISBN 978-8-1265-0645-3.

[16] **Data Vault**
A data modeling solution for data warehouses invented by Dan Linstedt.
Book: **Super Charge Your Data Warehouse: Invaluable Data Modeling Rules to Implement Your Data Vault**, 2011
Dan Linstedt, Kent Graziano
CreateSpace Independent Publishing Platform,
ISBN: 978-1463778682
Website: http://danlinstedt.com
Book: **The Business of Data Vault Modeling**, Second Edition, 2010
Linstedt, Graziano, Hultgren
Dan Linstedt, ISBN 978-1-4357-1914-9.

[17] **Anchor Modeling**
Website: http://www.anchormodeling.com.

B4 On Other Related Fields of Interest

[18] **Business Process Model and Notation (BPMN)**
A technique to model business processes with,
supported by the Object Management Group (OMG).
Website: http://www.omg.org/spec/SBVR
Book (for instance):
BPMN Method & Style, 2009,
Bruce Silver
Cody-Cassidy Press, ISBN 978-0-9823681-0-7
Software tool:
Bizagi Modeler, http://www.bizagi.com.

[19] **Use cases**
Essentially, each use case is a description of 'who can do what' if he/she uses the information system for one particular function. The description should state in a step-by-step way exactly *what* the user can do and *what* the system's responses are without giving any details about *how* this is done. Use cases can be given in more or less detail (brief, casual, fully dressed), ranging from the 'happy path' showing only the intended problem-free sequence of events or the fully boarded up version covering every possible mistake and safeguards against them.
Use Case Diagrams are a part of UML (see [13]).

[20] **Semantics of Business Vocabulary and Rules (SBVR)**
A technique to formulate Business Rules in, based on mathematical logic with a natural language interface, supported by the Object Management Group (OMG).
Website: http://www.omg.org/spec/SBVR.

[21] **Data quality**
Book: **Data Quality**, 1998,
Carlo Batini, Monica Scannapieco
Springer, ISBN 3-540-33172-7
Book: **Data Quality Assessment**, 2007,
Arkady Maydanchik
Technics Publications,
ISBN 978-0-9771400-2-2
Article **A Critical Success Factors Framework for Information Quality Management**, 2014
Baškarada, S, Koronios, A
Information Systems Management, vol. 31, no. 4, pp. 1-20

[22] **Organizational communication**
Book: **Rethinking the Theory of Organizational Communication:**

how to Read an Organization, 1993,
J.R. Taylor
Ablex Publishing, ISBN 9781567500028.

[23] **Conceptualization processes**
PHD thesis (original text 2003):
Freezing Language, Conceptualisation Processes across ICT-Supported Organisations, 2015
S.J.B.A Hoppenbrouwers,
Scholar's Press, ISBN 978-3-639-70304-7.

[24] **Semantic web**
Book: **A Semantic Web Primer**, 2nd Edition, 2008
Grigoris Antoniou, Frank van Harmelen
The MIT Press. ISBN 0-262-01242-1.

[25] **Ontologies**
Book chapter:
Advances in Web Semantics, Volume I, 2008
Chapter 3: **Ontology Engineering – The DOGMA Approach**
Mustafa Jarrar, Robert Meersman
LNCS 4891, Springer, ISBN 978-3-540-89783-5:
Article: **Formal Ontology in Information Systems**, 1998
Proceedings of FOIS'98, Trento, Italy, 6-8 June 1998
Amsterdam, IOS Press, pp. 3-15.

[26] **Data governance**
Collibra: https://www.collibra.com.

[27] **Interoperability**
Website: http://www.ariadne.ac.uk/issue24/interoperability.

[28] **Business process management**
Book: **Business Process Management:**
Concepts, Languages, Architectures (Second Edition), 2012
Mathias Weske
ISBN 978-3-642-28615-5.

[29] **Business intelligence**
Book: **Business Intelligence and Performance Management:**
Theory, Systems, and Industrial Applications, 2013
Peter Rausch, Alaa Sheta, Aladdin Ayesh
Springer Verlag U.K., ISBN 978-1-4471-4865-4.

[30] **NoSQL**
PDF: **NoSQL Databases**, 2012
Christof Strauch
http://www.christof-strauch.de/nosqldbs.pdf.

[31] **iTasks**
PHD thesis:
TOP to the Rescue: Task-Oriented Programming for Incident Response Applications, 2013
Bas Lijnse
PhD Thesis Radboud University Nijmegen. March 2013
Article: **CCL: A Lightweight ORM Embedding in Clean**, 2012
Bas Lijnse, Patrick van Bommel, Rinus Plasmeijer
In : On the Move to Meaningful Internet Systems:
OTM 2012 Workhops, Rome, Italy, Sep. 2012
P. Herrero, H. Panetto, R. Meersman, and T. Dillon, editors.

[32] **System dynamics**
Article: **Enhancing the System Dynamics Modeling Process with a Domain Modeling Method**, 2013
P. (Fiona) Tulinayo, Patrick van Bommel, Henderik Alex Proper
Int. J. Cooperative Inf. Syst. 22(2) (2013).

[33] **Scrum**
Book: **Agile software development with Scrum**, 2002
Ken Schwaber, Mike Beedle
Prentice Hall. ISBN 0-13-067634-9.

[34] **Concept mapping**
Book: **Learning, Creating, and Using Knowledge: Concept Maps as Facilitative Tools in Schools and Corporations**, 2nd ed. 2010
Joseph D. Novak
Routledge, New York
ISBN-13: 978-0415991858
Website: http://cmap.ihmc.us/docs/theory-of-concept-maps.

Index